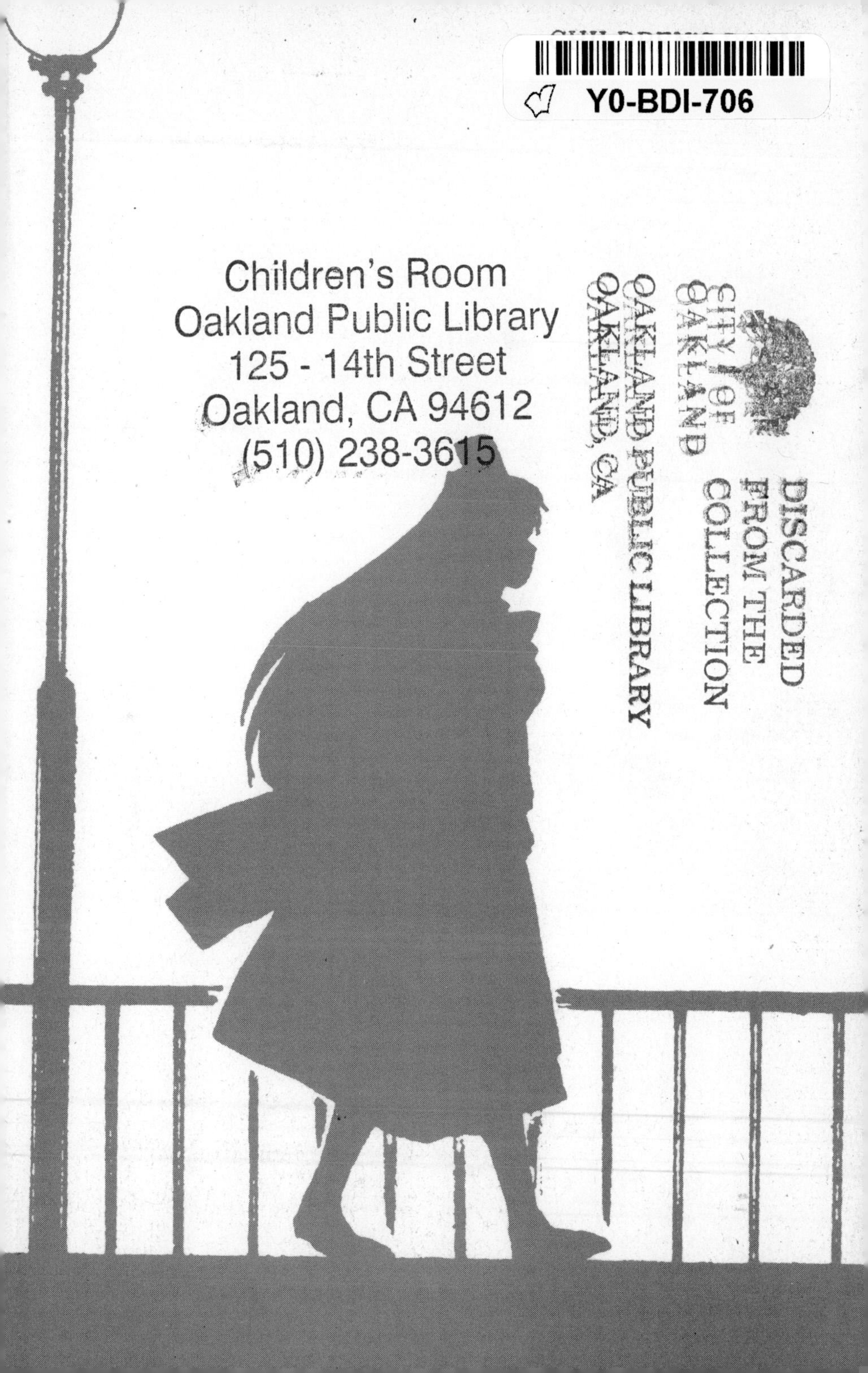

"*Sherlock Holmes* meets *The Maltese Falcon* meets *Mobile Suit Gundam* in Kia Asamiya's retro-Victorian world of gaslight and clockwork machines, film noir and steampunk...Narutaki's foes chew the scenery with vigor"
—Wizard Magazine

"*Steam Detectives* is always interesting, and the virtuoso artwork always helps."
—Anime News Network

"Just plain fun stories. Asamiya is terrific."
—Tony Isabella, comics critic

"This is one of the most attractive-looking books I've seen in a long time. Elegant inside pages, with a marvelous use of layout, great line and tone work, attractive designs and fun little extras. Asamiya has a lot to teach would-be artists about layout and technique."
—Manga Max

ANIMERICA EXTRA GRAPHIC NOVEL
STEAM DETECTIVES™
VOL. 3

This volume contains the STEAM DETECTIVES installments from
Animerica Extra Vol. 2, No. 4 through Vol. 3, No. 3 in their entirety.

STORY AND ART BY

KIA ASAMIYA

ENGLISH ADAPTATION BY

YUJI ONIHI

Touch-Up Art & Lettering/Bill Spicer
Cover Design/Hidemi Sahara
Layout & Graphics/Carolina Ugalde
Editor/William Flanagan

Director of Sales & Marketing/Oliver Chin
Editor-in-Chief/Hyoe Narita
Publisher/Seiji Horibuchi

Printed in Canada

APR 1 2 2007

Published by Viz Communications, Inc.
P.O. Box 77010 • San Francisco, CA 94107

10 9 8 7 6 5 4 3 2 1
First printing, June 2000

j-p☺p.com
www.j-pop.com

VIZ kids
www.vizkids.com

ANIMERICA
anime & manga monthly
ww.animerica-mag.com

VIZ
www.viz.com

• get your own vizmail.net email account
• register for the weekly email newsletter
• sign up for your free catalog
• voice 1-800-394-3042   fax 415-384-8936

ANIMERICA EXTRA GRAPHIC NOVEL

STEAM DETECTIVES™

VOL. 3

STORY AND ART BY

KIA ASAMIYA

CONTENTS

Steam-Punk Mysteries

The place is Steam City, a mixture of London and Tokyo's Asakusa district, and boy detective Narutaki is gaining quite a reputation as he solves the myriad of mysteries that come to his door.

In his first case, the evil Phantom Knight tricks beautiful nurse Ling Ling and her *megamaton* robot Goriki into luring Narutaki into a trap. Ling Ling thinks the Phantom Knight can rescue the brain of her father, the brilliant scientist Dr. Hsu, from the body of her steam-powered *megamaton*, but the treacherous Phantom Knight has no intention of helping her. After defeating the plans of the Phantom Knight, Ling Ling and Goriki ask to join Narutaki and his butler Kawakubo in the Narutaki Detective Agency, and together they formed the Steam Detectives.

But their work is just beginning and the agency must solve a dizzying array of mysteries including a hijack attempt by the machine fetishist, Machine Baron; two attacks by Dr. Guilty to defeat Goriki and prove his Shadow Bolt *megamaton* designs superior; Ling Ling's evil opposite Lang Lang's kidnapping of Narutaki, abetted by the boy criminal Le Bread; a second showdown with Phantom Knight, who bears a grudge against Narutaki's late father for some secret reason; and a pearl heist by the ingenious cat-burglar the Red Scorpion.

Since Narutaki and his friends solve every case with which they are presented, they have gained a good reputation throughout Steam City. But that means defeating the boy detective will make a criminal famous, and this lure is too much for the unhinged criminal element to resist!

Narutaki

Son of the greatest detective in the history of Steam City, his parents' murder has left him with only his butler's help in his quest to follow in his father's footsteps.

Ling Ling

It is known that the beautiful nurse Ling Ling's father is the great scientist Dr. Hsu, but her past is still a mystery.

Goriki

A steam-powered *megamaton* robot that is fiercely loyal to Ling Ling. Somewhere inside its body is the brain of Dr. Hsu.

Kawakubo

Narutaki's loyal butler and a man of many resources.

Inspector Onigawara

This gruff detective of the Steam City Police Force is infatuated with Ling Ling.

Emperor of Steam

A fictional murderer in a series of horror novels who seems to have been brought to life.

The Machine Baron

An insane machine fetishist who wants Goriki for his own.

Amanda Rose

A newspaper photographer who may not be all she seems to be.

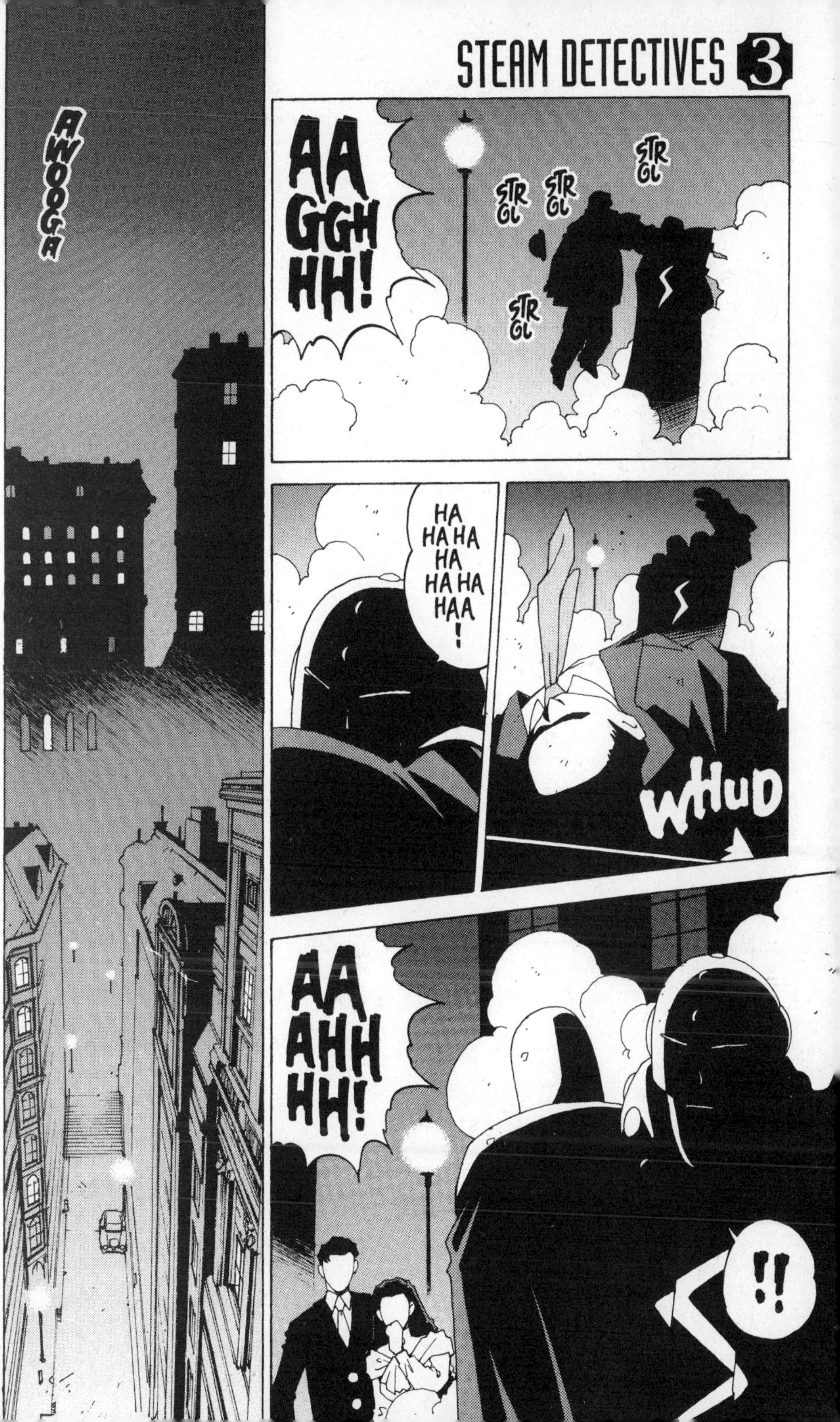
AWOOGA
AAGGHHH!
STRGL
STRGL
STRGL
STRGL
HA HA HA HA HA HA HA HAA!
WHUD
AAAHHHH!
!!

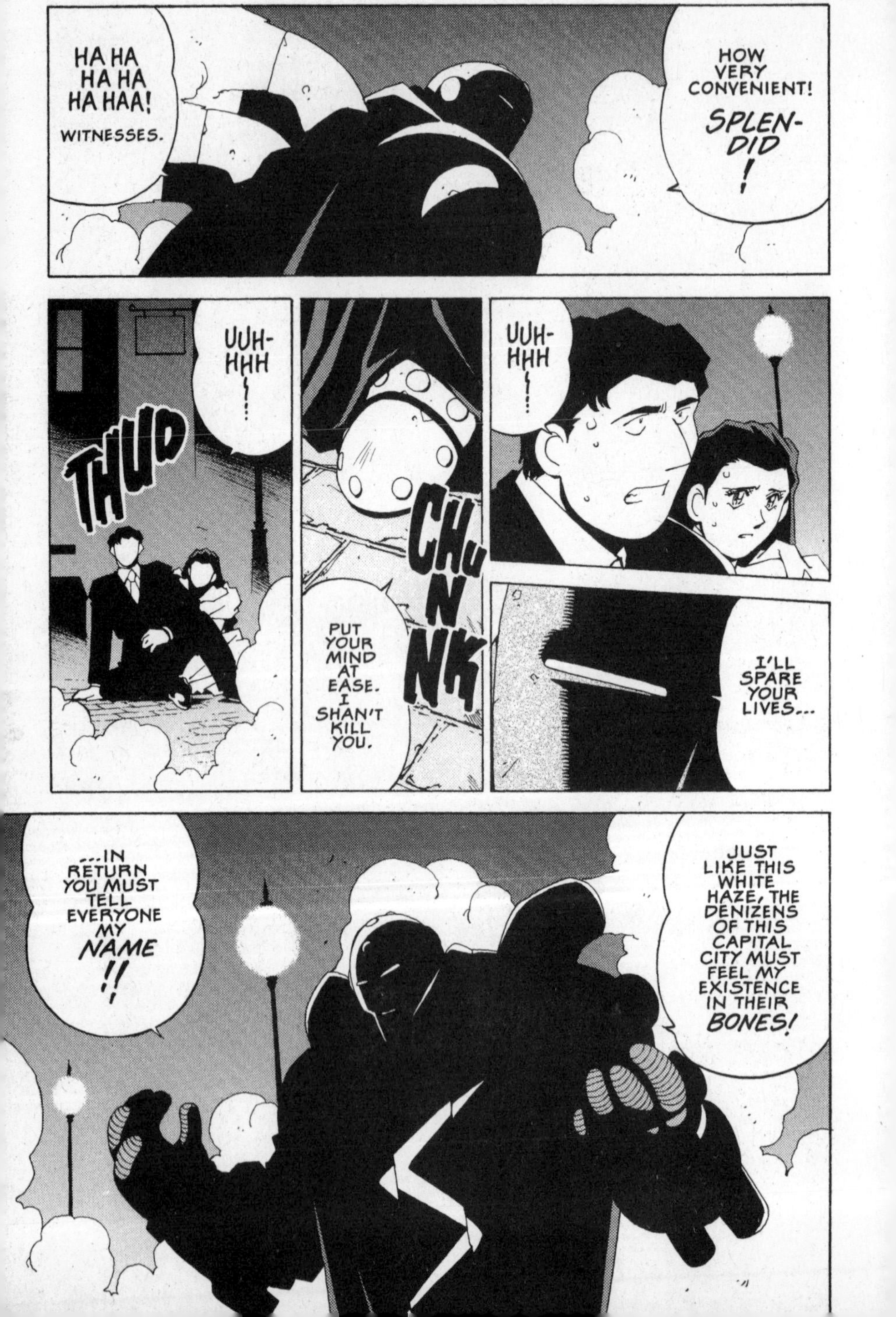
HA HA HA HA HA HAA!
WITNESSES.
HOW VERY CONVENIENT!
SPLEN-DID !
UUH-HHH...!
THUD
CHUNNK
PUT YOUR MIND AT EASE. I SHAN'T KILL YOU.
UUH-HHH...!
I'LL SPARE YOUR LIVES...
...IN RETURN YOU MUST TELL EVERYONE MY NAME !!
JUST LIKE THIS WHITE HAZE, THE DENIZENS OF THIS CAPITAL CITY MUST FEEL MY EXISTENCE IN THEIR BONES!

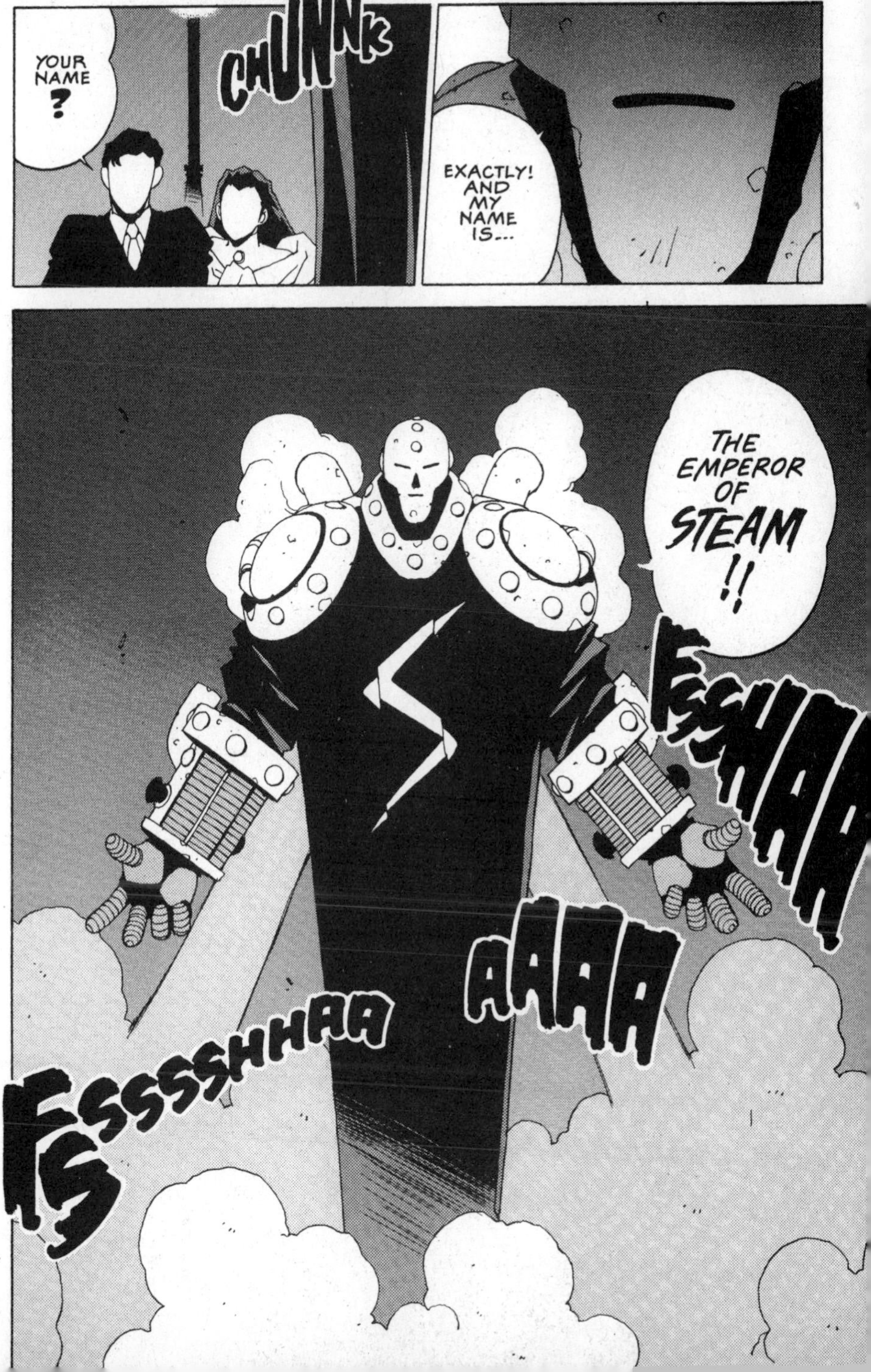
YOUR NAME ?
CHUNNK
EXACTLY! AND MY NAME IS...
THE EMPEROR OF STEAM !!
FSSSHAA
AAAA
FSSSSSHHAA

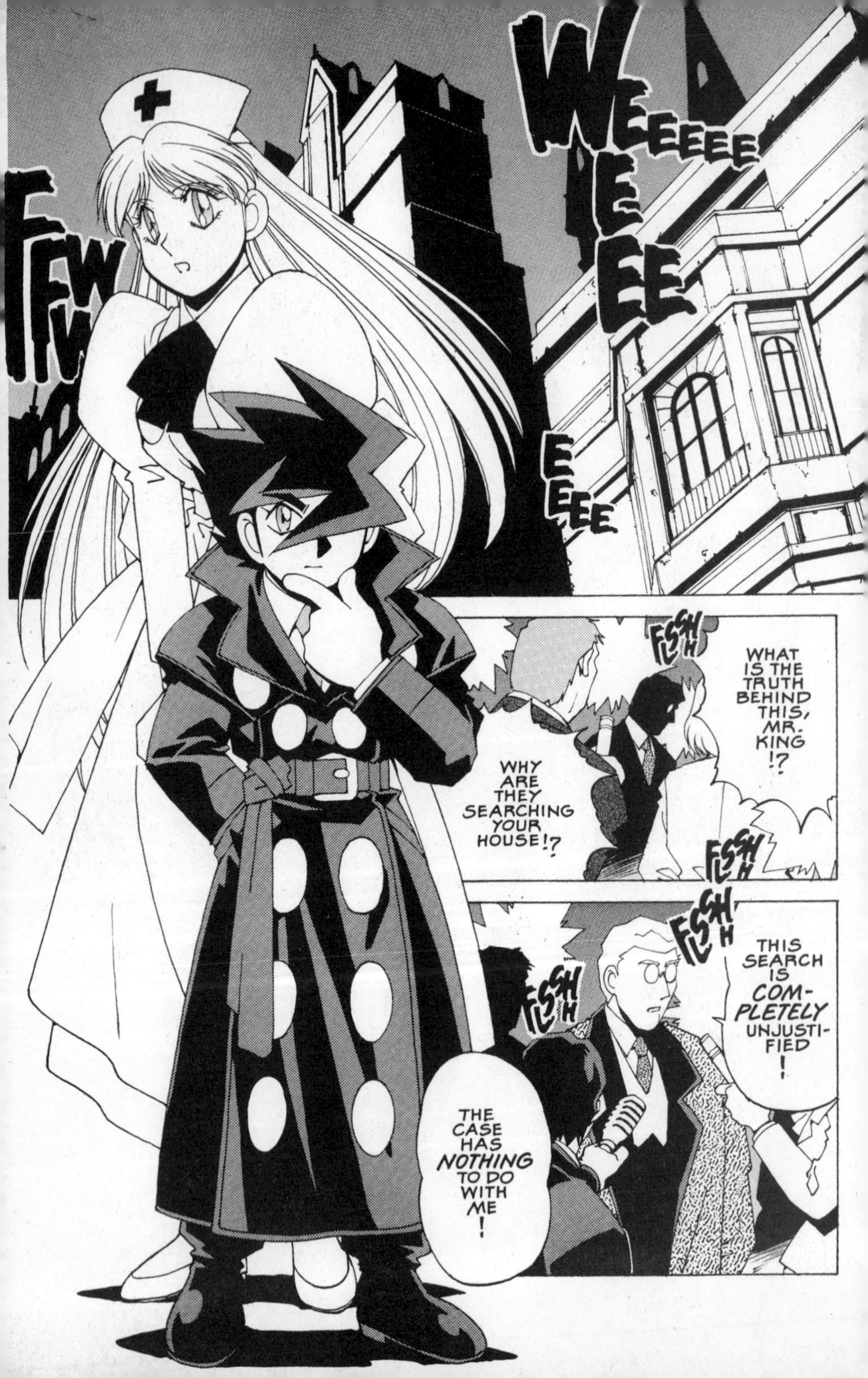
FWFW
WEEEEEEEEEEEEEE
FLSSHH
WHY ARE THEY SEARCHING YOUR HOUSE!?
WHAT IS THE TRUTH BEHIND THIS, MR. KING!?
FLSSHH
FLSSHH
FLSSHH
THIS SEARCH IS COMPLETELY UNJUSTIFIED!
THE CASE HAS NOTHING TO DO WITH ME!

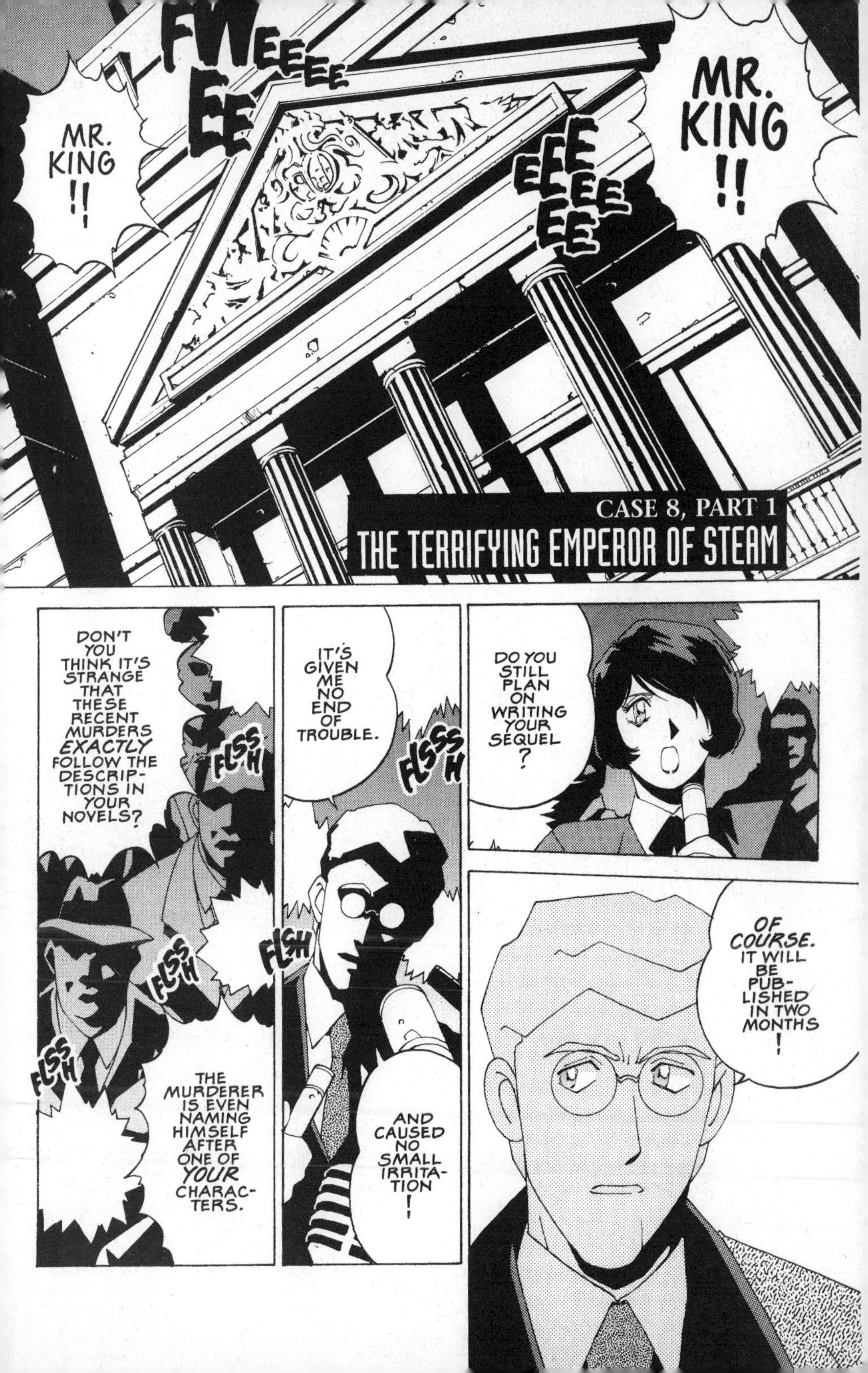
FWEEEEEE
EE
MR. KING !!
EEEEEE
EE
MR. KING !!
CASE 8, PART 1
THE TERRIFYING EMPEROR OF STEAM
DON'T YOU THINK IT'S STRANGE THAT THESE RECENT MURDERS EXACTLY FOLLOW THE DESCRIPTIONS IN YOUR NOVELS?
FLSSH
FLSSH
FLSH
FLSSH
THE MURDERER IS EVEN NAMING HIMSELF AFTER ONE OF YOUR CHARACTERS.
IT'S GIVEN ME NO END OF TROUBLE.
FLSSSH
AND CAUSED NO SMALL IRRITATION!
DO YOU STILL PLAN ON WRITING YOUR SEQUEL?
OF COURSE. IT WILL BE PUBLISHED IN TWO MONTHS!

STEAM KING?

THE HORROR FICTION WRITER? SURE, I KNOW OF HIM. I'VE READ HIS BOOKS.

HIS BLOCKBUSTER "EMPEROR OF STEAM" WAS ABOUT AN ANTI-HERO WHO COMMITS A SERIES OF GROTESQUE MURDERS TARGETING FAMOUS POLITICIANS AND CELEBRITIES.

THAT'S RIGHT. THE MURDER CASES RESEMBLE THE CONTENTS OF HIS LATEST BOOK, THE ONE THAT HAS HIM KILLING CORPORATE PRESIDENTS.

I THINK THAT KING IS SOMEHOW CONNECTED TO THESE SERIAL KILLINGS.

KING, HIMSELF?

CONNECTED, NOTHING. I THINK *HE'S* THE MURDERER!!

SSSSUP

YUK! WHAT THE HELL IS THIS COFFEE!?

YOU'RE STILL A KID! YOU SHOULDN'T BE DRINKING THIS KIND OF MUD!

SO YOU'RE SAYING MR. KING IS THE EMPEROR OF STEAM?

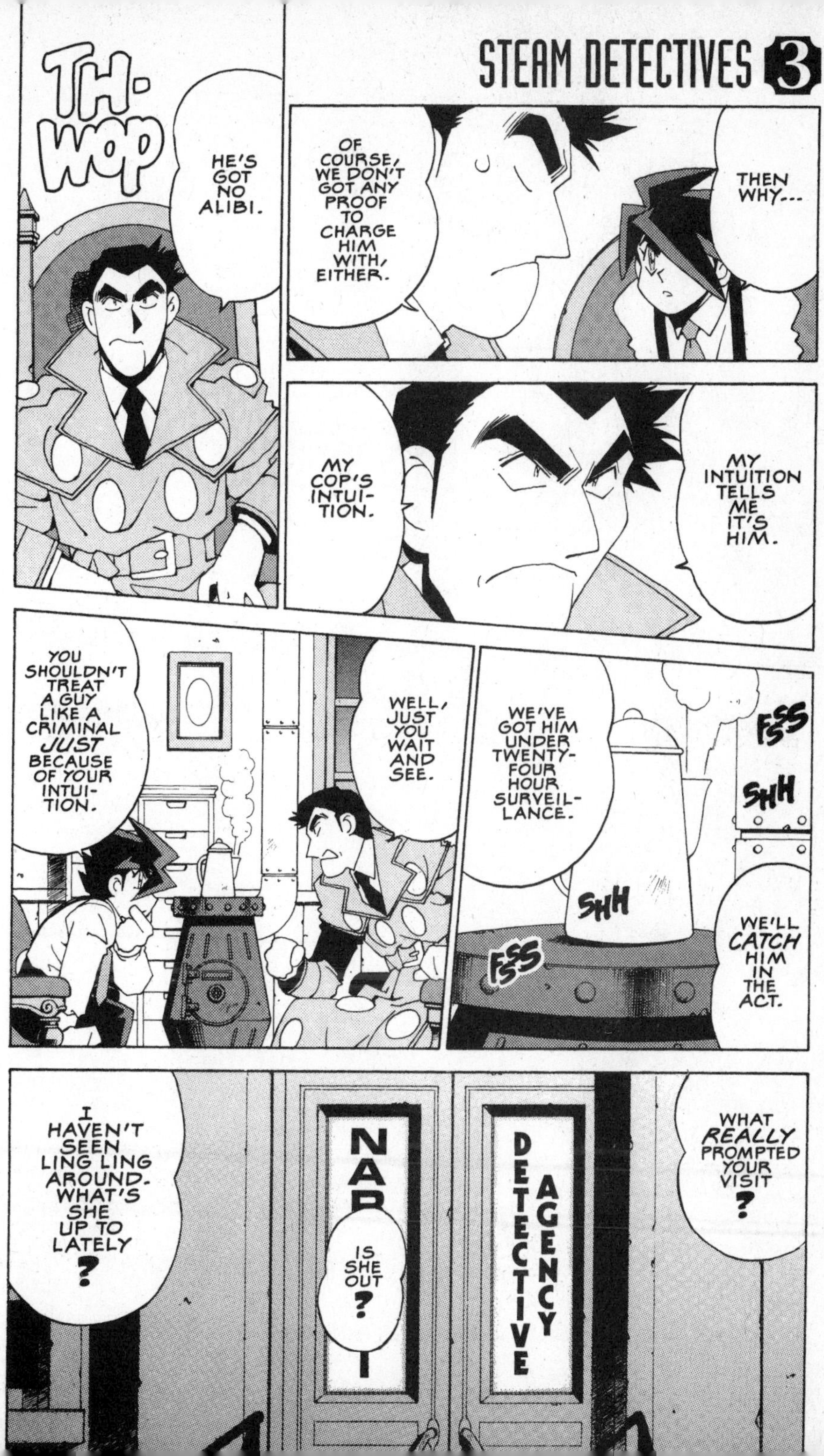
TH-WOP
HE'S GOT NO ALIBI.
OF COURSE, WE DON'T GOT ANY PROOF TO CHARGE HIM WITH, EITHER.
THEN WHY...
MY COP'S INTUITION.
MY INTUITION TELLS ME IT'S HIM.
YOU SHOULDN'T TREAT A GUY LIKE A CRIMINAL JUST BECAUSE OF YOUR INTUITION.
WELL, JUST YOU WAIT AND SEE.
WE'VE GOT HIM UNDER TWENTY-FOUR HOUR SURVEILLANCE.
FSSS
SHH
SHH
FSSS
WE'LL CATCH HIM IN THE ACT.
I HAVEN'T SEEN LING LING AROUND. WHAT'S SHE UP TO LATELY?
NAR
I
IS SHE OUT?
DETECTIVE AGENCY
WHAT REALLY PROMPTED YOUR VISIT?

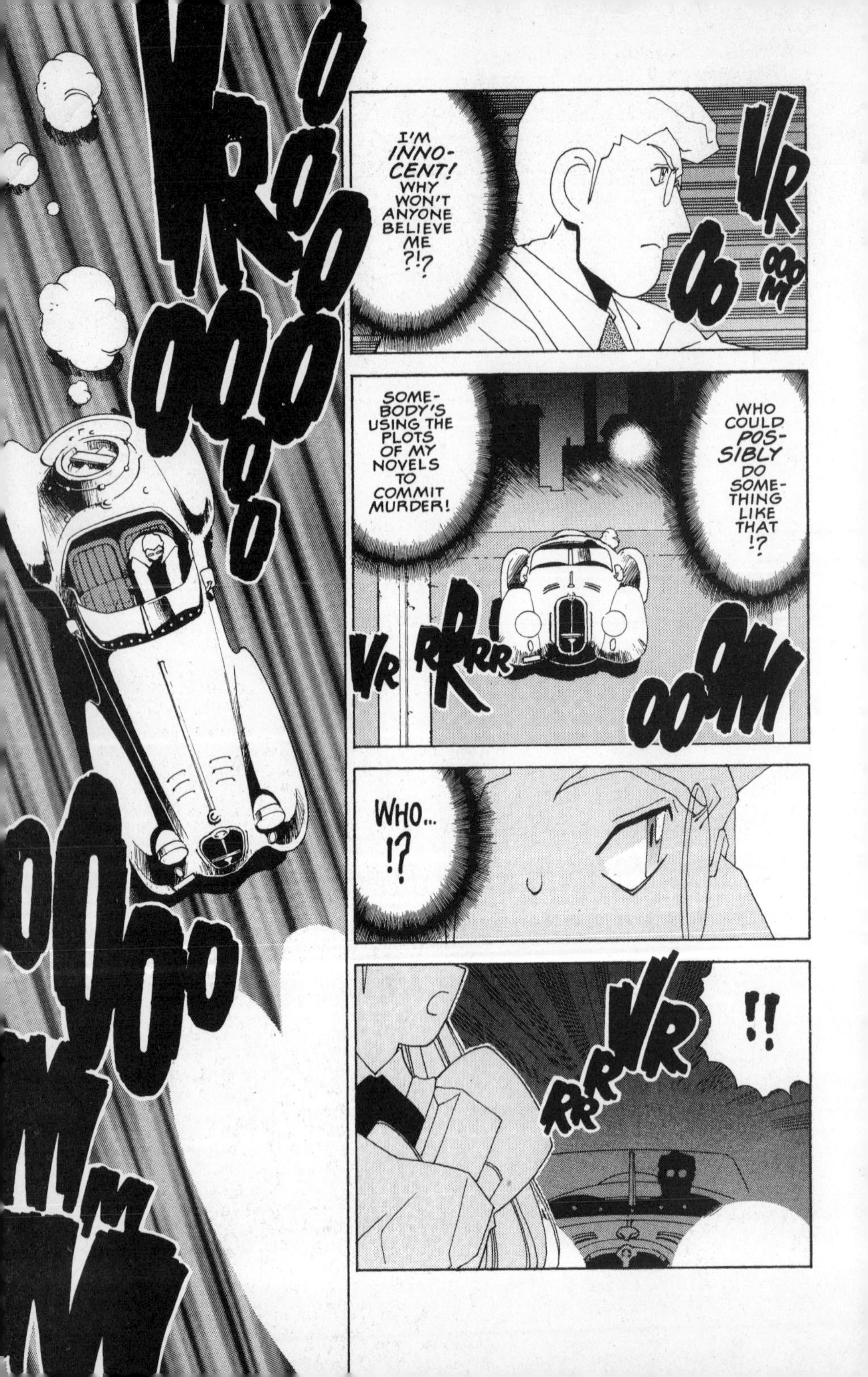
VROOOOOOOOOOOOOOOOOOMMM
I'M INNOCENT! WHY WON'T ANYONE BELIEVE ME ?!?
VROOOOOM
SOMEBODY'S USING THE PLOTS OF MY NOVELS TO COMMIT MURDER!
WHO COULD POSSIBLY DO SOMETHING LIKE THAT !?
VRRRRRR
OOOOM
WHO... !?
RRRRVR
!!

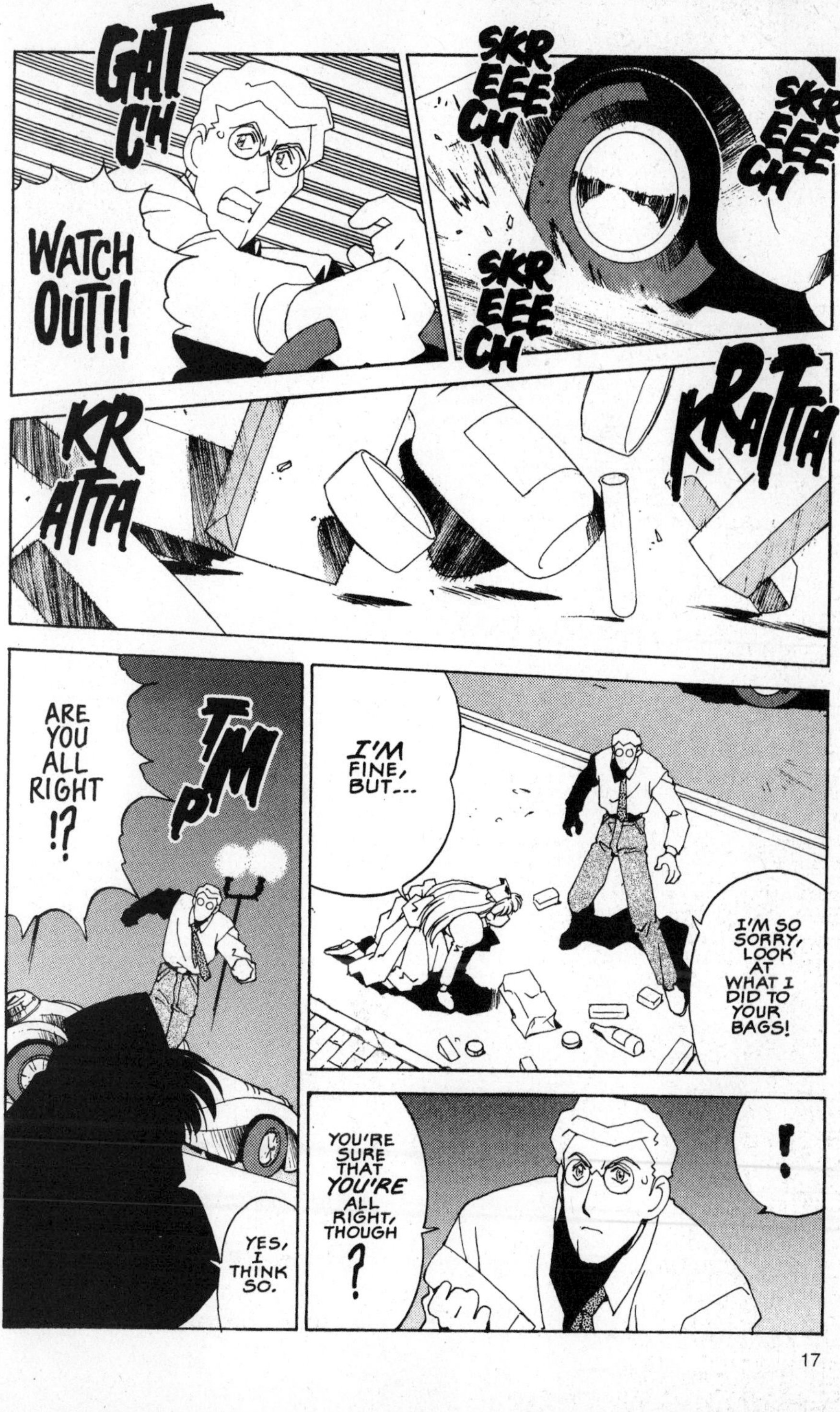
GATCH
WATCH OUT!!
SKREEECH
SKREEECH
SKREEECH
KRATTA
KRATTA
ARE YOU ALL RIGHT !?
TMP
YES, I THINK SO.
I'M FINE, BUT...
I'M SO SORRY, LOOK AT WHAT I DID TO YOUR BAGS!
YOU'RE SURE THAT *YOU'RE* ALL RIGHT, THOUGH ?
!

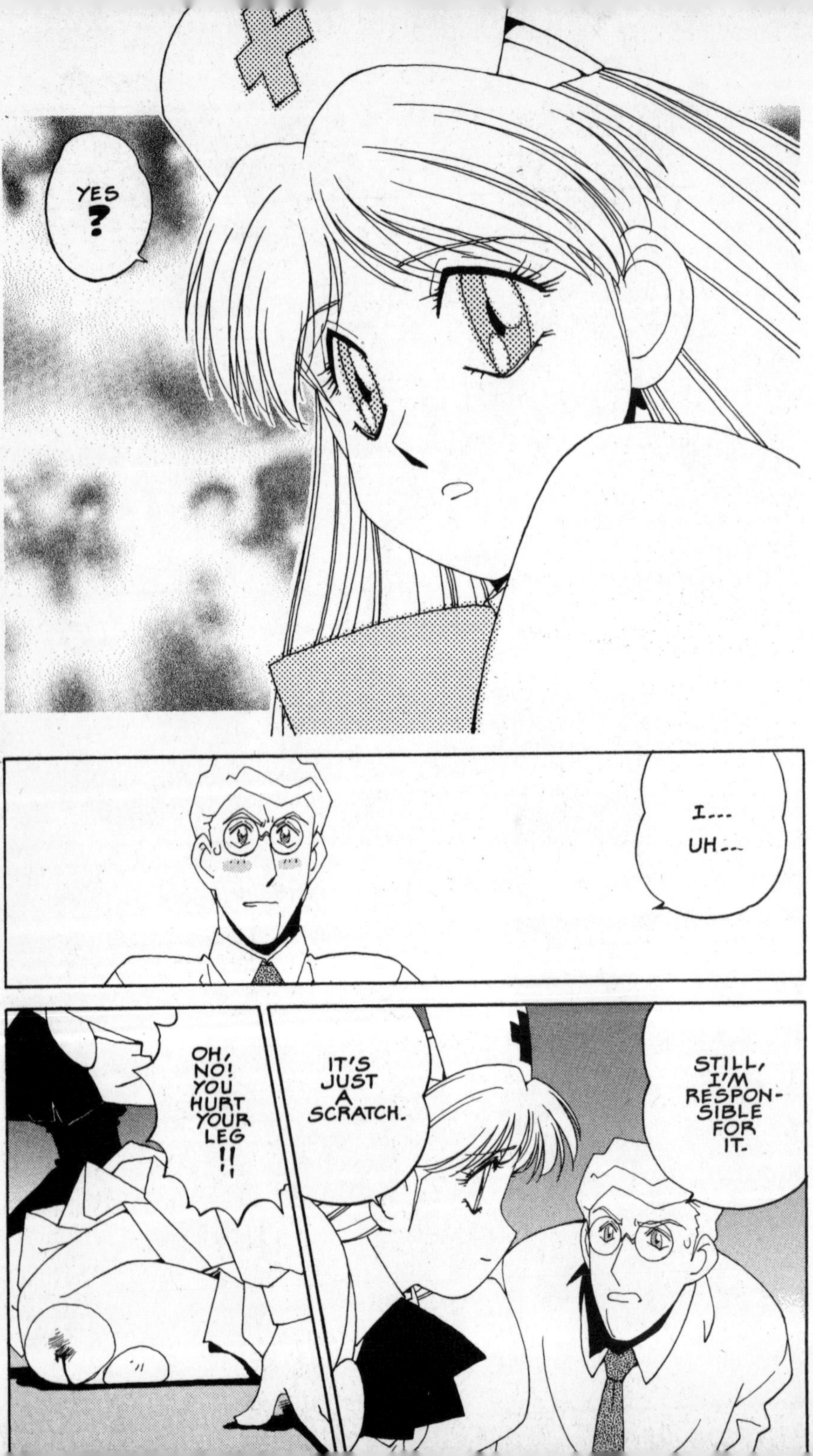
YES?
I... UH...
OH, NO! YOU HURT YOUR LEG!!
IT'S JUST A SCRATCH.
STILL, I'M RESPONSIBLE FOR IT.

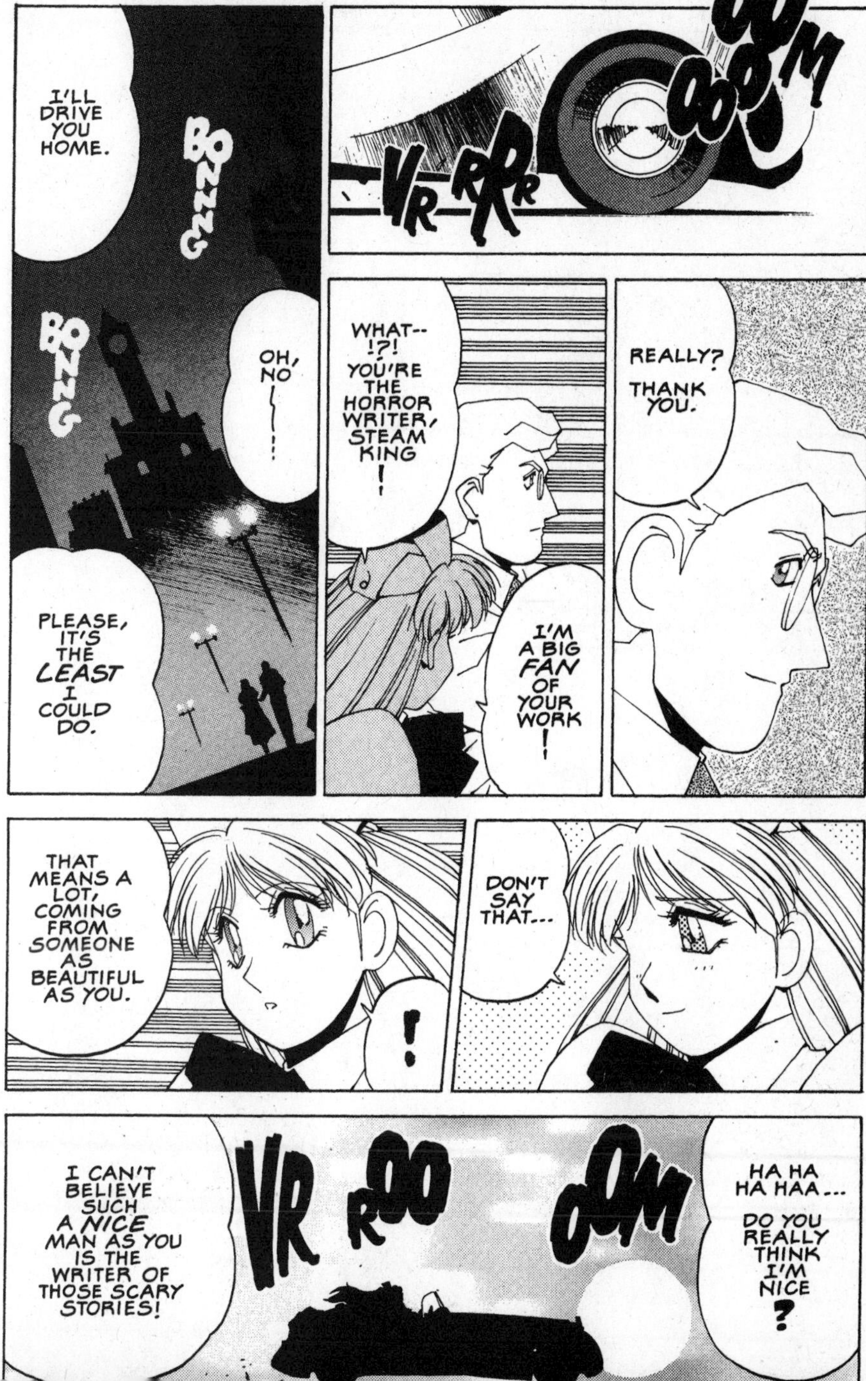
I'LL DRIVE YOU HOME.
BONNNG
BONNG
OH, NO!!
PLEASE, IT'S THE LEAST I COULD DO.
VRRRRR
OOOOOOM!
WHAT--!?! YOU'RE THE HORROR WRITER, STEAM KING!
I'M A BIG FAN OF YOUR WORK!
REALLY? THANK YOU.
THAT MEANS A LOT, COMING FROM SOMEONE AS BEAUTIFUL AS YOU.
!
DON'T SAY THAT...
I CAN'T BELIEVE SUCH A NICE MAN AS YOU IS THE WRITER OF THOSE SCARY STORIES!
VRROOOOM
HA HA HA HAA... DO YOU REALLY THINK I'M NICE?

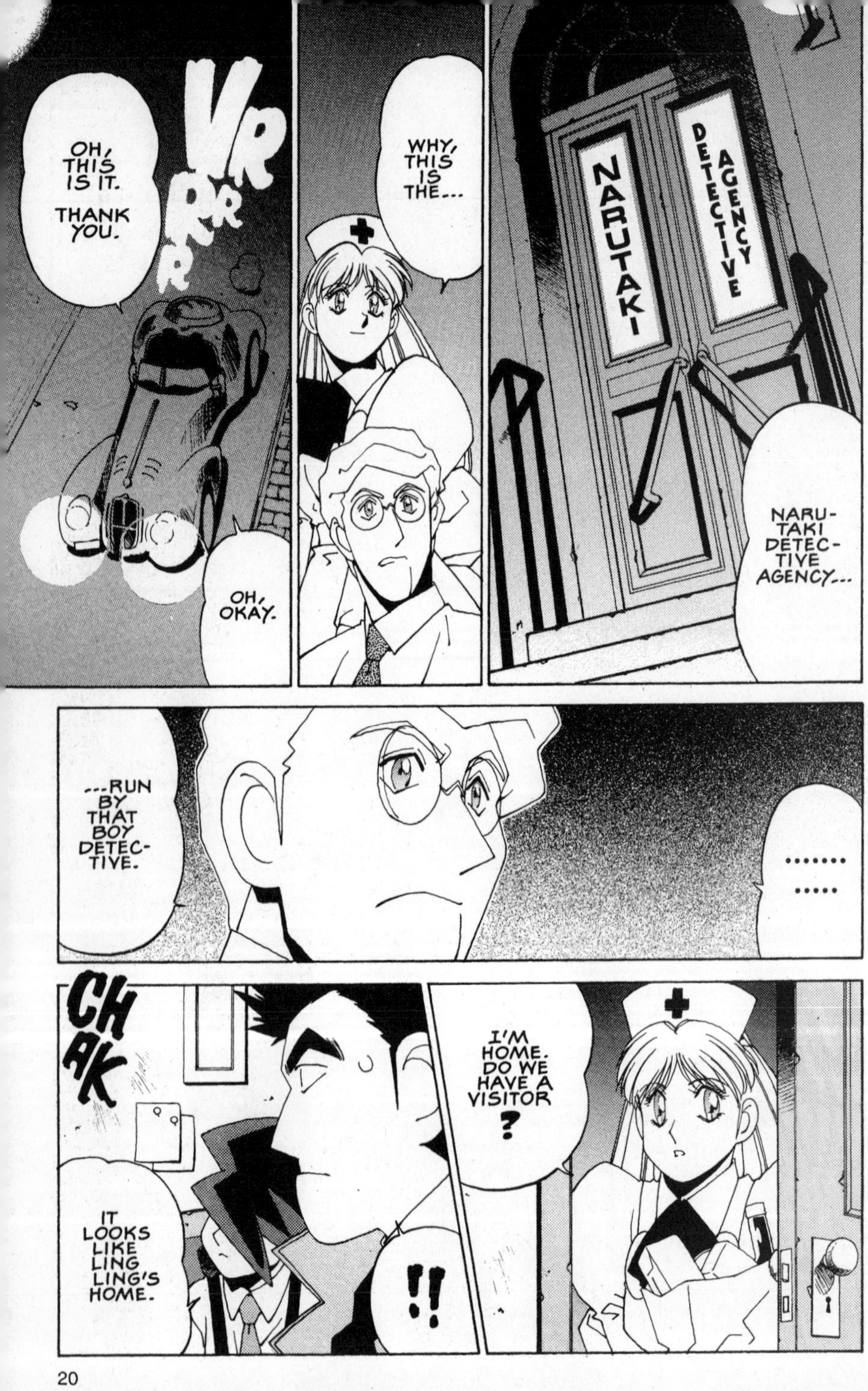
OH, THIS IS IT.
THANK YOU.
VRRRRR
OH, OKAY.
WHY, THIS IS THE...
NARUTAKI DETECTIVE AGENCY
NARUTAKI DETECTIVE AGENCY...
...RUN BY THAT BOY DETECTIVE.
....
.....
CHAK
IT LOOKS LIKE LING LING'S HOME.
!!
I'M HOME. DO WE HAVE A VISITOR?

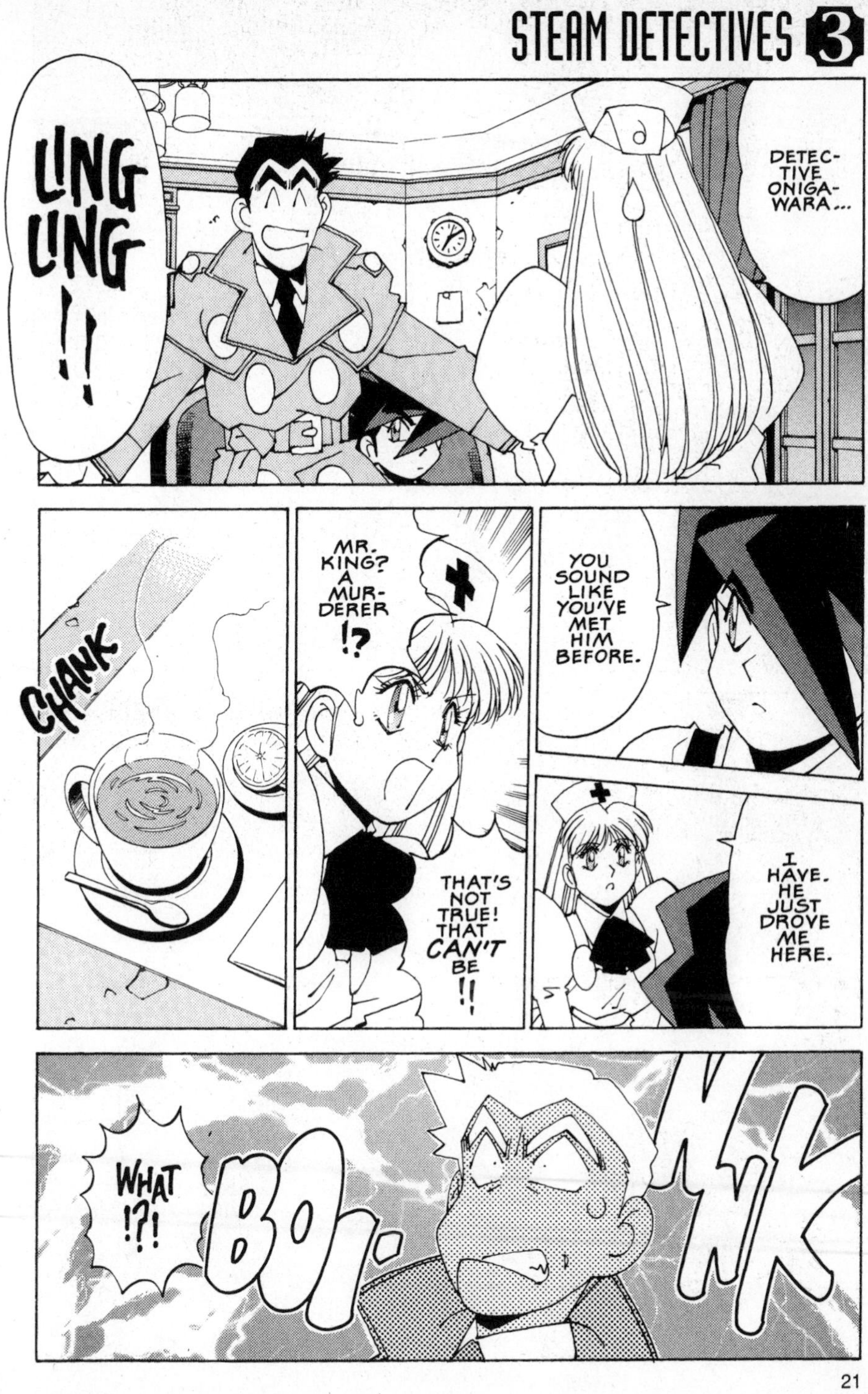
LING LING !!
DETECTIVE ONIGAWARA...
CHANK
MR. KING? A MURDERER !?
THAT'S NOT TRUE! THAT CAN'T BE !!
YOU SOUND LIKE YOU'VE MET HIM BEFORE.
I HAVE. HE JUST DROVE ME HERE.
WHAT !?!
BOI-NK

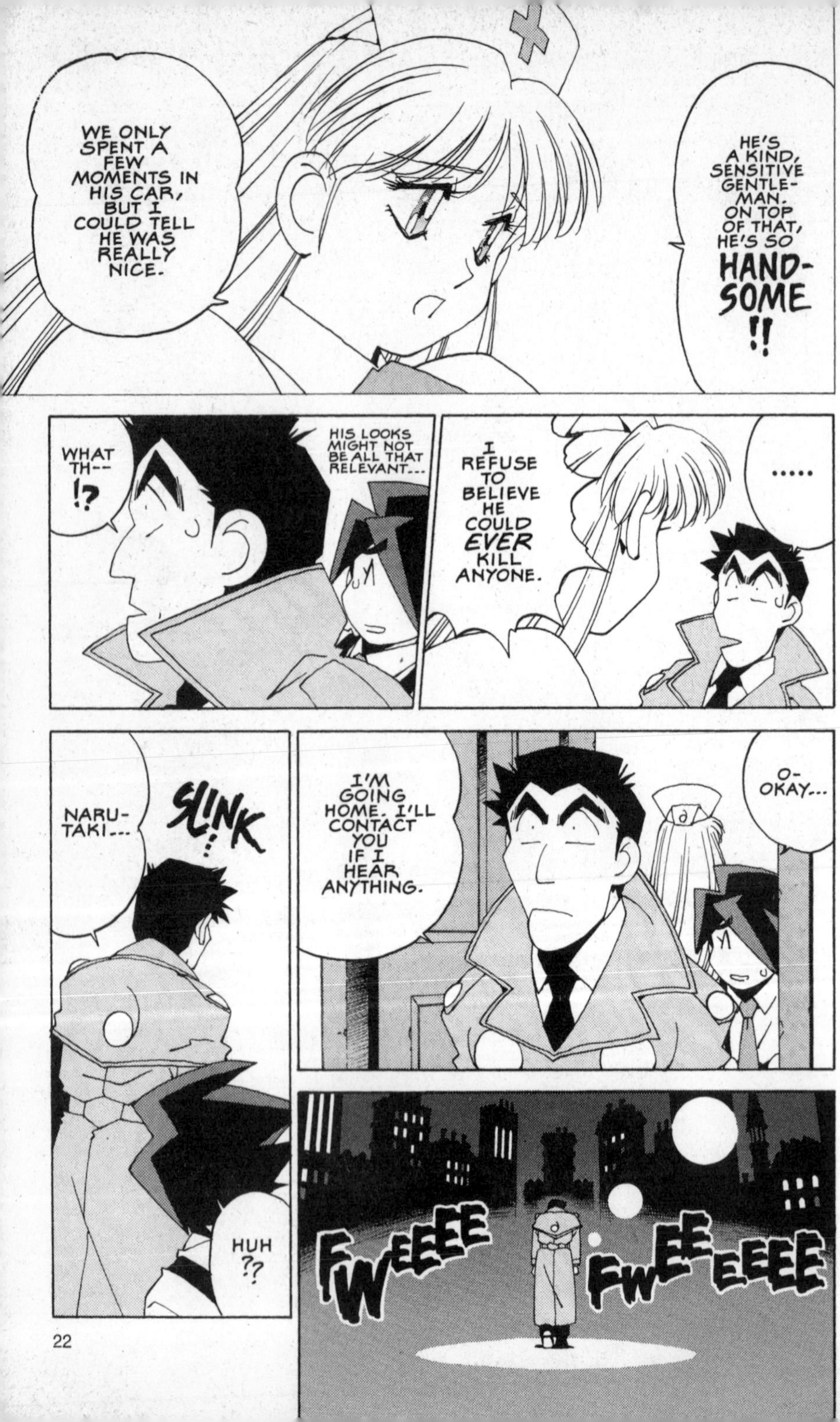
WE ONLY SPENT A FEW MOMENTS IN HIS CAR, BUT I COULD TELL HE WAS REALLY NICE.
HE'S A KIND, SENSITIVE GENTLE-MAN. ON TOP OF THAT, HE'S SO HAND-SOME !!
WHAT TH-- !?
HIS LOOKS MIGHT NOT BE ALL THAT RELEVANT...
I REFUSE TO BELIEVE HE COULD EVER KILL ANYONE.
.....
NARU-TAKI...
SLINK
HUH ??
I'M GOING HOME. I'LL CONTACT YOU IF I HEAR ANYTHING.
O-OKAY...
FWEEEEE
FWEEEEEEE

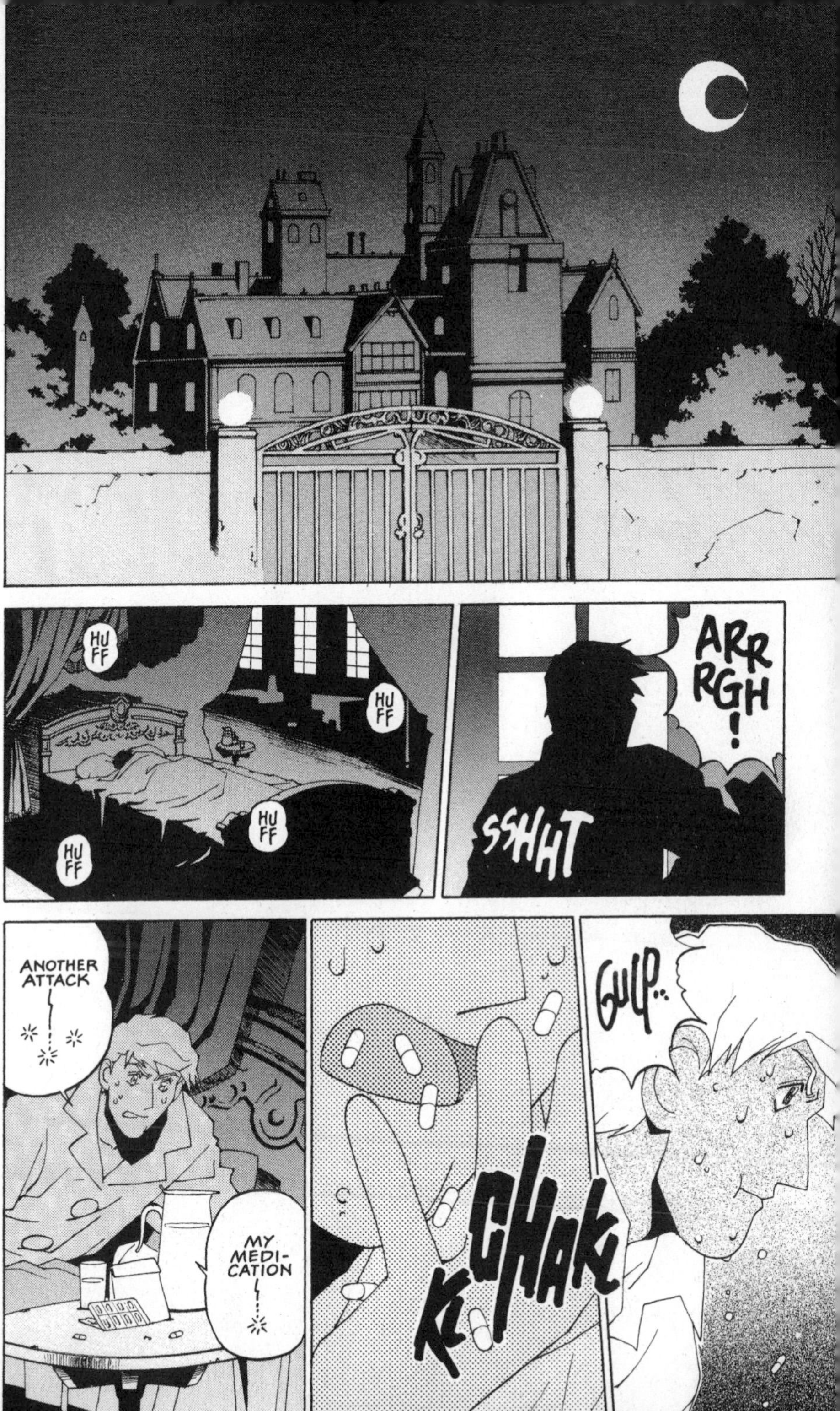
HUFF
HUFF
HUFF
HUFF
ARRRGH!
SSHHT
ANOTHER ATTACK
MY MEDI-CATION
GULP..
KCHAK

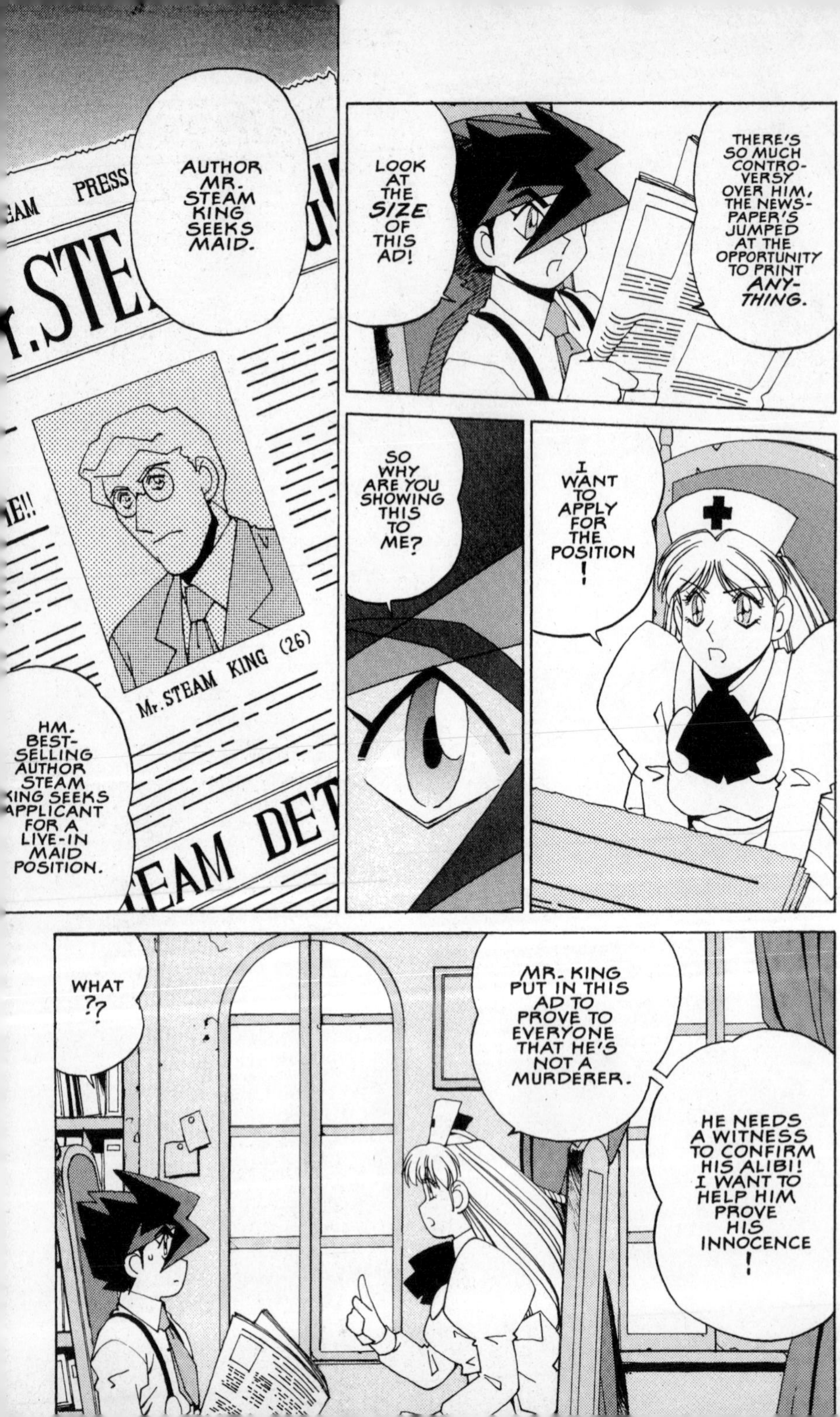
AUTHOR MR. STEAM KING SEEKS MAID.
PRESS
Mr. STEAM KING (26)
HM. BEST-SELLING AUTHOR STEAM KING SEEKS APPLICANT FOR A LIVE-IN MAID POSITION.
LOOK AT THE *SIZE* OF THIS AD!
THERE'S SO MUCH CONTROVERSY OVER HIM, THE NEWSPAPER'S JUMPED AT THE OPPORTUNITY TO PRINT *ANYTHING*.
SO WHY ARE YOU SHOWING THIS TO ME?
I WANT TO APPLY FOR THE POSITION!
WHAT??
MR. KING PUT IN THIS AD TO PROVE TO EVERYONE THAT HE'S NOT A MURDERER.
HE NEEDS A WITNESS TO CONFIRM HIS ALIBI! I WANT TO HELP HIM PROVE HIS INNOCENCE!

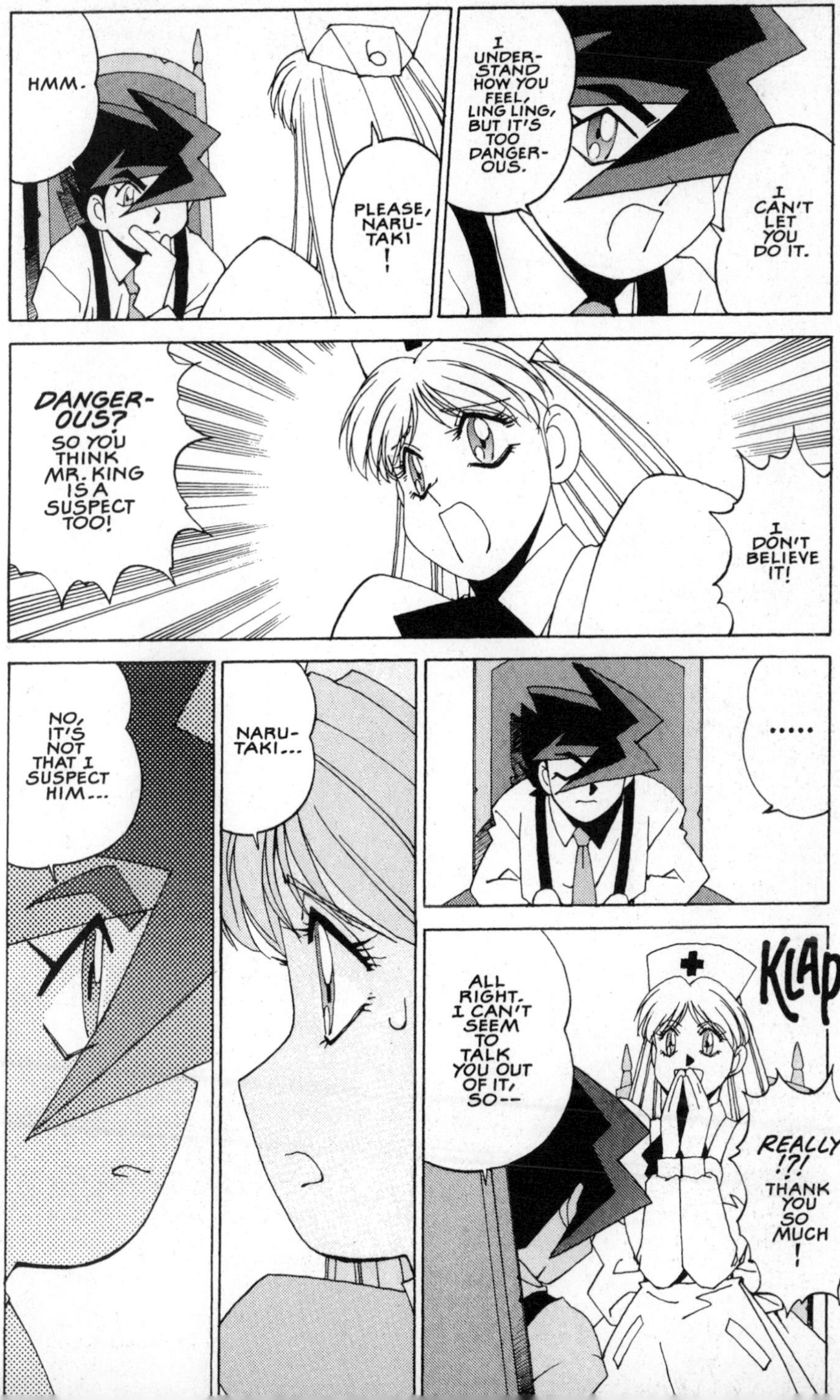
HMM.
PLEASE, NARUTAKI!
I UNDERSTAND HOW YOU FEEL, LING LING, BUT IT'S TOO DANGEROUS.
I CAN'T LET YOU DO IT.
DANGEROUS? SO YOU THINK MR. KING IS A SUSPECT TOO!
I DON'T BELIEVE IT!
NO, IT'S NOT THAT I SUSPECT HIM...
NARUTAKI...
.....
ALL RIGHT. I CAN'T SEEM TO TALK YOU OUT OF IT, SO--
KLAP
REALLY!?! THANK YOU SO MUCH!

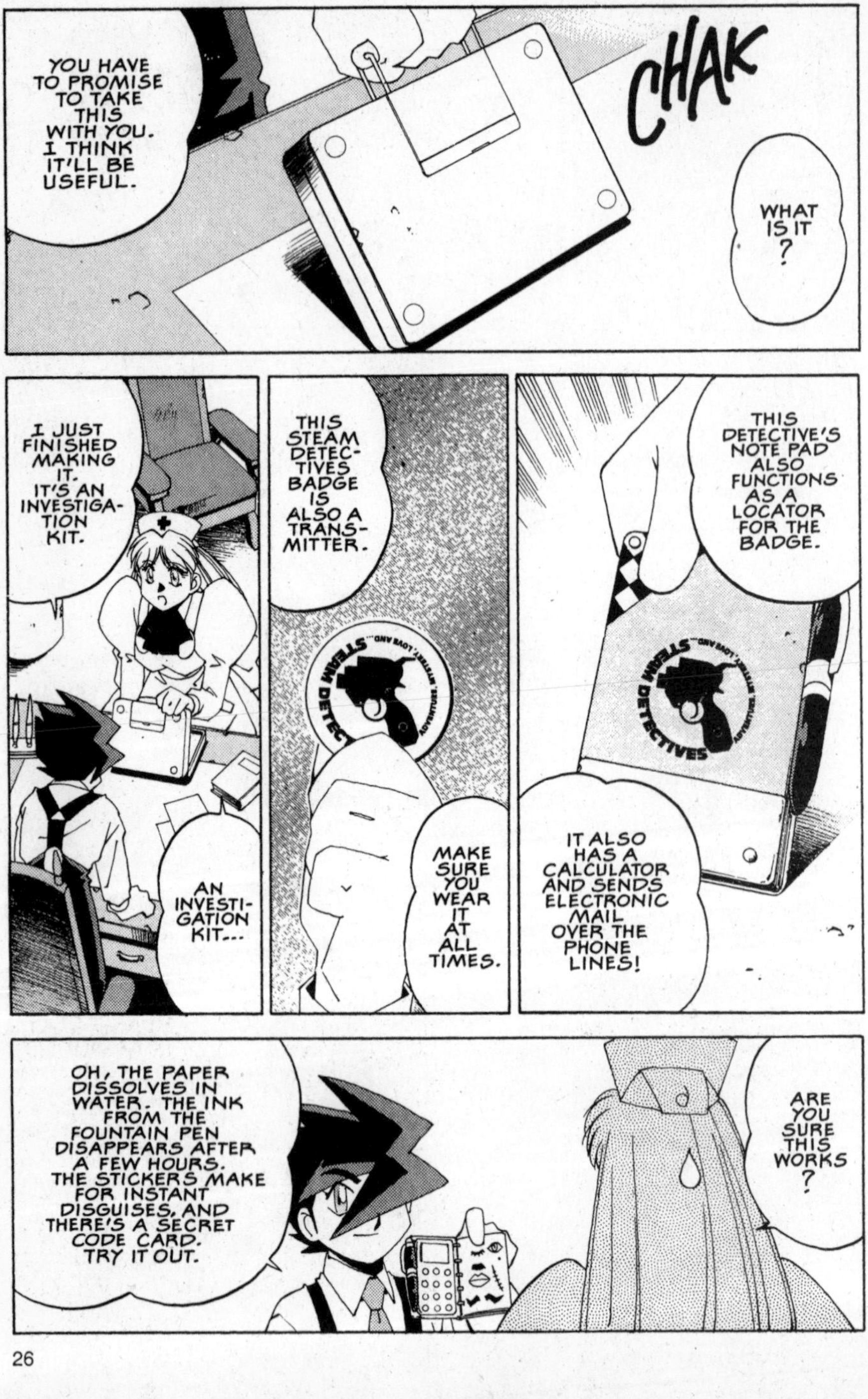
YOU HAVE TO PROMISE TO TAKE THIS WITH YOU. I THINK IT'LL BE USEFUL.
CHAK
WHAT IS IT?
I JUST FINISHED MAKING IT. IT'S AN INVESTIGATION KIT.
AN INVESTIGATION KIT...
THIS STEAM DETECTIVES BADGE IS ALSO A TRANSMITTER.
MAKE SURE YOU WEAR IT AT ALL TIMES.
THIS DETECTIVE'S NOTE PAD ALSO FUNCTIONS AS A LOCATOR FOR THE BADGE.
IT ALSO HAS A CALCULATOR AND SENDS ELECTRONIC MAIL OVER THE PHONE LINES!
OH, THE PAPER DISSOLVES IN WATER. THE INK FROM THE FOUNTAIN PEN DISAPPEARS AFTER A FEW HOURS. THE STICKERS MAKE FOR INSTANT DISGUISES, AND THERE'S A SECRET CODE CARD. TRY IT OUT.
ARE YOU SURE THIS WORKS?

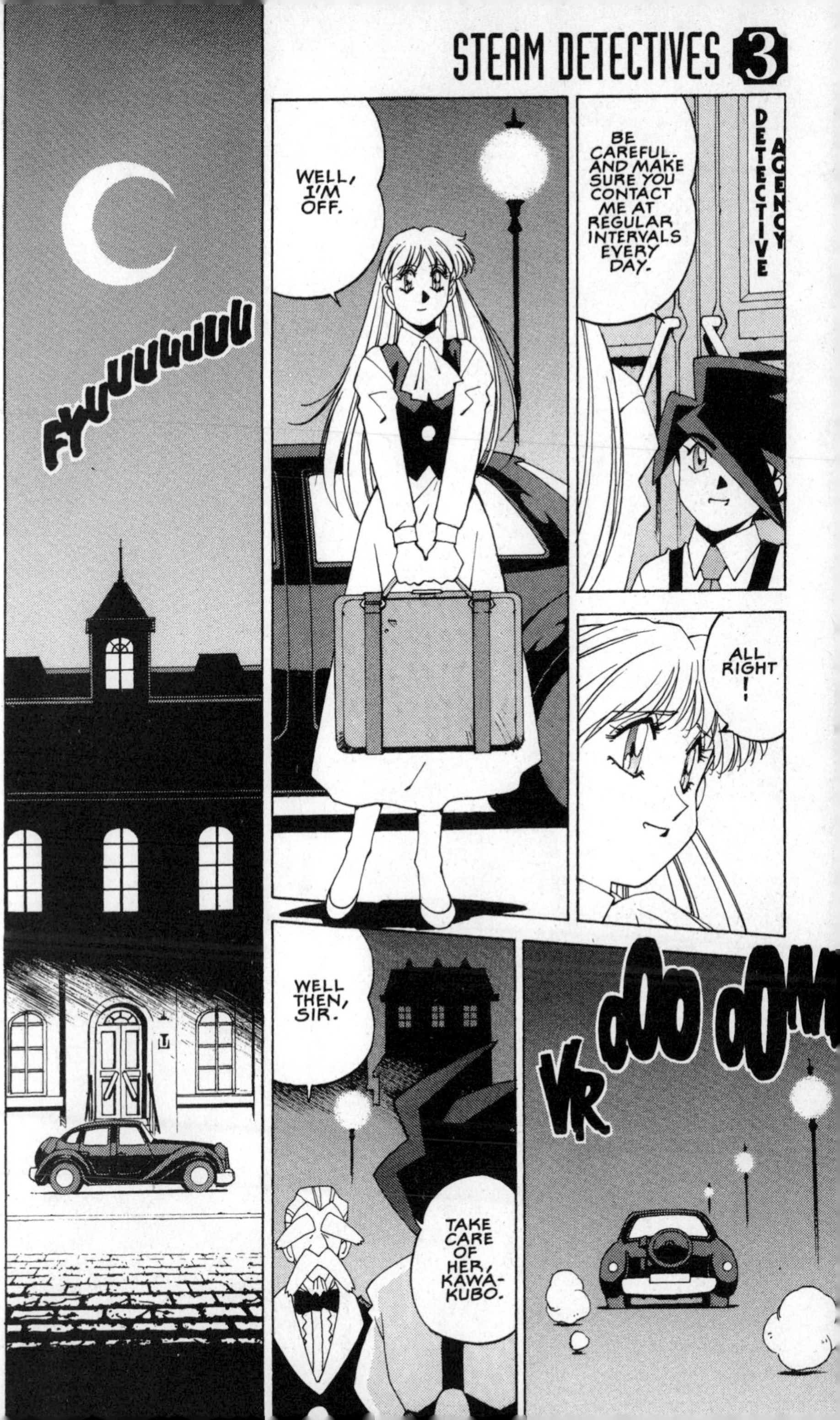
FYUUUUUU
WELL, I'M OFF.
BE CAREFUL. AND MAKE SURE YOU CONTACT ME AT REGULAR INTERVALS EVERY DAY.
DETECTIVE AGENCY
ALL RIGHT!
WELL THEN, SIR.
TAKE CARE OF HER, KAWAKUBO.
VROOO OOM

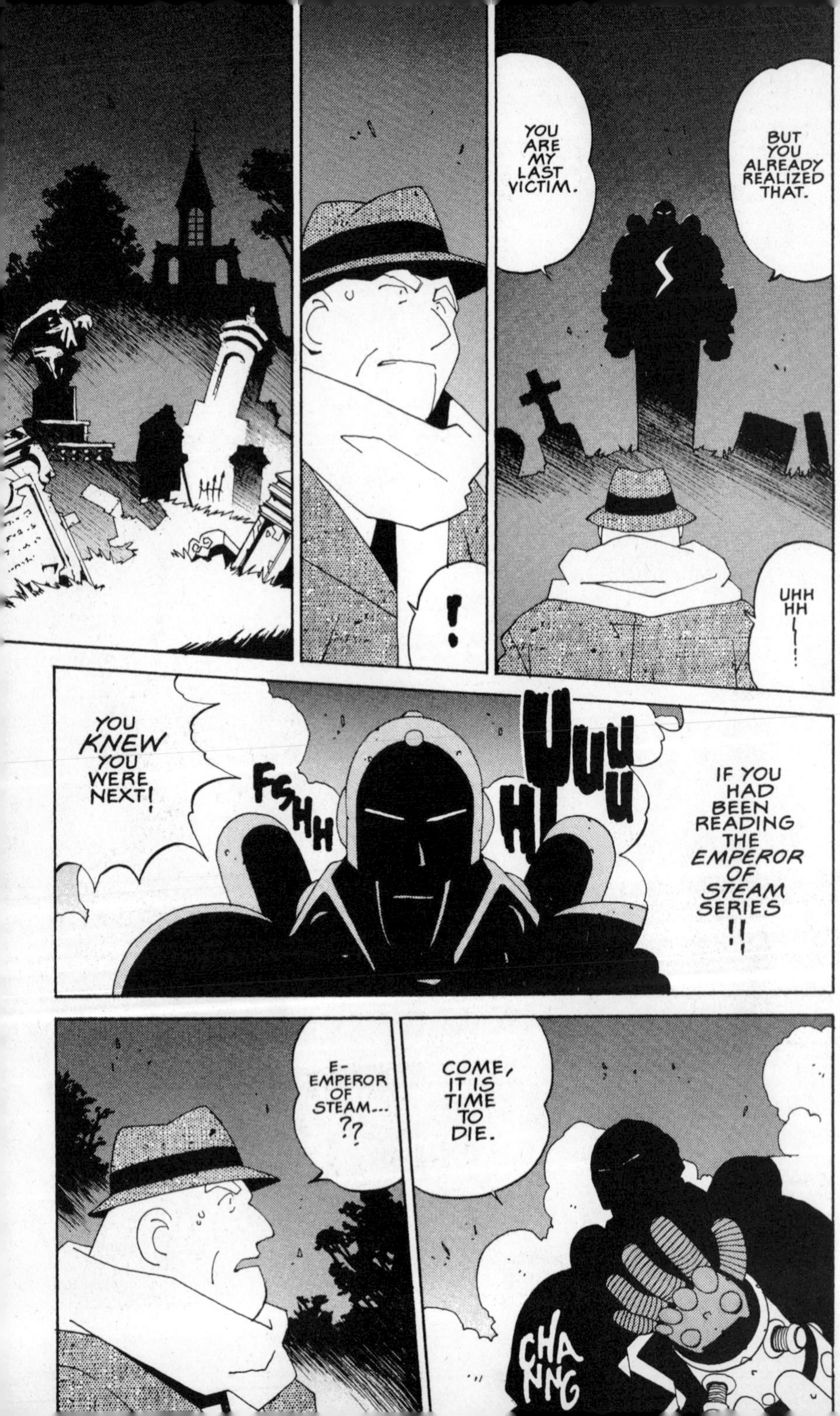
!
YOU ARE MY LAST VICTIM.
BUT YOU ALREADY REALIZED THAT.
UHHHH!!
YOU KNEW YOU WERE NEXT!
FSHHH
HUUUU
IF YOU HAD BEEN READING THE EMPEROR OF STEAM SERIES!!
E-EMPEROR OF STEAM...??
COME, IT IS TIME TO DIE.
CHANNG

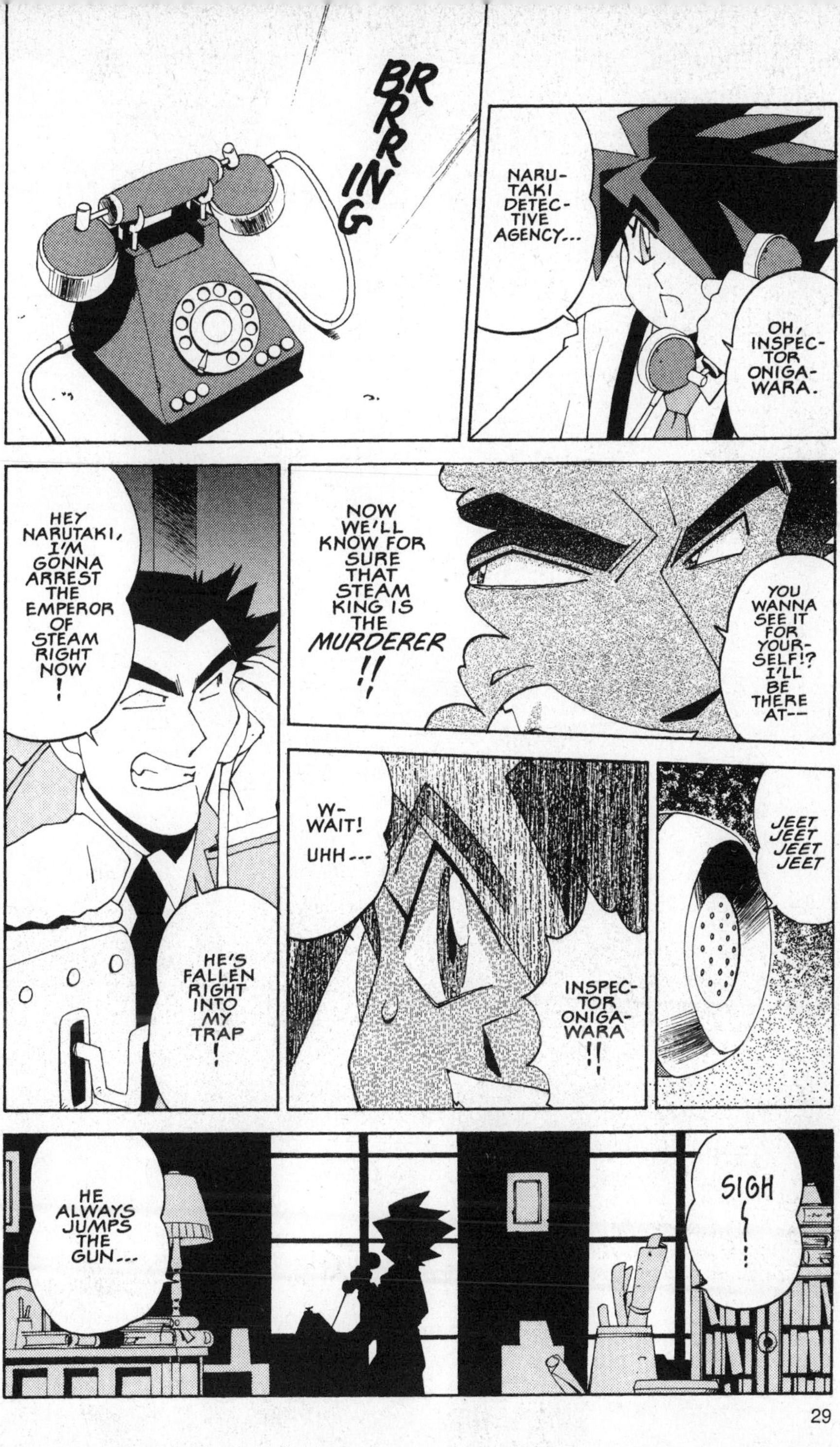
BRRRING
NARUTAKI DETECTIVE AGENCY...
OH, INSPECTOR ONIGAWARA.
HEY NARUTAKI, I'M GONNA ARREST THE EMPEROR OF STEAM RIGHT NOW!
HE'S FALLEN RIGHT INTO MY TRAP!
NOW WE'LL KNOW FOR SURE THAT STEAM KING IS THE MURDERER!!
YOU WANNA SEE IT FOR YOURSELF!? I'LL BE THERE AT--
W-WAIT! UHH...
INSPECTOR ONIGAWARA!!
JEET JEET JEET JEET
HE ALWAYS JUMPS THE GUN...
SIGH~...

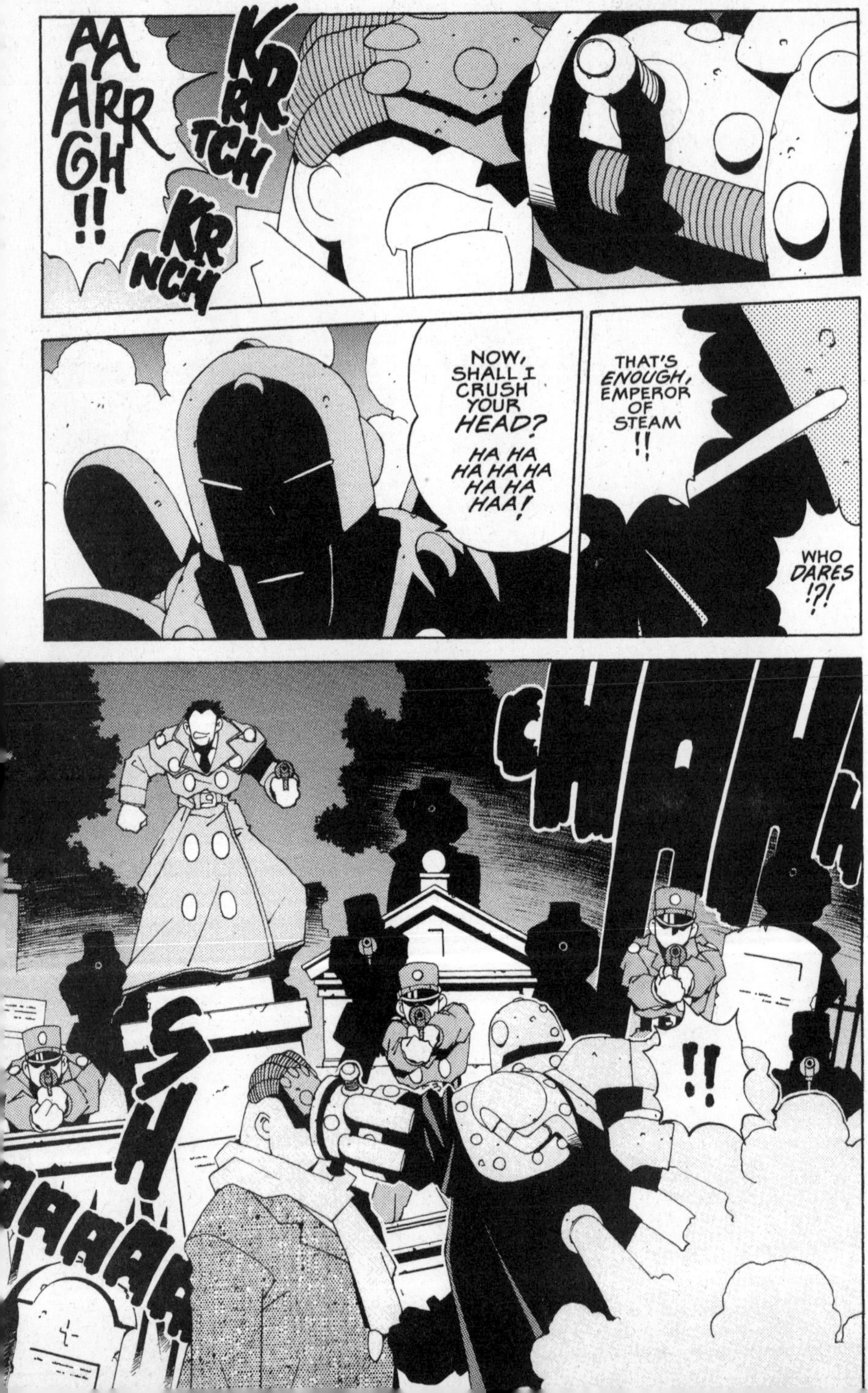
AAARRGH!!
KRRRTCH
KRNCH
NOW, SHALL I CRUSH YOUR *HEAD?*
HA HA HA HA HA HA HA HAA!
THAT'S *ENOUGH,* EMPEROR OF STEAM!!
WHO *DARES* !?!
!!

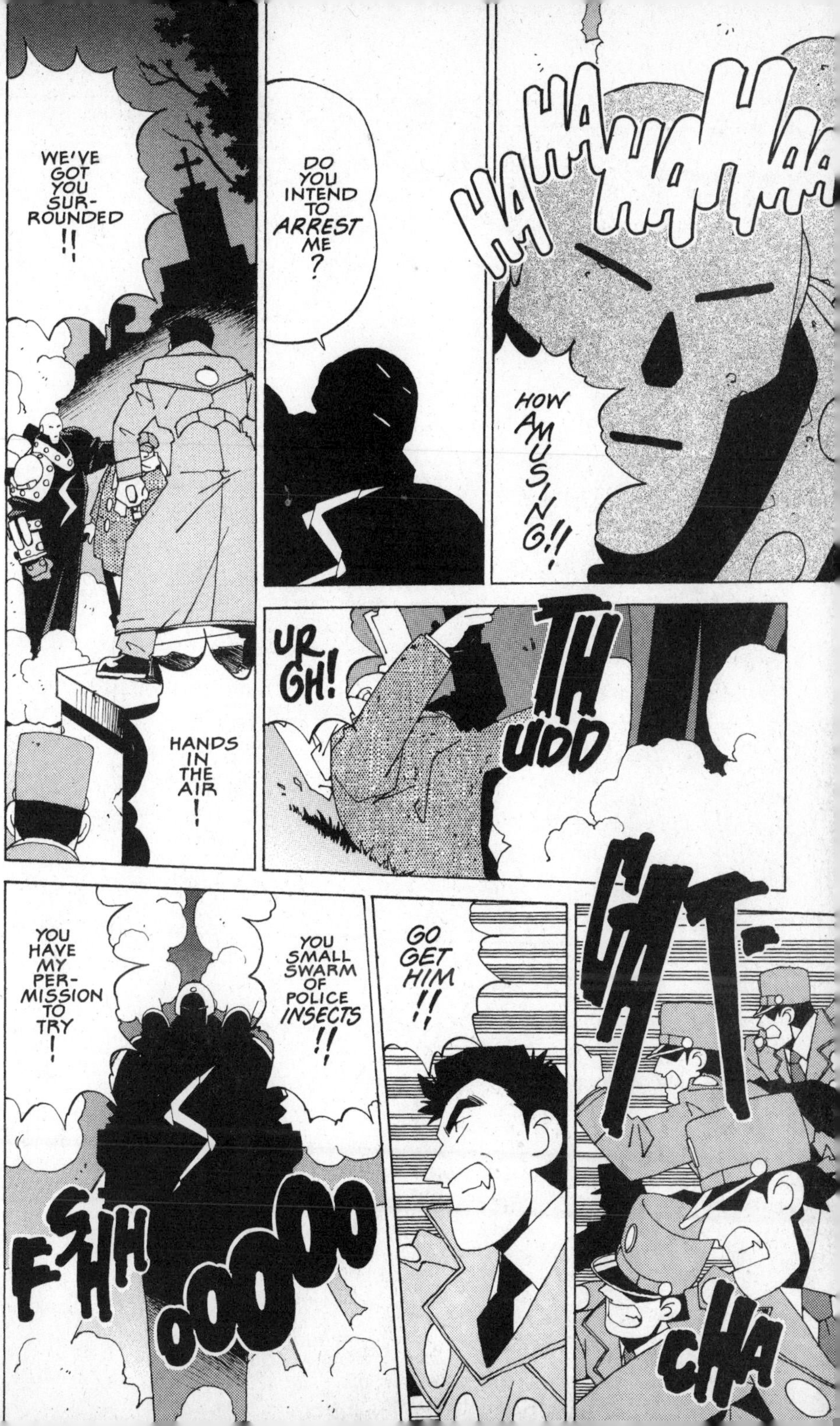
WE'VE GOT YOU SUR-ROUNDED!!
HANDS IN THE AIR!
DO YOU INTEND TO ARREST ME?
HAHAHAHAHAA
HOW AMUSING!!
URGH!
THUDD
YOU HAVE MY PER-MISSION TO TRY!
YOU SMALL SWARM OF POLICE INSECTS!!
FSHHOOOOOO
GO GET HIM!!
CHA-
CHA

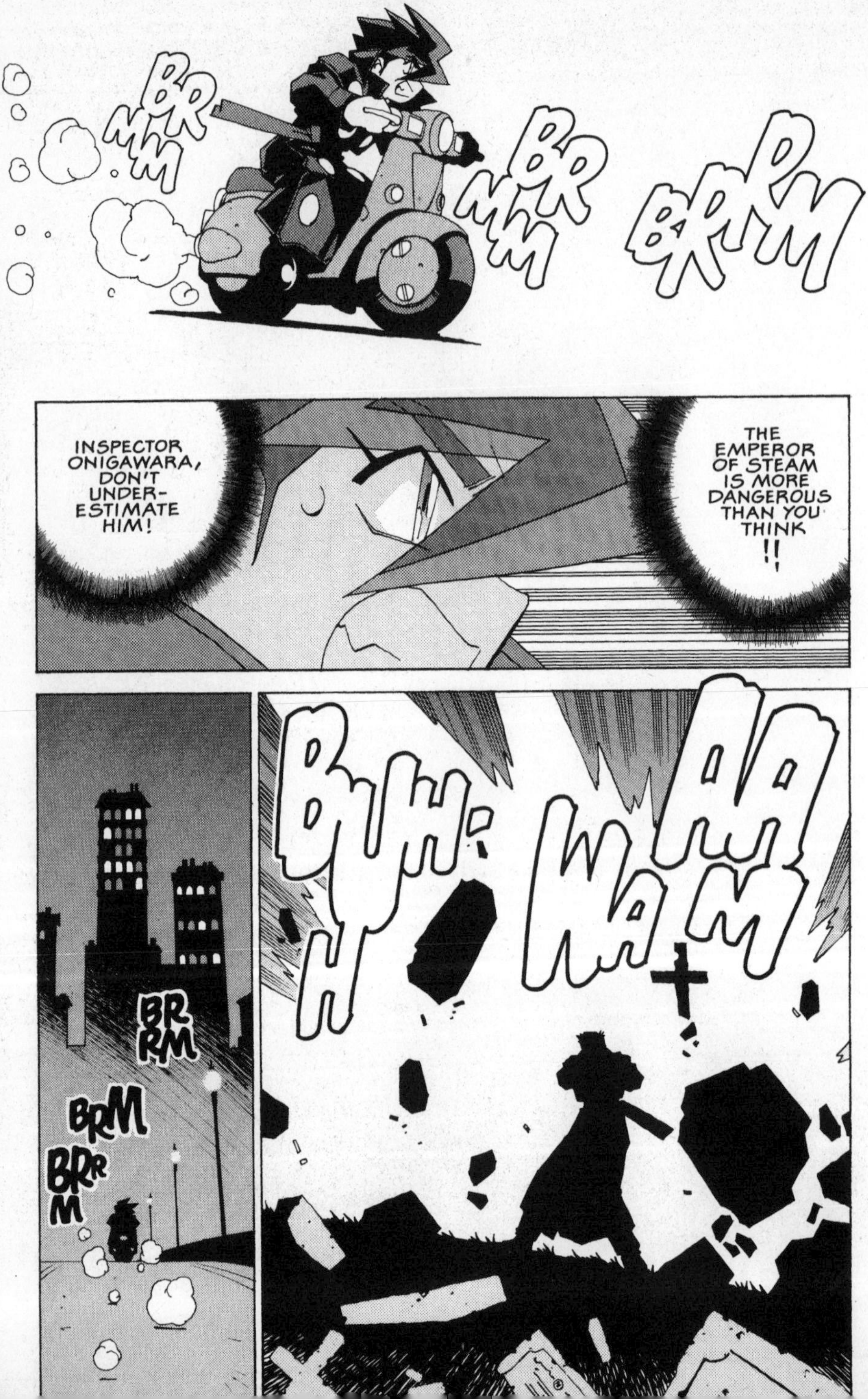
BRMM
BRMM
BRRM
INSPECTOR ONIGAWARA, DON'T UNDER-ESTIMATE HIM!
THE EMPEROR OF STEAM IS MORE DANGEROUS THAN YOU THINK!!
BRRM
BRM
BRRM

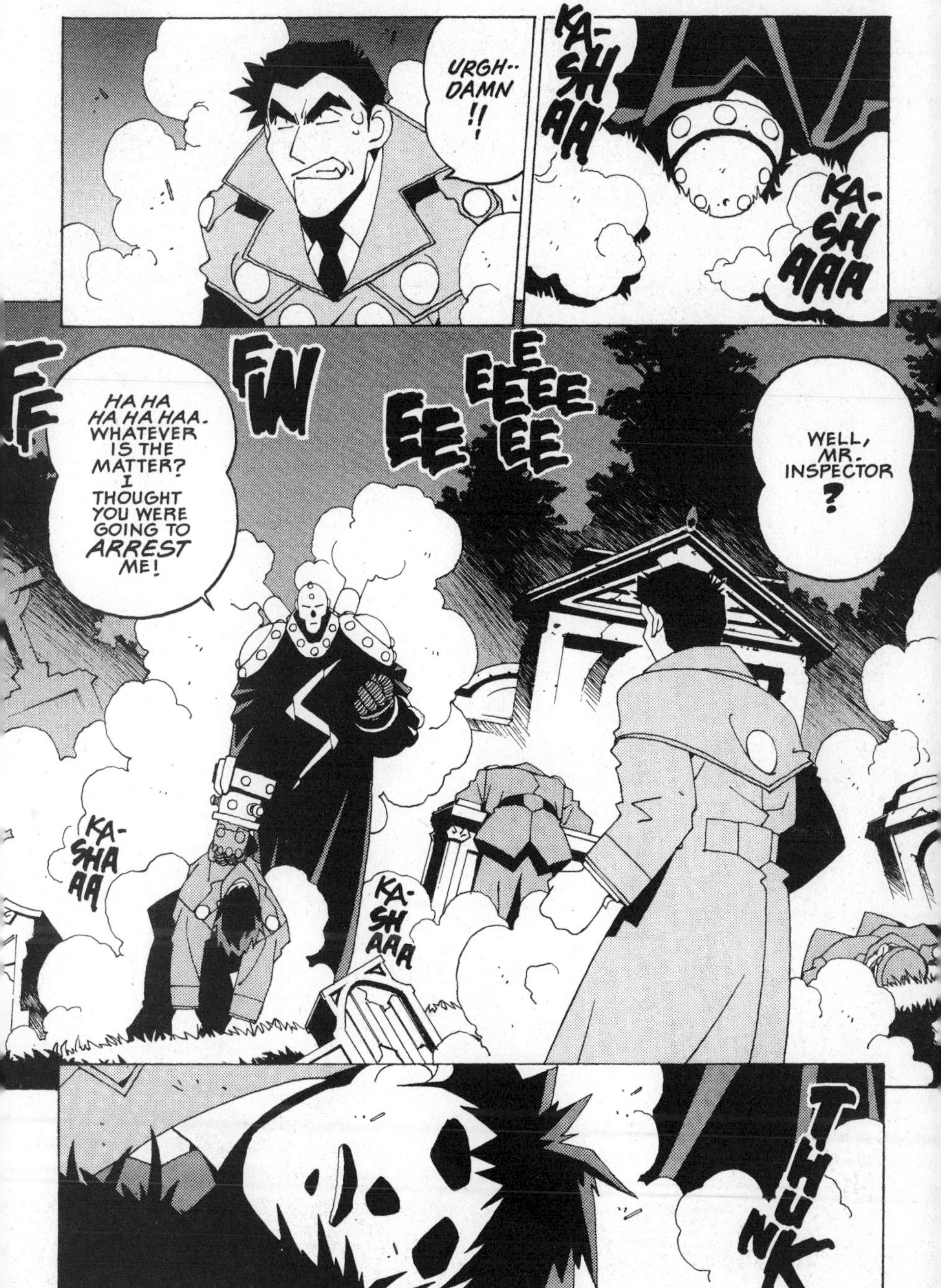
URGH.. DAMN !!
KA-SH AA
KA-SH AAA
FF
HA HA HA HA HAA. WHATEVER IS THE MATTER? I THOUGHT YOU WERE GOING TO ARREST ME!
FW
EE EEEEE EE
WELL, MR. INSPECTOR ?
KA-SHA AA
KA-SH AAA
THUNK

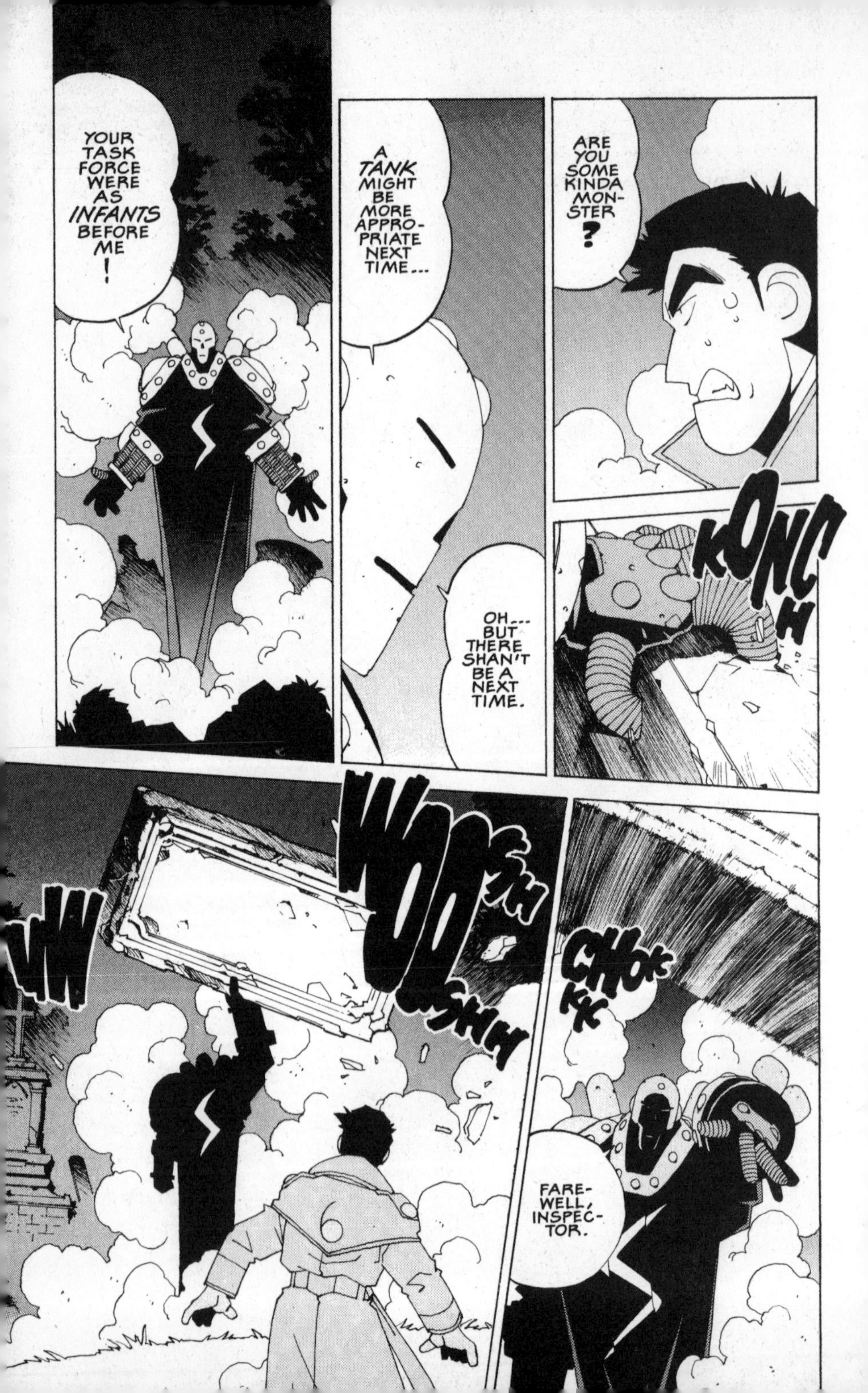
YOUR TASK FORCE WERE AS *INFANTS* BEFORE ME!
A *TANK* MIGHT BE MORE APPROPRIATE NEXT TIME...
OH... BUT THERE SHAN'T BE A NEXT TIME.
ARE YOU SOME KINDA MONSTER?
KONCH
WOOOSH
WOOSHH
CHOKK
FAREWELL, INSPECTOR.

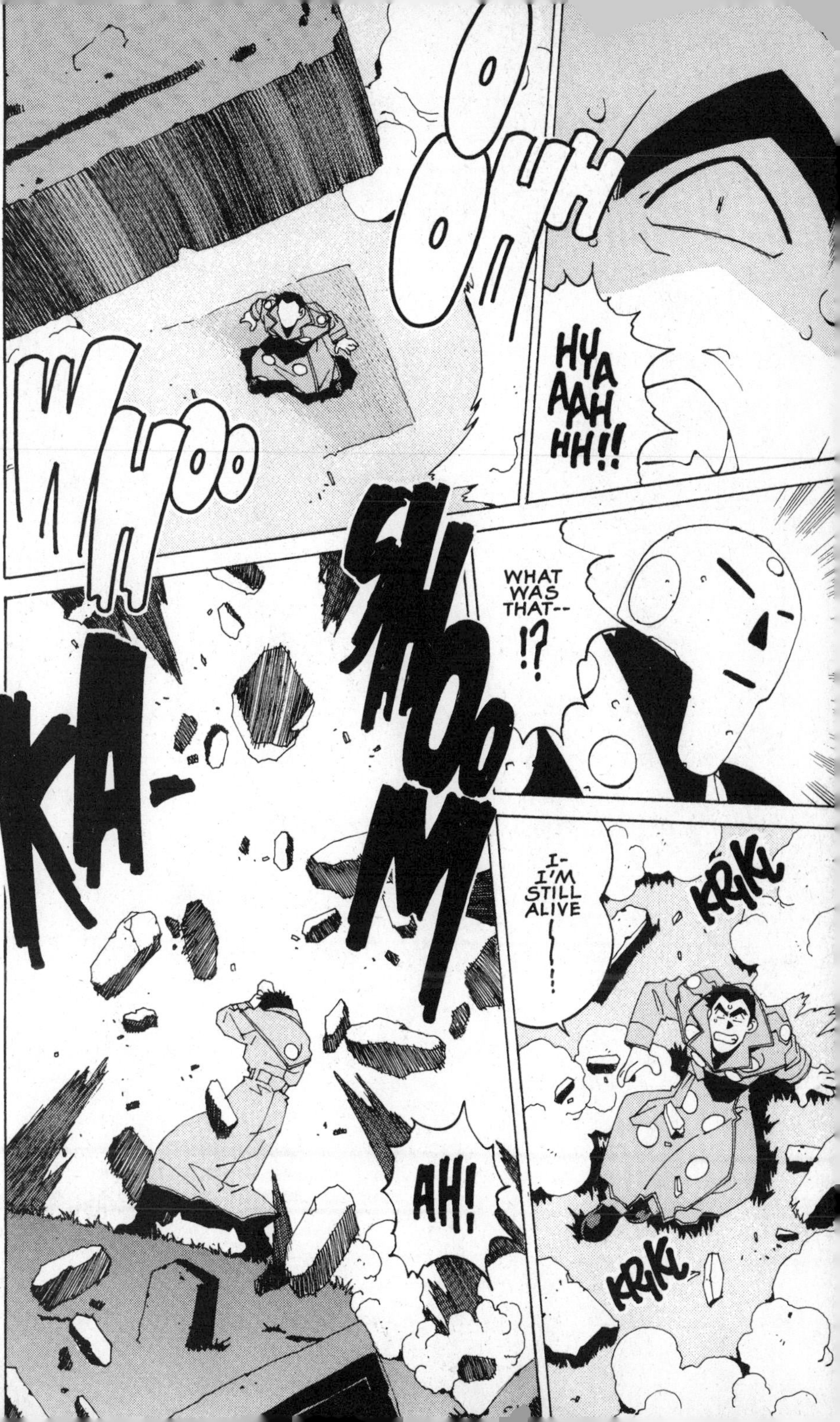
WHOO
OOHH
HYAAAHHH!!
KA-
SHOOM
AH!
WHAT WAS THAT--!?
I-I'M STILL ALIVE
KRIKI
KRIKI

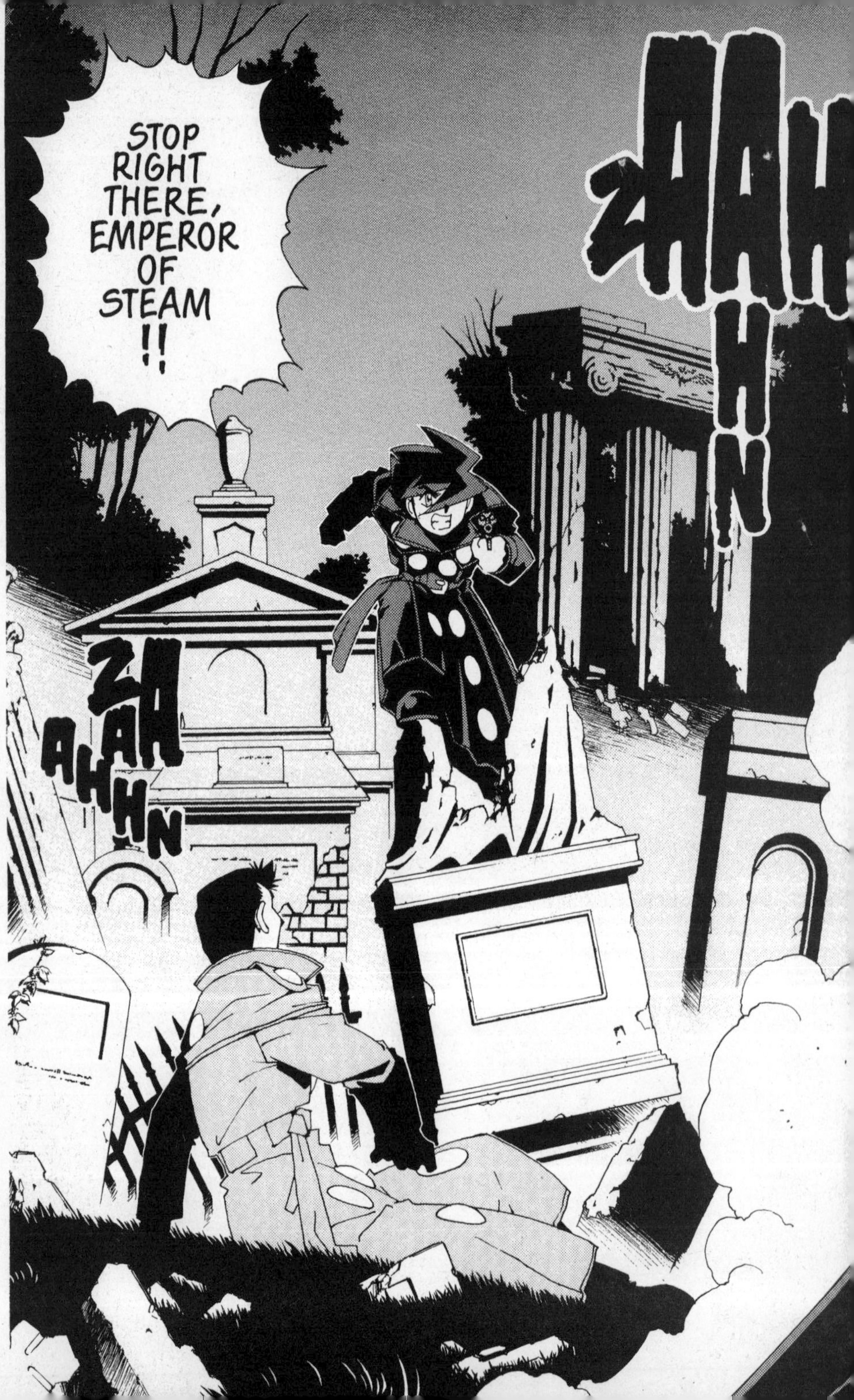
STOP RIGHT THERE, EMPEROR OF STEAM !!
ZAAHHHN
ZAAHHHN

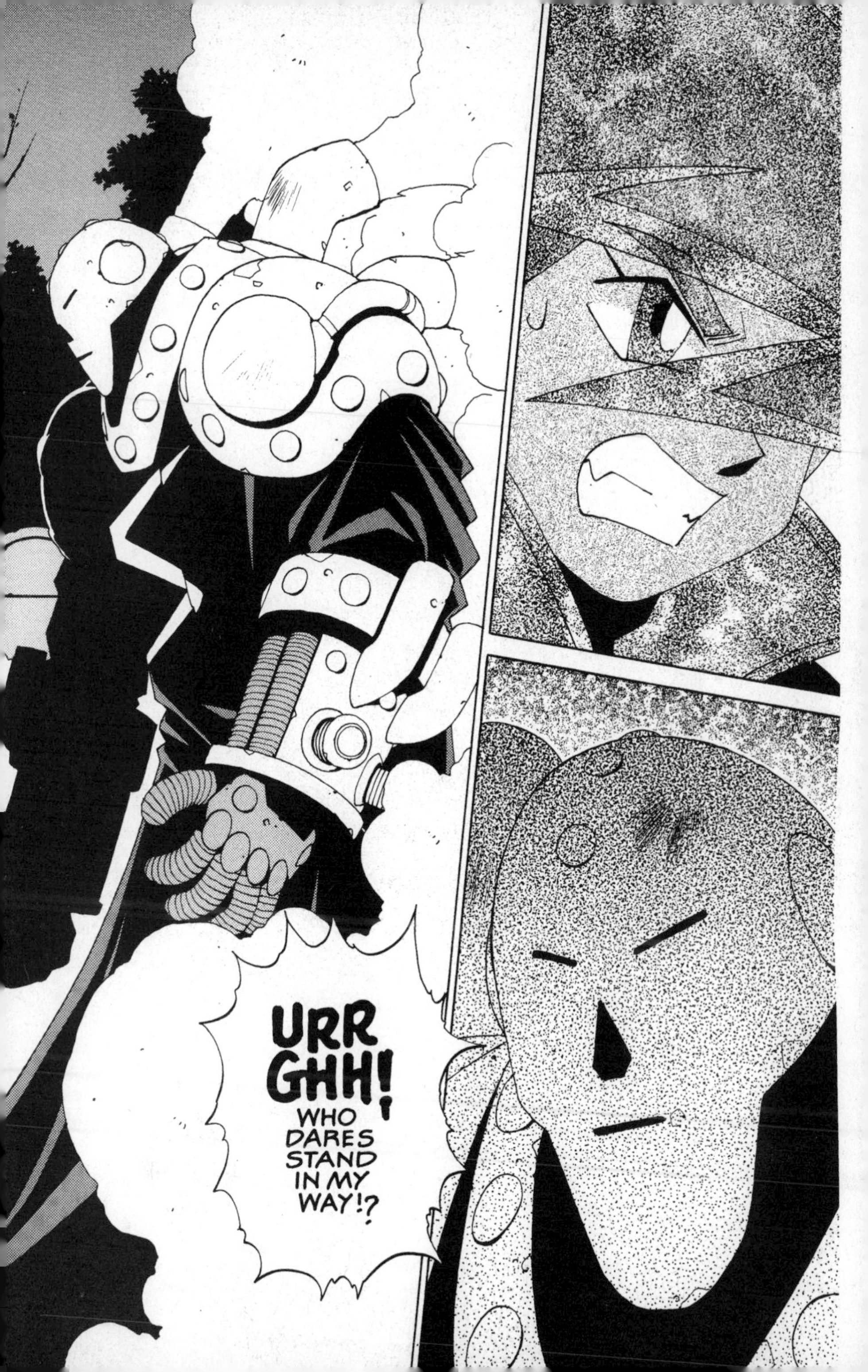
URR GHH! WHO DARES STAND IN MY WAY!?

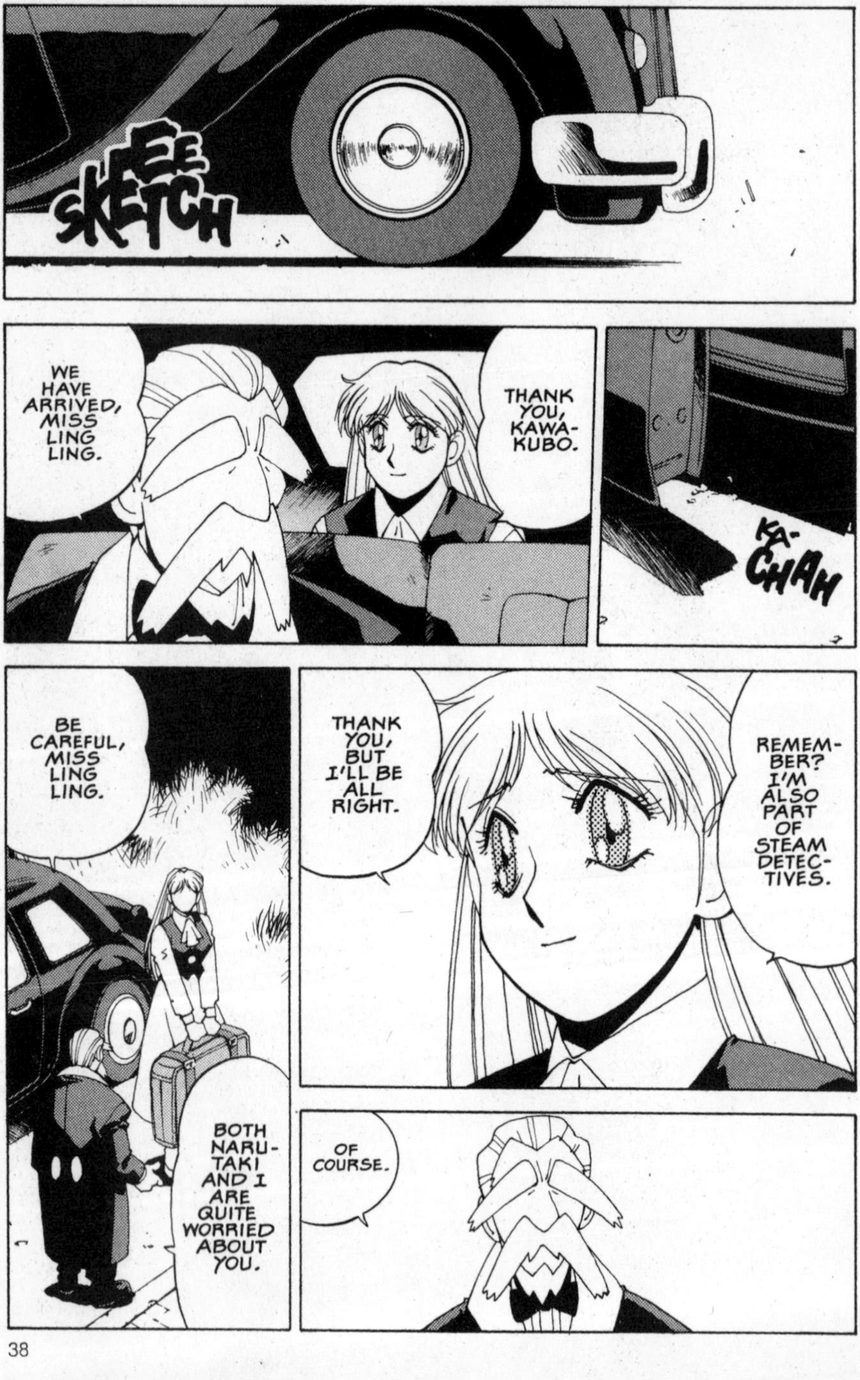
EEE
SKETCH
WE HAVE ARRIVED, MISS LING LING.
THANK YOU, KAWAKUBO.
KA-CHAH
BE CAREFUL, MISS LING LING.
BOTH NARUTAKI AND I ARE QUITE WORRIED ABOUT YOU.
THANK YOU, BUT I'LL BE ALL RIGHT.
REMEMBER? I'M ALSO PART OF STEAM DETECTIVES.
OF COURSE.

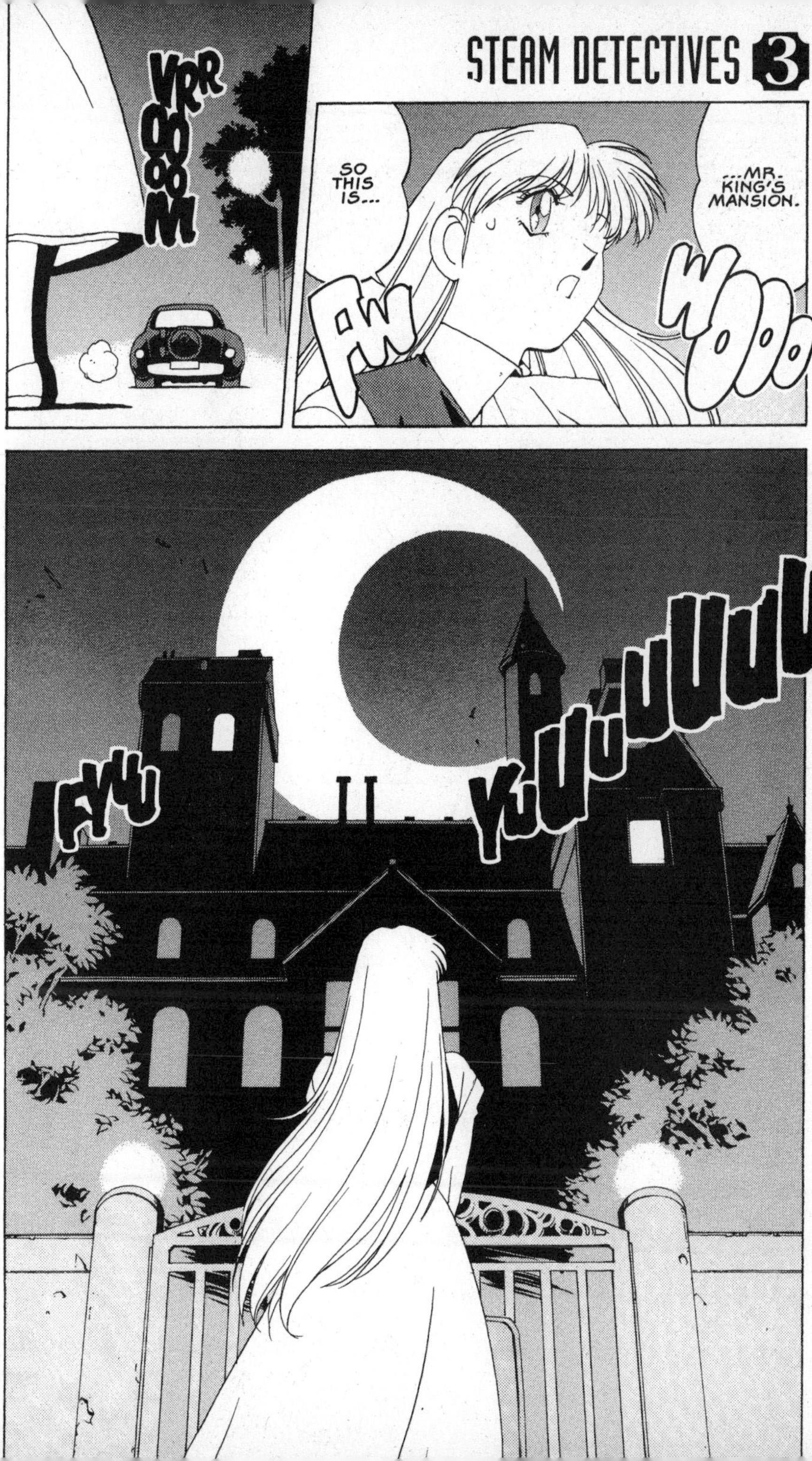
VRROOOOOM
SO THIS IS...
...MR. KING'S MANSION.
FW
WOOO
FYUU
YUUUUUUUUUU

STEAM DETECTIVES PRESS

The Secret Behind the Steam Detectives INVESTIGATION KIT

This investigation kit is absolutely essential for the Steam Detectives to maintain peace in our beloved Steam City! Even an elephant couldn't dent this shockproof and waterproof case which can withstand a depth of 200 meters. Any mystery can be solved with this kit! Here's the list of its features we secretly obtained!

ONLY STEAM DETECTIVES ARE PERMITTED TO USE THIS SPECIAL KIT

1. SD BADGE. This invaluable device can only be used by Steam Detectives in good standing. It contains a transmitter.
2. DETECTIVE NOTEPAD has 7 features:
a) Locator: Allows you to locate your badge.
b) Calculator: Essential for data analysis.
c) Electronic Mail Device: Allows data transmission (including maps and scheduled messages) through regular phone lines.
d) Water Soluble Paper: Destroy the evidence before the enemy finds it!
e) Fountain Pen with Disappearing Ink: Make your secret messages disappear or reappear!
f) Disguise Stickers: Disguise your face instantly using these 10 stickers; includes mustache, mole, scar, and more!
g) Secret Code Card: Code system that can only be read by Steam Detectives. Send the SOS code when in trouble!

READY FOR ANY AILMENT

YAMATO DRUG CORP.

Revives body and spirit! Be sure to read instructions carefully before taking medication.

With this incredible kit the Steam Detectives can solve any crime! This product was custom made by the Positive Corporation, a company that makes precision tools.

CASE 8, PART 2
LING LING AND STEAM KING

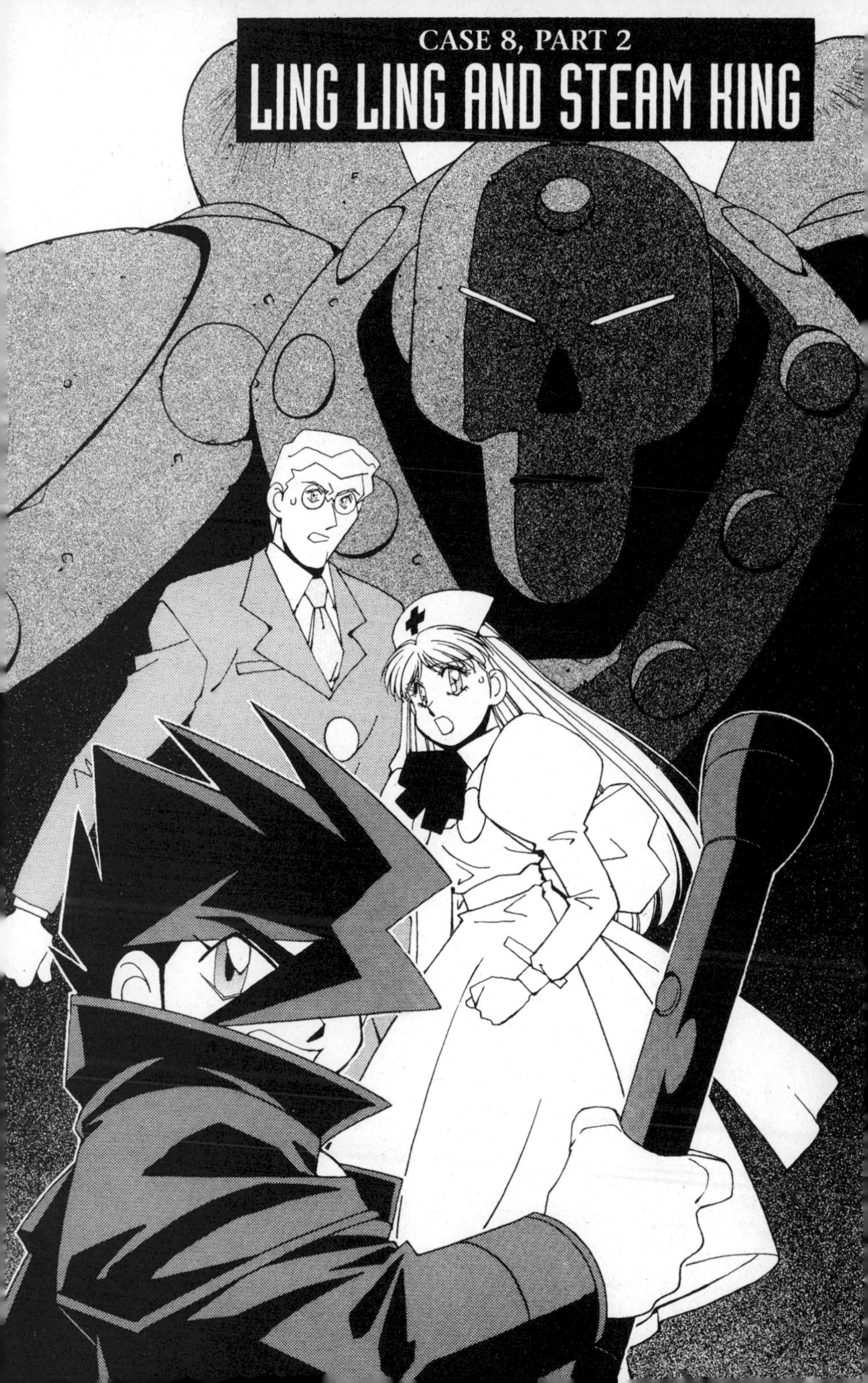

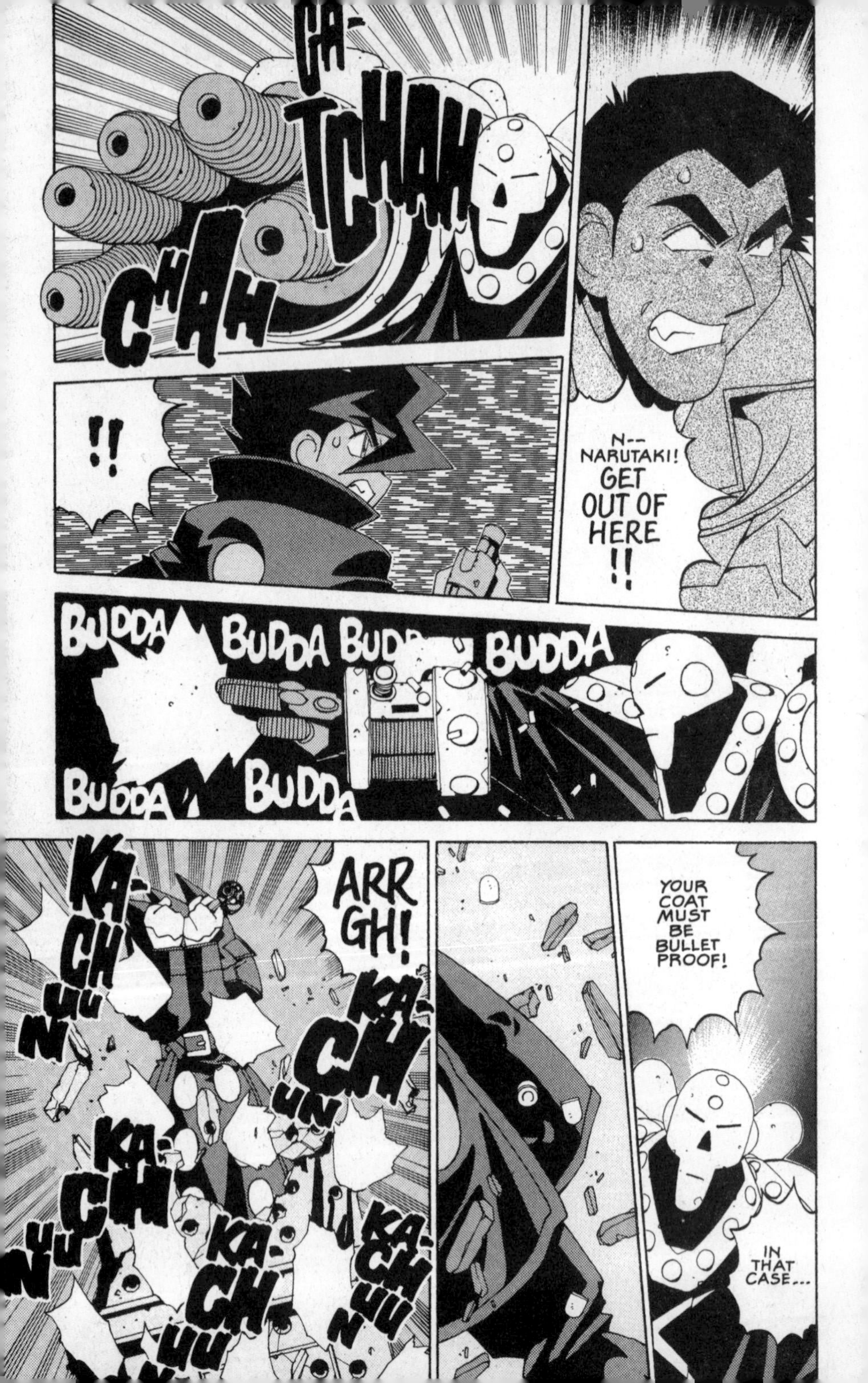

CA-TCHAH
CHAH
N-- NARUTAKI! GET OUT OF HERE !!
!!
BUDDA
BUDDA
BUDDA
BUDDA
BUDDA
BUDDA
KA-CHUUN
ARR GH!
KA-CHUUN
KA-CHUUN
KA-CHUUN
KA-CHUUN
YOUR COAT MUST BE BULLET PROOF!
IN THAT CASE...

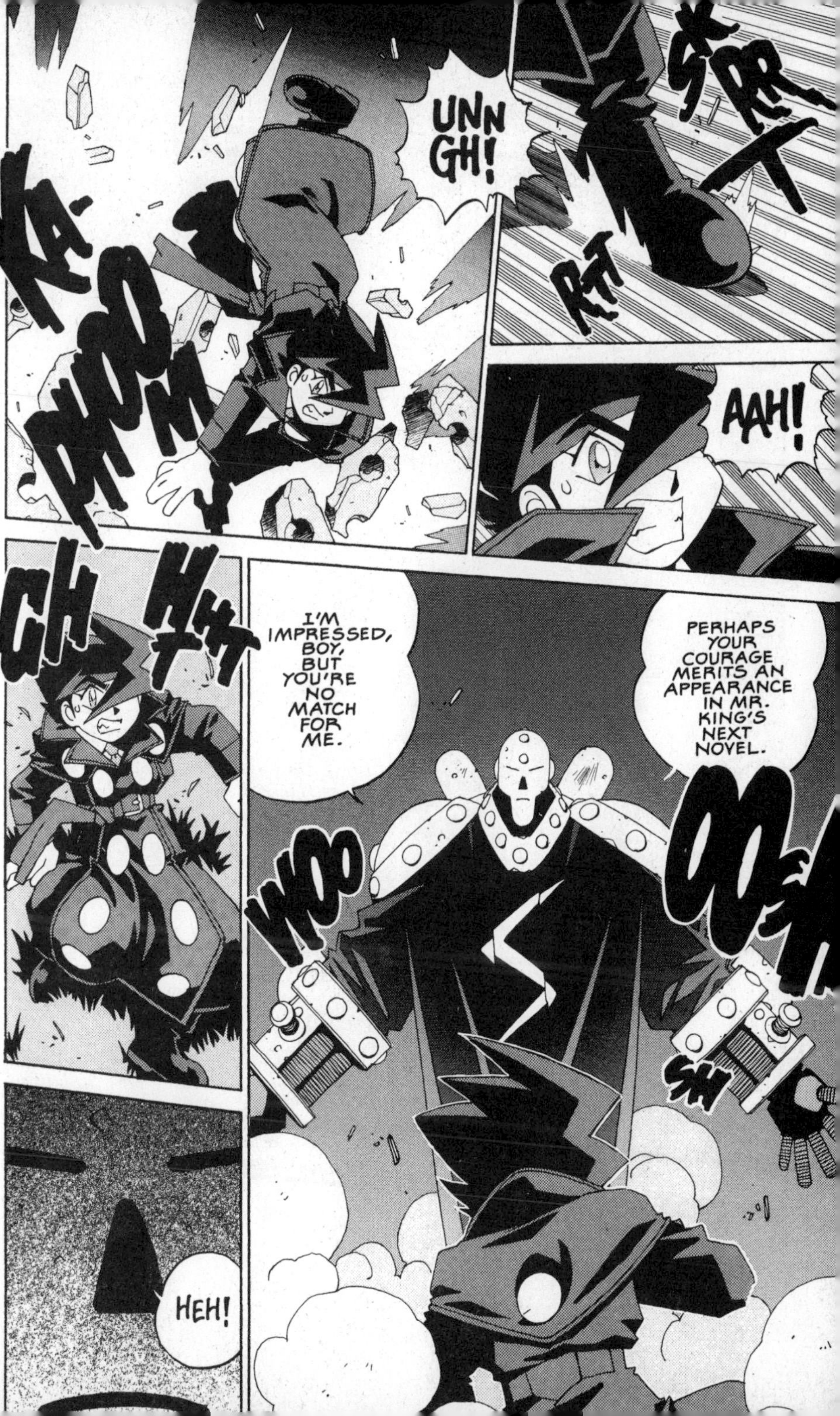
KA-PHOOOM
UNNGH!
AAH!
I'M IMPRESSED, BOY, BUT YOU'RE NO MATCH FOR ME.
PERHAPS YOUR COURAGE MERITS AN APPEARANCE IN MR. KING'S NEXT NOVEL.
HEH!

WHAT
!?!

I CAN BRING THE MATTER UP WITH HIM IF YOU LIKE!

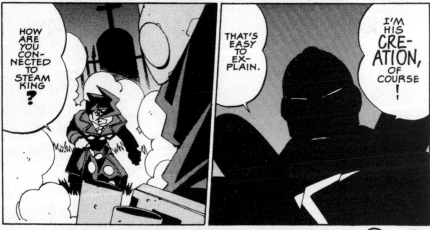

HOW ARE YOU CONNECTED TO STEAM KING?

THAT'S EASY TO EXPLAIN.

I'M HIS CREATION, OF COURSE!

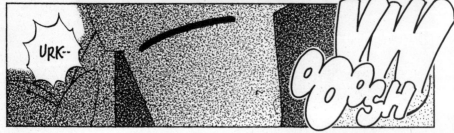

URK--

VWWOOSH!

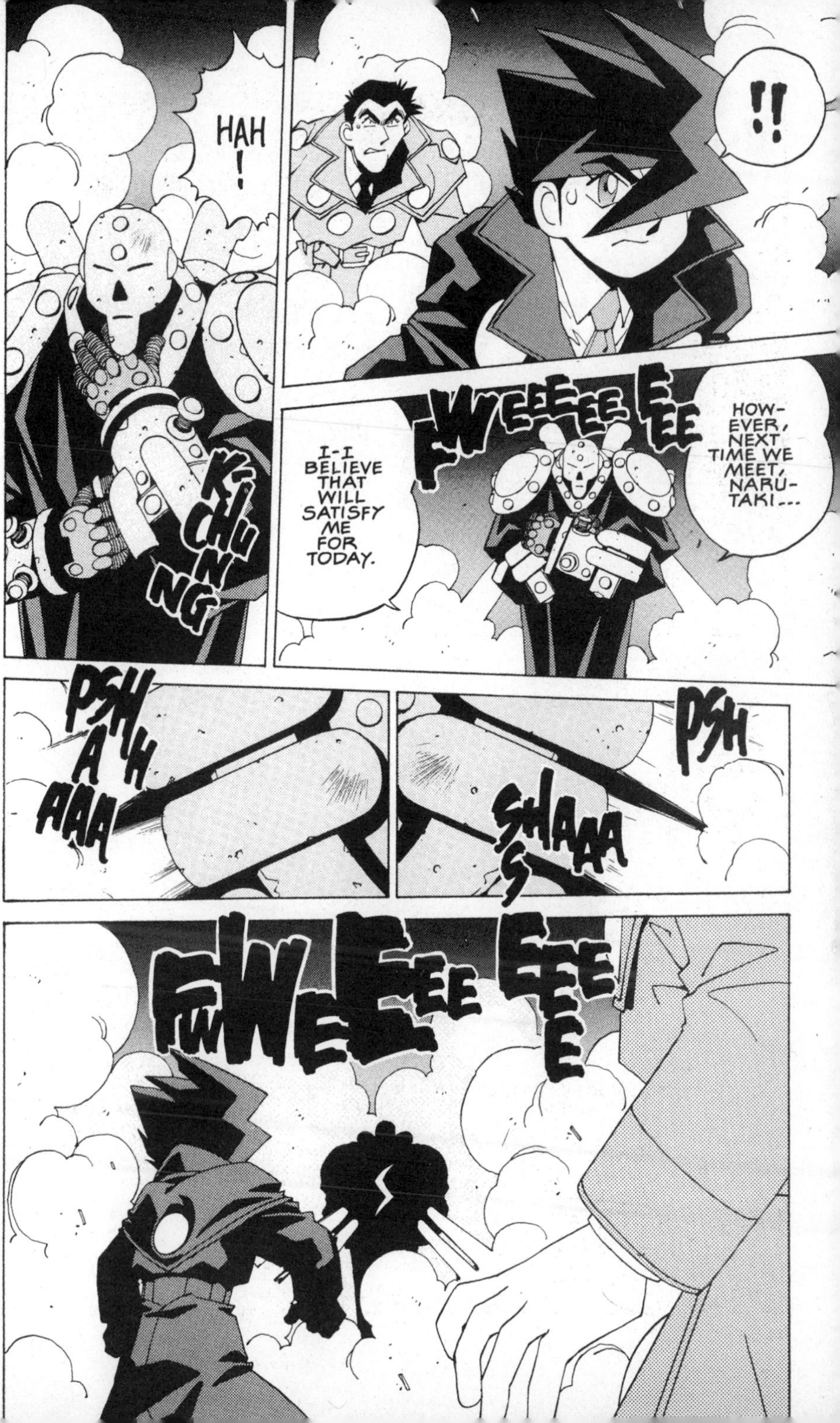
HAH!
K-CHUNNNG
!!
I-I BELIEVE THAT WILL SATISFY ME FOR TODAY.
FWEEEEE EEE
HOW-EVER, NEXT TIME WE MEET, NARU-TAKI...
PSHHAAAA
PSH
SHAAAAS
FWEEEEE EEEE

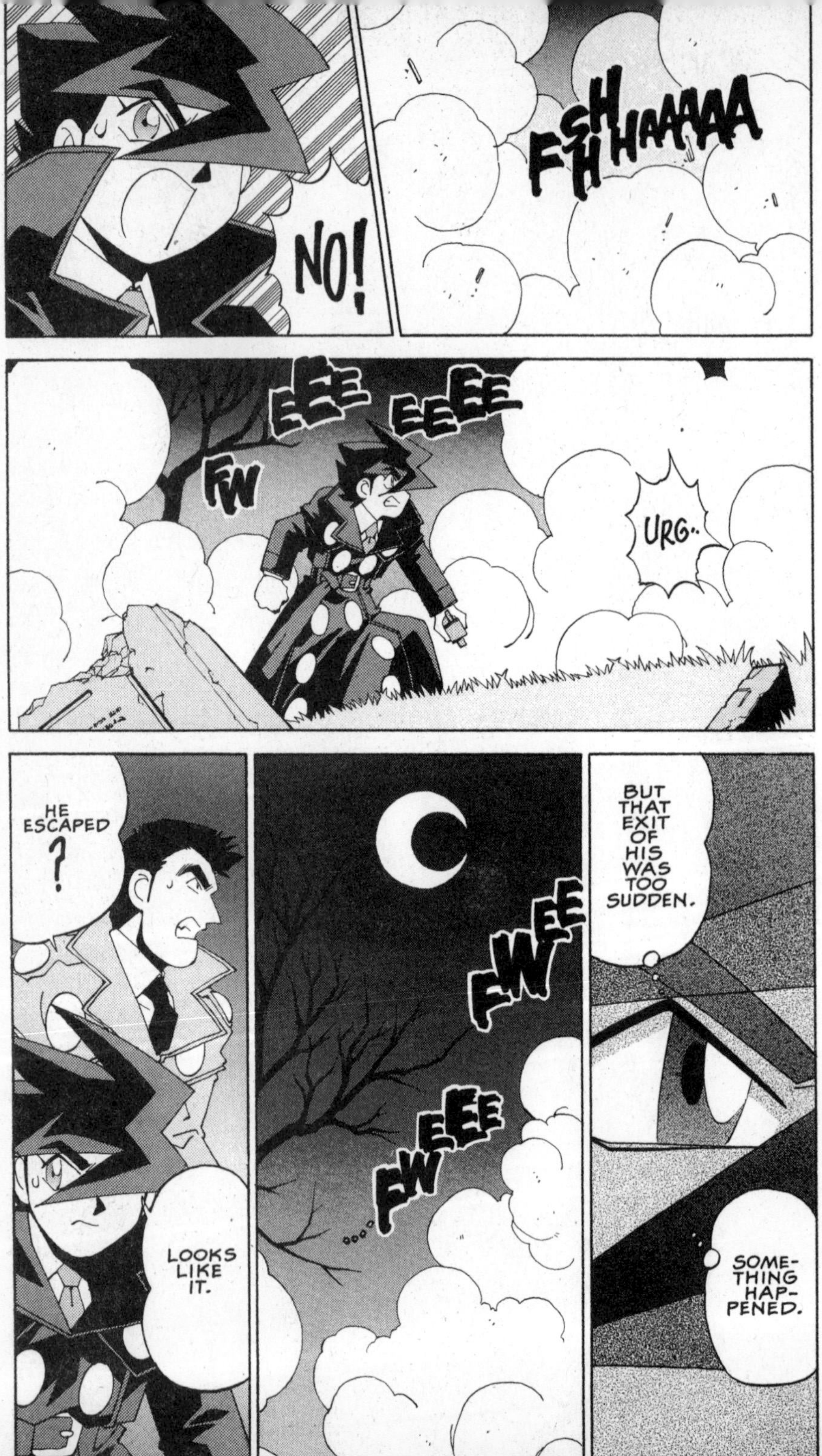
NO!
FSHHHAAAAA
EEE
EEEEE
FW
URG..
HE ESCAPED?
LOOKS LIKE IT.
FWEE
FWEEE
BUT THAT EXIT OF HIS WAS TOO SUDDEN.
SOMETHING HAPPENED.

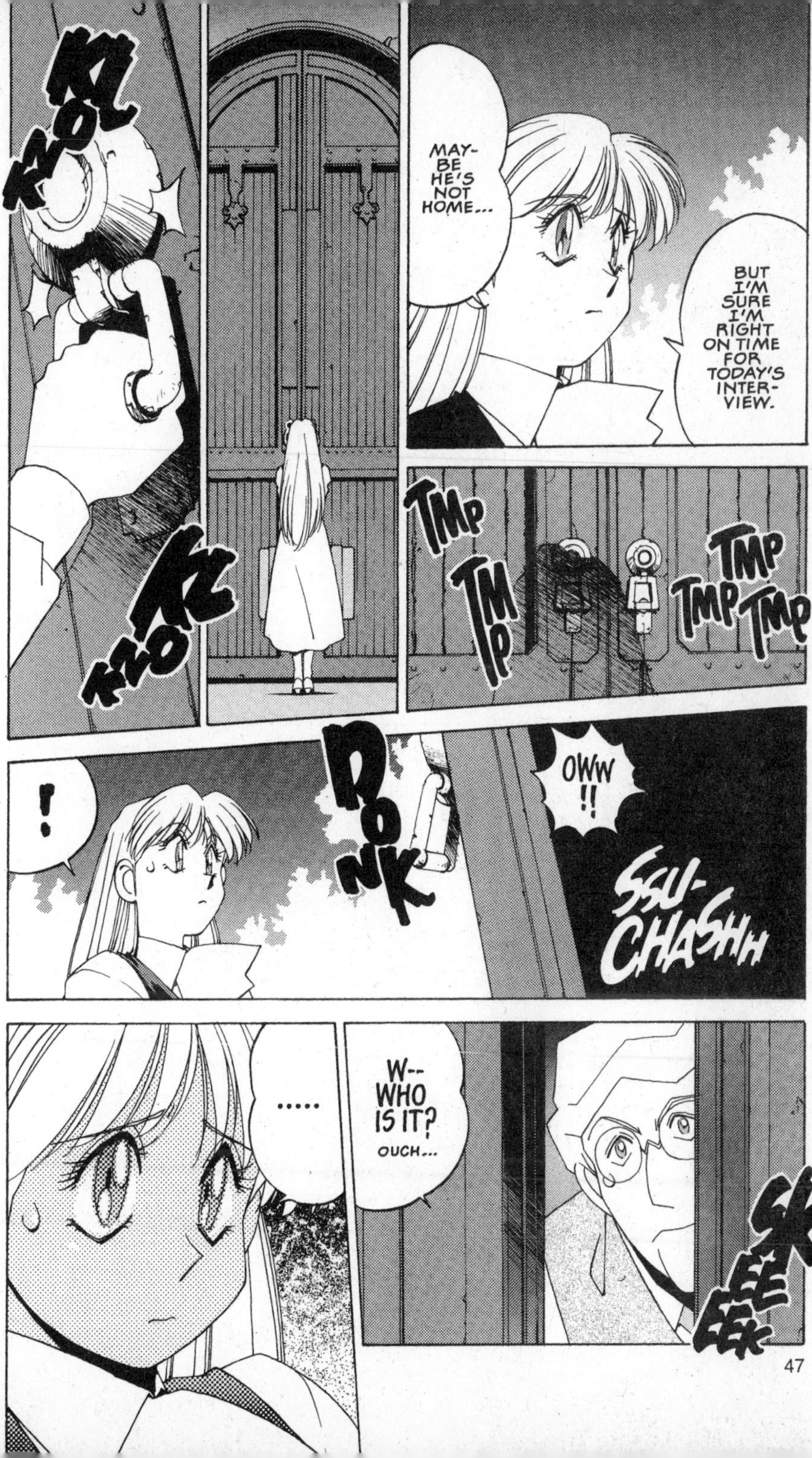
KNOCK
KNOCK
MAY-BE HE'S NOT HOME...
BUT I'M SURE I'M RIGHT ON TIME FOR TODAY'S INTER-VIEW.
TMP
TMP
TMP
TMP TMP
!
DONK
OWW !!
SSU-CHASHH
.....
W-- WHO IS IT?
OUCH...
SKEEEK

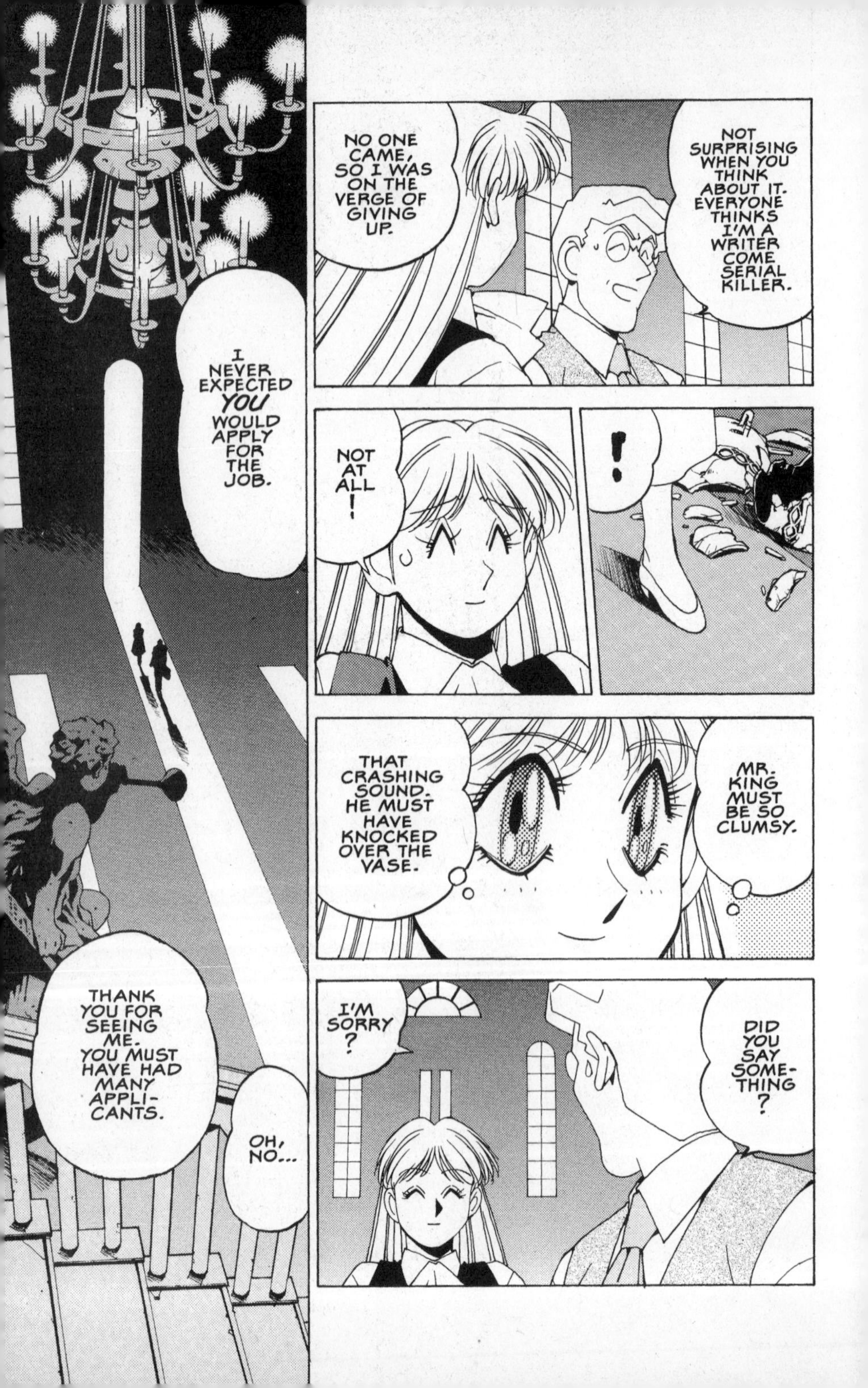
I NEVER EXPECTED YOU WOULD APPLY FOR THE JOB.
THANK YOU FOR SEEING ME. YOU MUST HAVE HAD MANY APPLICANTS.
OH, NO...
NO ONE CAME, SO I WAS ON THE VERGE OF GIVING UP.
NOT SURPRISING WHEN YOU THINK ABOUT IT. EVERYONE THINKS I'M A WRITER COME SERIAL KILLER.
NOT AT ALL!
!
THAT CRASHING SOUND. HE MUST HAVE KNOCKED OVER THE VASE.
MR. KING MUST BE SO CLUMSY.
I'M SORRY?
DID YOU SAY SOMETHING?

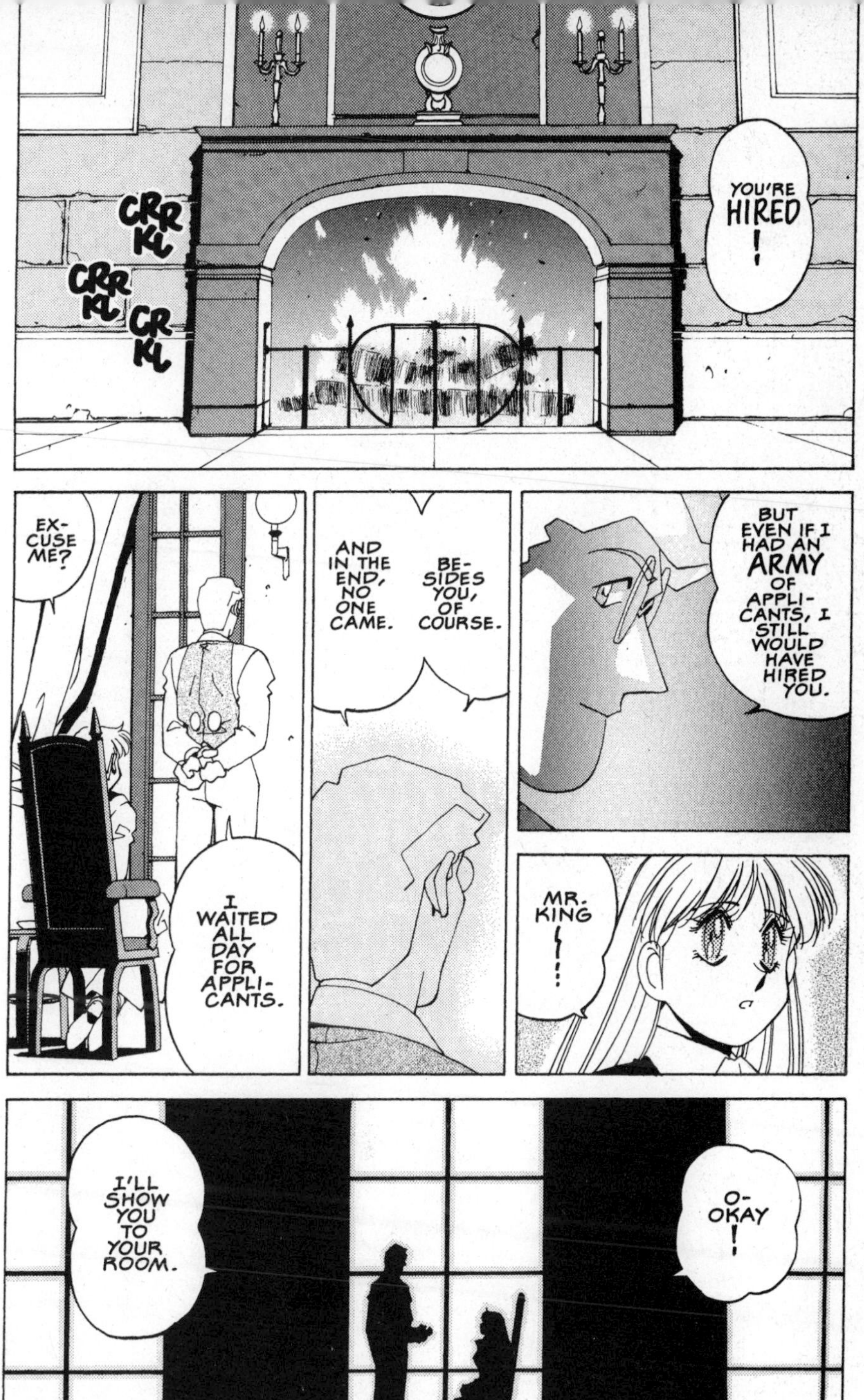
CRR KL
CRR KL
CR KL
YOU'RE HIRED!
EX-CUSE ME?
I WAITED ALL DAY FOR APPLI-CANTS.
AND IN THE END, NO ONE CAME.
BE-SIDES YOU, OF COURSE.
BUT EVEN IF I HAD AN ARMY OF APPLI-CANTS, I STILL WOULD HAVE HIRED YOU.
MR. KING!!
I'LL SHOW YOU TO YOUR ROOM.
O-OKAY!

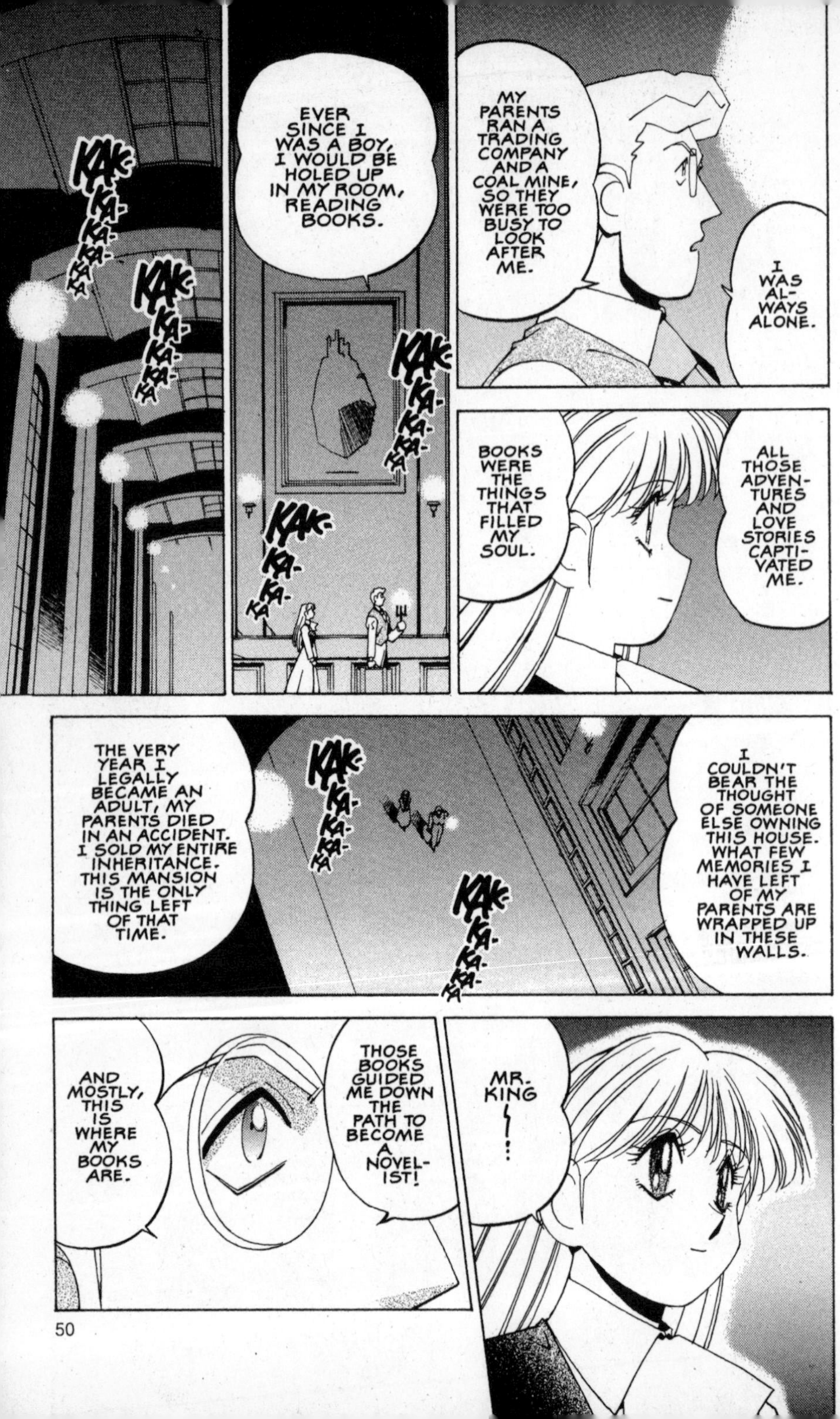

KAK-KA-KA-KA-KA
KAK-KA-KA-KA-KA
EVER SINCE I WAS A BOY, I WOULD BE HOLED UP IN MY ROOM, READING BOOKS.
KAK-KA-KA-KA-KA
KAK-KA-KA-KA
MY PARENTS RAN A TRADING COMPANY AND A COAL MINE, SO THEY WERE TOO BUSY TO LOOK AFTER ME.
I WAS ALWAYS ALONE.
BOOKS WERE THE THINGS THAT FILLED MY SOUL.
ALL THOSE ADVENTURES AND LOVE STORIES CAPTIVATED ME.
THE VERY YEAR I LEGALLY BECAME AN ADULT, MY PARENTS DIED IN AN ACCIDENT. I SOLD MY ENTIRE INHERITANCE. THIS MANSION IS THE ONLY THING LEFT OF THAT TIME.
KAK-KA-KA-KA-KA
KAK-KA-KA-KA-KA
I COULDN'T BEAR THE THOUGHT OF SOMEONE ELSE OWNING THIS HOUSE. WHAT FEW MEMORIES I HAVE LEFT OF MY PARENTS ARE WRAPPED UP IN THESE WALLS.
AND MOSTLY, THIS IS WHERE MY BOOKS ARE.
THOSE BOOKS GUIDED ME DOWN THE PATH TO BECOME A NOVELIST!
MR. KING...!

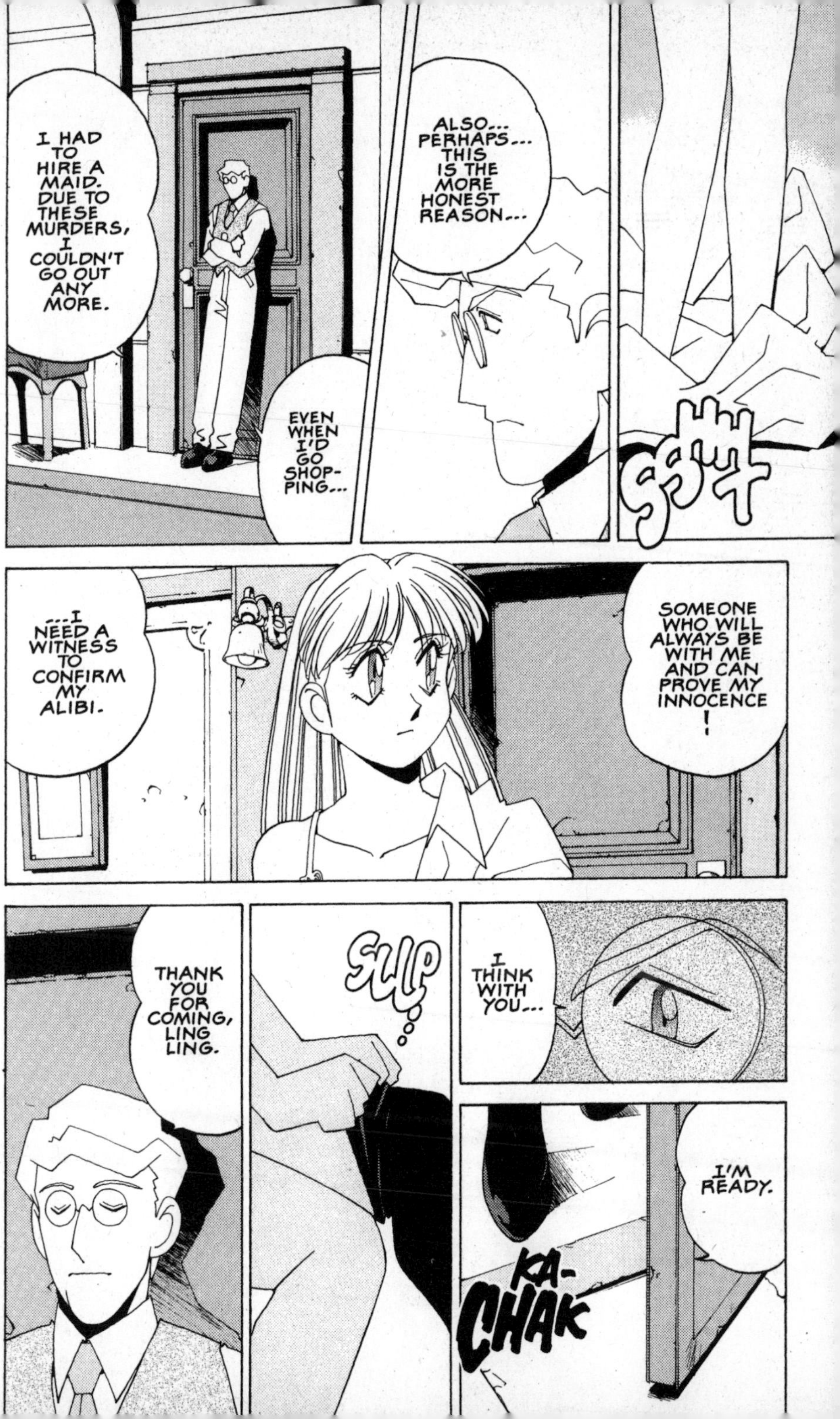
I HAD TO HIRE A MAID. DUE TO THESE MURDERS, I COULDN'T GO OUT ANY MORE.
EVEN WHEN I'D GO SHOP-PING...
ALSO... PERHAPS... THIS IS THE MORE HONEST REASON...
SQUIT
...I NEED A WITNESS TO CONFIRM MY ALIBI.
SOMEONE WHO WILL ALWAYS BE WITH ME AND CAN PROVE MY INNOCENCE!
THANK YOU FOR COMING, LING LING.
SLIP
I THINK WITH YOU...
I'M READY.
KA-CHAK

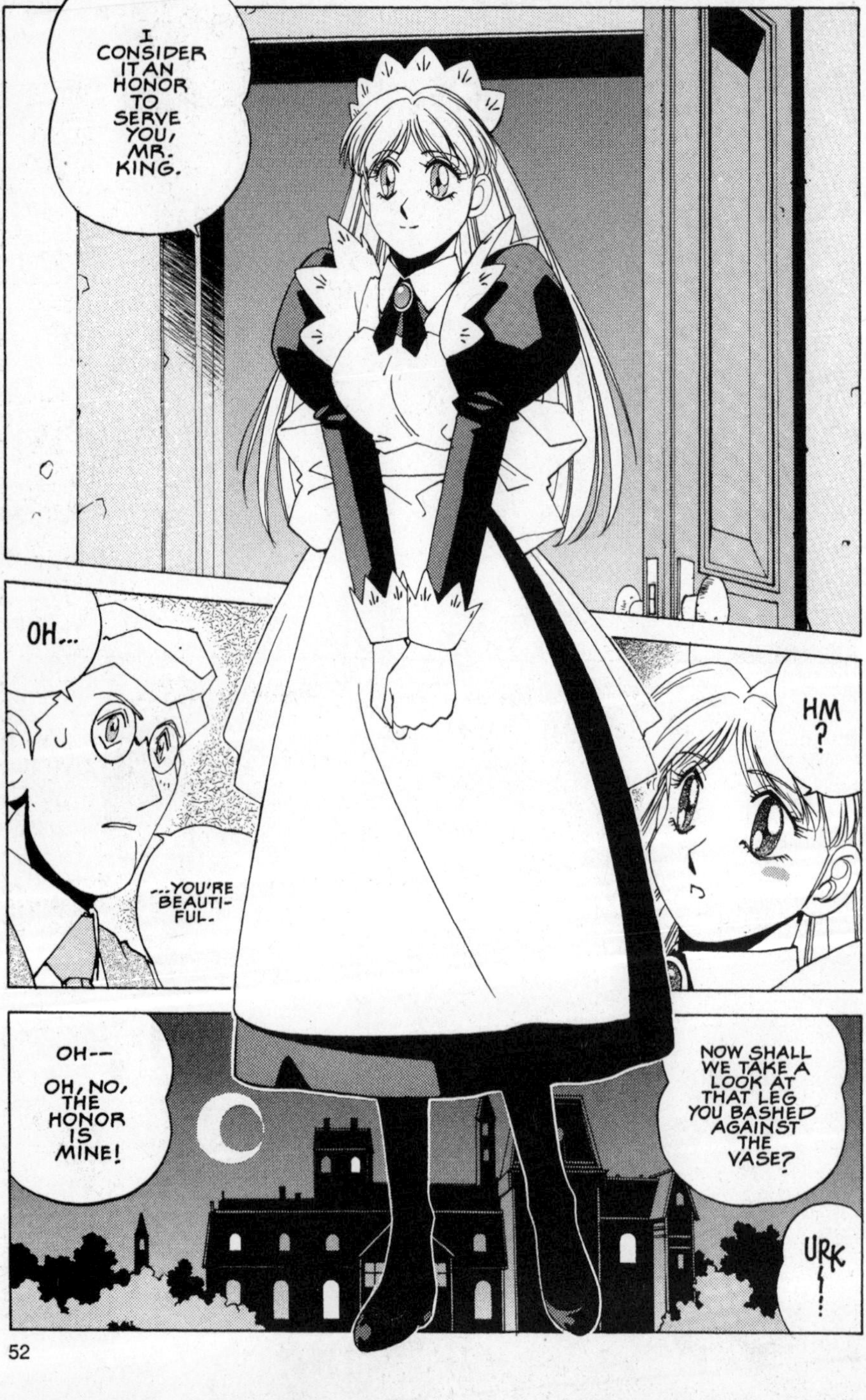
I CONSIDER IT AN HONOR TO SERVE YOU, MR. KING.
OH...
...YOU'RE BEAUTIFUL.
HM?
OH--
OH, NO, THE HONOR IS MINE!
NOW SHALL WE TAKE A LOOK AT THAT LEG YOU BASHED AGAINST THE VASE?
URK!!

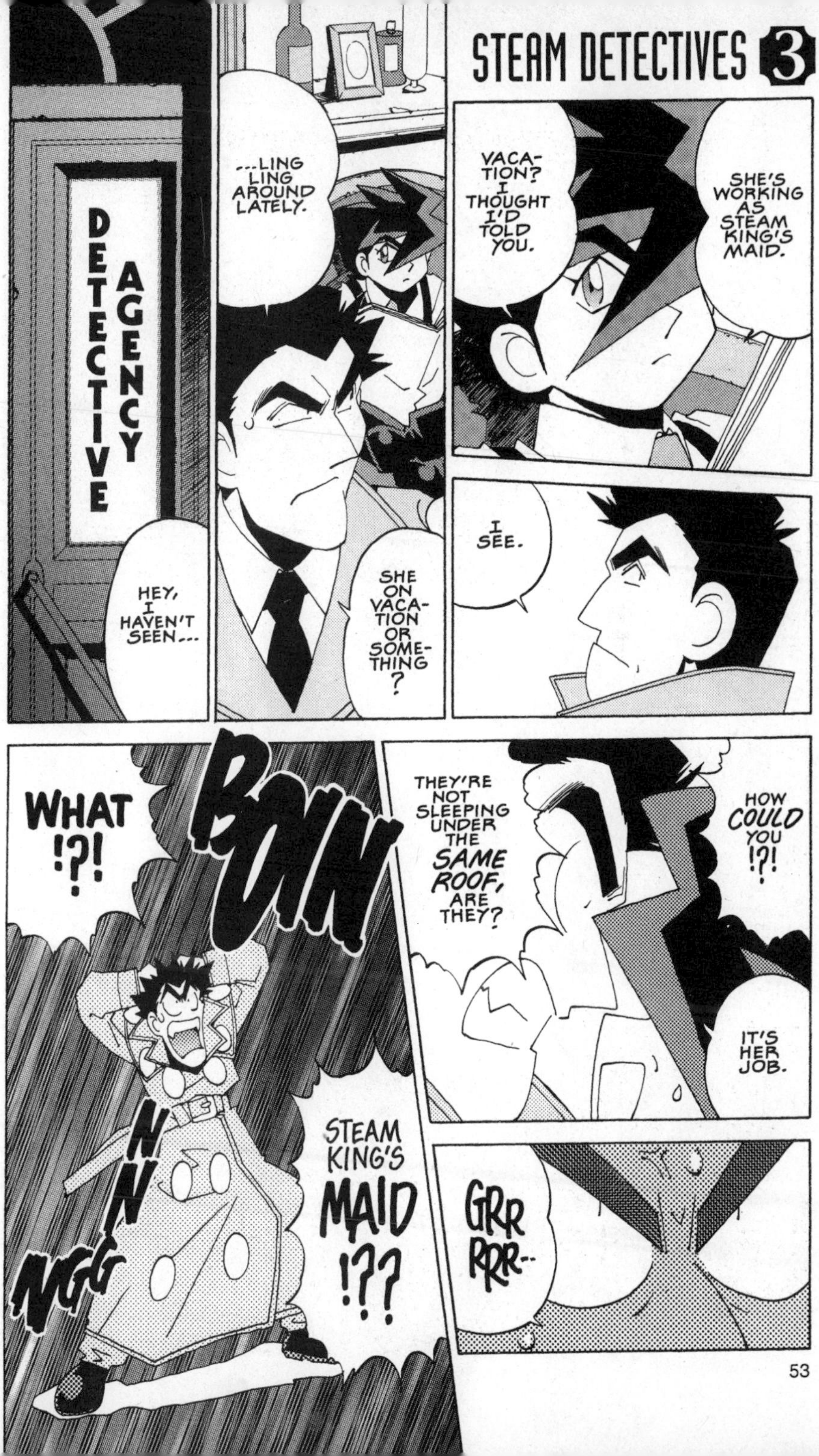
DETECTIVE AGENCY
HEY, I HAVEN'T SEEN...
...LING LING AROUND LATELY.
SHE ON VACATION OR SOMETHING?
VACATION? I THOUGHT I'D TOLD YOU.
SHE'S WORKING AS STEAM KING'S MAID.
I SEE.
WHAT!?!
BWANNNNGG
STEAM KING'S MAID!??
THEY'RE NOT SLEEPING UNDER THE SAME ROOF, ARE THEY?
HOW COULD YOU!?!
IT'S HER JOB.
GRRRRR--

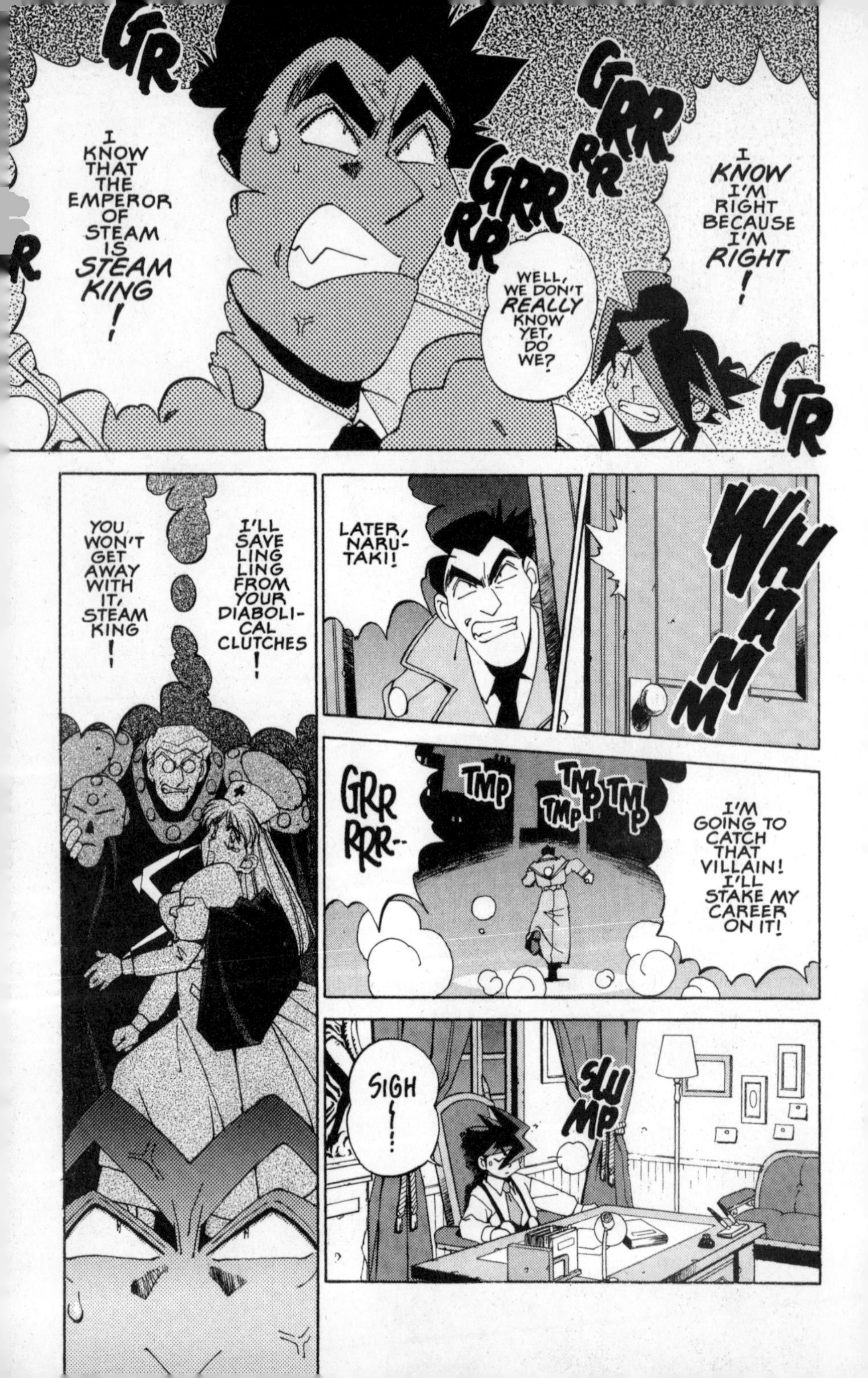
GR
I KNOW THAT THE EMPEROR OF STEAM IS STEAM KING!
GRRRR
GRRRR
WELL, WE DON'T REALLY KNOW YET, DO WE?
I KNOW I'M RIGHT BECAUSE I'M RIGHT!
GR
YOU WON'T GET AWAY WITH IT, STEAM KING!
I'LL SAVE LING LING FROM YOUR DIABOLICAL CLUTCHES!
LATER, NARUTAKI!
WHAMM
GRRRRR--
TMP
TMP TMP
TMP
I'M GOING TO CATCH THAT VILLAIN! I'LL STAKE MY CAREER ON IT!
SIGH!
SLUMP

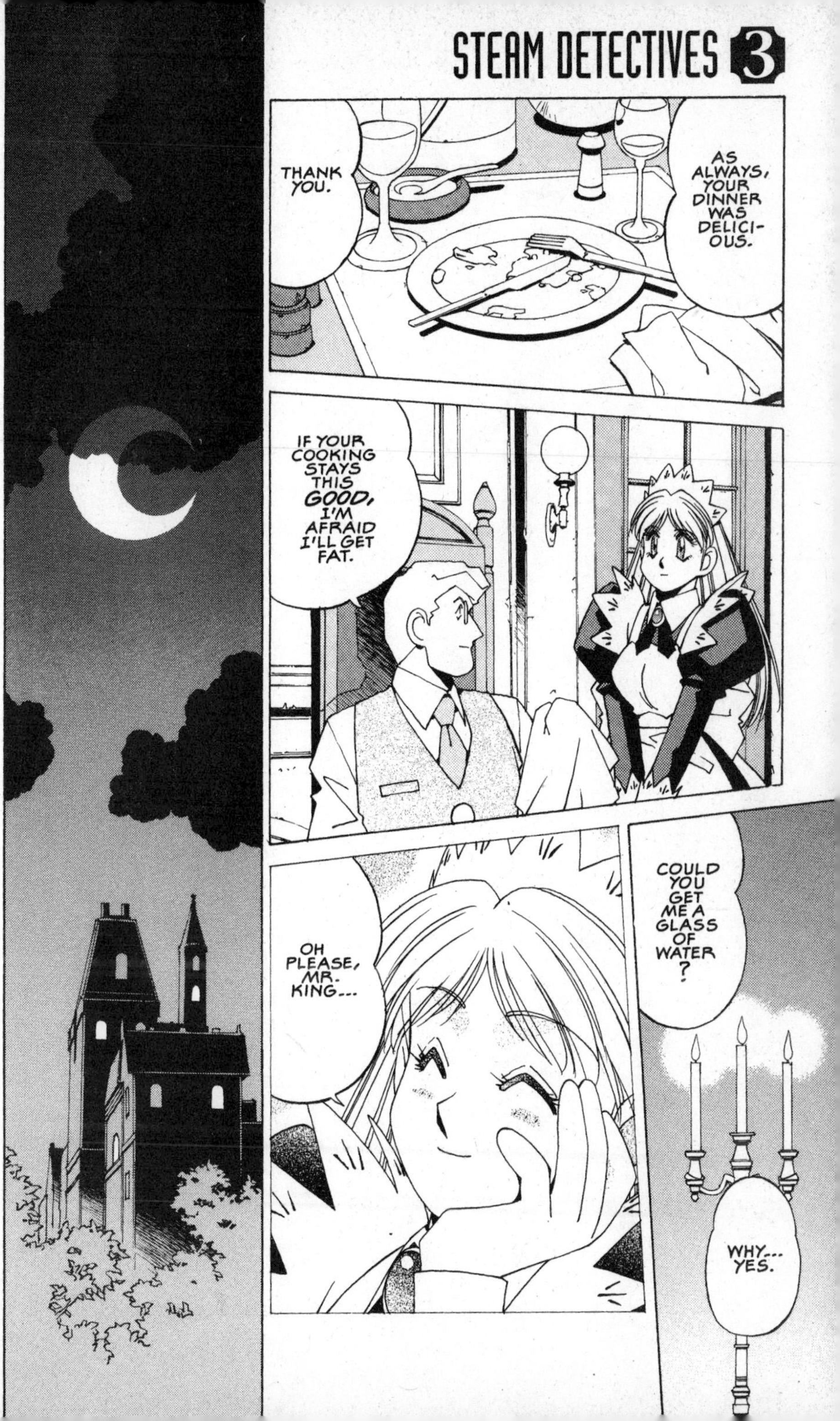
THANK YOU.
AS ALWAYS, YOUR DINNER WAS DELICI-OUS.
IF YOUR COOKING STAYS THIS GOOD, I'M AFRAID I'LL GET FAT.
OH PLEASE, MR. KING...
COULD YOU GET ME A GLASS OF WATER?
WHY... YES.

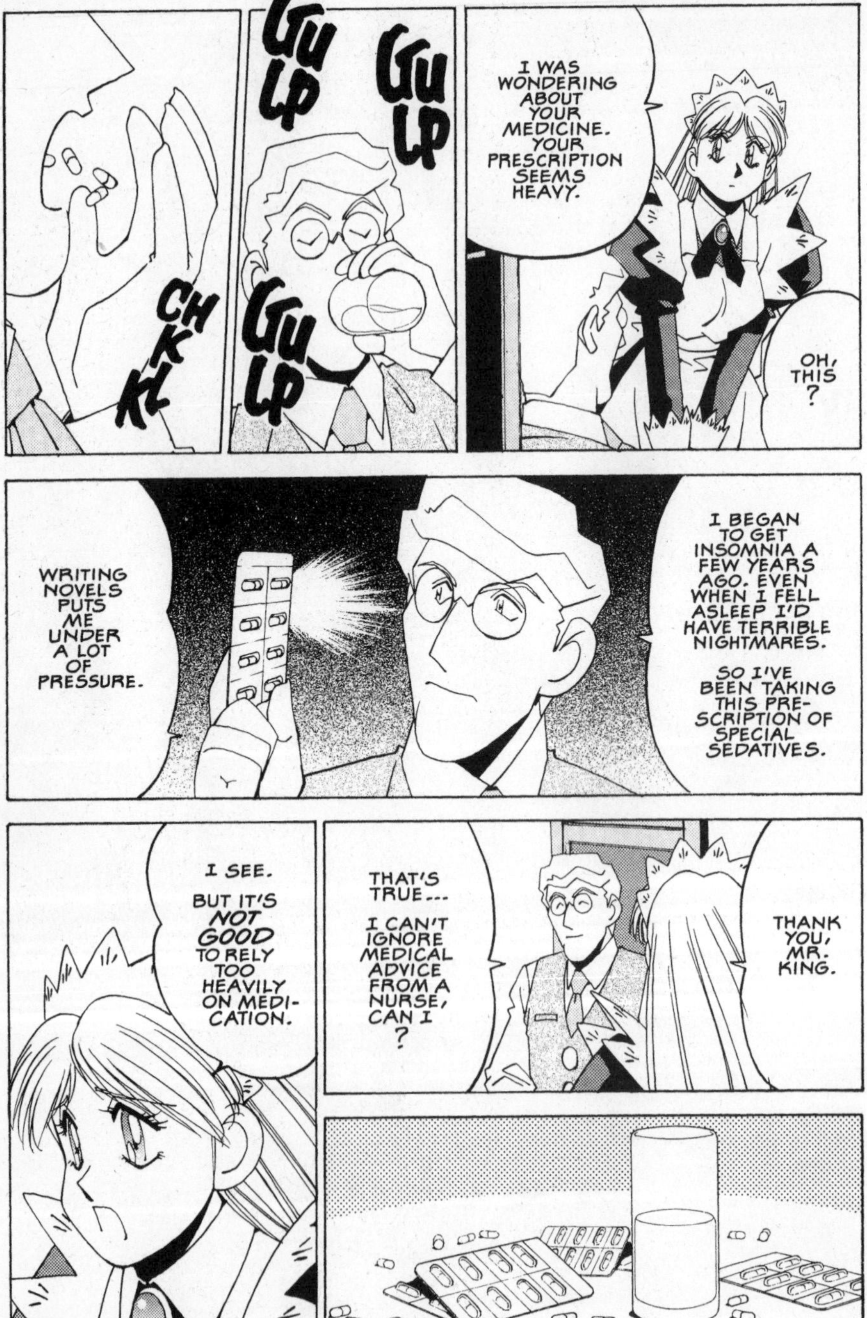
CHKKL
GULP
GULP
GULP
I WAS WONDERING ABOUT YOUR MEDICINE. YOUR PRESCRIPTION SEEMS HEAVY.
OH, THIS?
WRITING NOVELS PUTS ME UNDER A LOT OF PRESSURE.
I BEGAN TO GET INSOMNIA A FEW YEARS AGO. EVEN WHEN I FELL ASLEEP I'D HAVE TERRIBLE NIGHTMARES.
SO I'VE BEEN TAKING THIS PRESCRIPTION OF SPECIAL SEDATIVES.
I SEE.
BUT IT'S NOT GOOD TO RELY TOO HEAVILY ON MEDICATION.
THAT'S TRUE...
I CAN'T IGNORE MEDICAL ADVICE FROM A NURSE, CAN I?
THANK YOU, MR. KING.

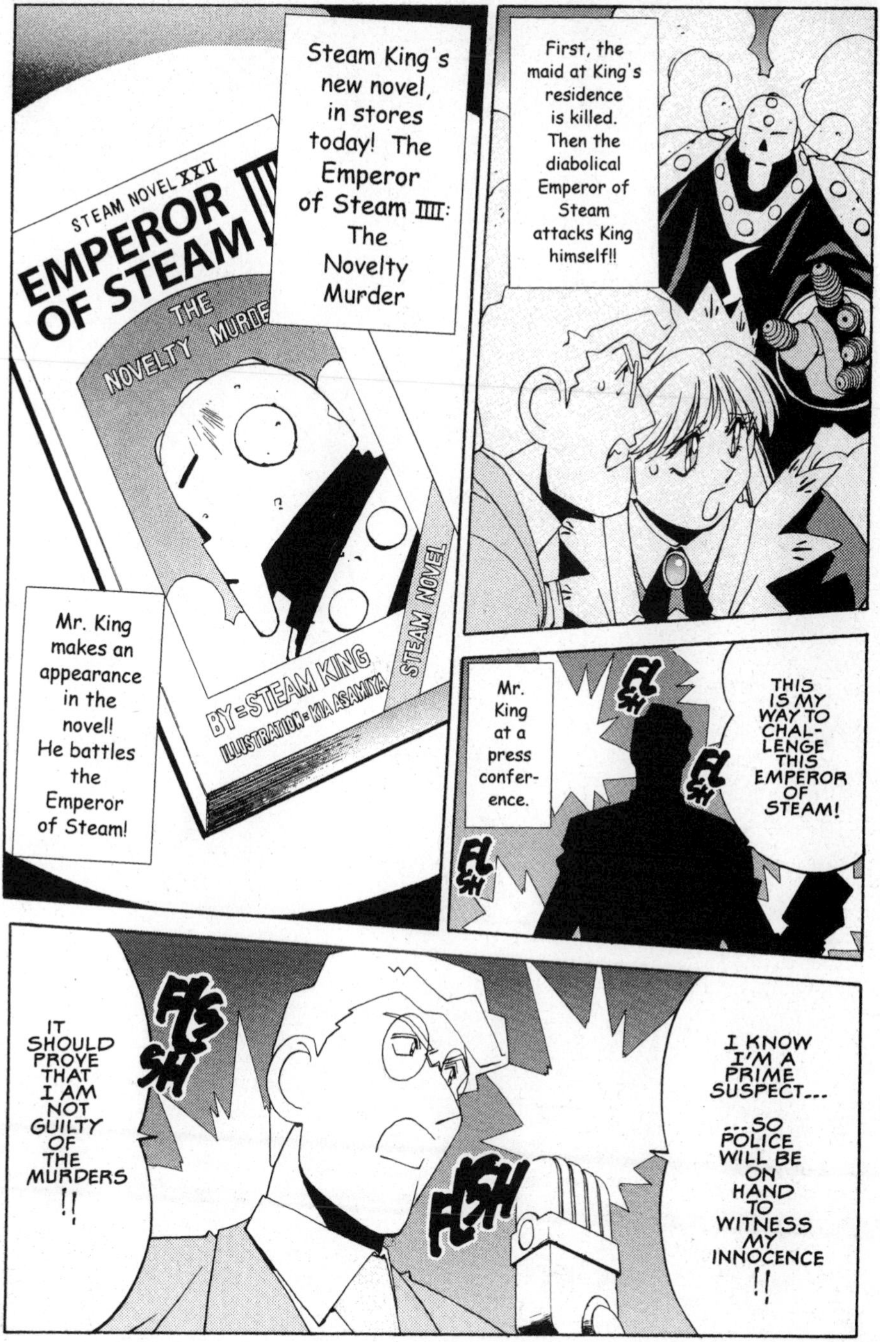
STEAM NOVEL XXII
EMPEROR OF STEAM IIII
Steam King's new novel, in stores today! The Emperor of Steam IIII: The Novelty Murder
BY=STEAM KING
ILLUSTRATION=KIA ASAMIYA
STEAM NOVEL
Mr. King makes an appearance in the novel! He battles the Emperor of Steam!
First, the maid at King's residence is killed. Then the diabolical Emperor of Steam attacks King himself!!
Mr. King at a press confer-ence.
THIS IS MY WAY TO CHAL-LENGE THIS EMPEROR OF STEAM!
IT SHOULD PROVE THAT I AM NOT GUILTY OF THE MURDERS !!
I KNOW I'M A PRIME SUSPECT...
...SO POLICE WILL BE ON HAND TO WITNESS MY INNOCENCE !!

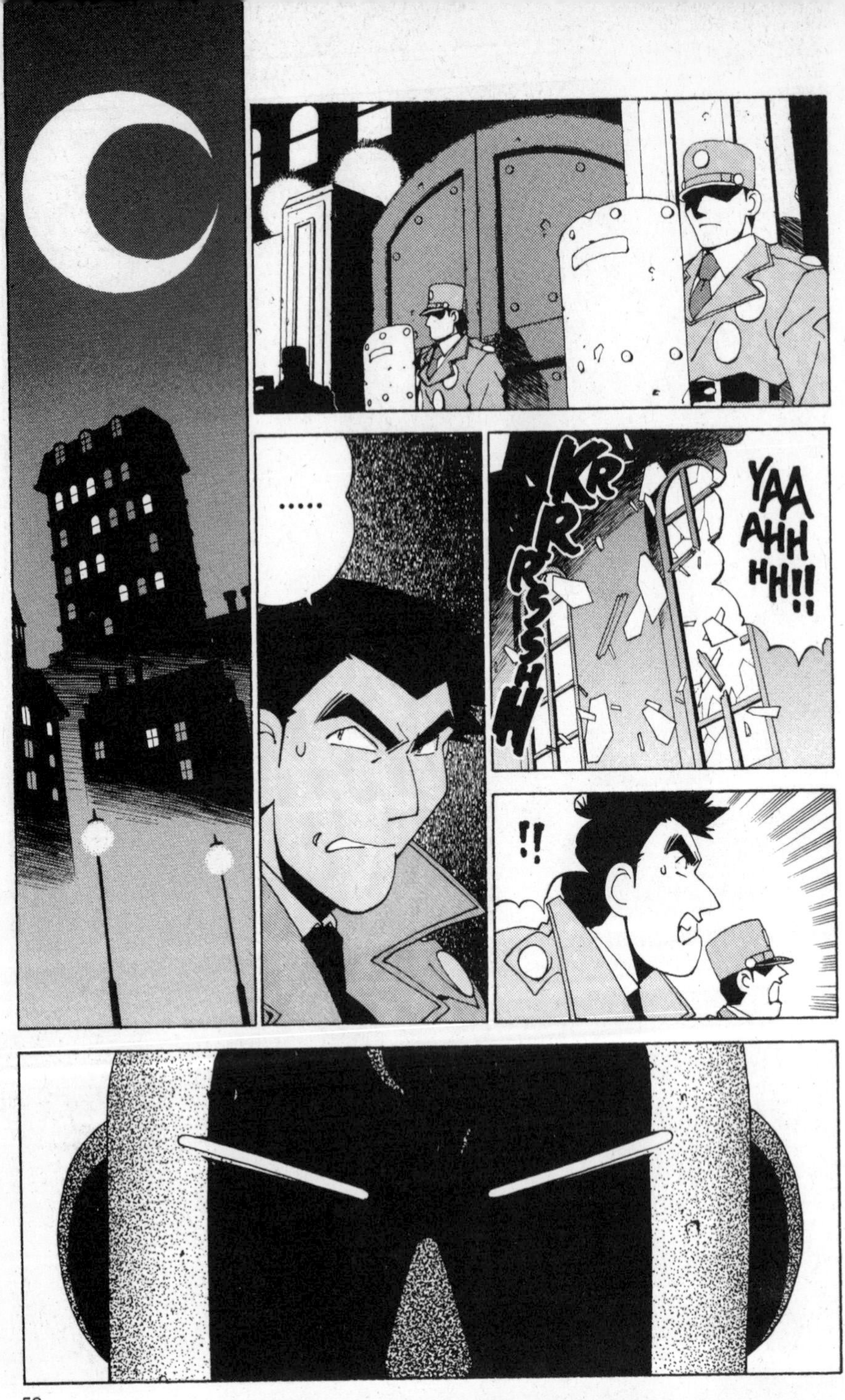
.....
KRRRRSSSHHH
YAAAHHHHH!!
!!

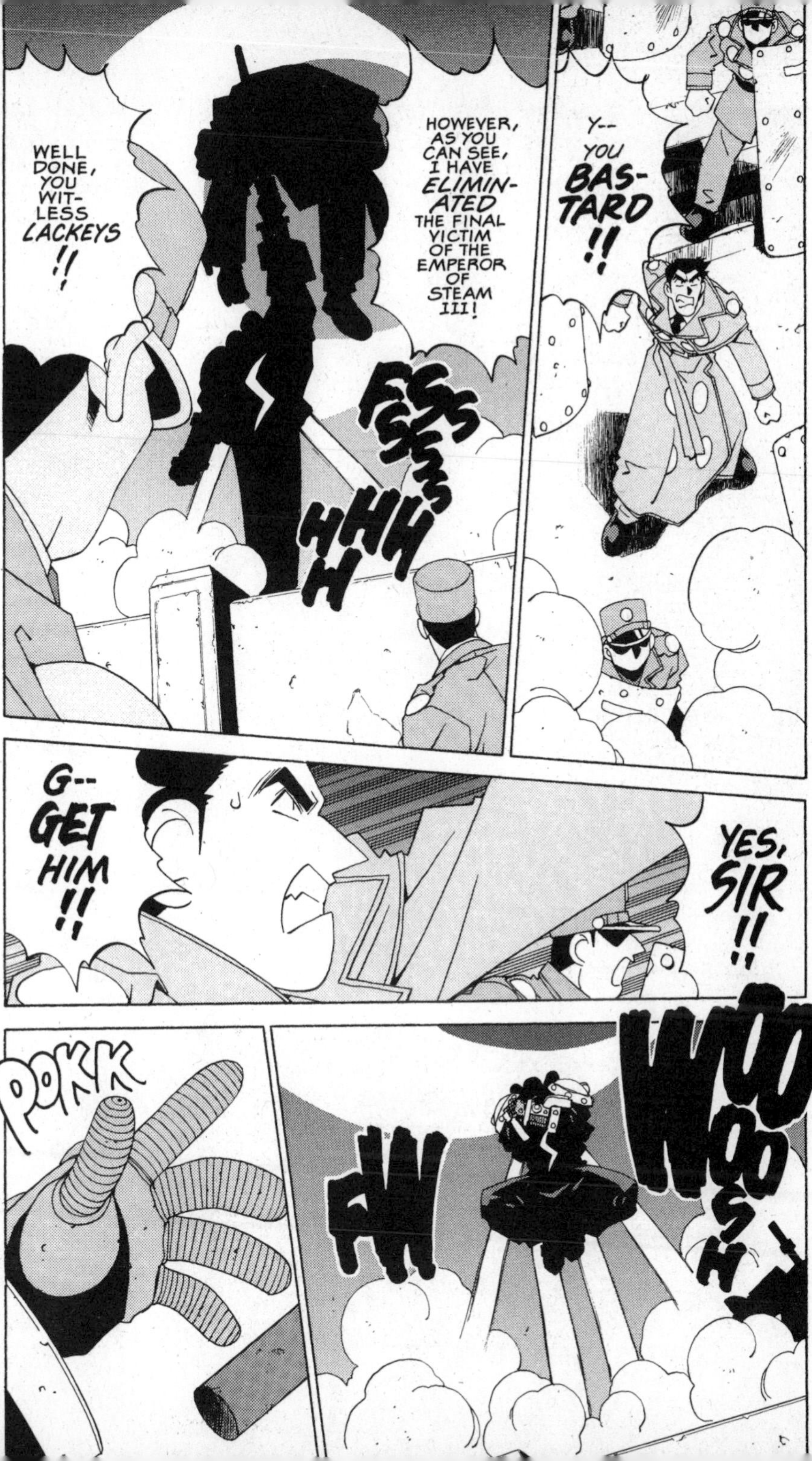
WELL DONE, YOU WIT-LESS LACKEYS !!
HOWEVER, AS YOU CAN SEE, I HAVE ELIMIN-ATED THE FINAL VICTIM OF THE EMPEROR OF STEAM III!
FSSSSSSSHHHH
Y-- YOU BAS-TARD !!
G-- GET HIM !!
YES, SIR !!
POKK
FWN
WOOWOOSH

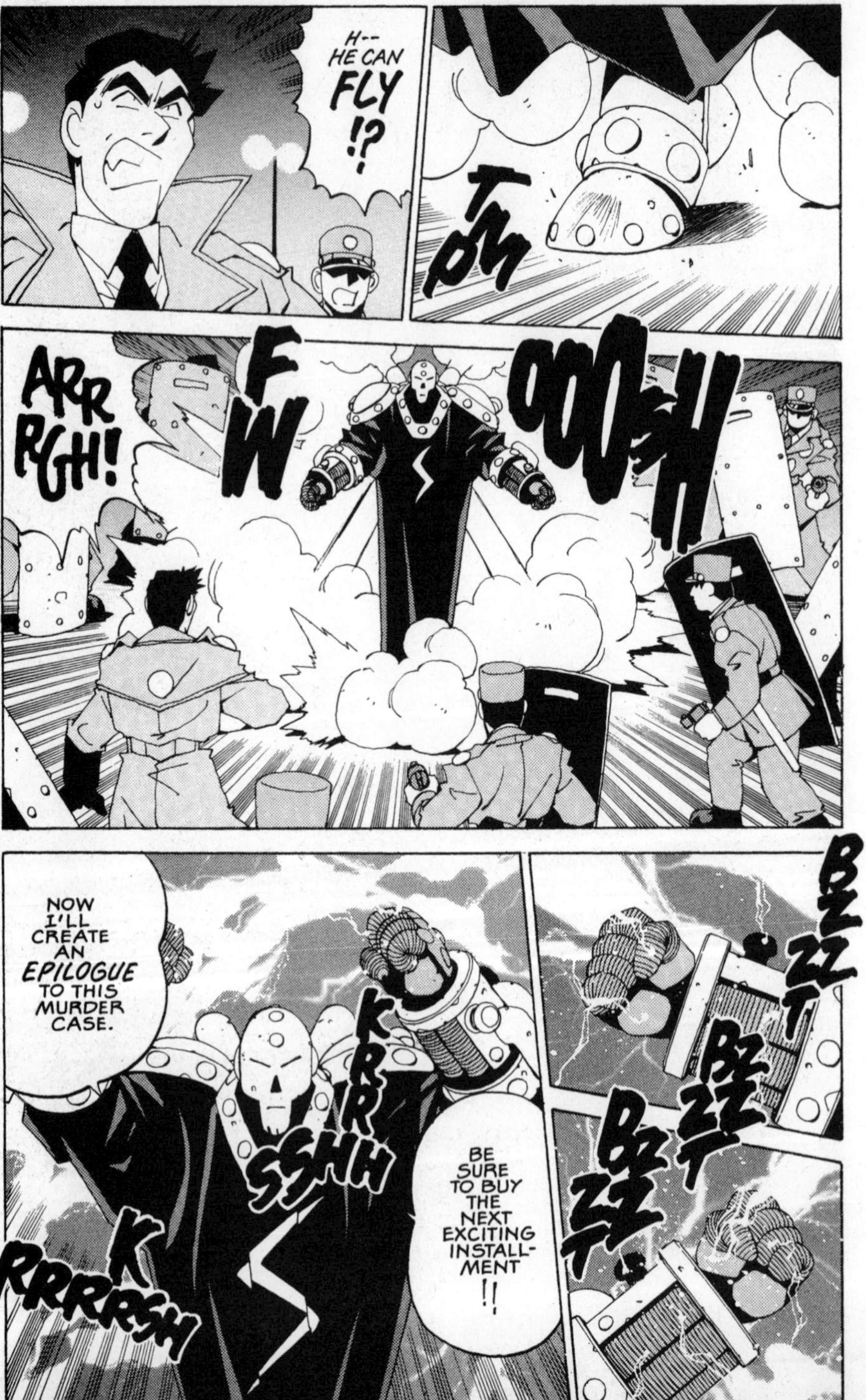
H-- HE CAN FLY !?
FWOOOSH
ARRRGH!
BZZT BZZT BZZT
NOW I'LL CREATE AN *EPILOGUE* TO THIS MURDER CASE.
KRRSSHH
BE SURE TO BUY THE NEXT EXCITING INSTALLMENT !!
KRRRRSH

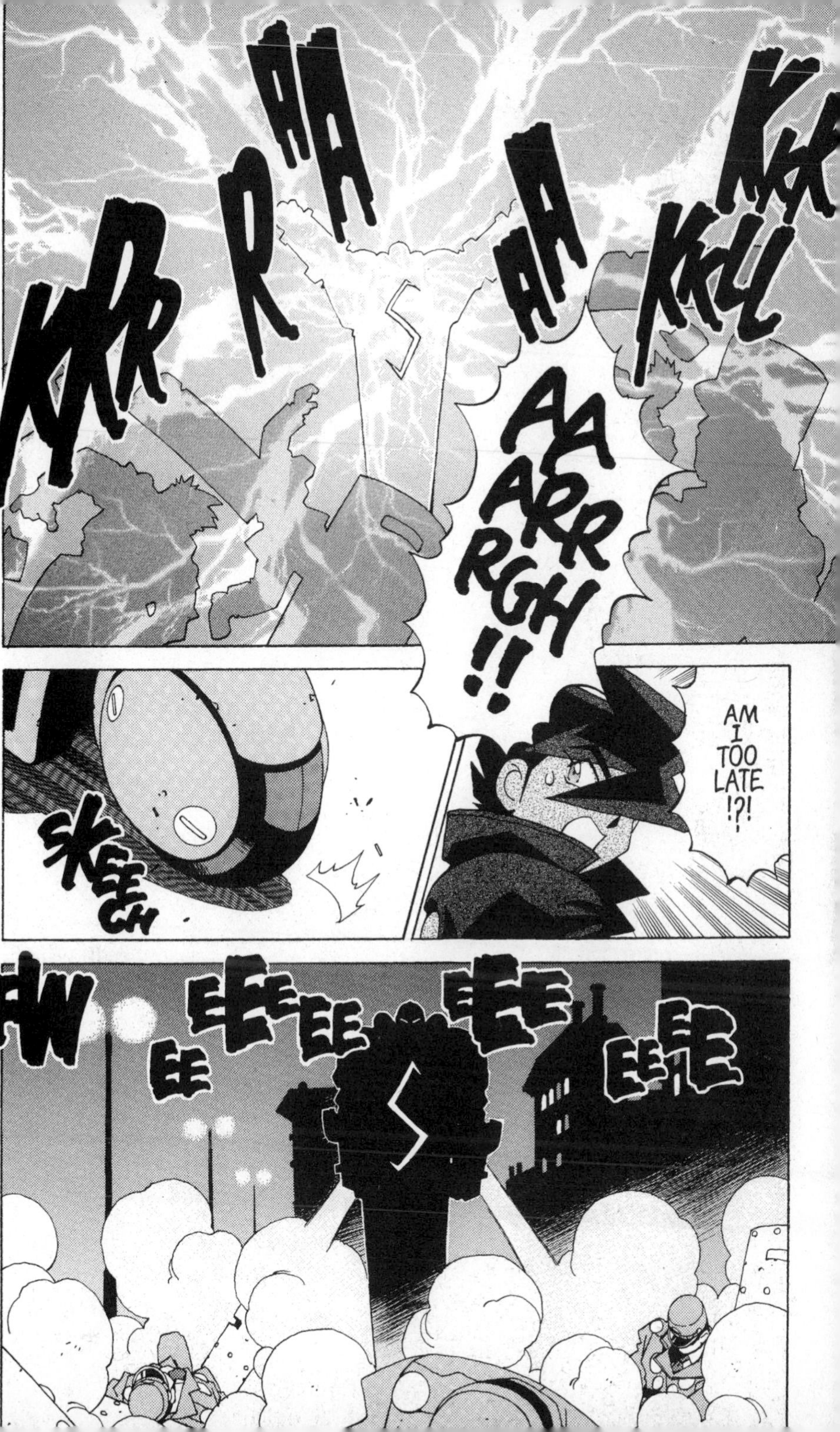
KKKKKUL
KRRRAAAAA
AAARRRGH!!
AM I TOO LATE!?!
SKEECH
EEEEEEEEEEEEE
FWEE

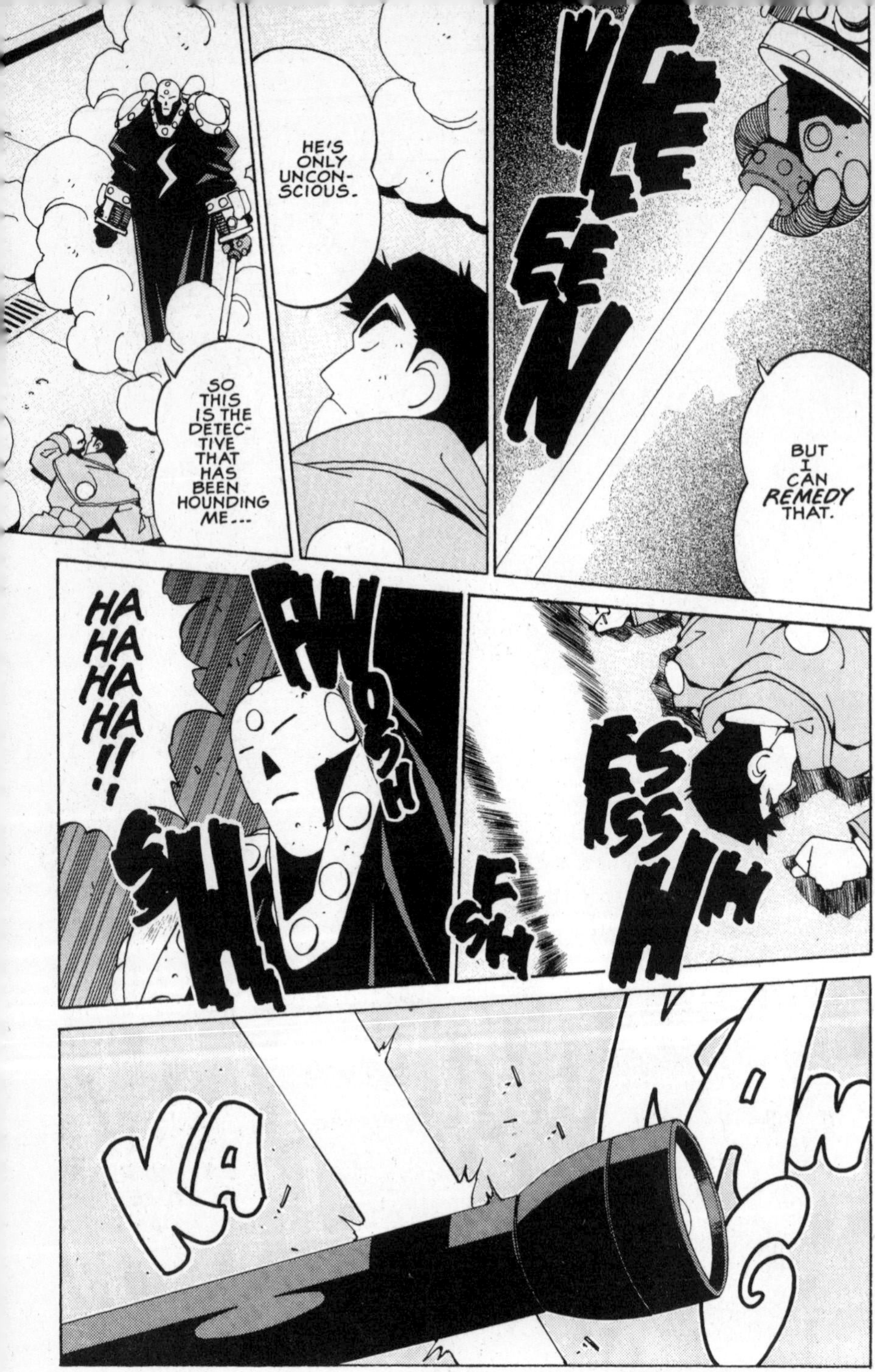
SO THIS IS THE DETECTIVE THAT HAS BEEN HOUNDING ME...
HE'S ONLY UNCONSCIOUS.
VVEEEEN
BUT I CAN REMEDY THAT.
HA HA HA HA!!
SH
FWOOSH
FSH
FSSSHH
KA
KAN

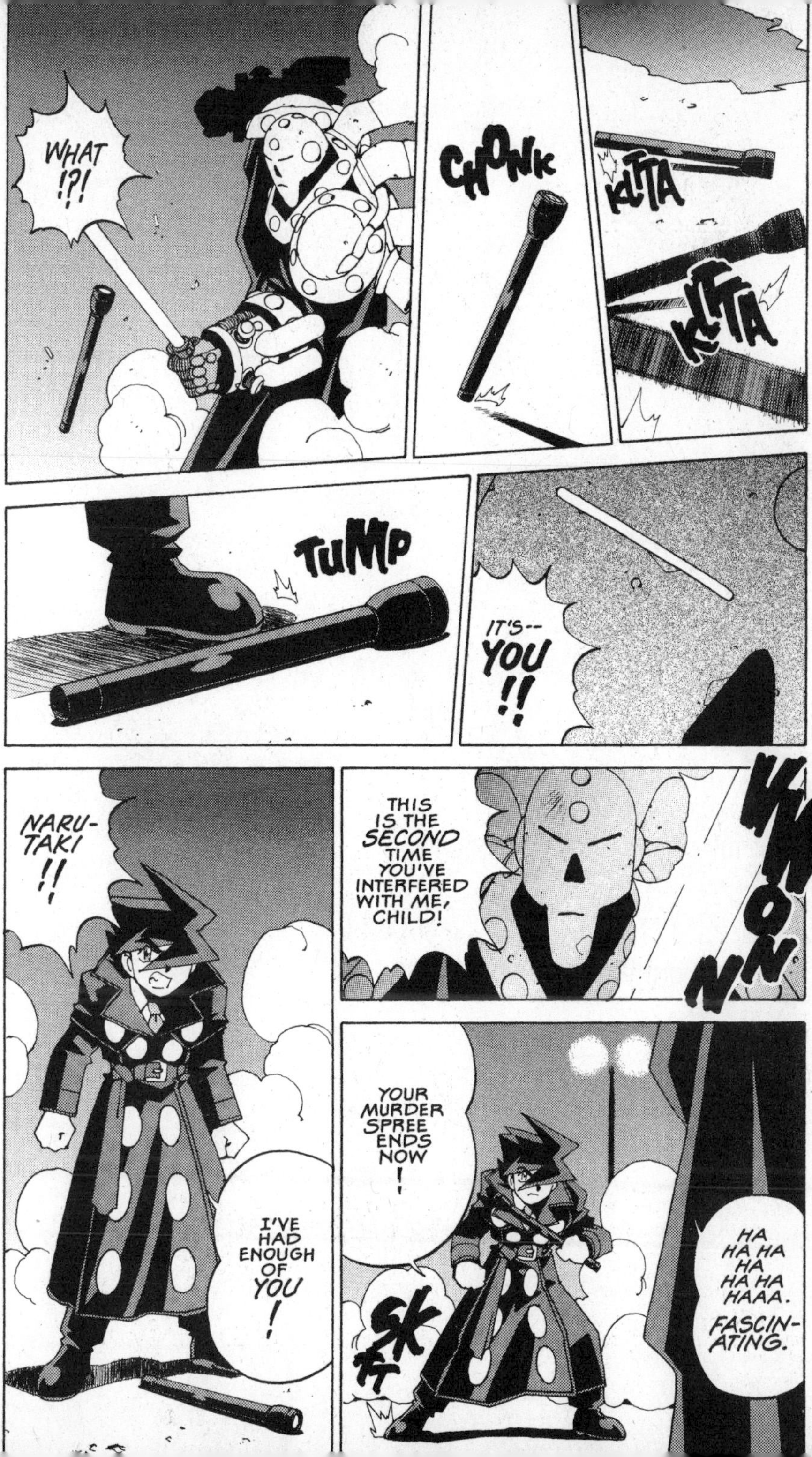
WHAT !?!
CHONK
KLITTA
KLITTA
TUMP
IT'S-- YOU !!
NARU-TAKI !!
THIS IS THE SECOND TIME YOU'VE INTERFERED WITH ME, CHILD!
WWONNN
I'VE HAD ENOUGH OF YOU!
YOUR MURDER SPREE ENDS NOW!
SKTT
HA HA HA HA HA HA HAAA.
FASCIN-ATING.

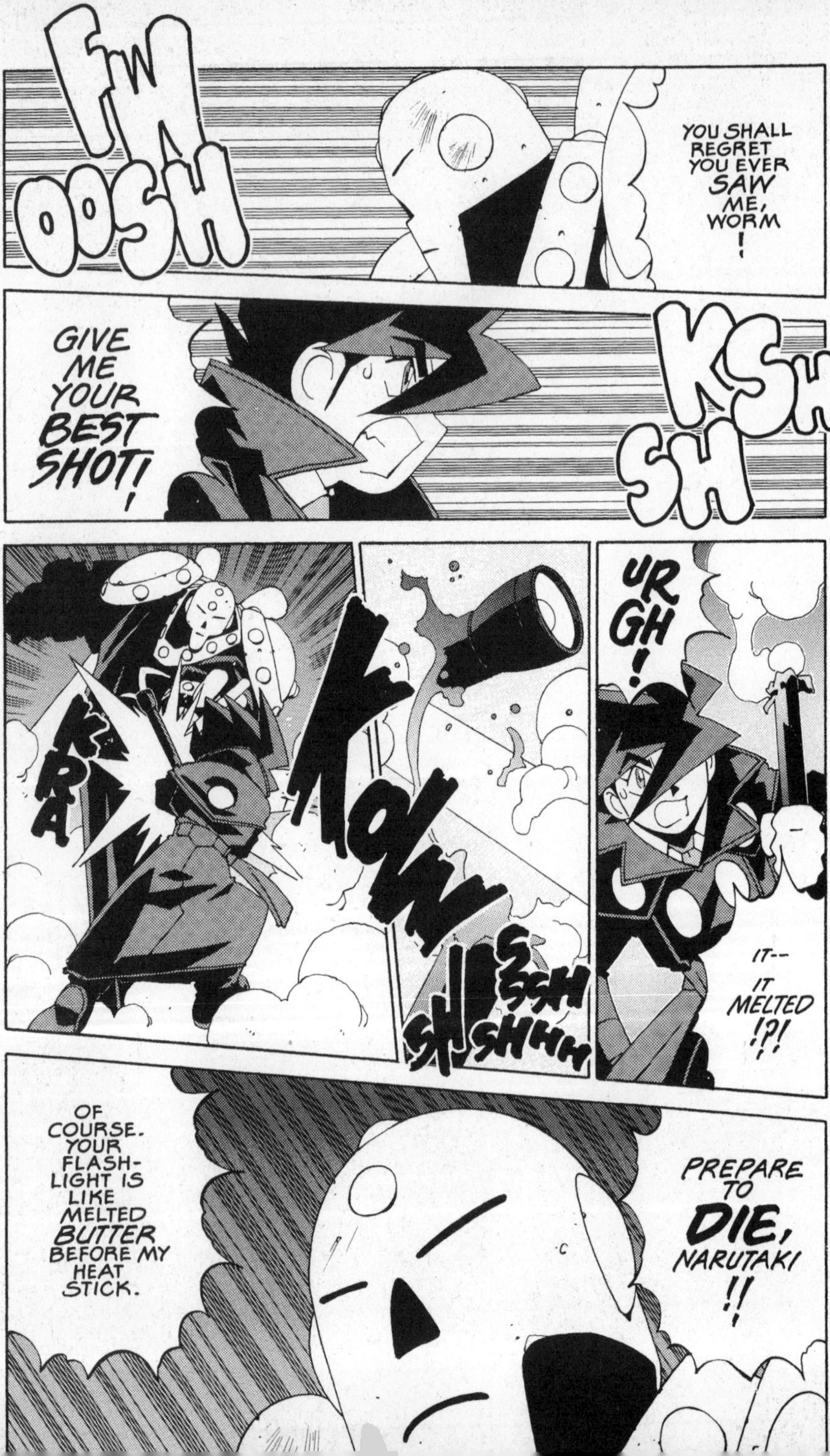
FWAOOSH
YOU SHALL REGRET YOU EVER SAW ME, WORM!
GIVE ME YOUR BEST SHOT!
KSHSH
KRA
KOWW
URGH!
SSSH SH SHHHH
IT--
IT MELTED!?!
OF COURSE. YOUR FLASH-LIGHT IS LIKE MELTED BUTTER BEFORE MY HEAT STICK.
PREPARE TO DIE, NARUTAKI!!

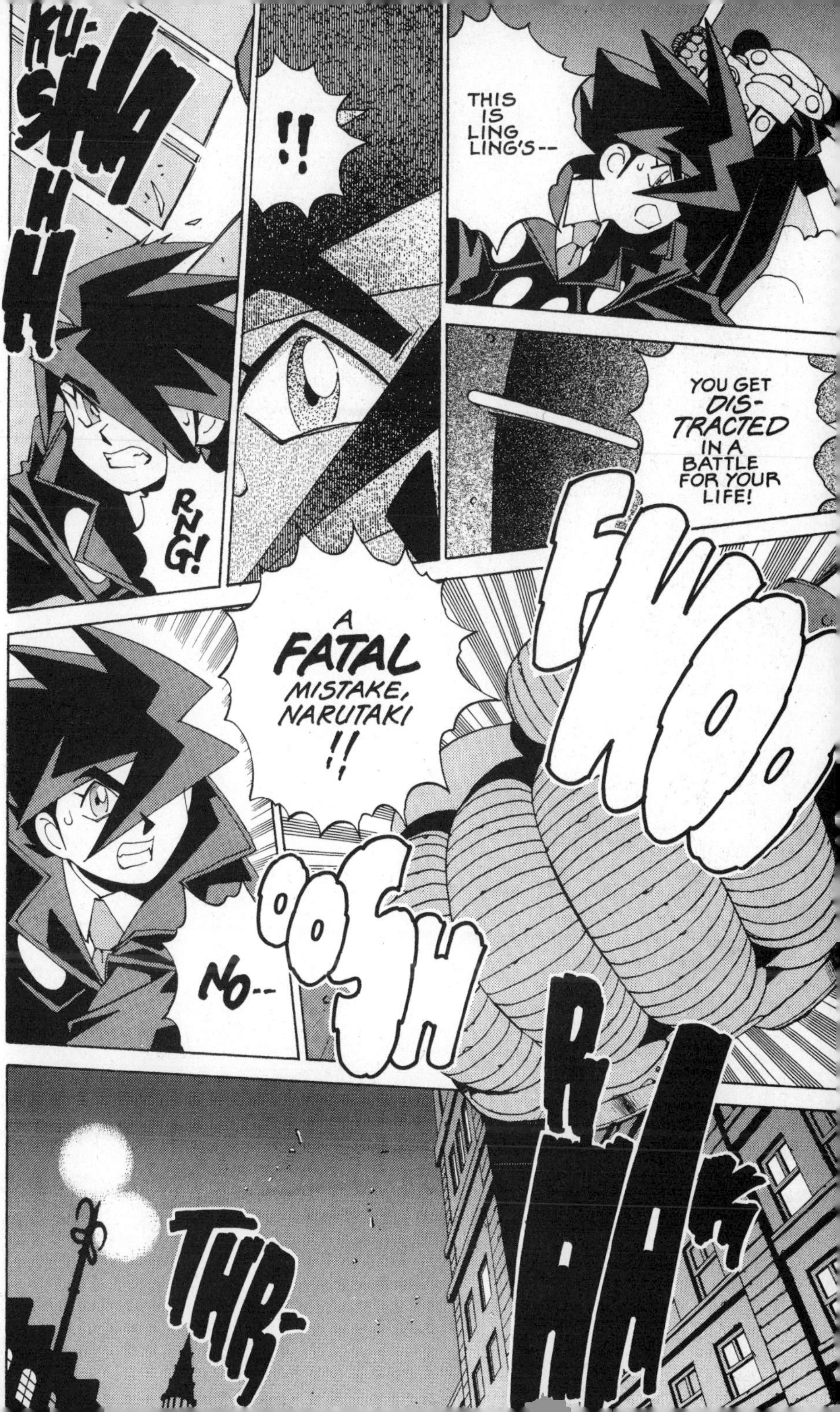
KU-SHA HHHH
RNG!
!!
THIS IS LING LING'S--
YOU GET DIS-TRACTED IN A BATTLE FOR YOUR LIFE!
A FATAL MISTAKE, NARUTAKI !!
NO--
FWOOO
OOSH
THR-
RAAAK

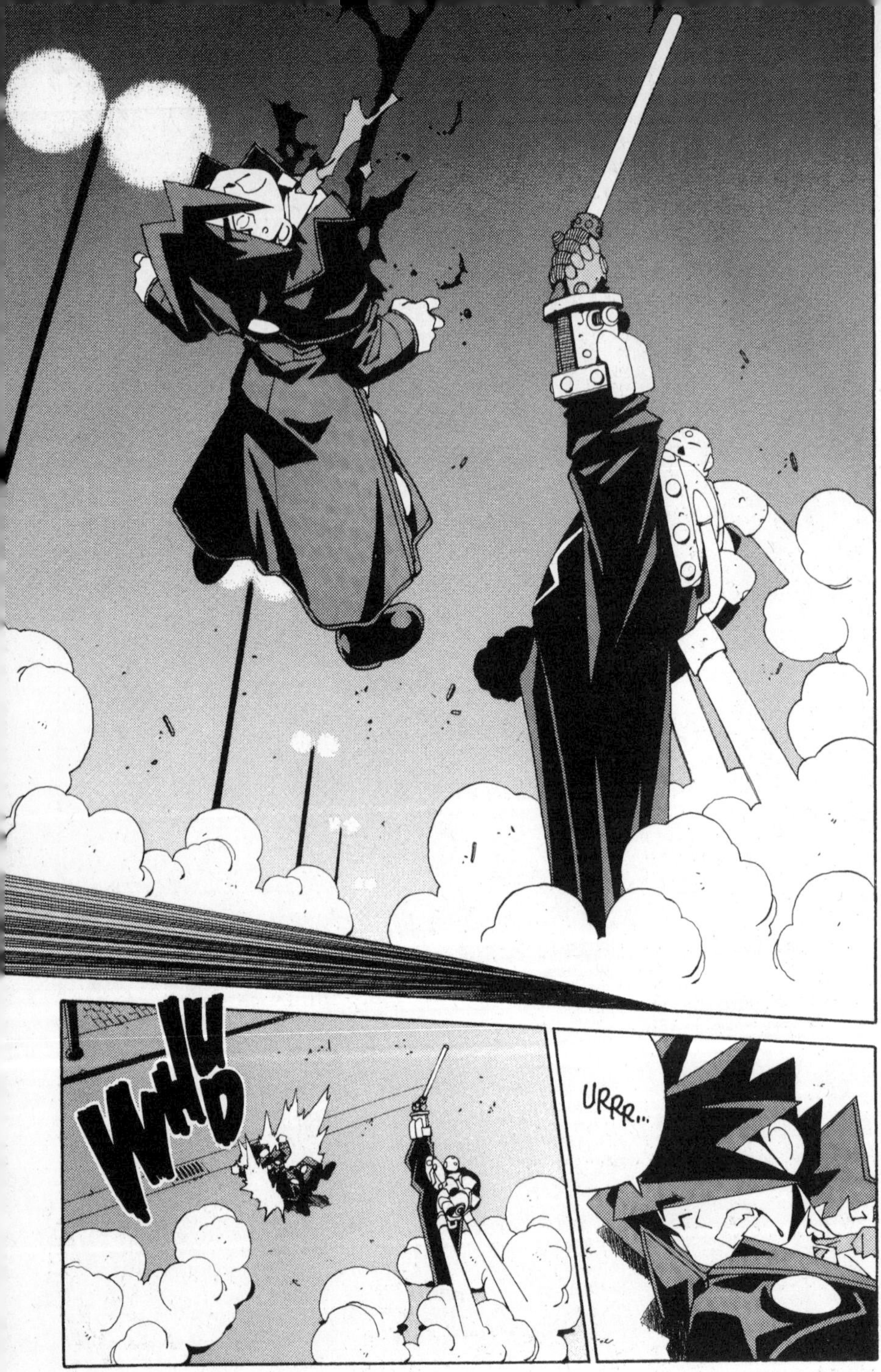
WHUD
URRR...

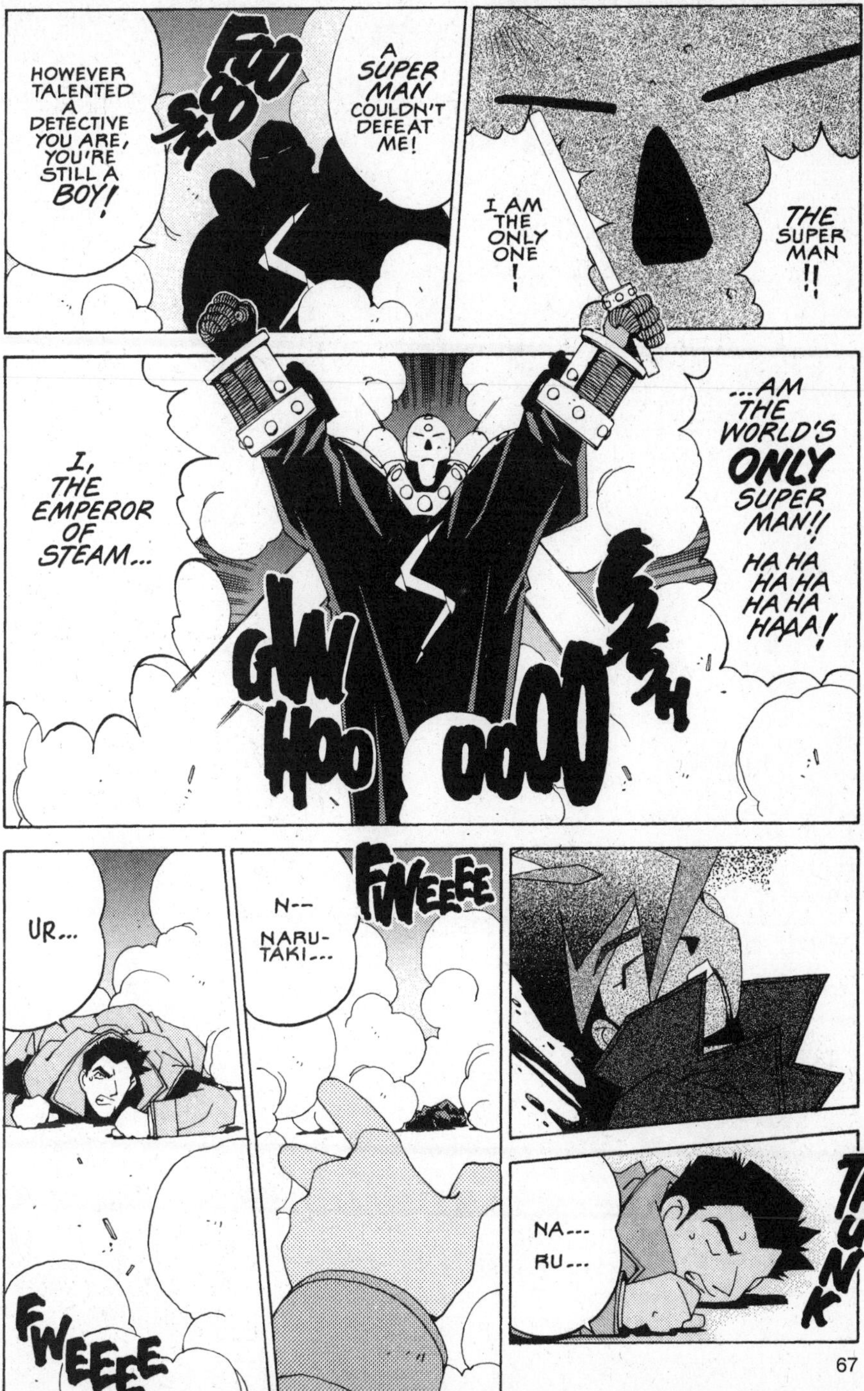
HOWEVER TALENTED A DETECTIVE YOU ARE, YOU'RE STILL A BOY!
A SUPER MAN COULDN'T DEFEAT ME!
I AM THE ONLY ONE!
THE SUPER MAN!!
I, THE EMPEROR OF STEAM...
...AM THE WORLD'S ONLY SUPER MAN!!
HA HA HA HA HA HA HAAA!
UR...
FWEEEEE
N-- NARU-TAKI...
FWEEEEE
NA--- RU---
THUNK

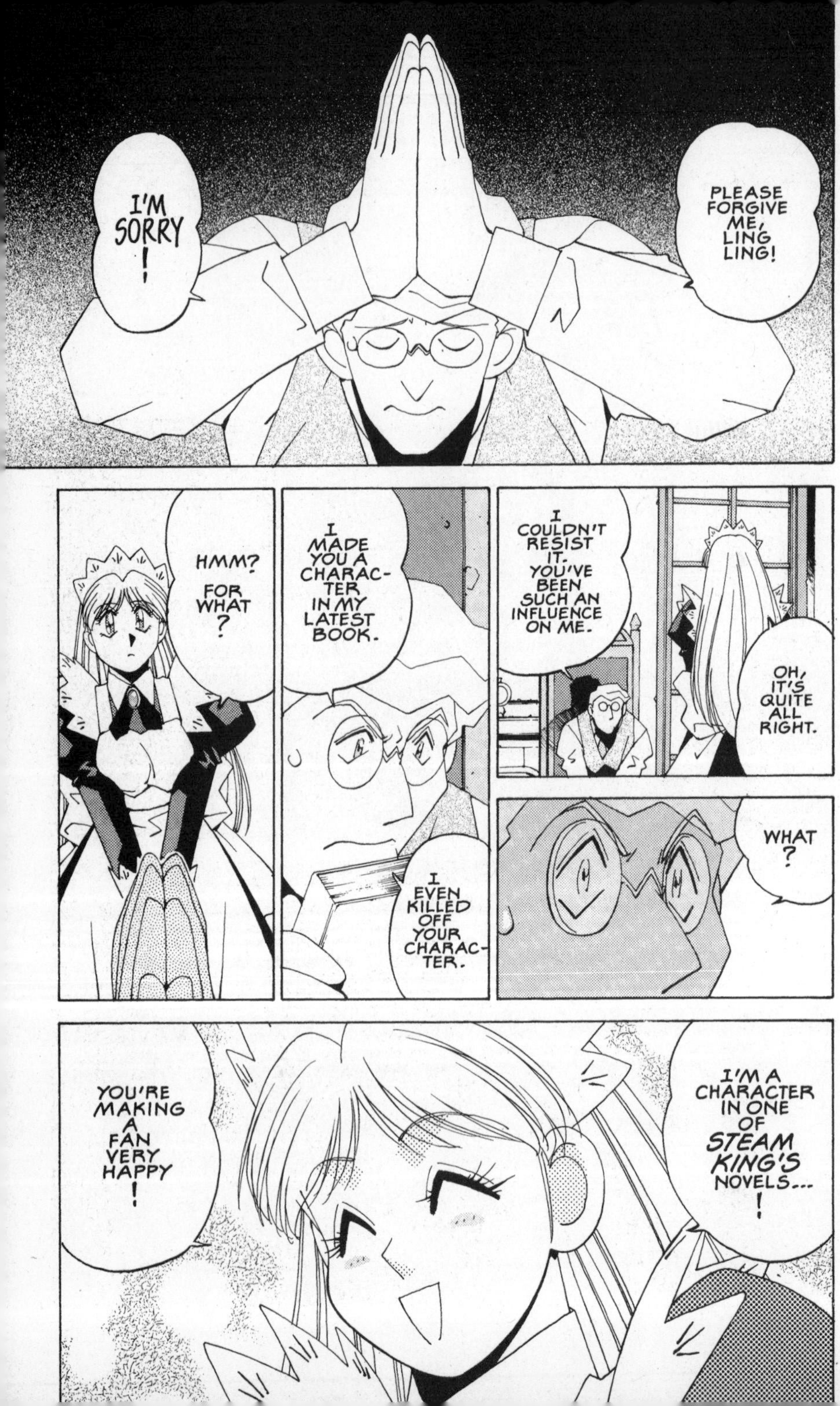
I'M SORRY!
PLEASE FORGIVE ME, LING LING!
HMM? FOR WHAT?
I MADE YOU A CHARACTER IN MY LATEST BOOK.
I EVEN KILLED OFF YOUR CHARACTER.
I COULDN'T RESIST IT. YOU'VE BEEN SUCH AN INFLUENCE ON ME.
OH, IT'S QUITE ALL RIGHT.
WHAT?
YOU'RE MAKING A FAN VERY HAPPY!
I'M A CHARACTER IN ONE OF *STEAM KING'S* NOVELS...!

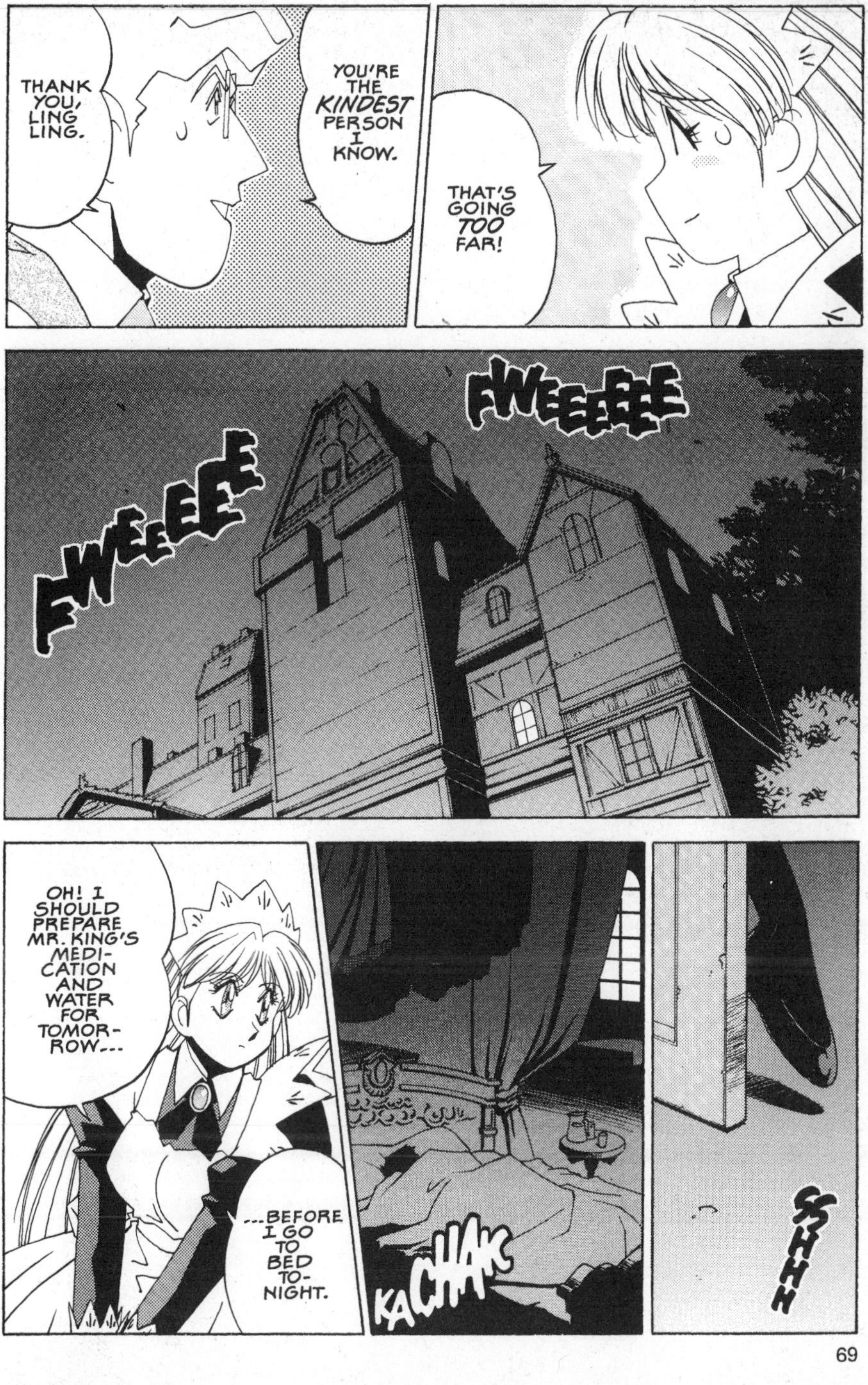
THANK YOU, LING LING.
YOU'RE THE KINDEST PERSON I KNOW.
THAT'S GOING TOO FAR!
FWEEEEE
FWEEEEEE
OH! I SHOULD PREPARE MR. KING'S MEDICATION AND WATER FOR TOMORROW...
...BEFORE I GO TO BED TONIGHT.
KACHAK
SSHHHH

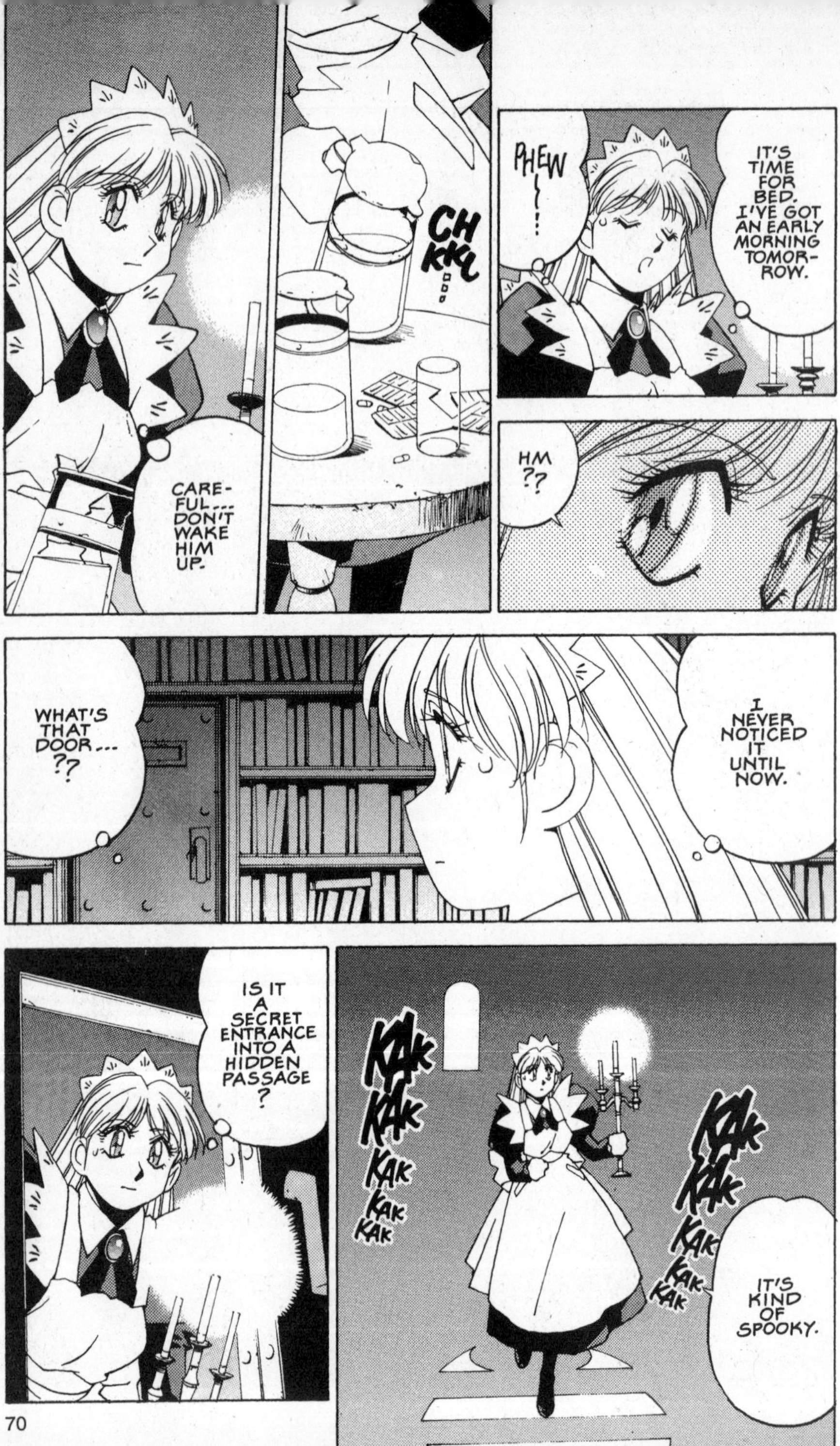
CARE-FUL... DON'T WAKE HIM UP.
CHKKK...
PHEW...!
IT'S TIME FOR BED. I'VE GOT AN EARLY MORNING TOMOR-ROW.
HM ??
WHAT'S THAT DOOR... ??
I NEVER NOTICED IT UNTIL NOW.
IS IT A SECRET ENTRANCE INTO A HIDDEN PASSAGE ?
KAK KAK KAK KAK KAK
KAK KAK KAK KAK KAK
IT'S KIND OF SPOOKY.

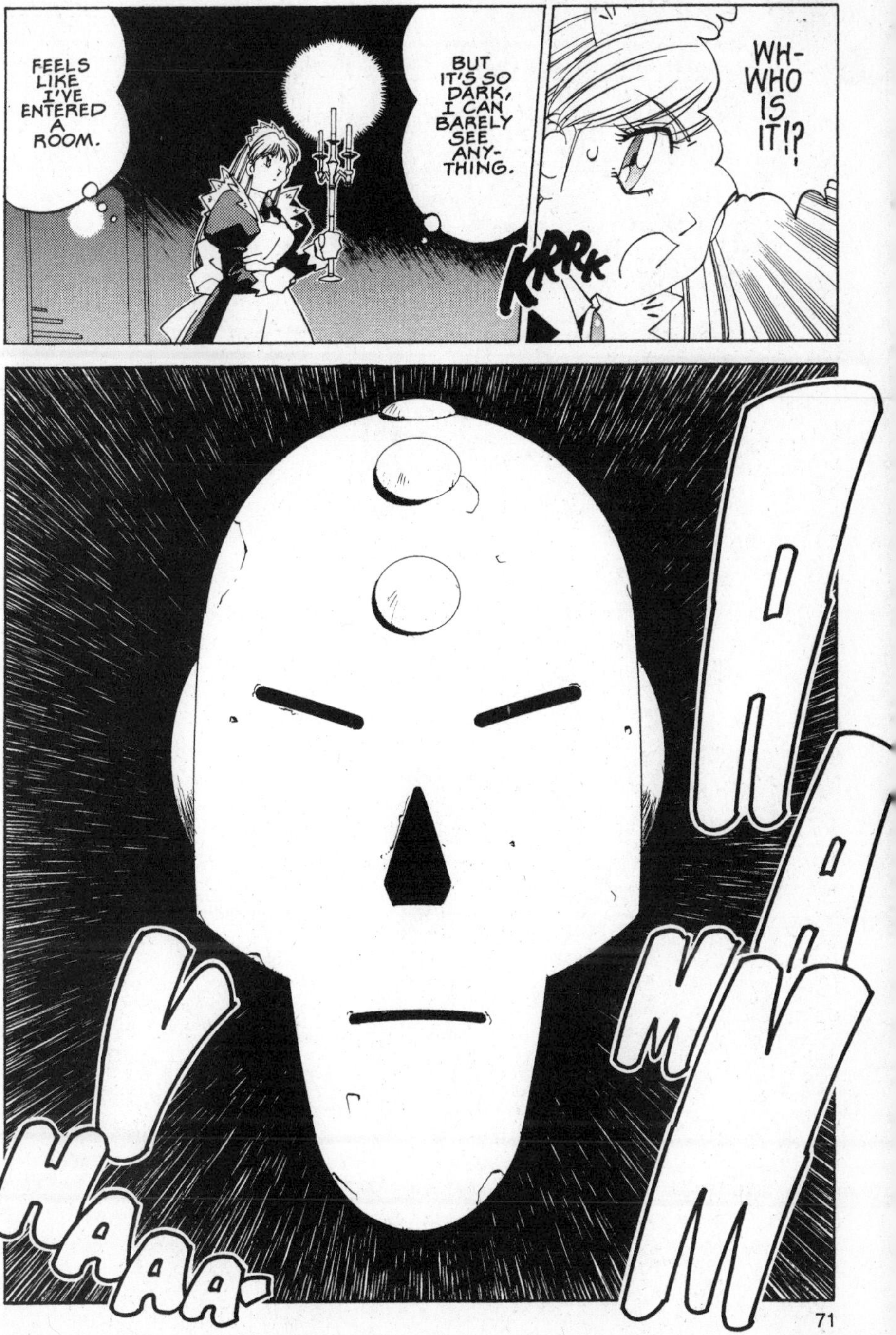
FEELS LIKE I'VE ENTERED A ROOM.
BUT IT'S SO DARK, I CAN BARELY SEE ANY-THING.
WH-WHO IS IT!?
KRRRK
HAAAA-

STEAM DETECTIVES PRESS

THE MYSTERY BEHIND MEGA-BEST-SELLING AUTHOR, STEAM KING!

CENTER OF THE POLICE INVESTI-GATION, MR. STEAM KING

Most readers are aware of the controversial serial murders occurring in the City. The murderer allegedly refers to himself as Emperor of Steam, the protagonist of the horror novels written by the best-selling author Steam King (28). Local authorities have been investigating the connection between the Emperor of Steam and Mr. Steam King. Mr. King denies any knowledge of the murders, insisting that the police suspicions are unfounded.

Mystery 1: HIDDEN PRIVATE LIFE
Born into a wealthy family which owned trading and mining companies, Mr. King enjoyed a privileged childhood. Both of his parents died when King was 20. He currently lives alone. After the deaths of his parents, King dedicated himself to his writing, shunning contact with the outside world.

Mystery 2: THE WRITER, STEAM KING
King published his first work at the age of 22 with a short story in a pulp science fiction magazine. Using over 50 pseudonyms, King wrote for many magazines. He published books in a wide range of genres including science fiction, literary non-fiction and criticism.

Mystery 3: THE POLICE INVESTIGATION
The police have advocated the following three theories:
A: A plot for revenge against Mr. King. B: A fan obsessed with King's work. C: A normal mental-case murder case.
The mass media has been pursuing rumors that King himself is the culprit, but this theory seems implausible in light of his reputation as a well established author. The police will be requesting a second interview with Mr. King.

KING RESIDENCE

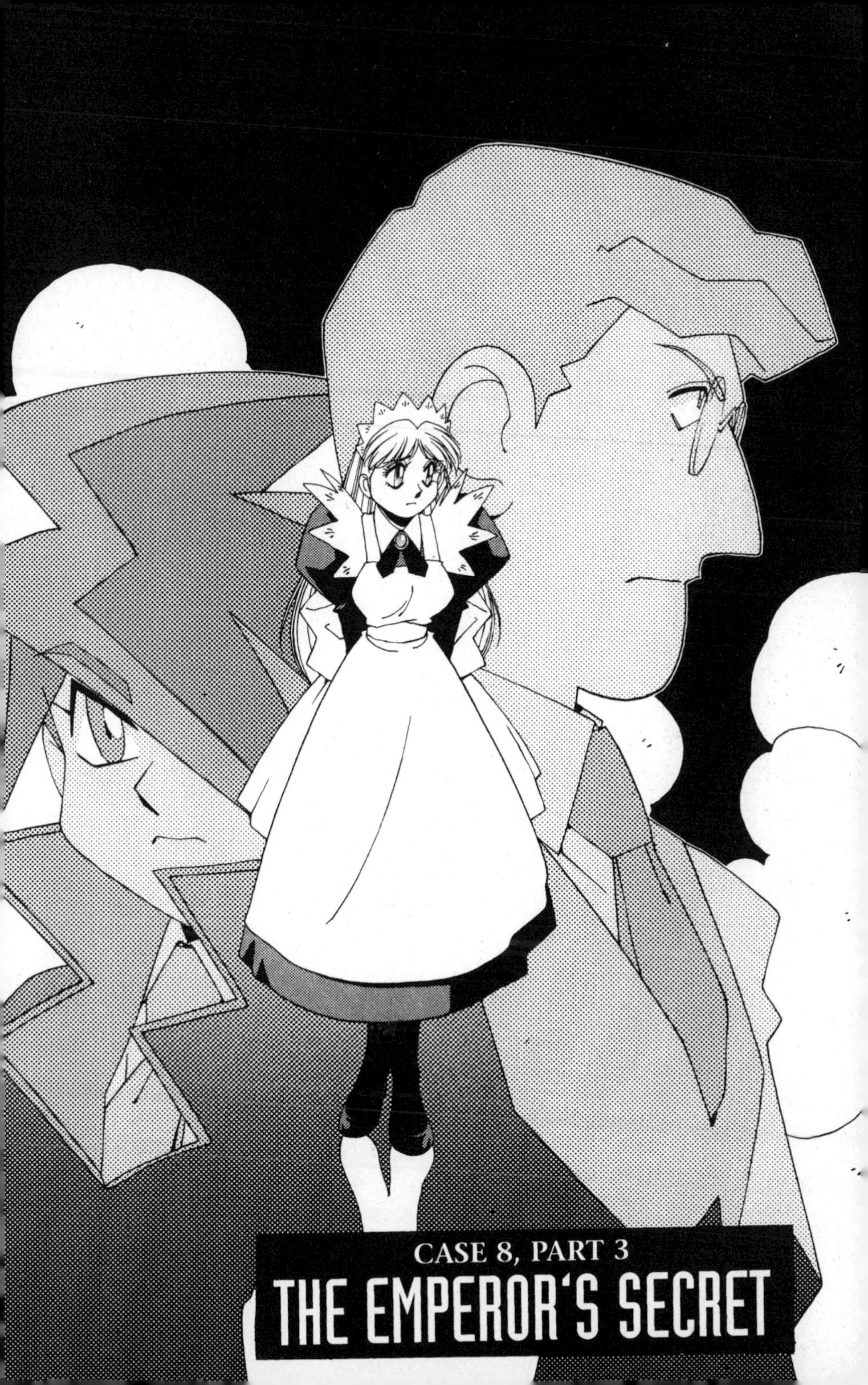
CASE 8, PART 3
THE EMPEROR'S SECRET

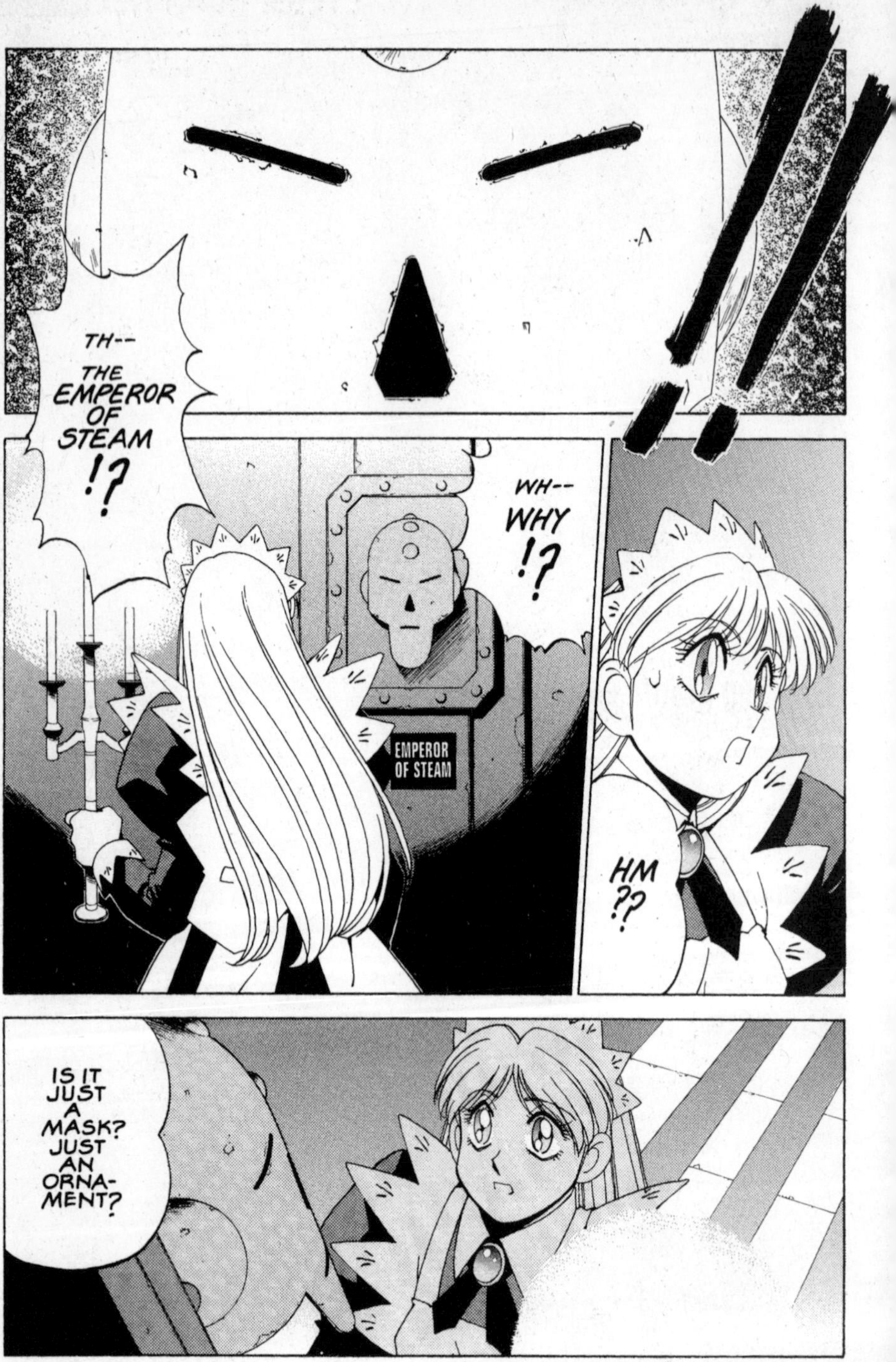
TH-- THE EMPEROR OF STEAM !?
WH-- WHY !?
EMPEROR OF STEAM
HM ??
IS IT JUST A MASK? JUST AN ORNA-MENT?

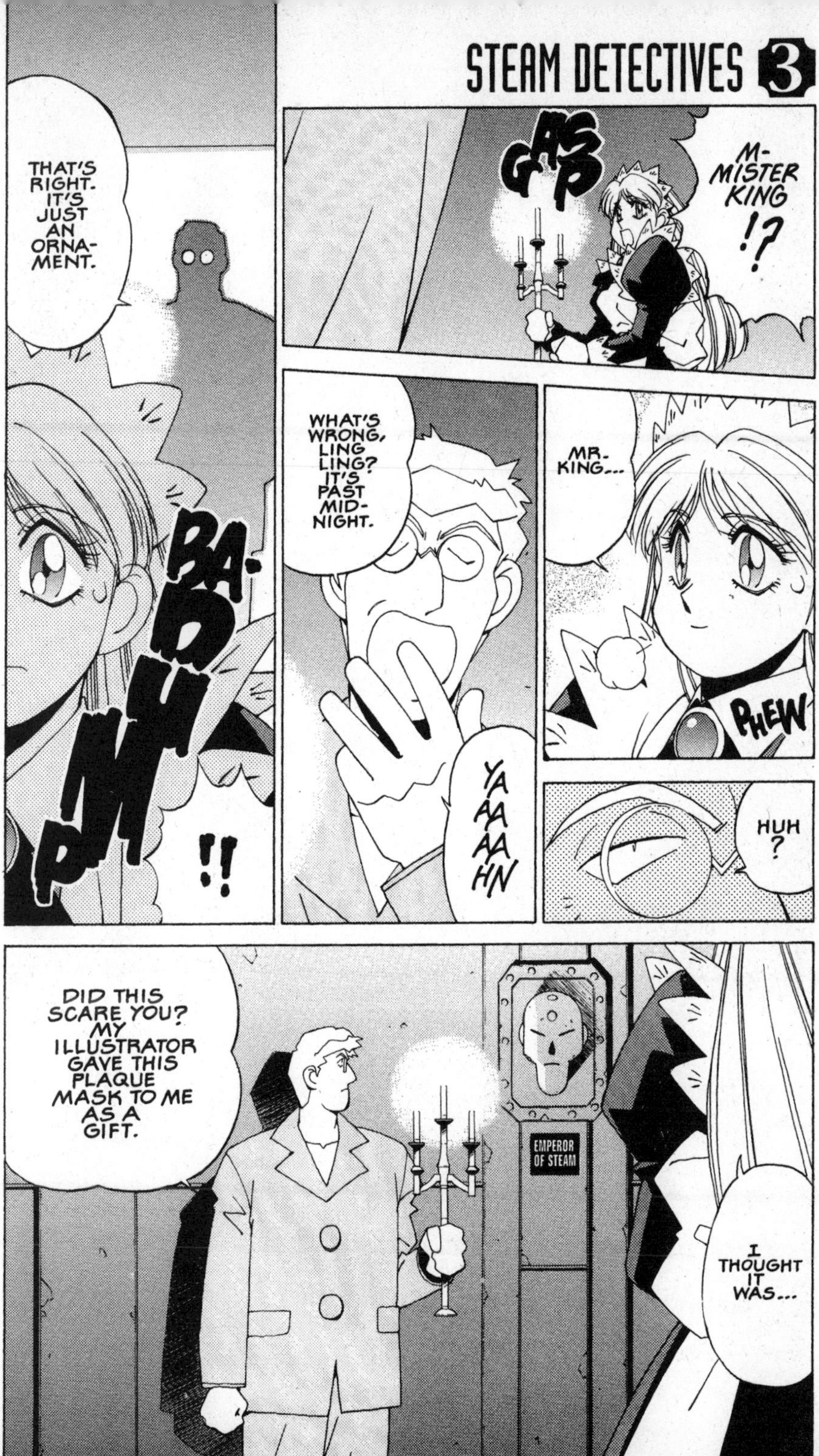
THAT'S RIGHT. IT'S JUST AN ORNAMENT.
BA-DUMP
!!
GASP
M-MISTER KING !?
WHAT'S WRONG, LING LING? IT'S PAST MIDNIGHT.
YAAAAAHN
MR. KING...
PHEW
HUH?
DID THIS SCARE YOU? MY ILLUSTRATOR GAVE THIS PLAQUE MASK TO ME AS A GIFT.
EMPEROR OF STEAM
I THOUGHT IT WAS...

SO YOU THOUGHT I WAS THE EMPEROR OF STEAM AS WELL?

NO, NOT AT ALL.

I THOUGHT THAT THE EMPEROR OF STEAM HAD COME TO GET ME.

EMPEROR OF STE

HA HA HA HA. THAT'LL *NEVER* HAPPEN. YOU'RE SUCH A WORRY-WORT.

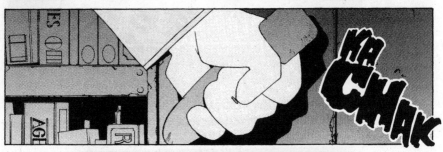

KA CHAK

I USE THAT ROOM TO CONCENTRATE. SOMETIMES I GET IDEAS FOR MY NOVELS HERE.

SOMETIMES I JUST RELAX. IT'S ONE OF THOSE THINGS I NEED.

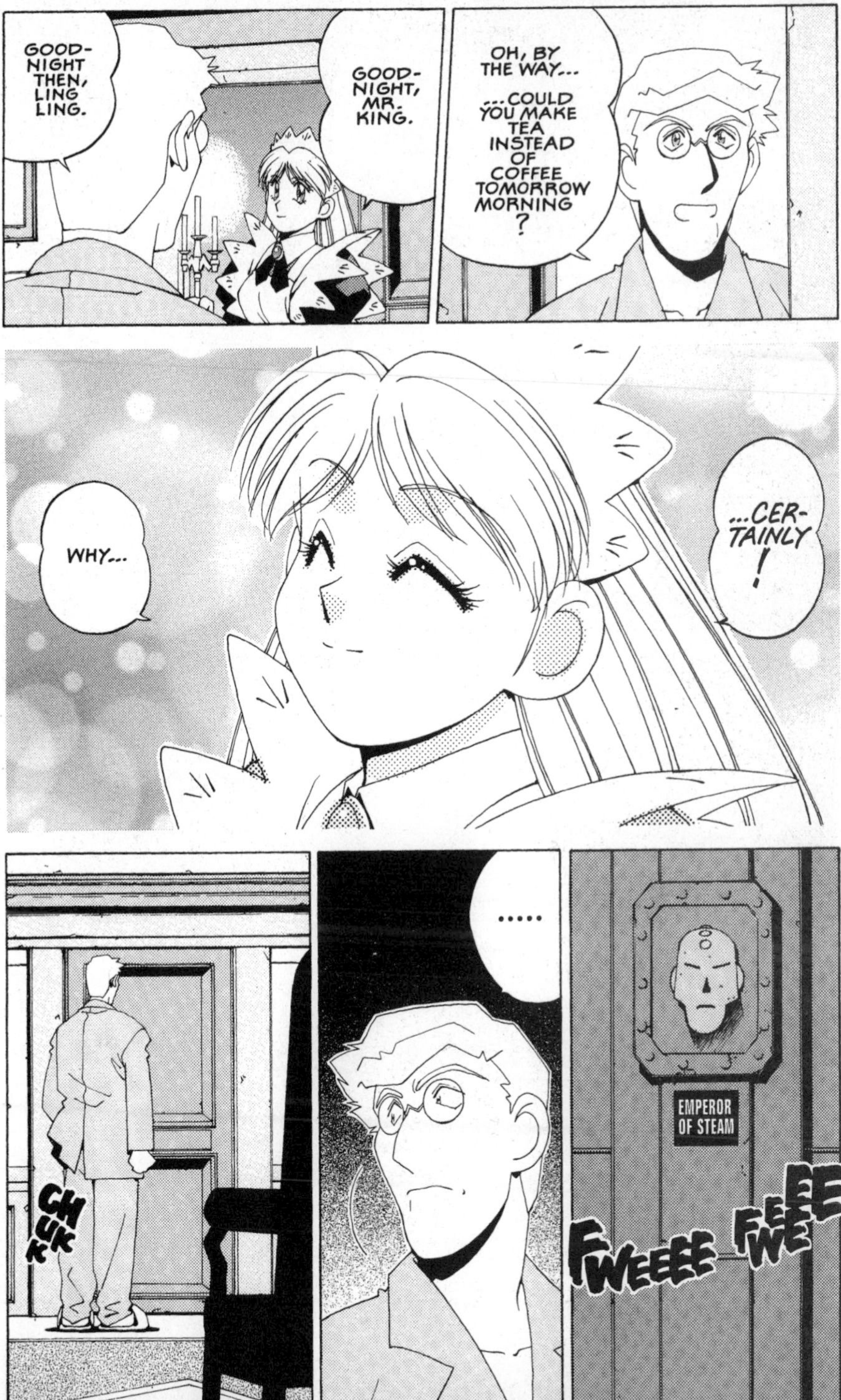
GOOD-NIGHT THEN, LING LING.
GOOD-NIGHT, MR. KING.
OH, BY THE WAY...
...COULD YOU MAKE TEA INSTEAD OF COFFEE TOMORROW MORNING?
WHY...
...CERTAINLY!
CHUK
.....
EMPEROR OF STEAM
FWEEEE FWEEEE

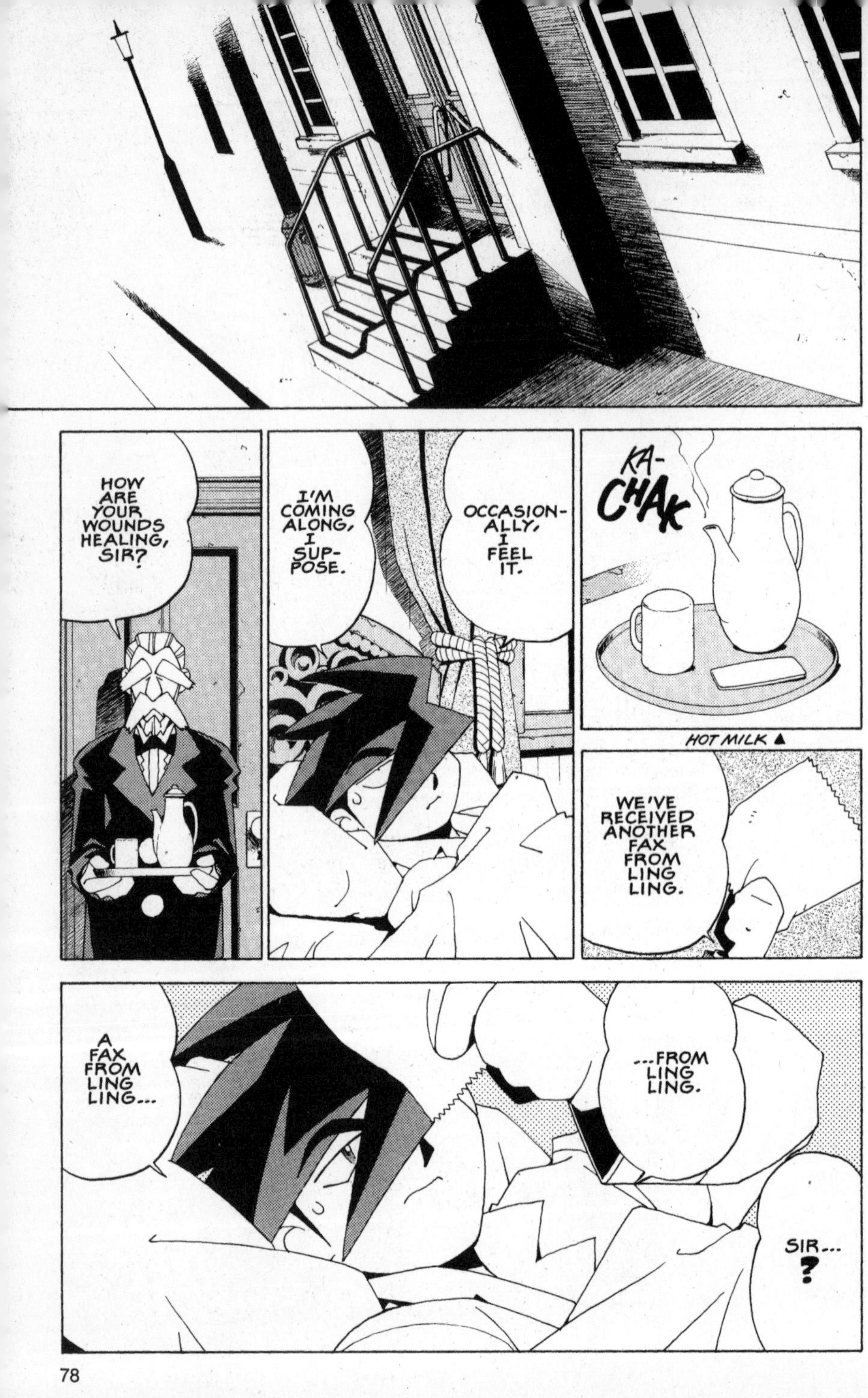
HOW ARE YOUR WOUNDS HEALING, SIR?
I'M COMING ALONG, I SUP-POSE.
OCCASION-ALLY, I FEEL IT.
KA-CHAK
HOT MILK ▲
WE'VE RECEIVED ANOTHER FAX FROM LING LING.
A FAX FROM LING LING...
...FROM LING LING.
SIR...?

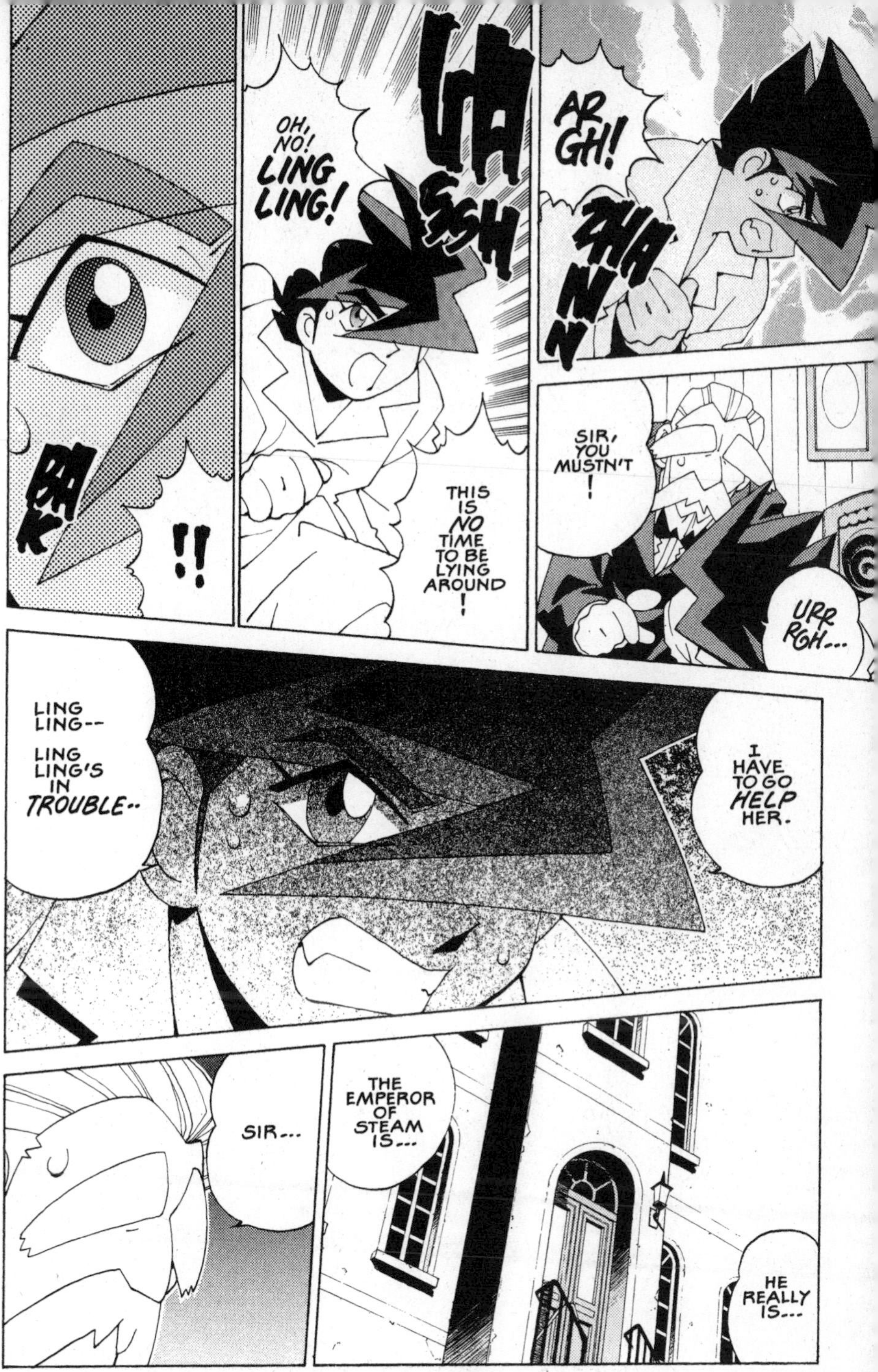
!!
OH, NO! LING LING!
THIS IS NO TIME TO BE LYING AROUND!
ARGH!
ZHANNN
SIR, YOU MUSTN'T!
URRRGH...
LING LING-- LING LING'S IN TROUBLE..
I HAVE TO GO HELP HER.
SIR...
THE EMPEROR OF STEAM IS...
HE REALLY IS...

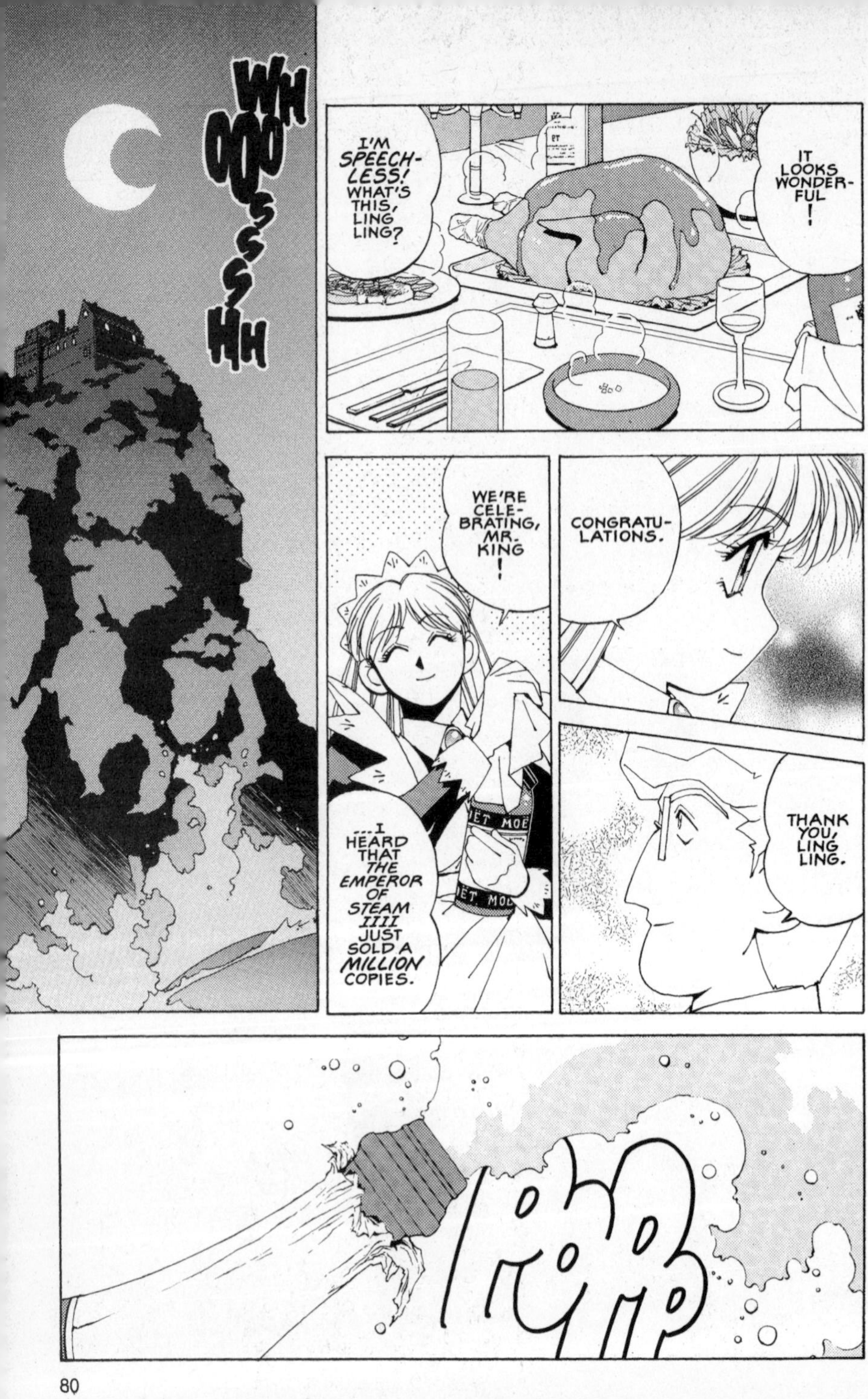
WHOOOOSSSHH
I'M SPEECHLESS! WHAT'S THIS, LING LING?
IT LOOKS WONDERFUL!
WE'RE CELEBRATING, MR. KING!
...I HEARD THAT THE EMPEROR OF STEAM IIII JUST SOLD A MILLION COPIES.
CONGRATULATIONS.
THANK YOU, LING LING.
POP

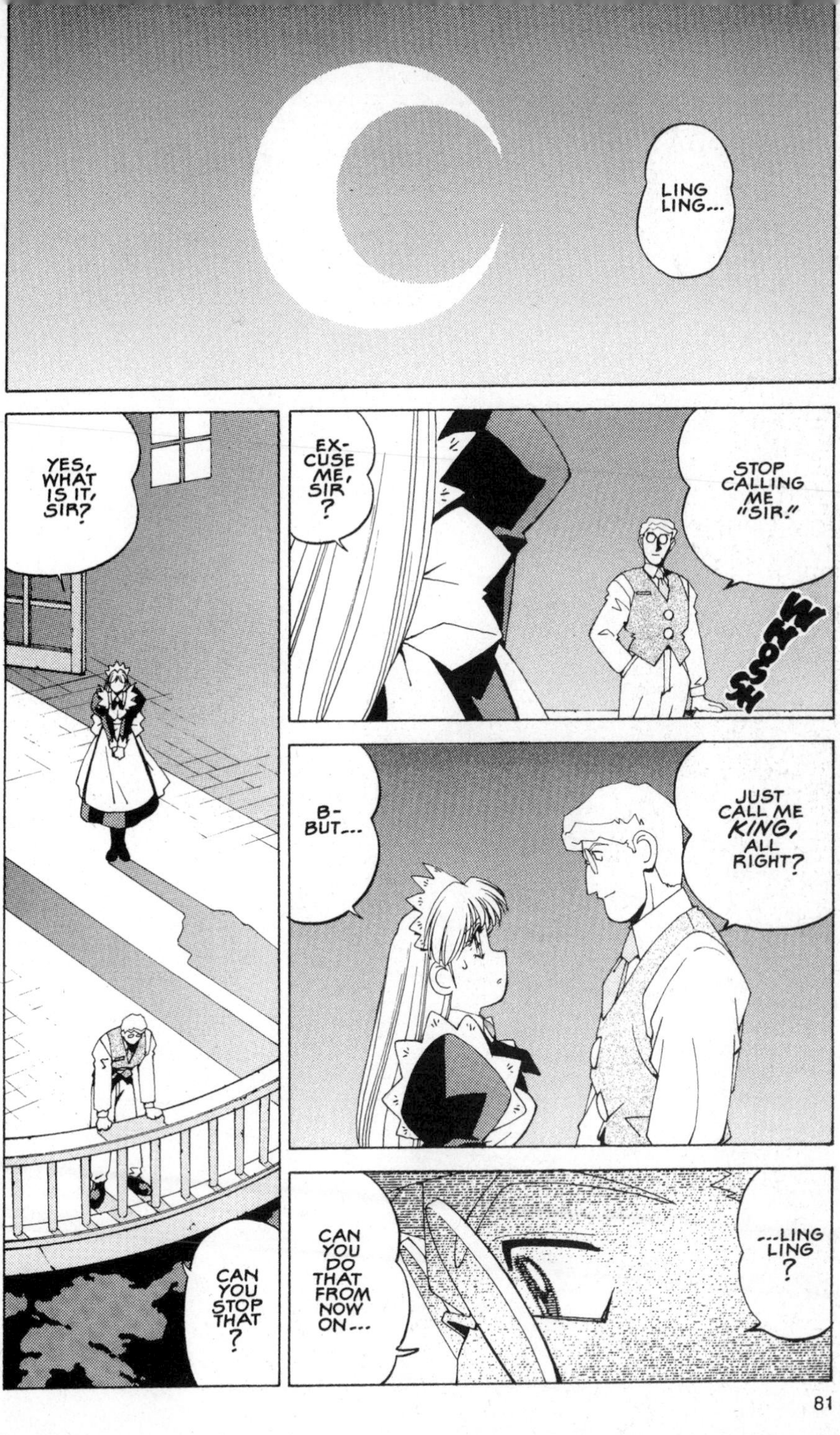
LING LING...
YES, WHAT IS IT, SIR?
CAN YOU STOP THAT?
EX-CUSE ME, SIR?
STOP CALLING ME "SIR!"
WHOOSH
B-BUT...
JUST CALL ME KING, ALL RIGHT?
CAN YOU DO THAT FROM NOW ON...
...LING LING?

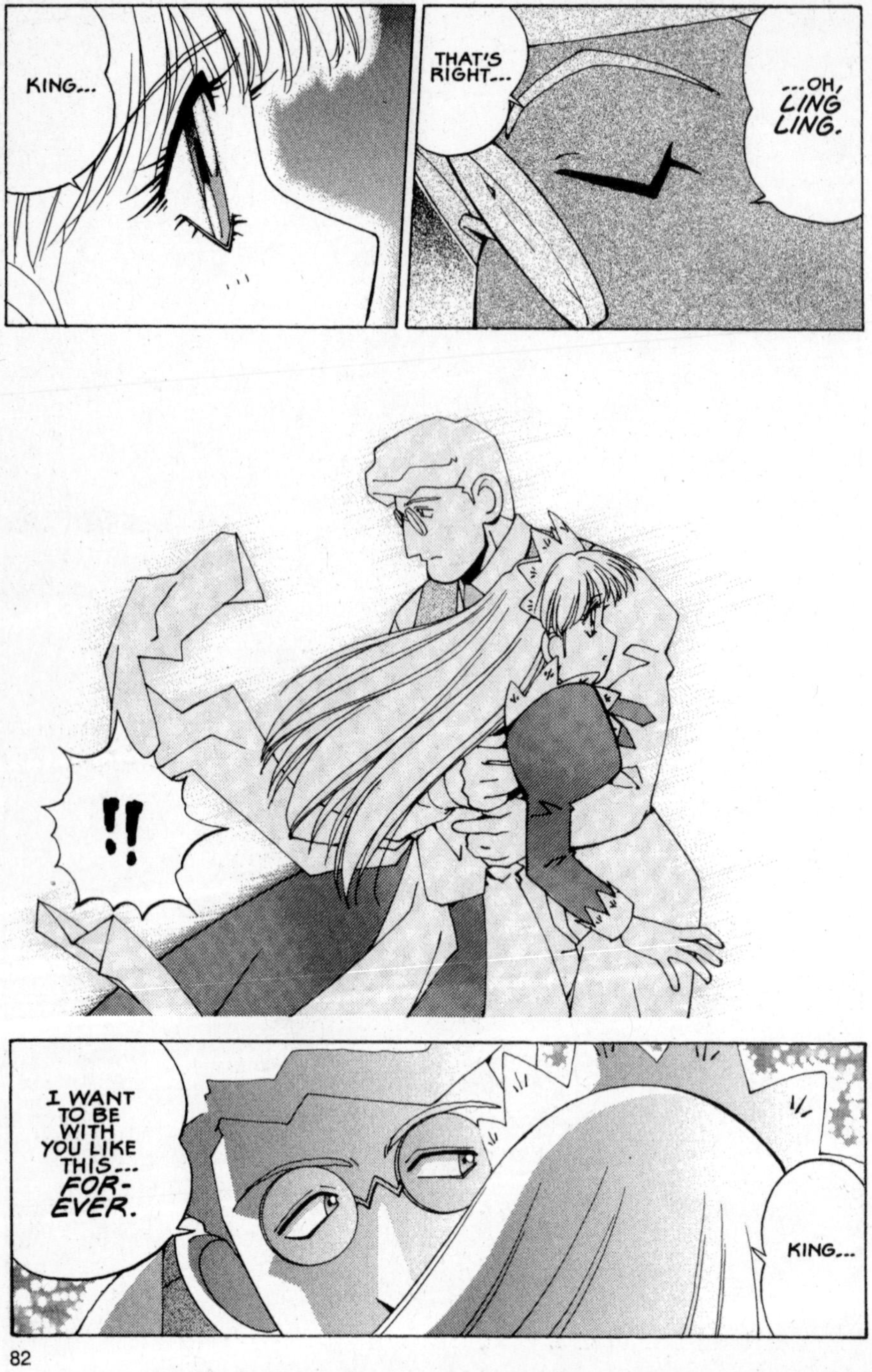
KING...
THAT'S RIGHT...
...OH, LING LING.
!!
I WANT TO BE WITH YOU LIKE THIS... FOR-EVER.
KING...

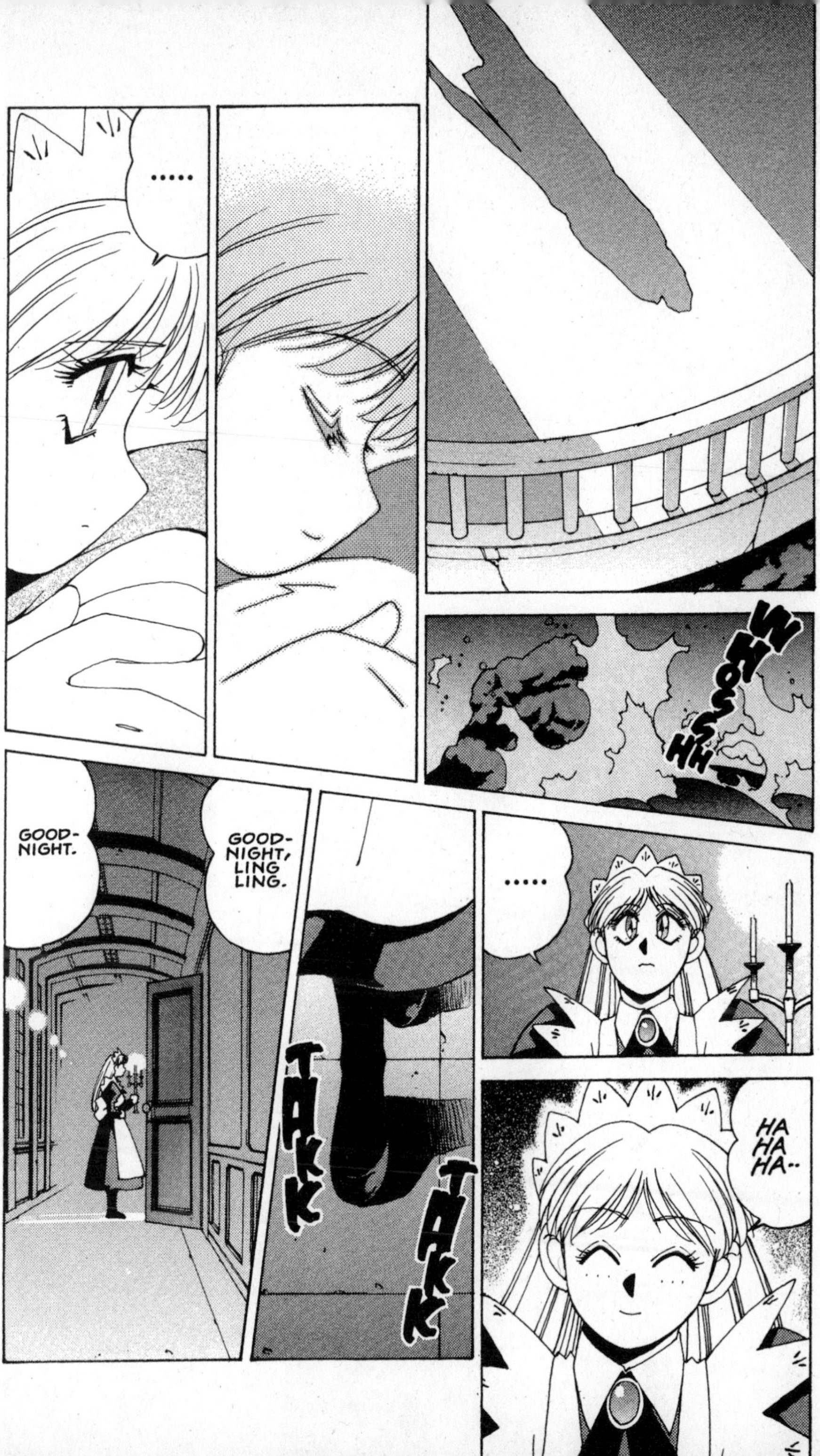
.....
WHOOSHH
GOOD-NIGHT.
GOOD-NIGHT, LING LING.
TAKK
TAKK
.....
HA HA HA HA..

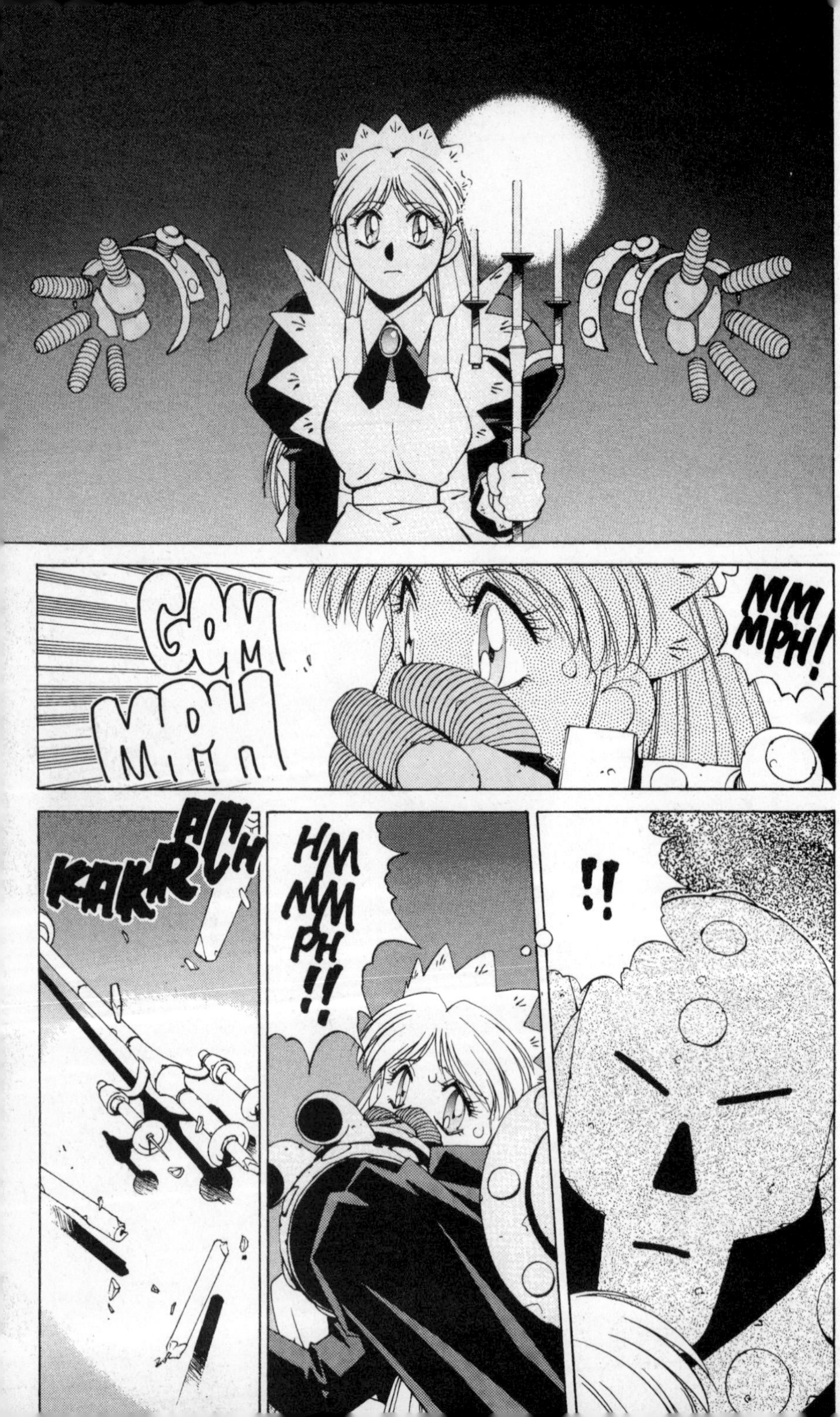
COMMMPH MMM
MMMPH!
KAKRACH
HMMMMPH!!
!!

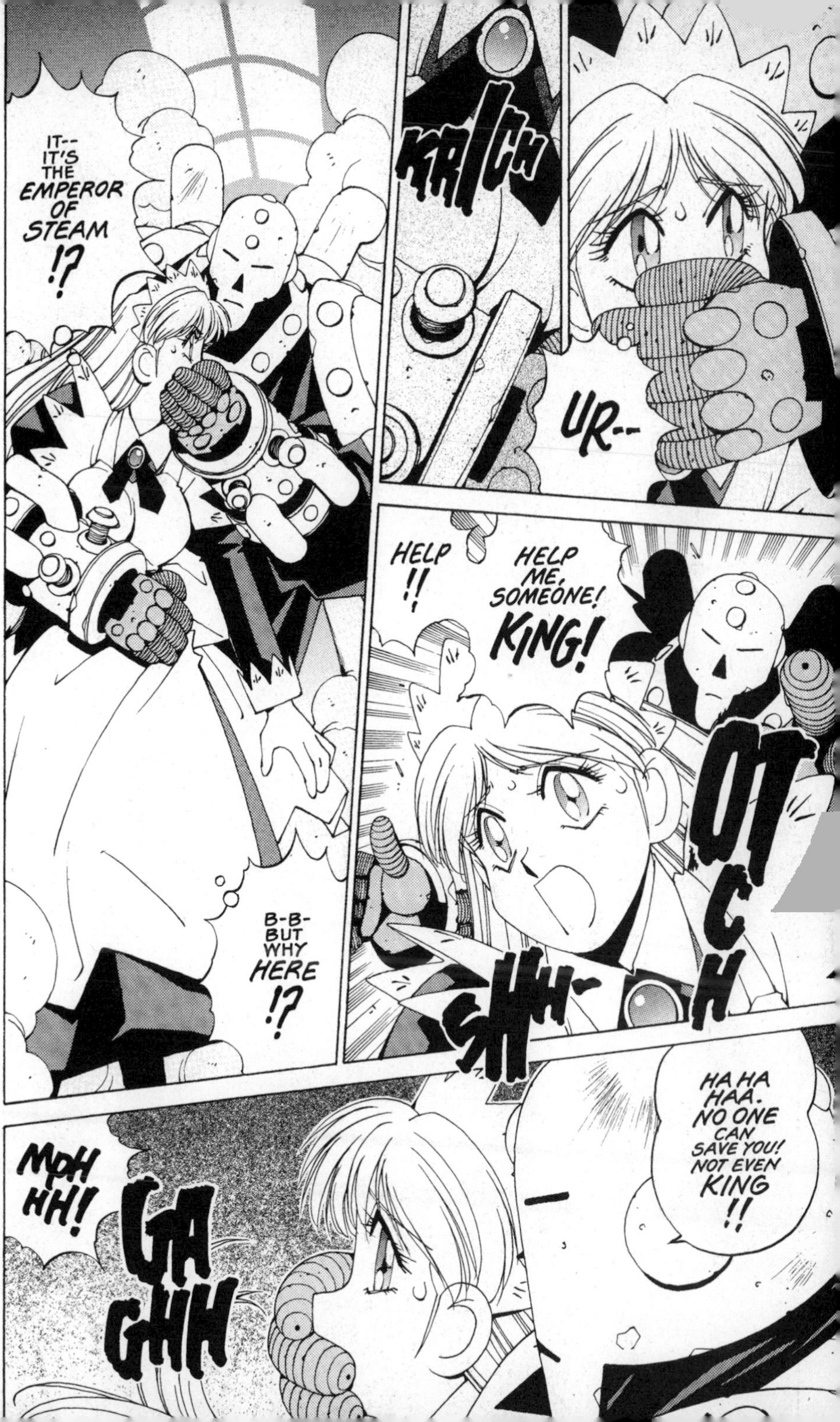

IT-- IT'S THE EMPEROR OF STEAM !?
B-B-BUT WHY HERE !?
KRITCH
UR--
HELP !!
HELP ME, SOMEONE! KING!
OTCH
SHH
MPHHH!
GA GHH
HA HA HAA. NO ONE CAN SAVE YOU! NOT EVEN KING !!

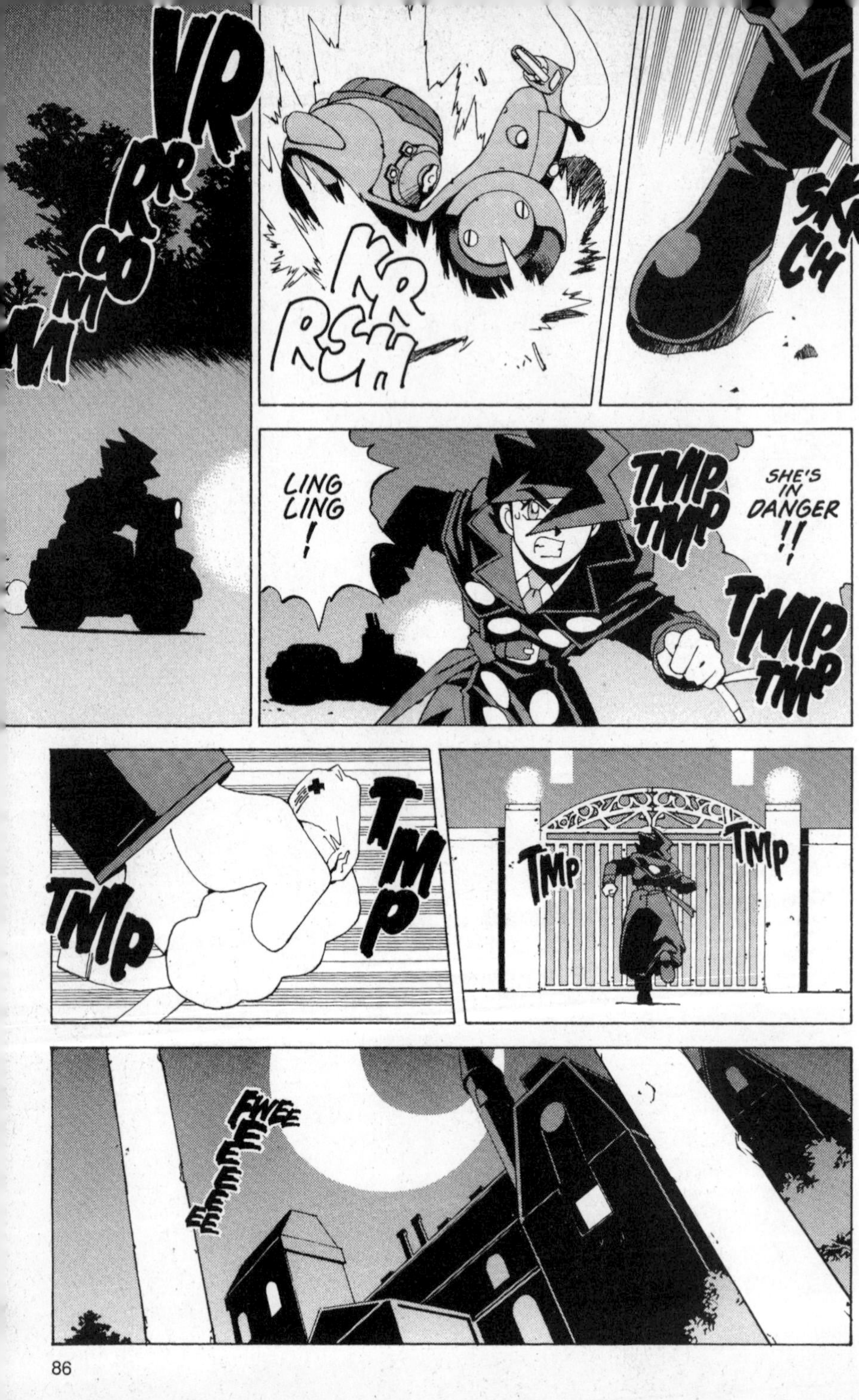
VRPR
ROOM
MM
KRRRCH
SKRCH
LING LING!
TMP TMP
SHE'S IN DANGER!!
TMP TMP
TMP
TMP
TMP
TMP
FWEEEEEE

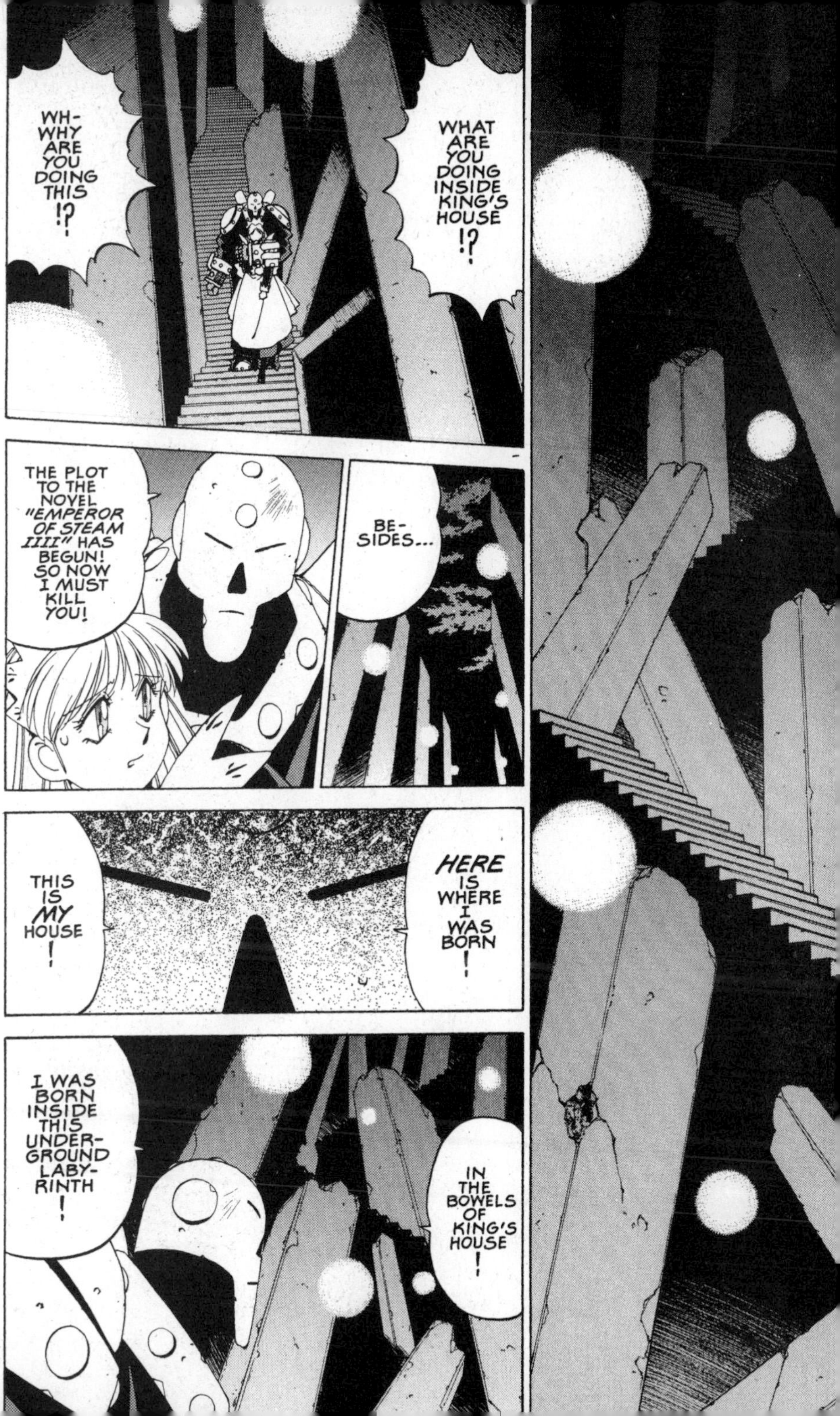
WH-WHY ARE YOU DOING THIS!?
WHAT ARE YOU DOING INSIDE KING'S HOUSE!?
THE PLOT TO THE NOVEL "EMPEROR OF STEAM IIII" HAS BEGUN! SO NOW I MUST KILL YOU!
BE-SIDES...
THIS IS MY HOUSE!
HERE IS WHERE I WAS BORN!
I WAS BORN INSIDE THIS UNDER-GROUND LABY-RINTH!
IN THE BOWELS OF KING'S HOUSE!

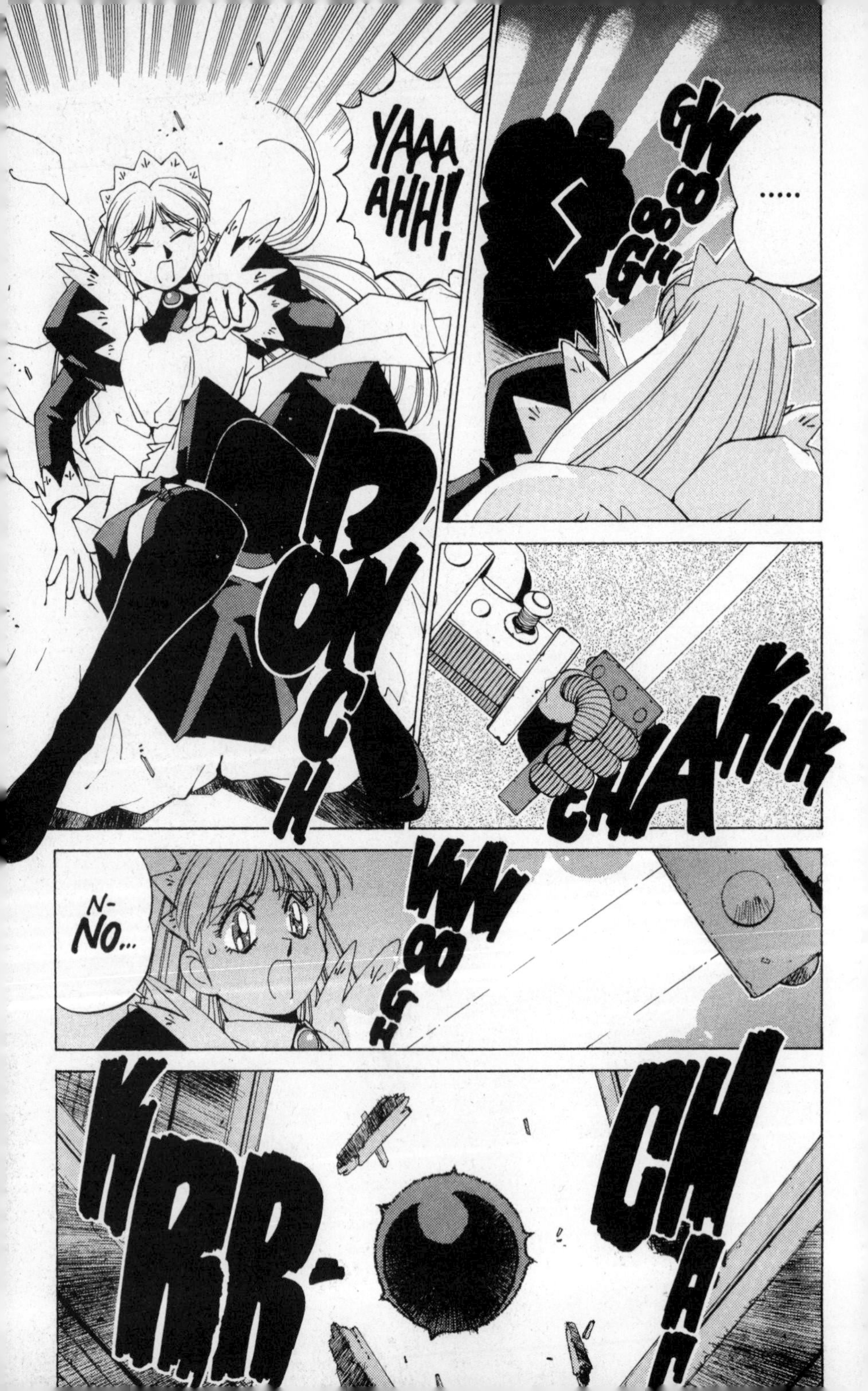
YAAA AHH!
DONCH
GWOOOOGH
......
CHAKIK
N-NO...
WWOOGH
KRR-
CHAA

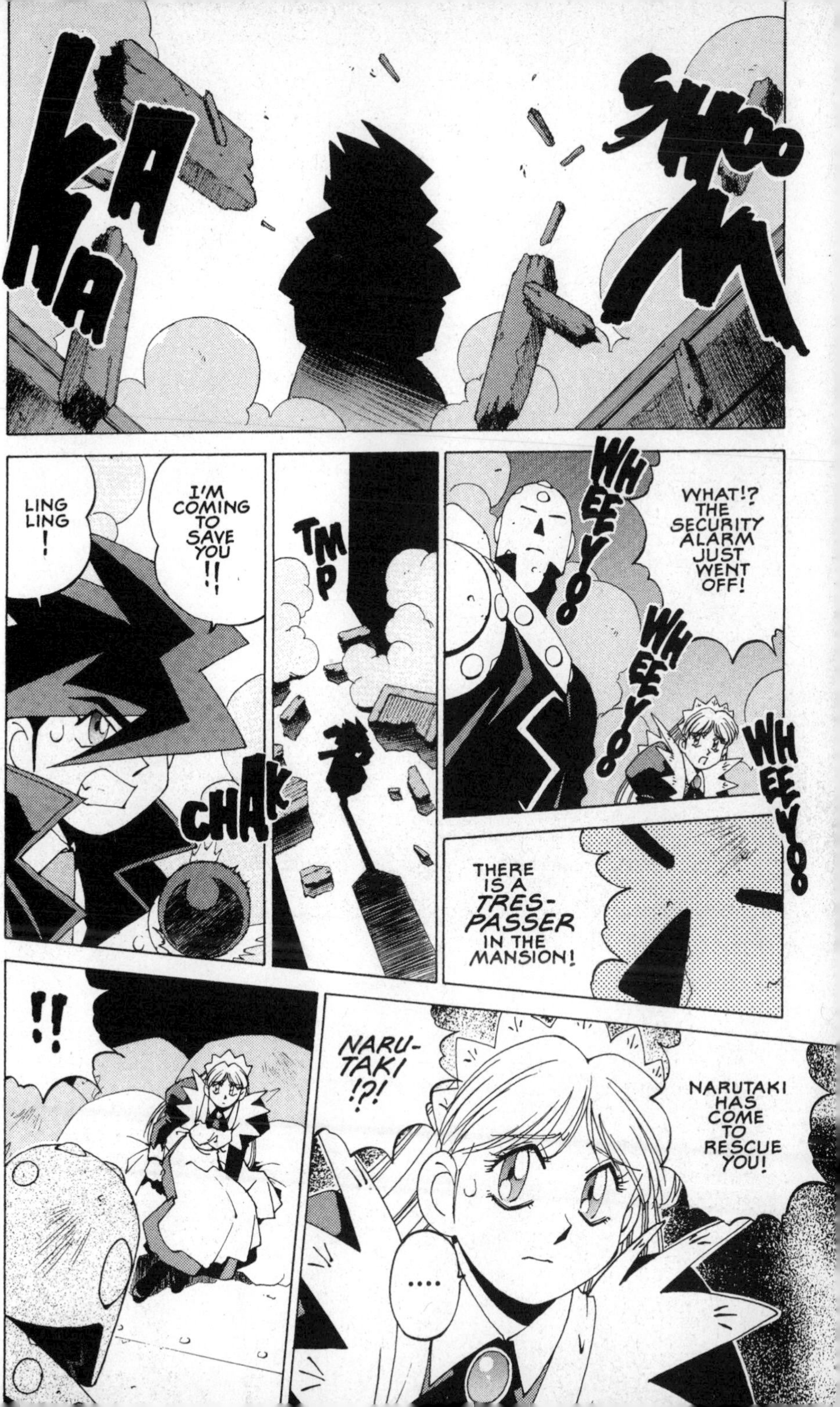
KA
NA
SHOOK
LING LING!
I'M COMING TO SAVE YOU!!
CHAK
TMP
WHEEYOO
WHEEYOO
WHAT!? THE SECURITY ALARM JUST WENT OFF!
WHEEYOO
THERE IS A *TRES-PASSER* IN THE MANSION!
!!
NARU-TAKI!?!
NARUTAKI HAS COME TO RESCUE YOU!
....

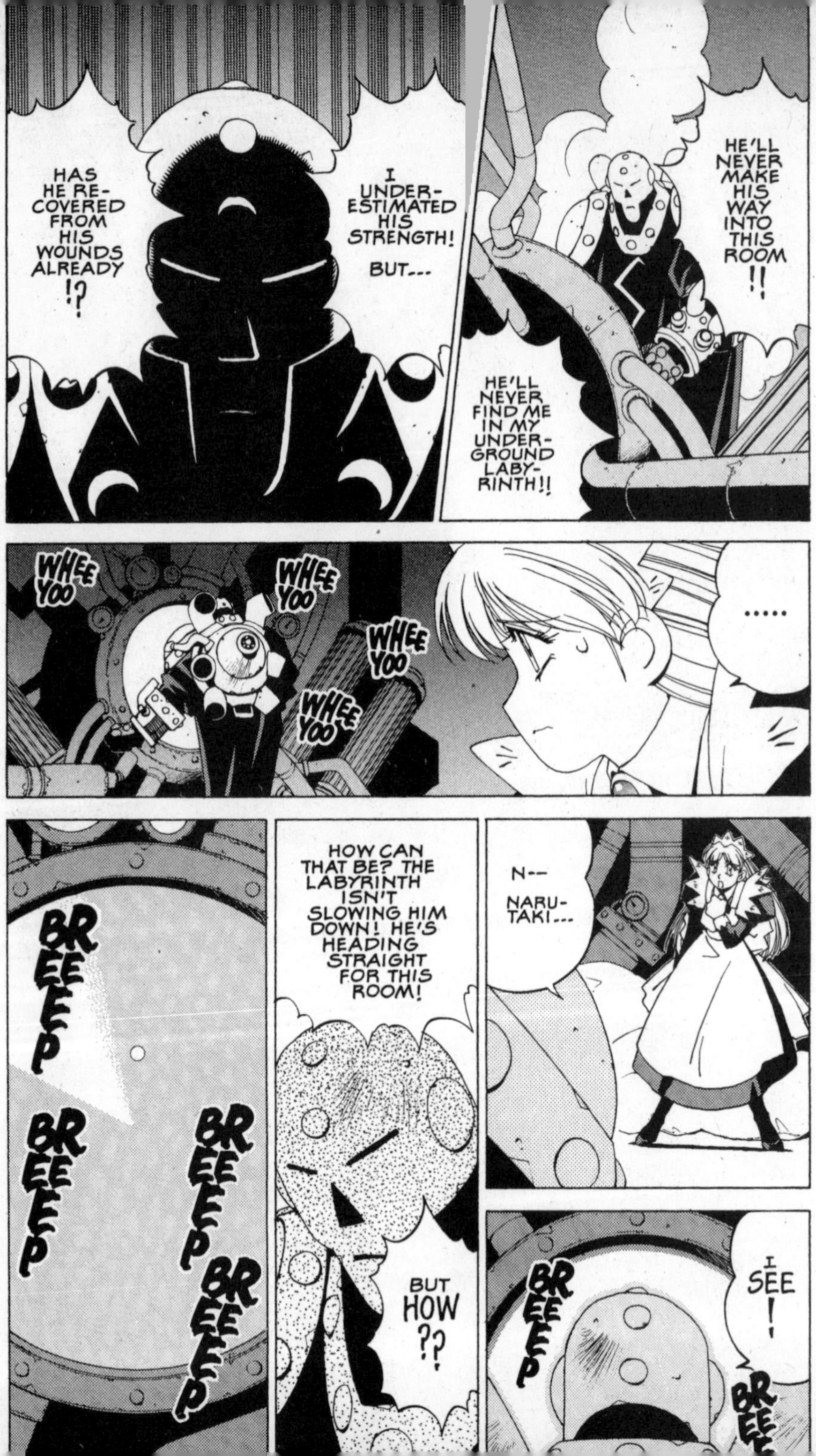
HAS HE RE-COVERED FROM HIS WOUNDS ALREADY !?
I UNDER-ESTIMATED HIS STRENGTH!
BUT...
HE'LL NEVER MAKE HIS WAY INTO THIS ROOM !!
HE'LL NEVER FIND ME IN MY UNDER-GROUND LABY-RINTH!!
WHEE YOO
WHEE YOO
WHEE YOO
WHEE YOO
.....
BREEEP
BREEEP
BREEEP
BREEEP
HOW CAN THAT BE? THE LABYRINTH ISN'T SLOWING HIM DOWN! HE'S HEADING STRAIGHT FOR THIS ROOM!
BUT HOW ??
N--
NARU-TAKI...
BREEEP
I SEE !

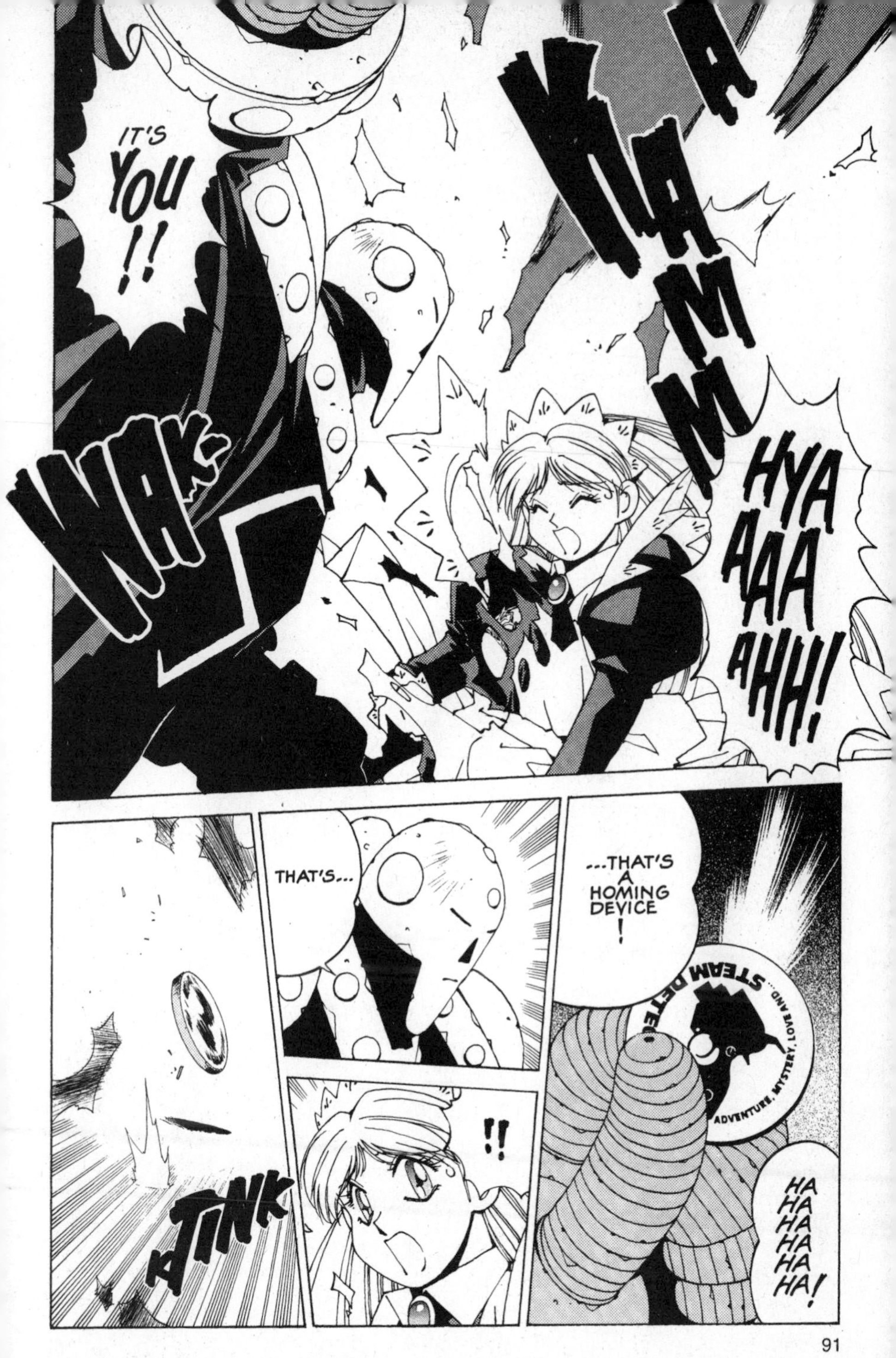
IT'S YOU!!
WHAK
WHAMMM
HYAAAAAHH!
KATINK
THAT'S...
!!
...THAT'S A HOMING DEVICE!
...ADVENTURE, MYSTERY, LOVE AND...
HAHAHAHAHAHA!

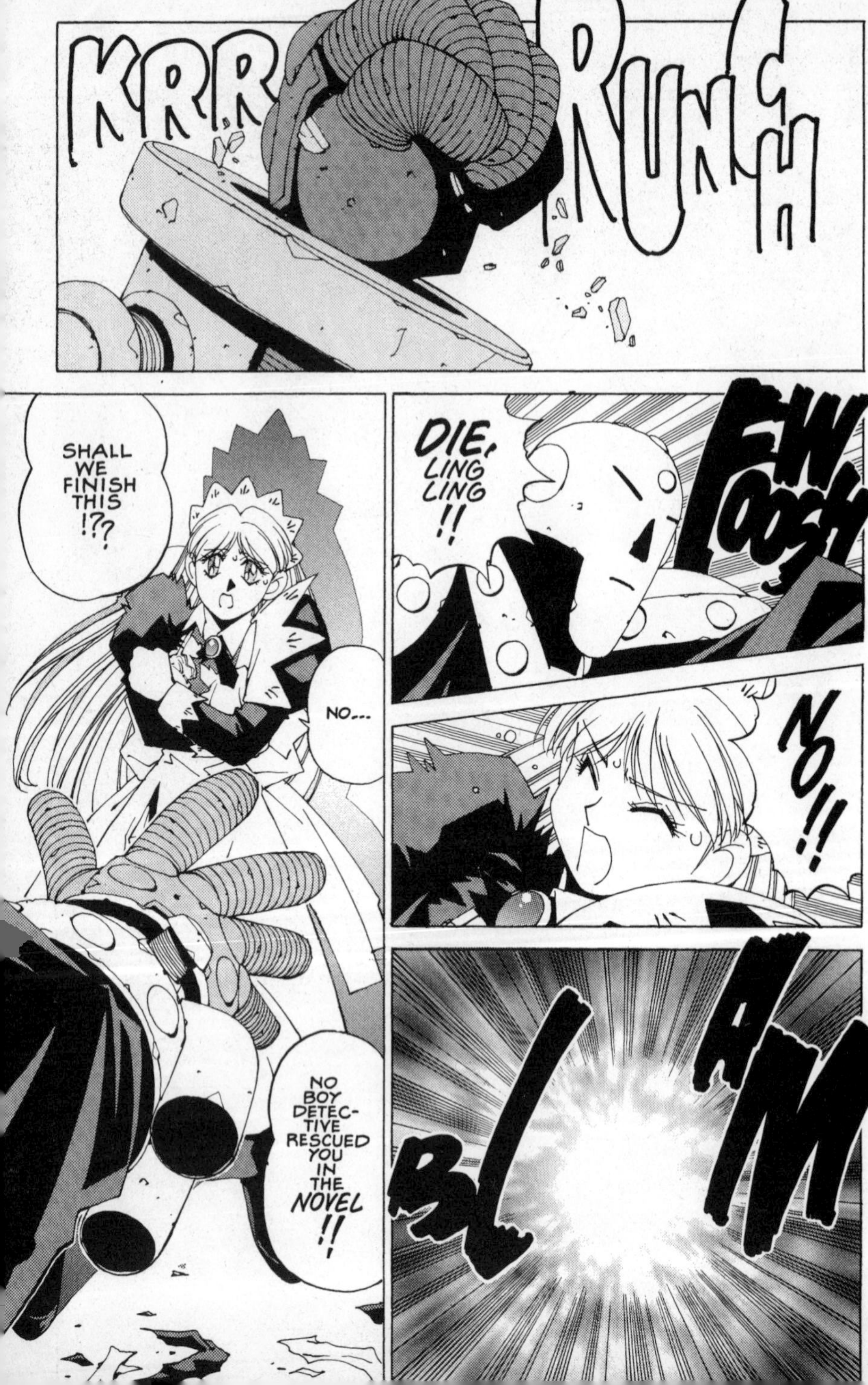
KRRRUNCH
SHALL WE FINISH THIS !??
NO...
NO BOY DETECTIVE RESCUED YOU IN THE NOVEL !!
DIE, LING LING !!
FWOOSH
NO!!
BLAM

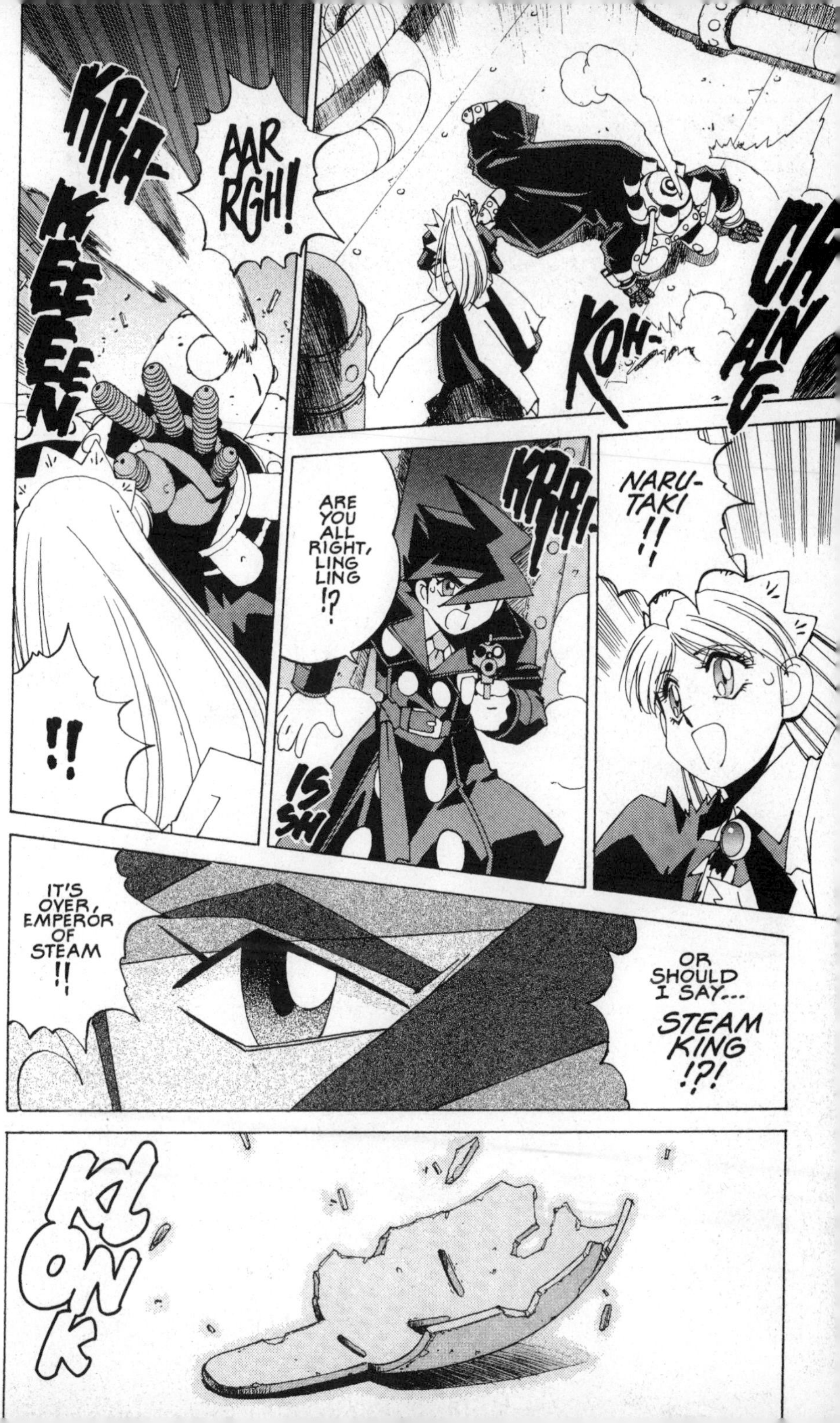
KRA-KEEEEN
AAR-RGH!
!!
KOH-
CHANG
ARE YOU ALL RIGHT, LING LING!?
KRRRI-
ISSHI
NARU-TAKI!!
IT'S OVER, EMPEROR OF STEAM!!
OR SHOULD I SAY... STEAM KING!?!
KLONK

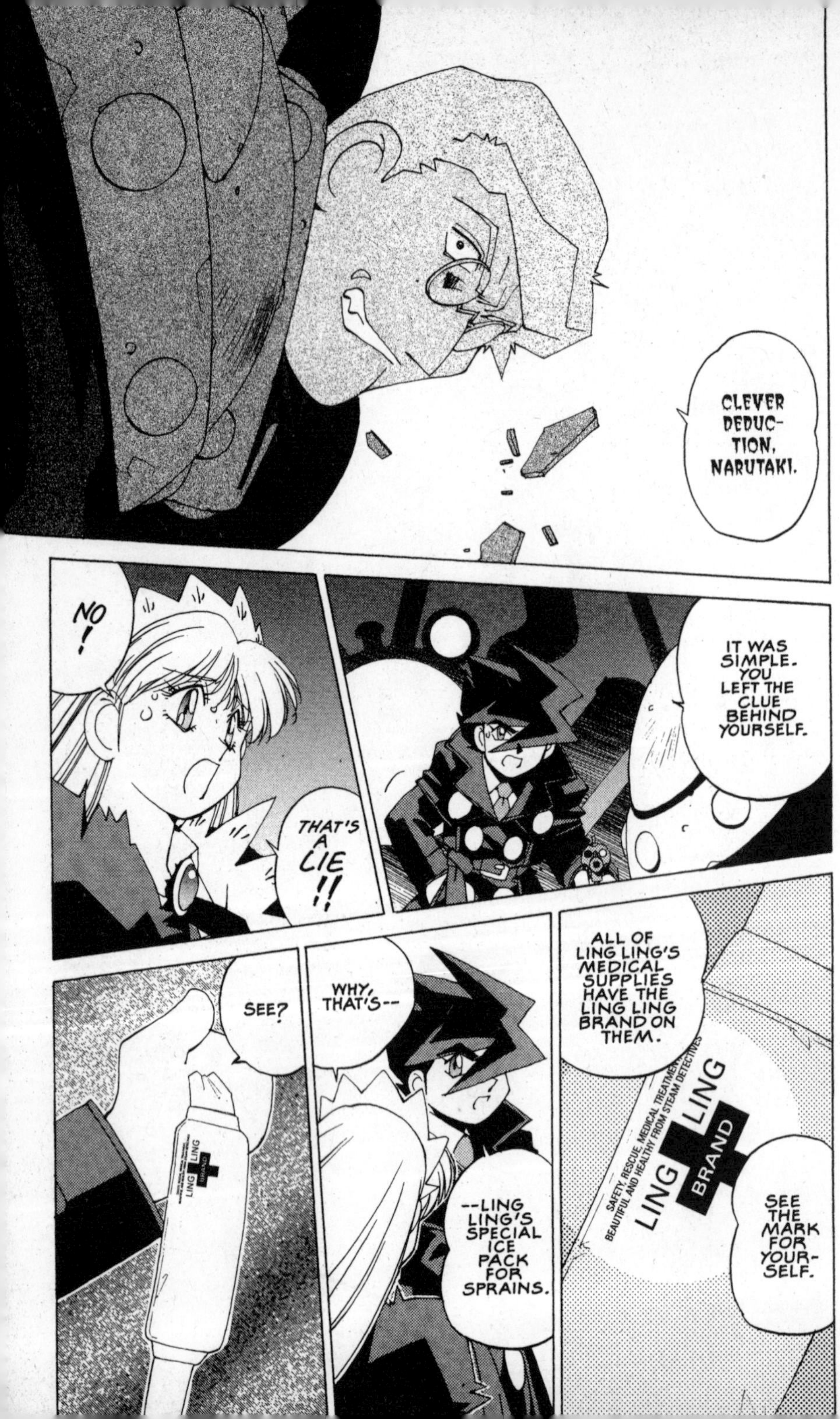
CLEVER DEDUCTION, NARUTAKI.
NO!
THAT'S A LIE!!
IT WAS SIMPLE. YOU LEFT THE CLUE BEHIND YOURSELF.
SEE?
WHY, THAT'S--
--LING LING'S SPECIAL ICE PACK FOR SPRAINS.
ALL OF LING LING'S MEDICAL SUPPLIES HAVE THE LING LING BRAND ON THEM.
SAFETY, RESCUE, MEDICAL TREATMENT
BEAUTIFUL AND HEALTHY FROM STEAM DETECTIVES
LING LING BRAND
SEE THE MARK FOR YOURSELF.

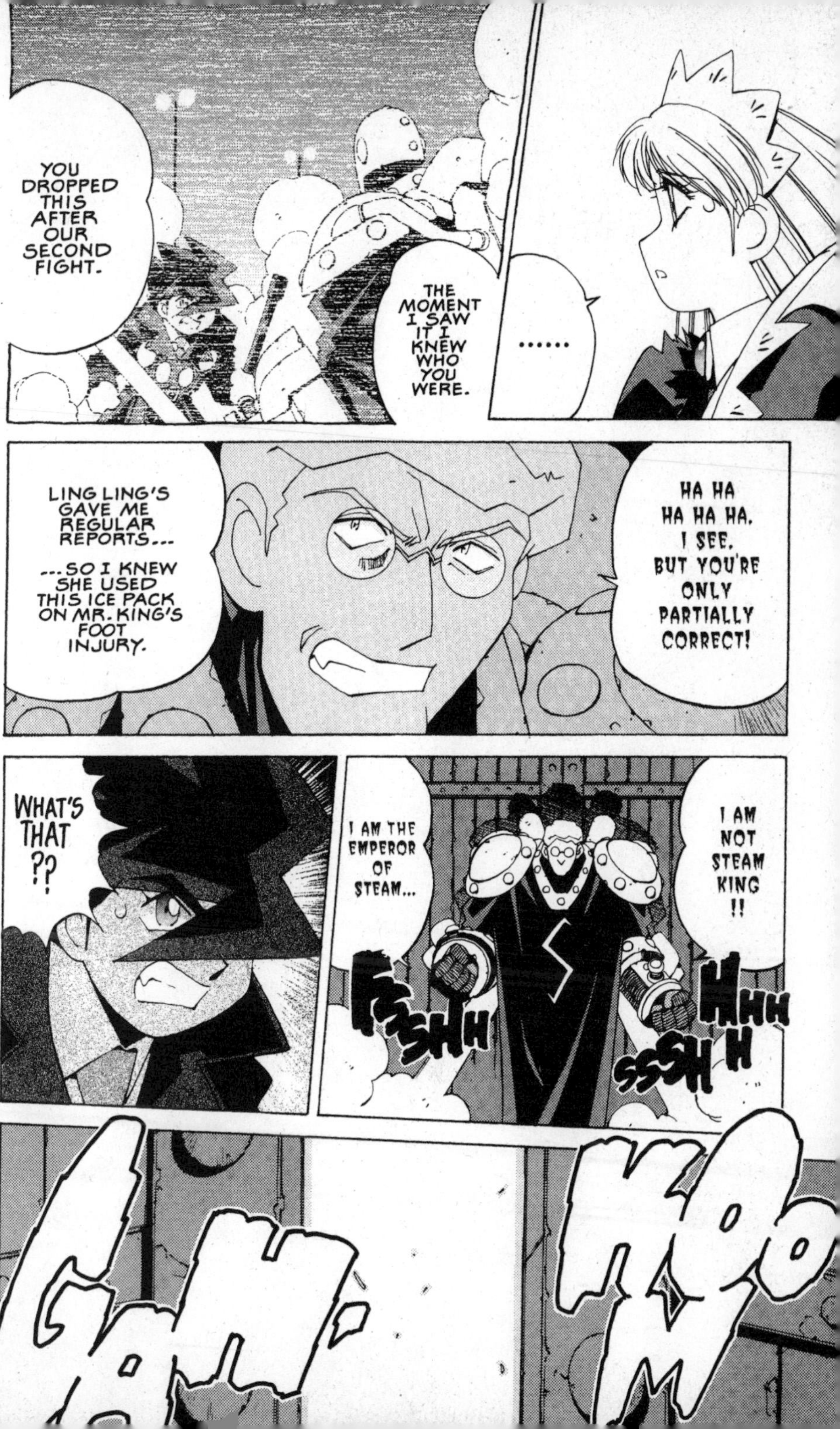
YOU DROPPED THIS AFTER OUR SECOND FIGHT.
THE MOMENT I SAW IT I KNEW WHO YOU WERE.
......
LING LING'S GAVE ME REGULAR REPORTS...
...SO I KNEW SHE USED THIS ICE PACK ON MR. KING'S FOOT INJURY.
HA HA HA HA HA. I SEE. BUT YOU'RE ONLY PARTIALLY CORRECT!
WHAT'S THAT ??
I AM THE EMPEROR OF STEAM...
I AM NOT STEAM KING !!
FSSHH
SSSHHHHH
GAH!

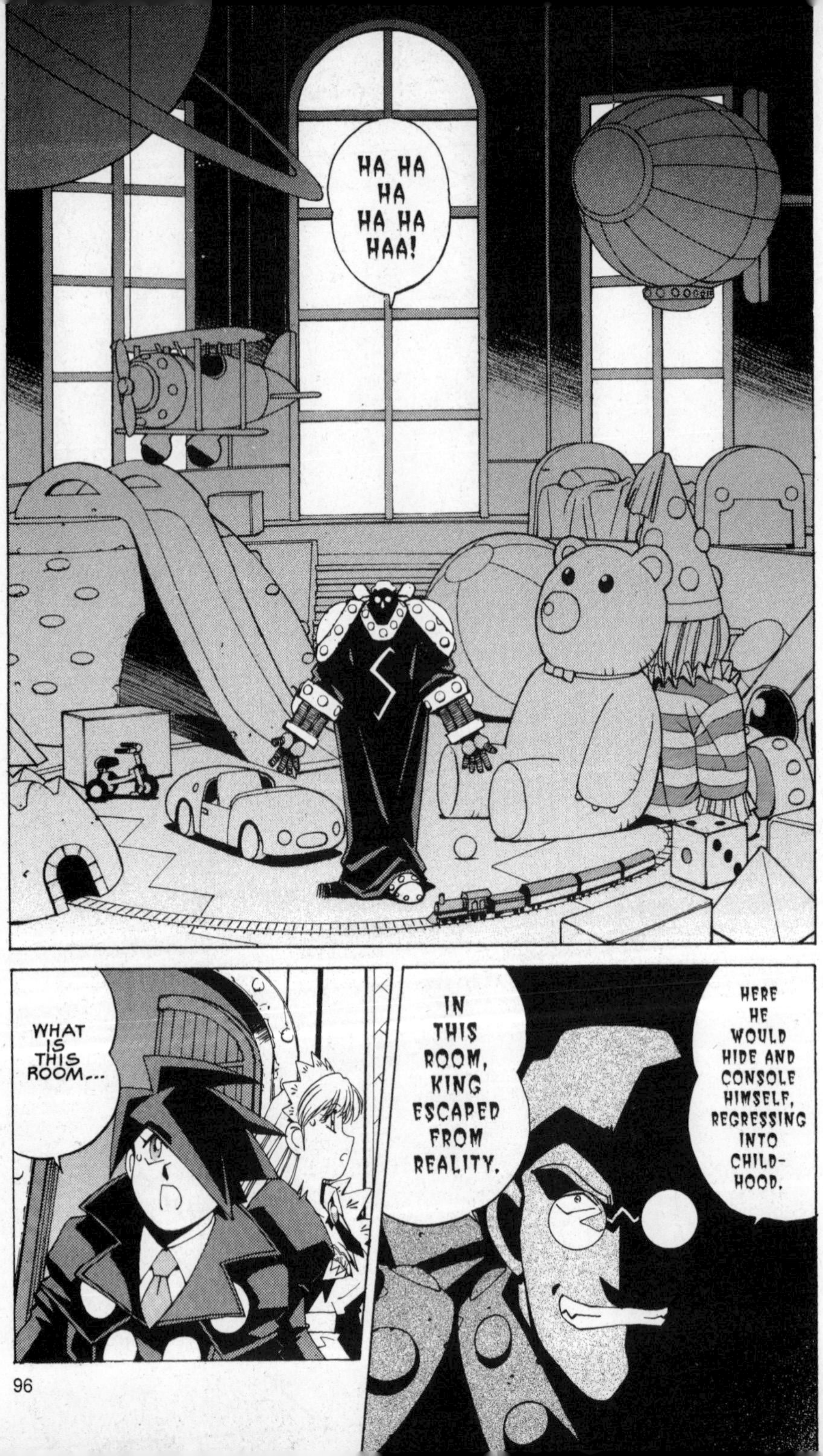

HA HA HA HA HA HAA!
WHAT IS THIS ROOM...
IN THIS ROOM, KING ESCAPED FROM REALITY.
HERE HE WOULD HIDE AND CONSOLE HIMSELF, REGRESSING INTO CHILD-HOOD.

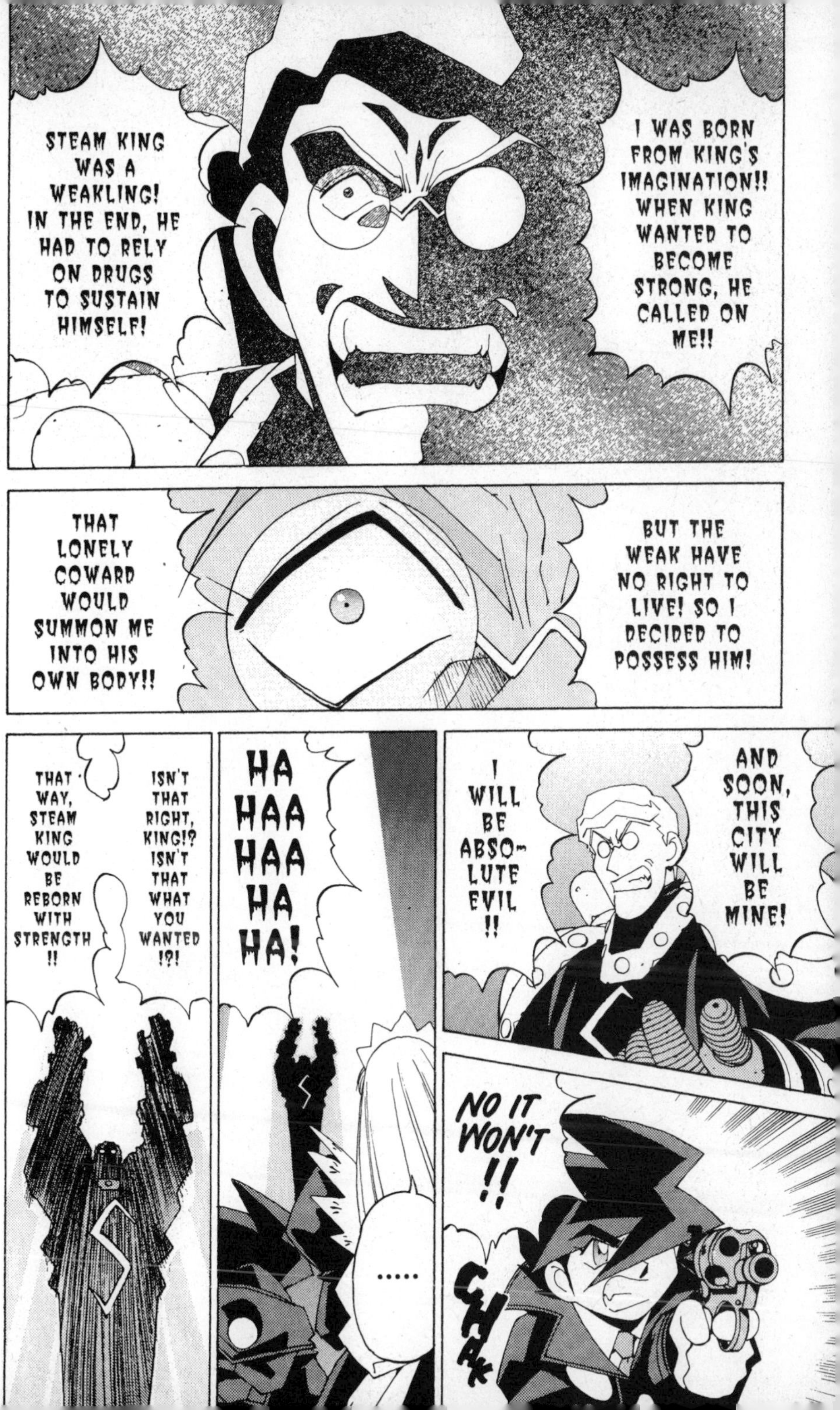
STEAM KING WAS A WEAKLING! IN THE END, HE HAD TO RELY ON DRUGS TO SUSTAIN HIMSELF!
I WAS BORN FROM KING'S IMAGINATION!! WHEN KING WANTED TO BECOME STRONG, HE CALLED ON ME!!
THAT LONELY COWARD WOULD SUMMON ME INTO HIS OWN BODY!!
BUT THE WEAK HAVE NO RIGHT TO LIVE! SO I DECIDED TO POSSESS HIM!
THAT WAY, STEAM KING WOULD BE REBORN WITH STRENGTH!!
ISN'T THAT RIGHT, KING!? ISN'T THAT WHAT YOU WANTED!?!
HA HAA HAA HA HA!
.....
I WILL BE ABSO-LUTE EVIL!!
AND SOON, THIS CITY WILL BE MINE!
NO IT WON'T!!
CHAK

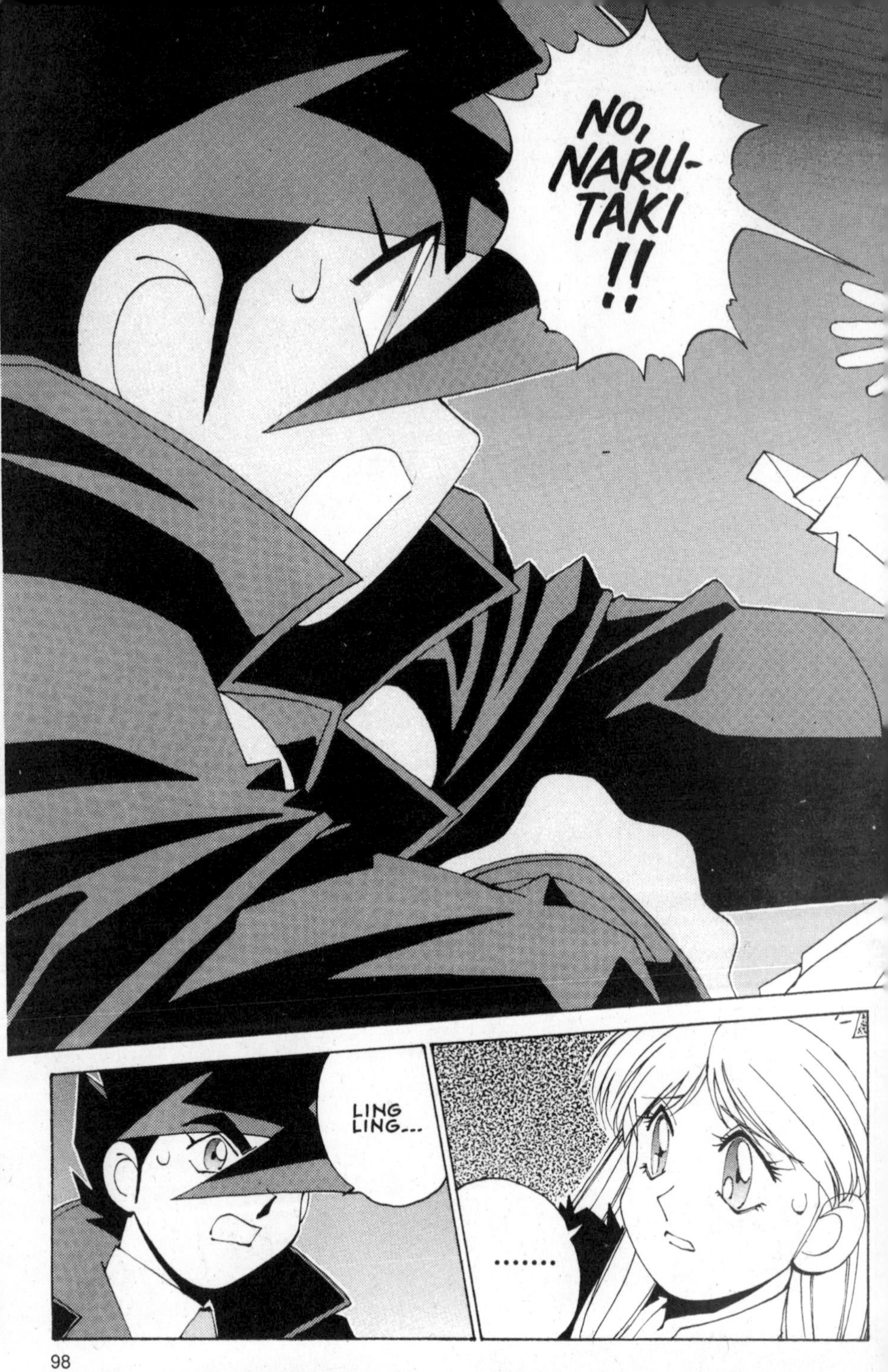
NO, NARU-TAKI!!
LING LING...
....

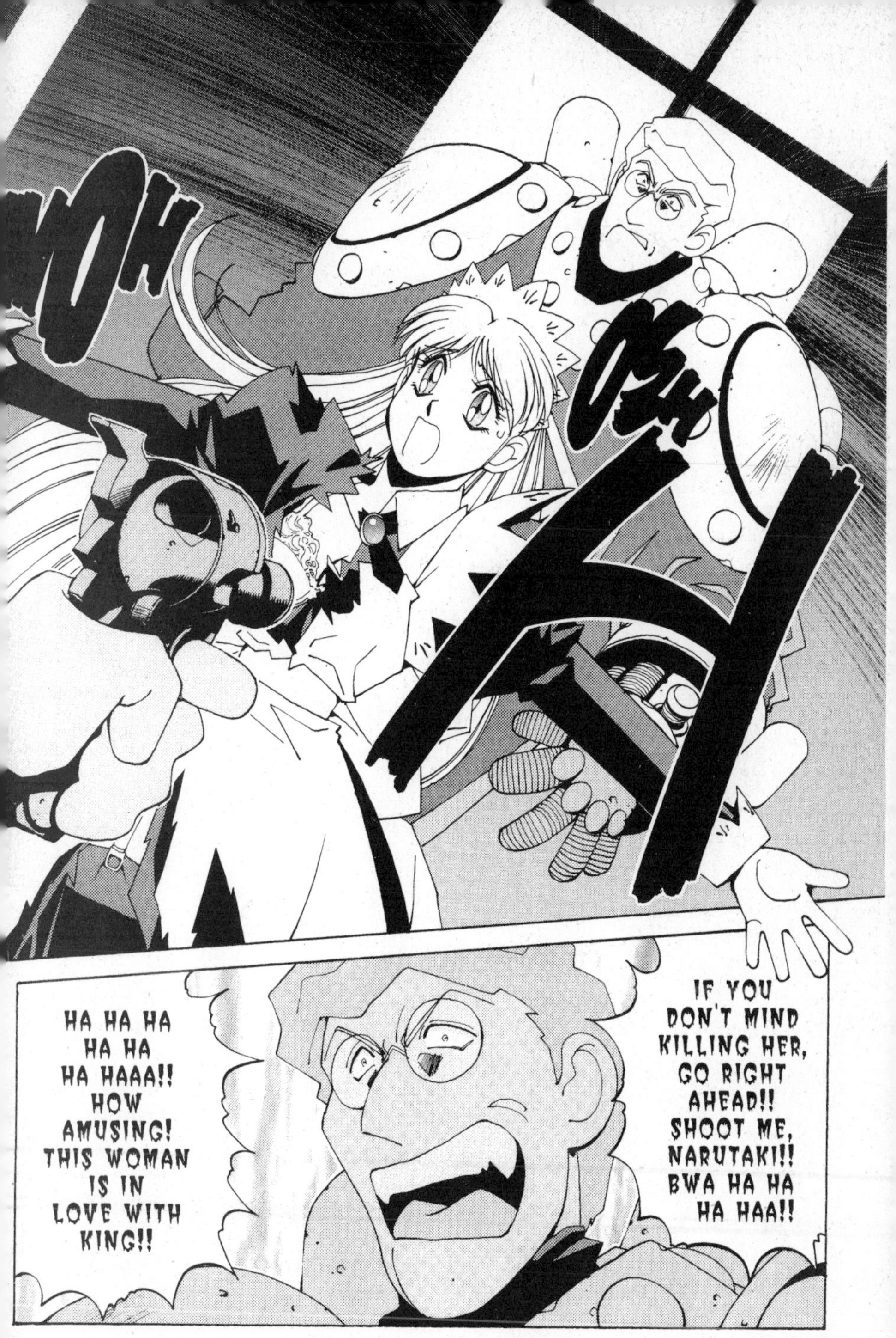
WOH
OPH
HA HA HA HA HA HA HAAA!! HOW AMUSING! THIS WOMAN IS IN LOVE WITH KING!!
IF YOU DON'T MIND KILLING HER, GO RIGHT AHEAD!! SHOOT ME, NARUTAKI!!! BWA HA HA HA HAA!!

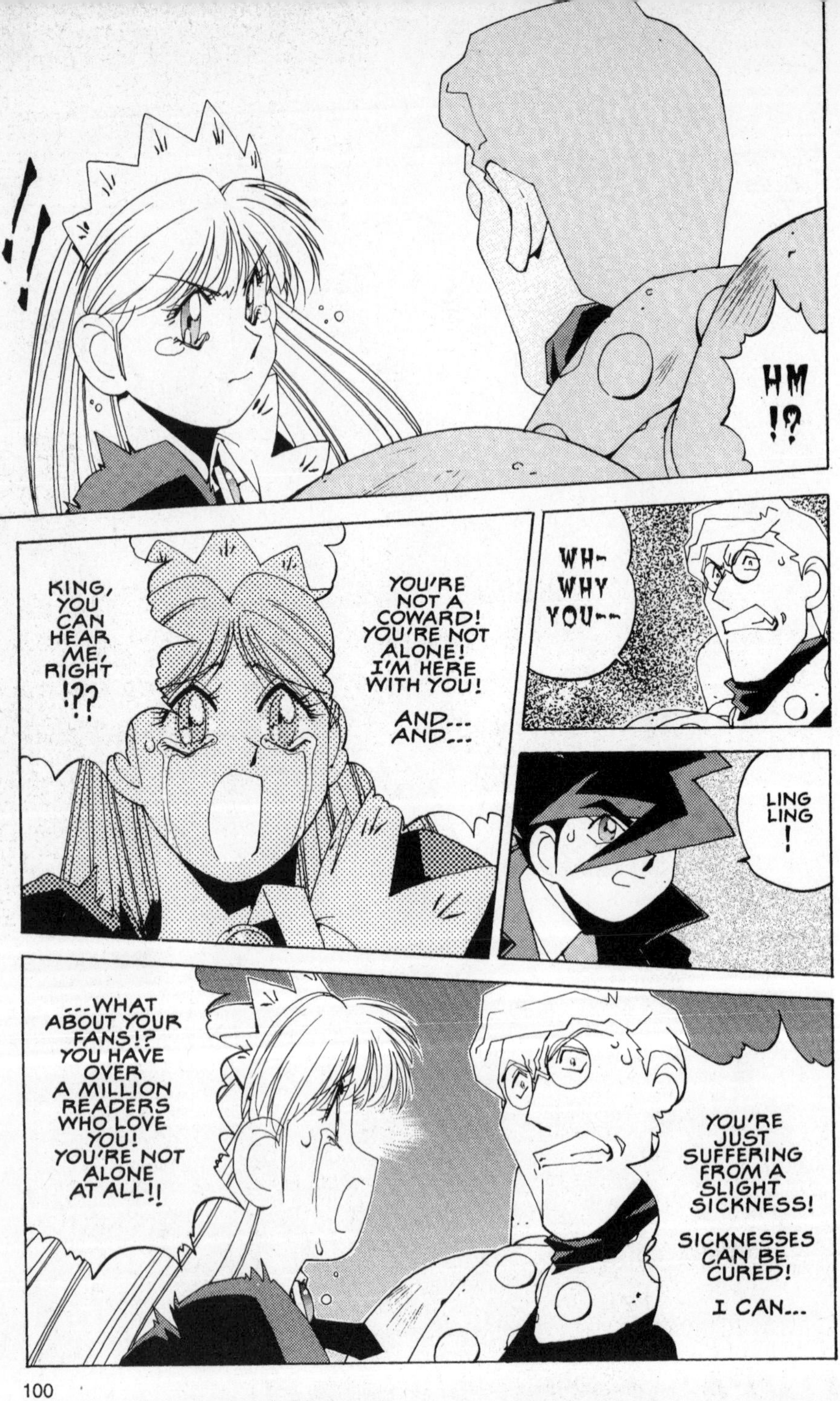
!!
HM !?
KING, YOU CAN HEAR ME, RIGHT !??
YOU'RE NOT A COWARD! YOU'RE NOT ALONE! I'M HERE WITH YOU!
AND... AND...
WH- WHY YOU--
LING LING !
...WHAT ABOUT YOUR FANS!? YOU HAVE OVER A MILLION READERS WHO LOVE YOU! YOU'RE NOT ALONE AT ALL!!
YOU'RE JUST SUFFERING FROM A SLIGHT SICKNESS!
SICKNESSES CAN BE CURED!
I CAN...

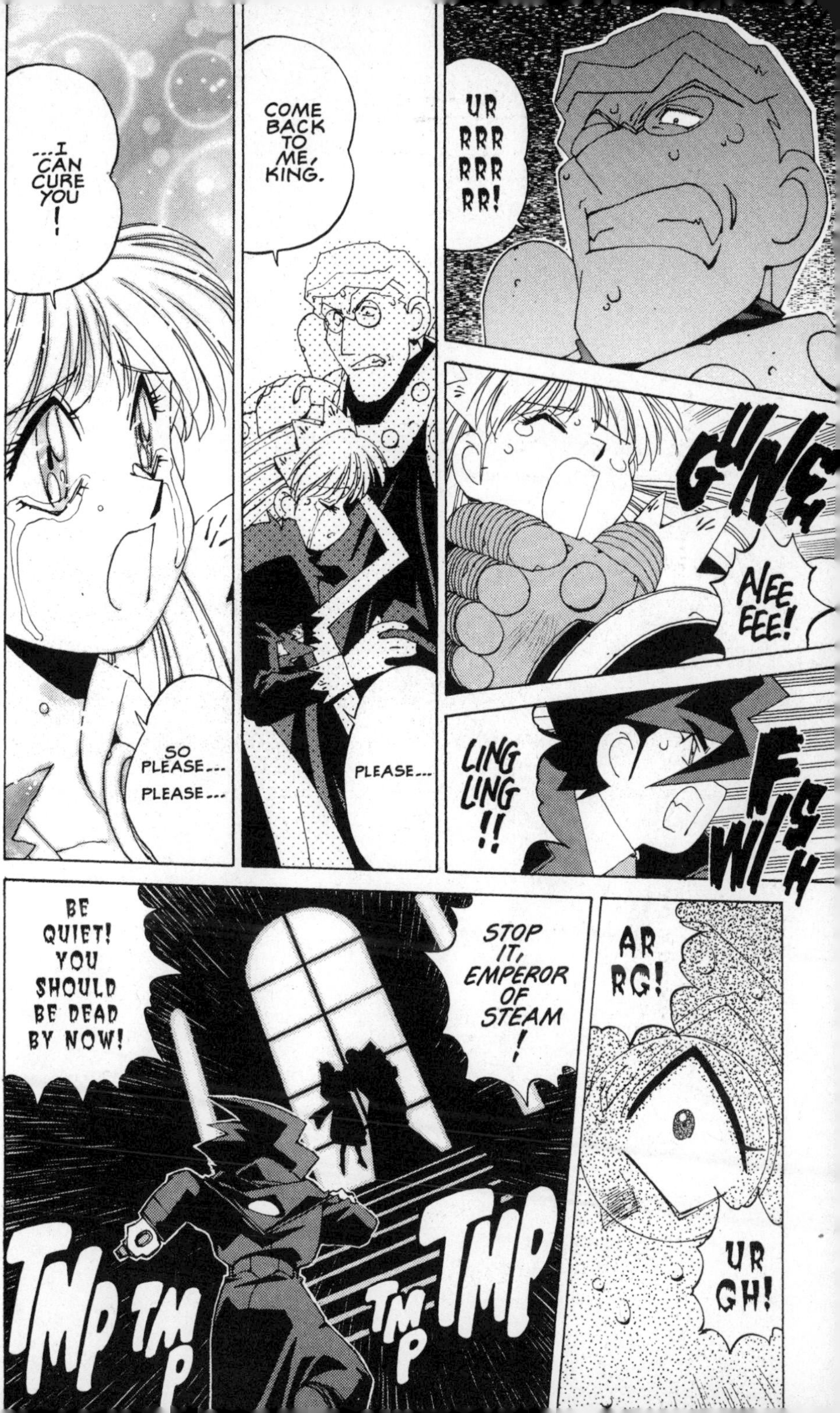
...I CAN CURE YOU!
SO PLEASE...
PLEASE...
COME BACK TO ME, KING.
PLEASE...
UR RRR RRR RR!
AIEE EEE!
LING LING!!
BE QUIET! YOU SHOULD BE DEAD BY NOW!
STOP IT, EMPEROR OF STEAM!
TMP TMP
TMP TMP
AR RG!
UR GH!

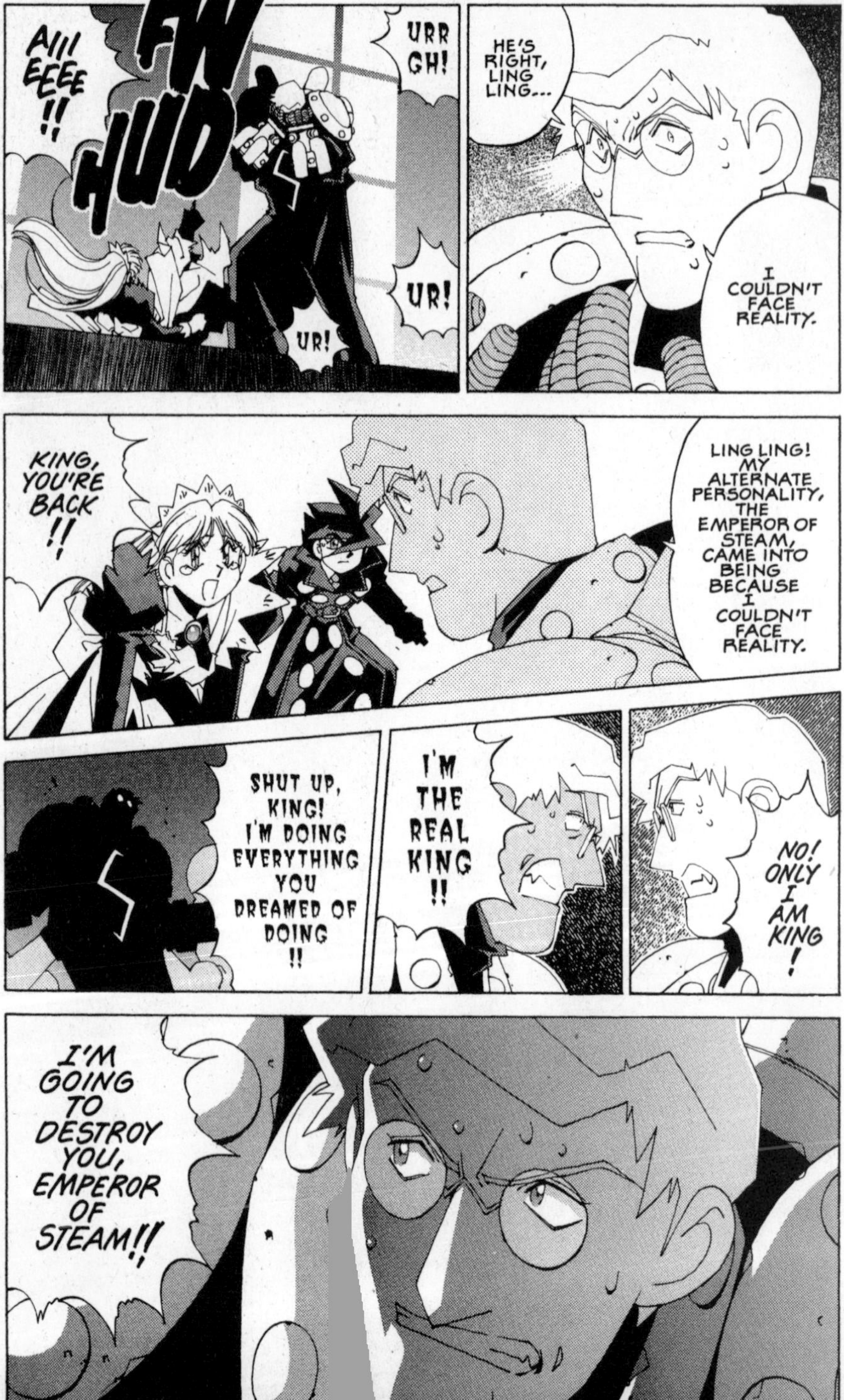

AIII EEEE!!
FWHUD
URRGH!
UR!
UR!
HE'S RIGHT, LING LING...
I COULDN'T FACE REALITY.
KING, YOU'RE BACK!!
LING LING! MY ALTERNATE PERSONALITY, THE EMPEROR OF STEAM, CAME INTO BEING BECAUSE I COULDN'T FACE REALITY.
SHUT UP, KING! I'M DOING EVERYTHING YOU DREAMED OF DOING!!
I'M THE REAL KING!!
NO! ONLY I AM KING!
I'M GOING TO DESTROY YOU, EMPEROR OF STEAM!!

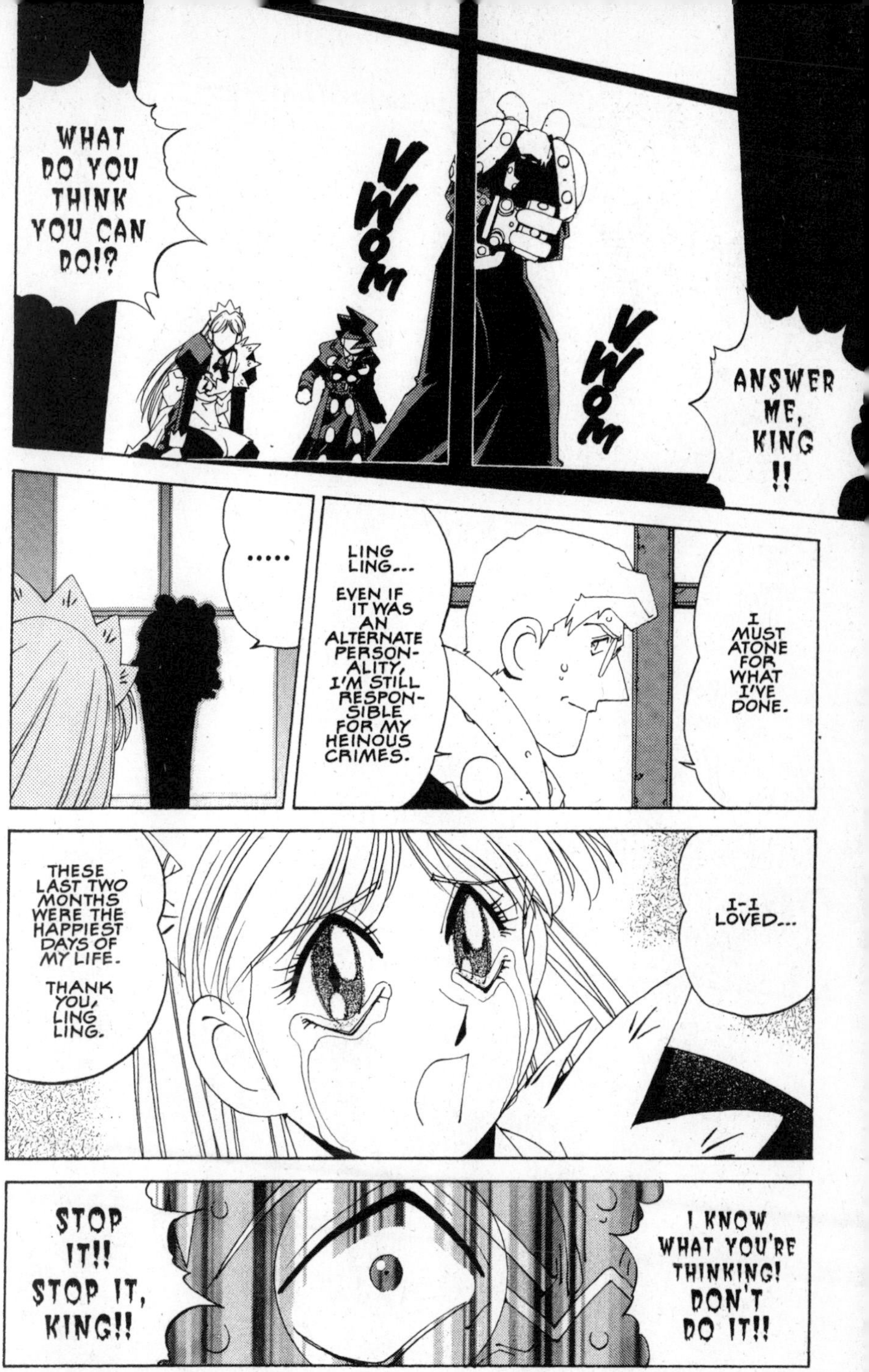
WHAT DO YOU THINK YOU CAN DO!?
VWOM
VWOM
ANSWER ME, KING!!
.....
LING LING... EVEN IF IT WAS AN ALTERNATE PERSONALITY, I'M STILL RESPONSIBLE FOR MY HEINOUS CRIMES.
I MUST ATONE FOR WHAT I'VE DONE.
THESE LAST TWO MONTHS WERE THE HAPPIEST DAYS OF MY LIFE. THANK YOU, LING LING.
I-I LOVED...
STOP IT!! STOP IT, KING!!
I KNOW WHAT YOU'RE THINKING! DON'T DO IT!!

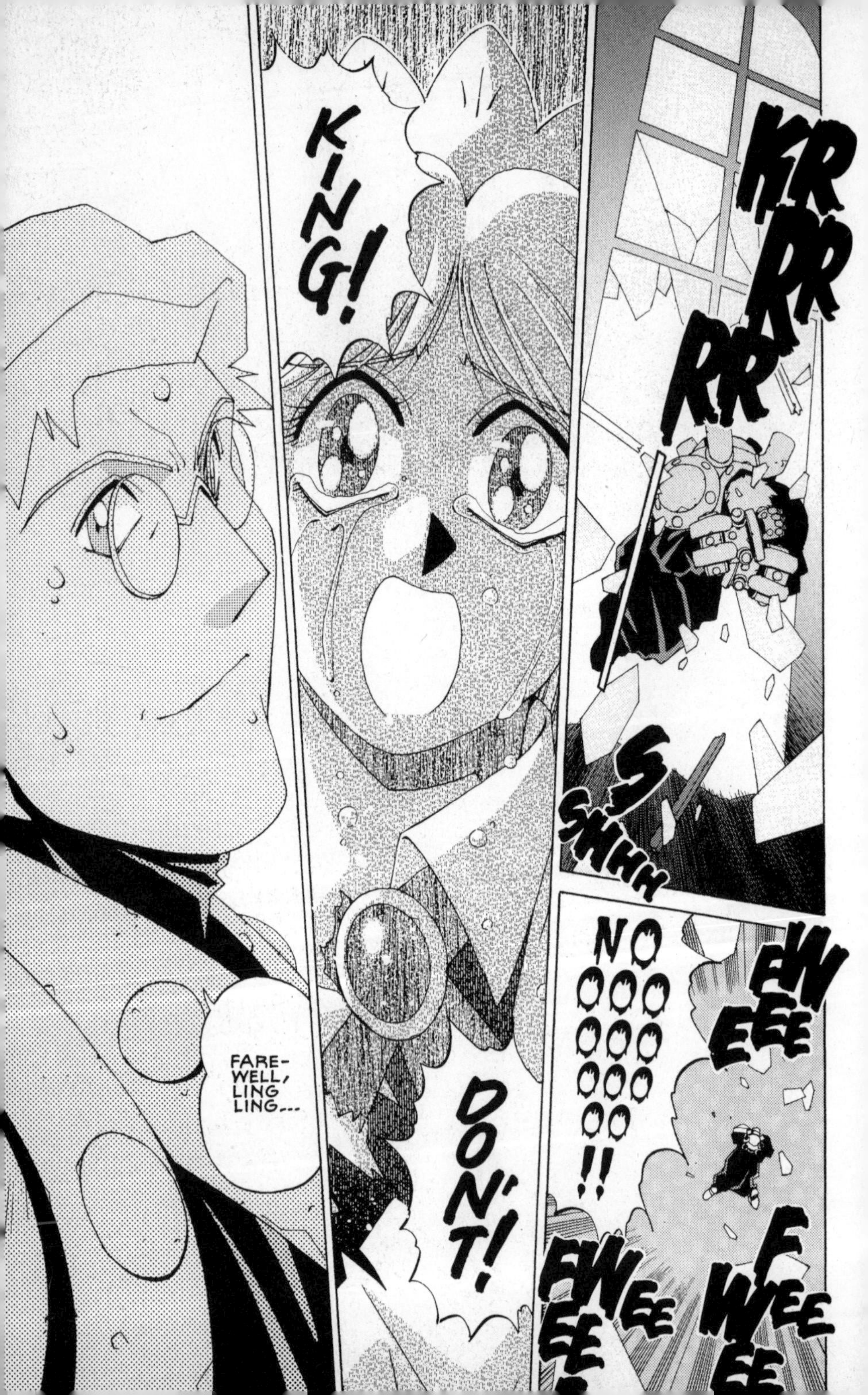
FARE-WELL, LING LING...
KING!
DON'T!
KRRRRRRR
SSHHHH
NOOOOOOOOOOOOOO!!
FWEEE
FWEEEE
FWEEEE

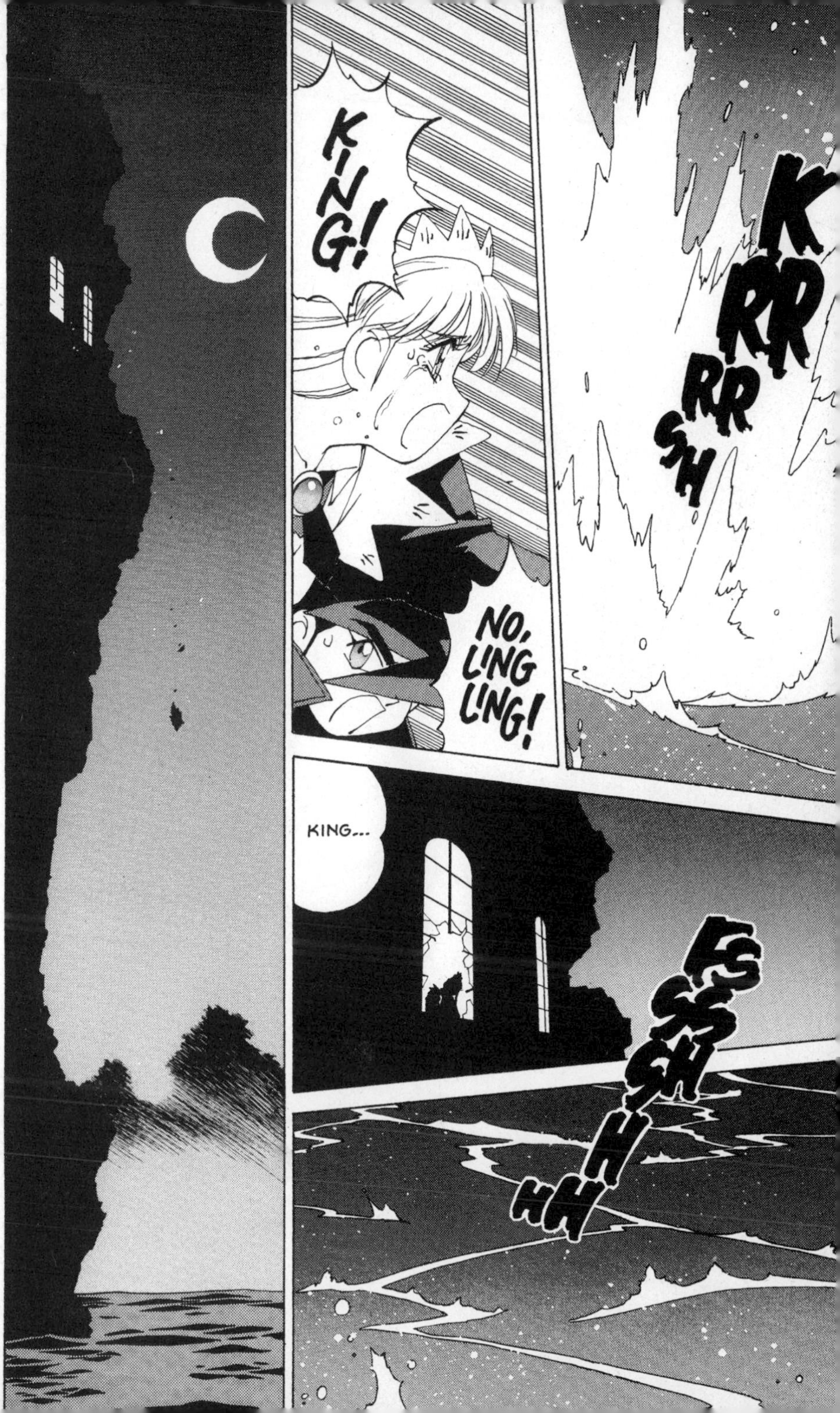
KING!
NO, LING LING!
KRRRRSH
KING...
FSSSSHHHH

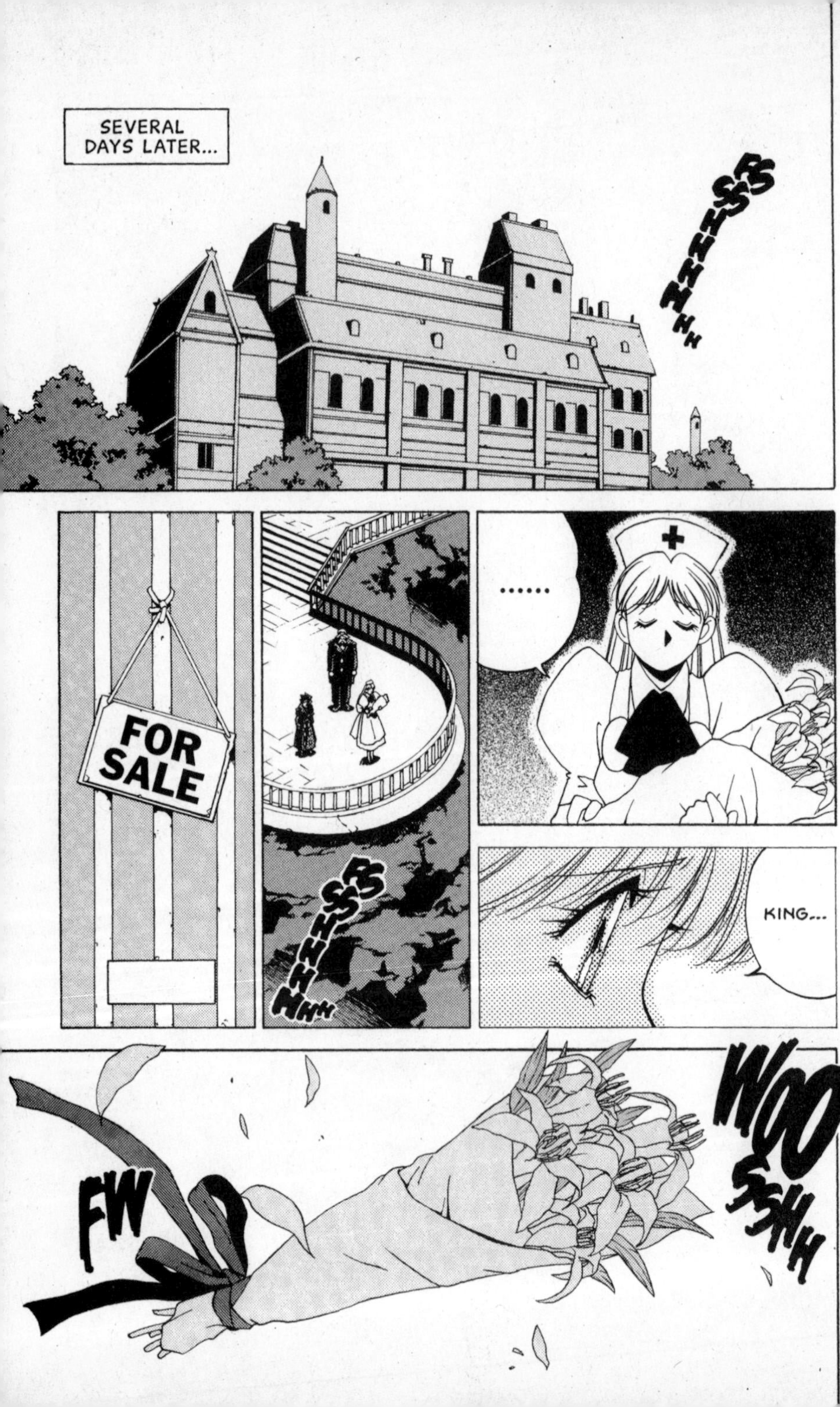
SEVERAL DAYS LATER...
RSSSHHHHHHHH
FOR SALE
RSSSHHHHHH
......
KING...
FW
WOOSSSHHH

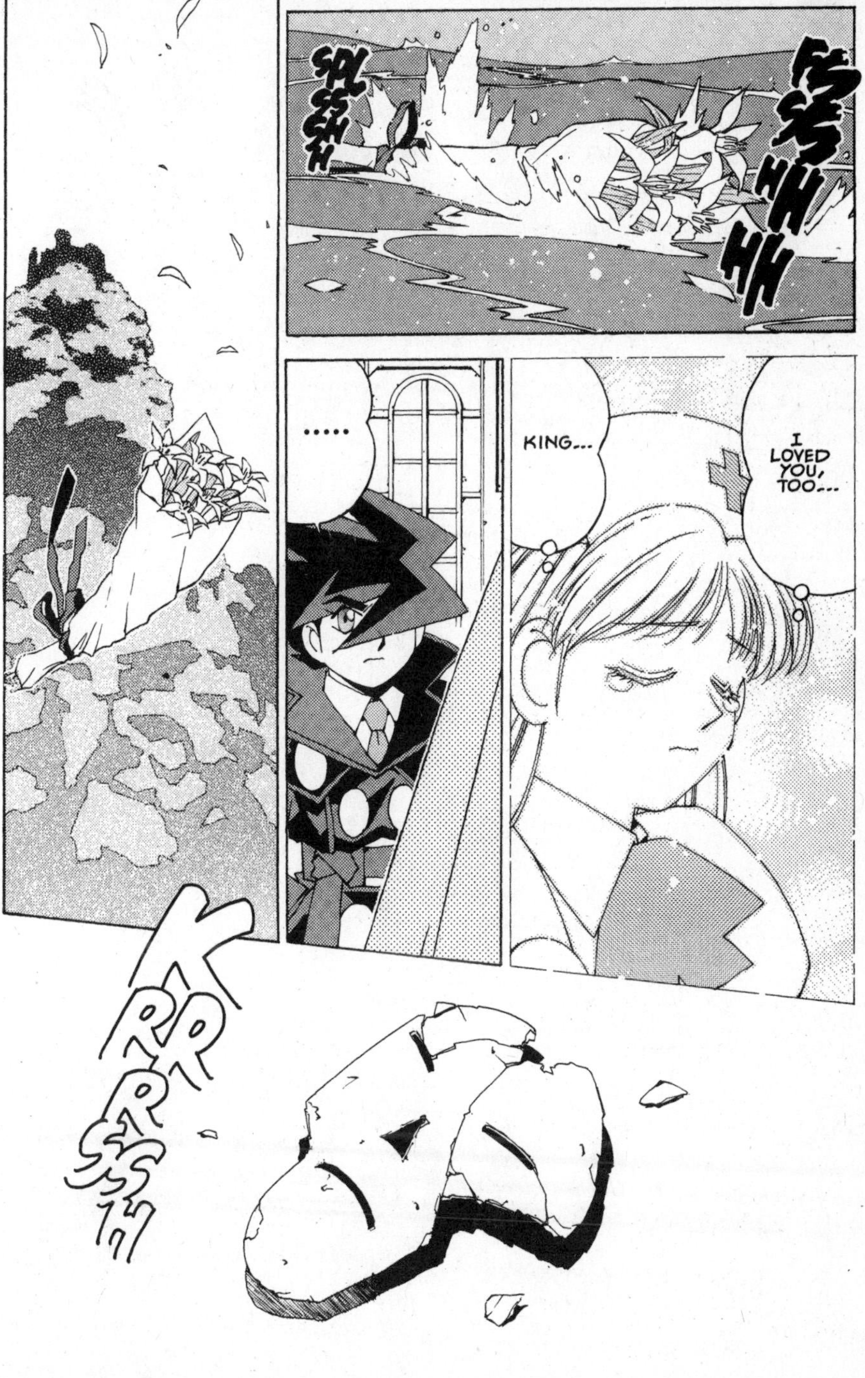
......
KING...
I LOVED YOU, TOO...

STEAM DETECTIVES PRESS

LING LING SOLVES THE MYSTERY!

Narutaki, the Boy Detective, was away from the office investigating the "Mystery of the Vanishing Steam Freighter," when a strange incident occurred. Ten-year-old Yukimi's pet cat Kyami disappeared in the Daily district of Steam City. But the mystery was solved by the beautiful secretary/nurse at the detective agency, Ling Ling.

After listening to Yukimi's report, Ling Ling had the idea to search the sewer system. Two days into the search she found the cat and managed to draw it out of hiding with a buttercake. Yukimi was overjoyed.

Residents of the district had heard strange crying sounds coming from underground, and they reported it to the police, but before the police could investigate, the mystery was solved. Now it seems that Steam City's very own Ling Ling is gaining popularity day by day!

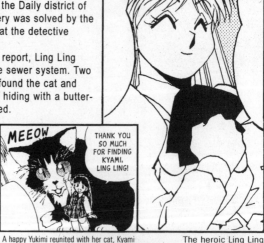

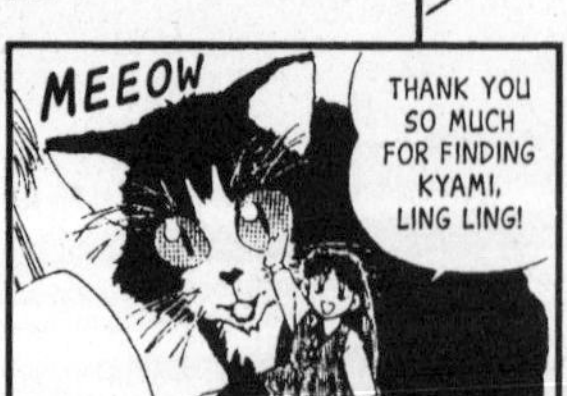
MEEOW
THANK YOU SO MUCH FOR FINDING KYAMI, LING LING!
A happy Yukimi reunited with her cat, Kyami

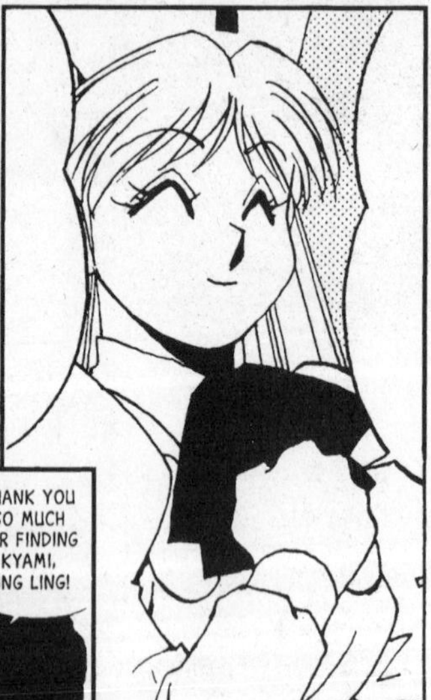
The heroic Ling Ling

CAFE SHOP

SORCA

DELICIOUS HOMEMADE BUTTERCAKES

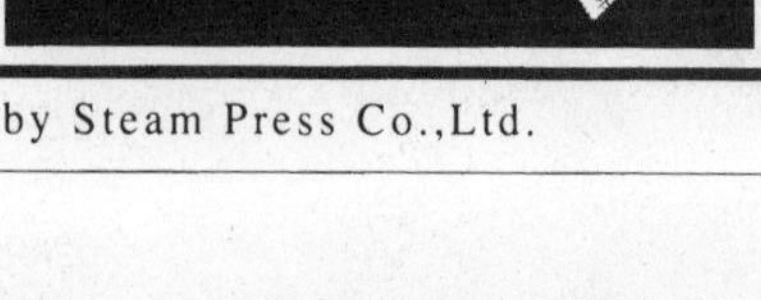
KYAMI LOVES IT TOO! ♥

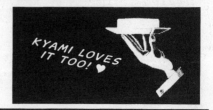

Volume 012 • Issued by Steam Press Co.,Ltd.

CASE 9 GORIKI AND THE MACHINE BARON

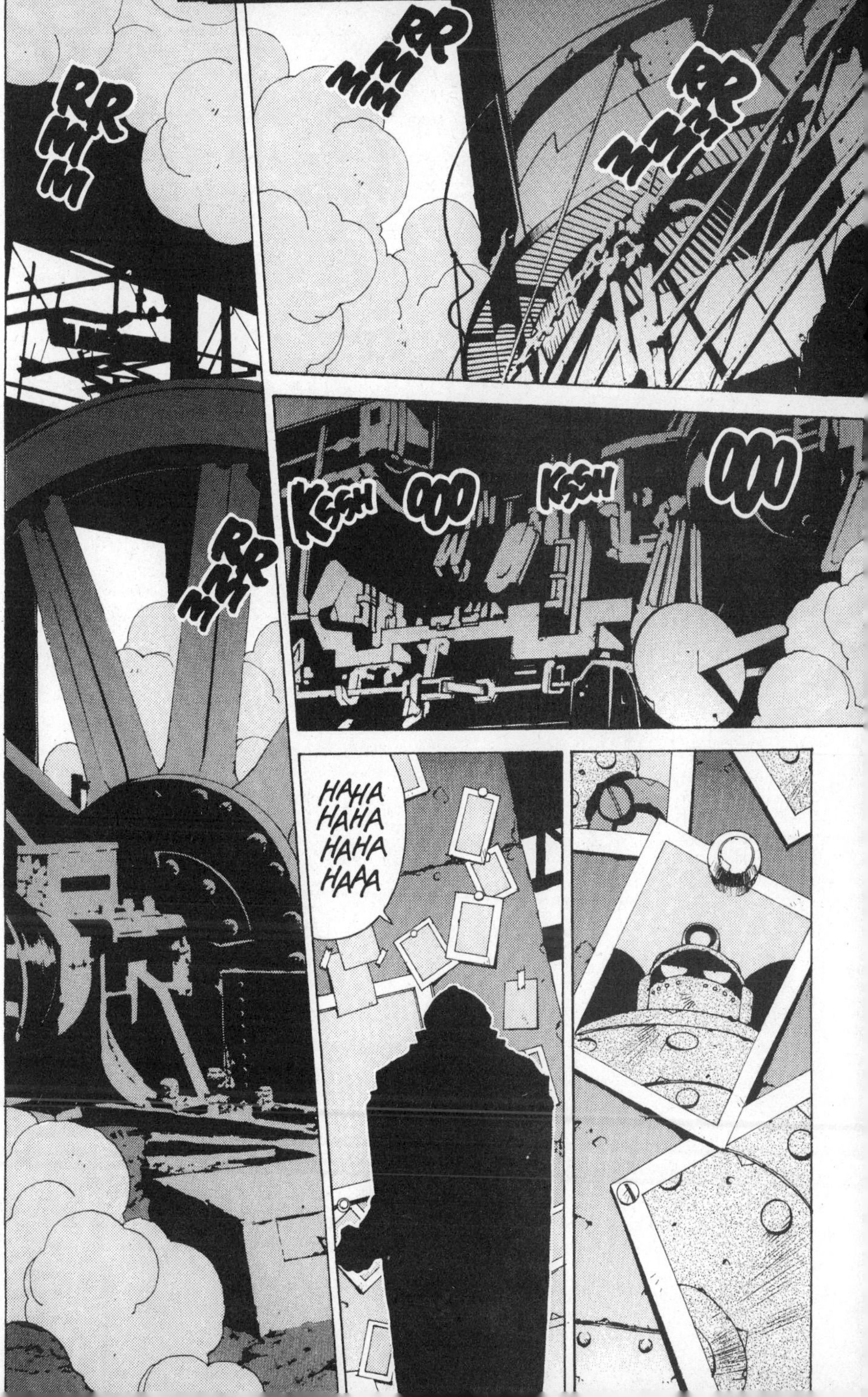
RRMMM
RRMMM
OOO
KSSH
OOO
KSSH
HAHA HAHA HAHA HAAA
RRMM
RRMM

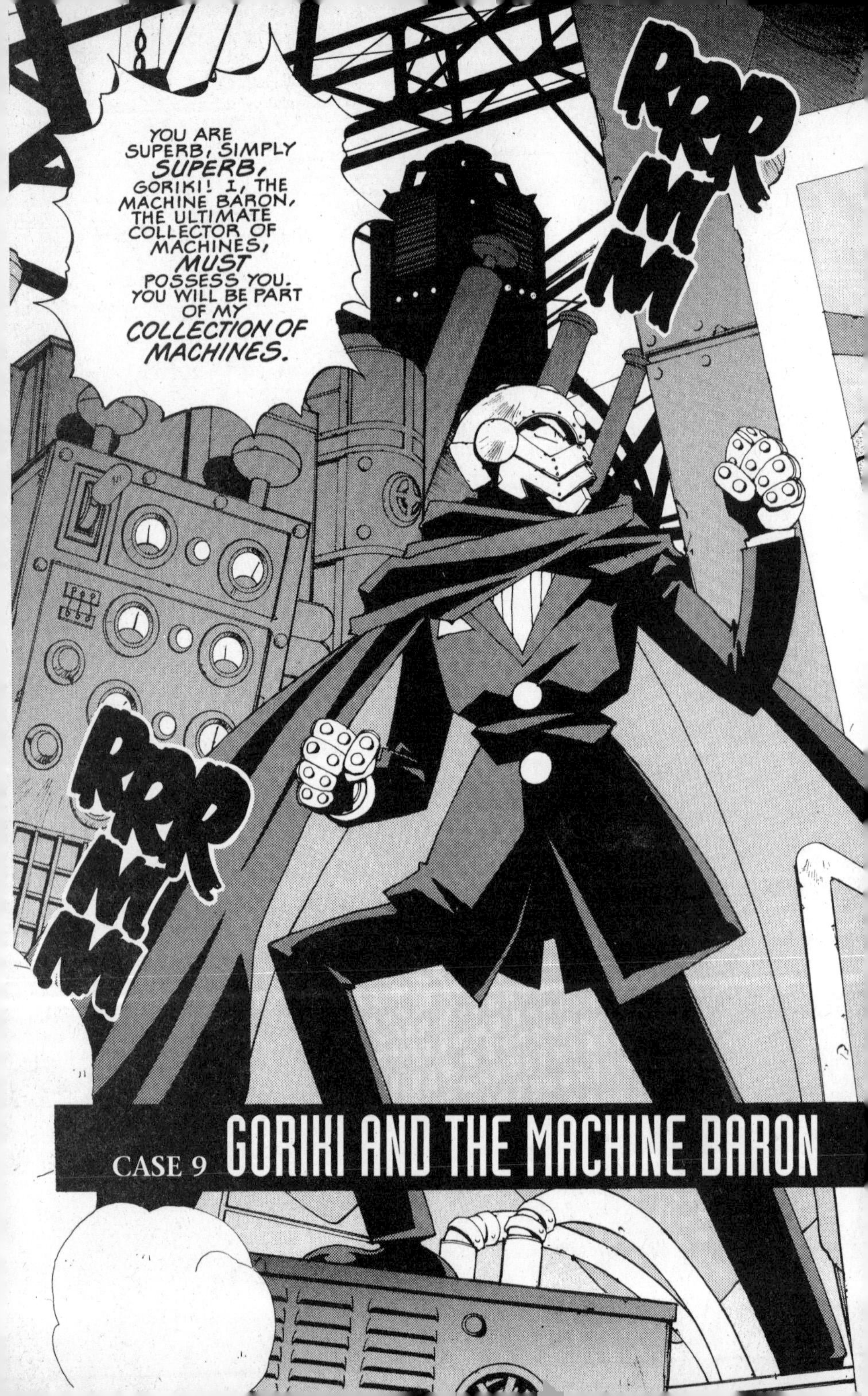
YOU ARE SUPERB, SIMPLY SUPERB, GORIKI! I, THE MACHINE BARON, THE ULTIMATE COLLECTOR OF MACHINES, MUST POSSESS YOU. YOU WILL BE PART OF MY COLLECTION OF MACHINES.
RRRRMMMM
RRRRMMMM
CASE 9 GORIKI AND THE MACHINE BARON

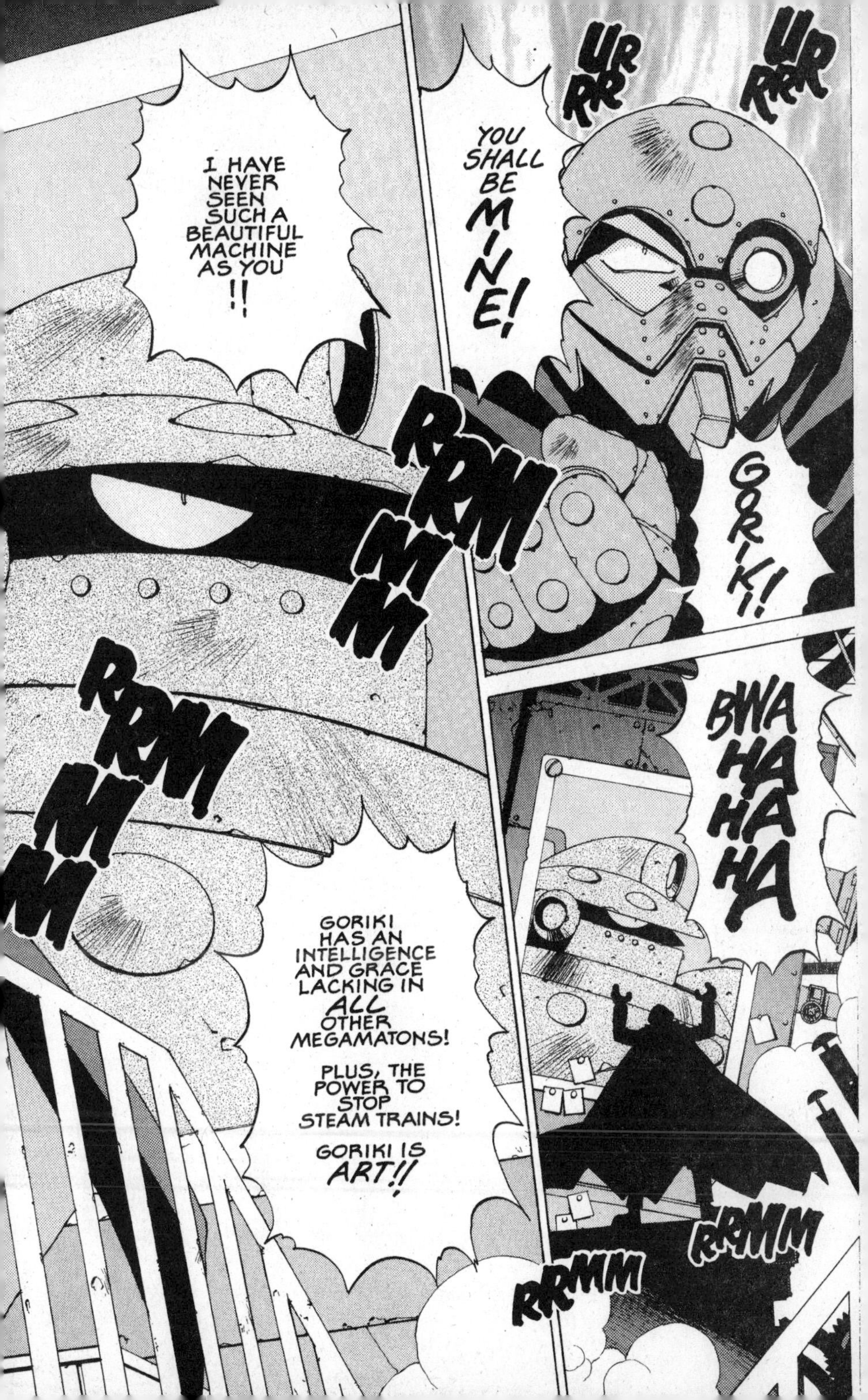
I HAVE NEVER SEEN SUCH A BEAUTIFUL MACHINE AS YOU !!
RRMMM
RRMMM
GORIKI HAS AN INTELLIGENCE AND GRACE LACKING IN ALL OTHER MEGAMATONS!
PLUS, THE POWER TO STOP STEAM TRAINS!
GORIKI IS ART!!
URRR
URRR
YOU SHALL BE MINE!
GORIKI!
BWAHAHAHAHA
RRMMM
RRMMM

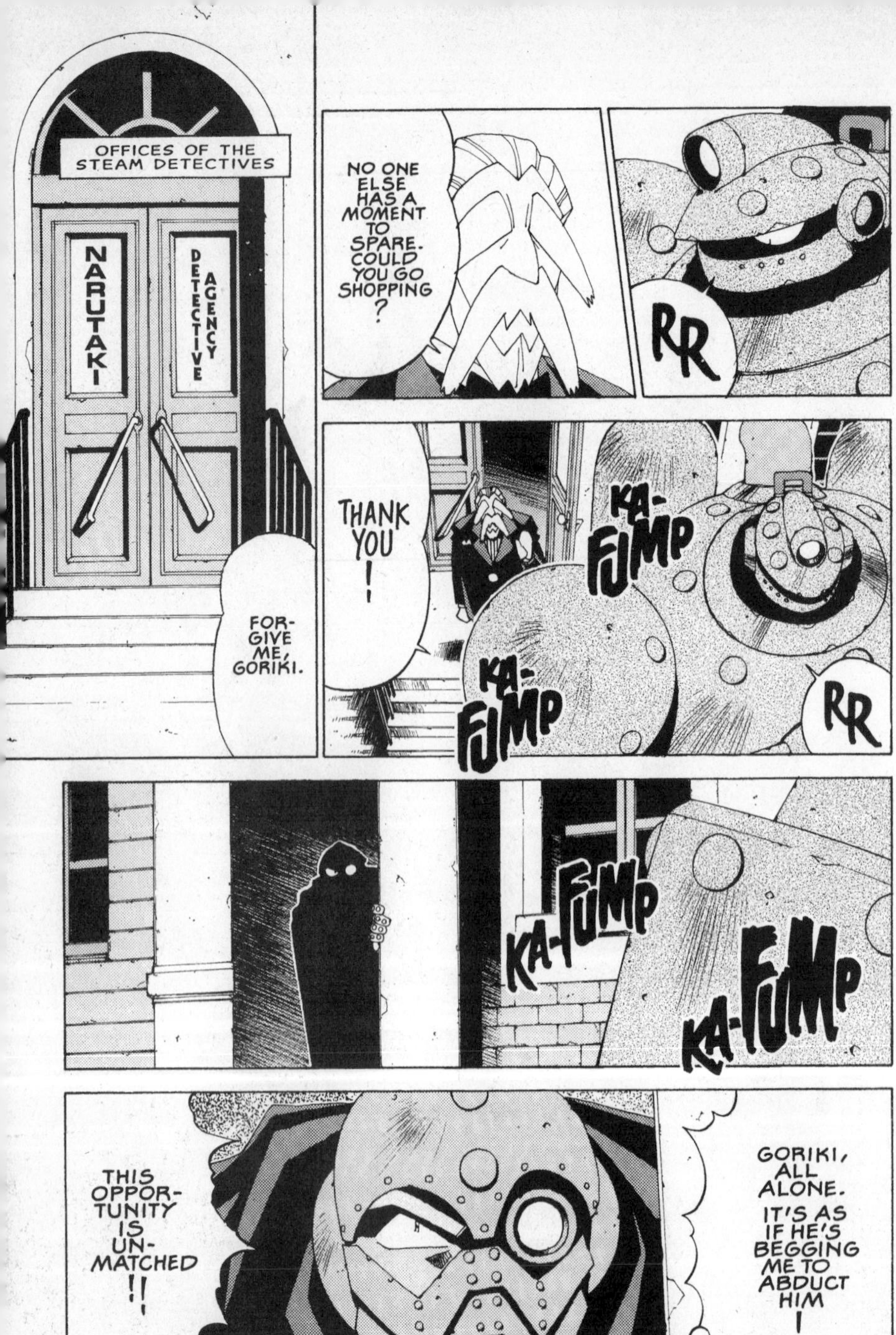
OFFICES OF THE STEAM DETECTIVES
NARUTAKI DETECTIVE AGENCY
FOR-GIVE ME, GORIKI.
NO ONE ELSE HAS A MOMENT TO SPARE. COULD YOU GO SHOPPING?
RR
THANK YOU!
KA-FUMP
KA-FUMP
RR
KA-FUMP
KA-FUMP
THIS OPPOR-TUNITY IS UN-MATCHED!!
GORIKI, ALL ALONE.
IT'S AS IF HE'S BEGGING ME TO ABDUCT HIM!

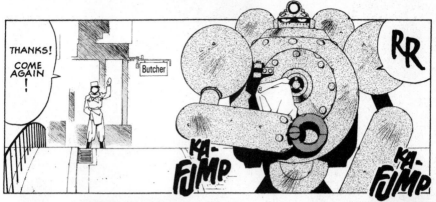

THANKS! COME AGAIN!

RR

KA-FUMP

KA-FUMP

H-HOW COULD THEY LOWER GORIKI TO A MENIAL ERRAND BOY!?

YOU'RE SADLY MISTAKEN, NARUTAKI!

ONLY I CAN POSSIBLY UNDERSTAND THE FULL POTENTIAL OF GORIKI!

ZING

FWEEE...!

KA-FUMP

KA-FUMP

HERE HE COMES!!

KN'CH

STEP INTO MY NOOSE!!

FUMP

KA-

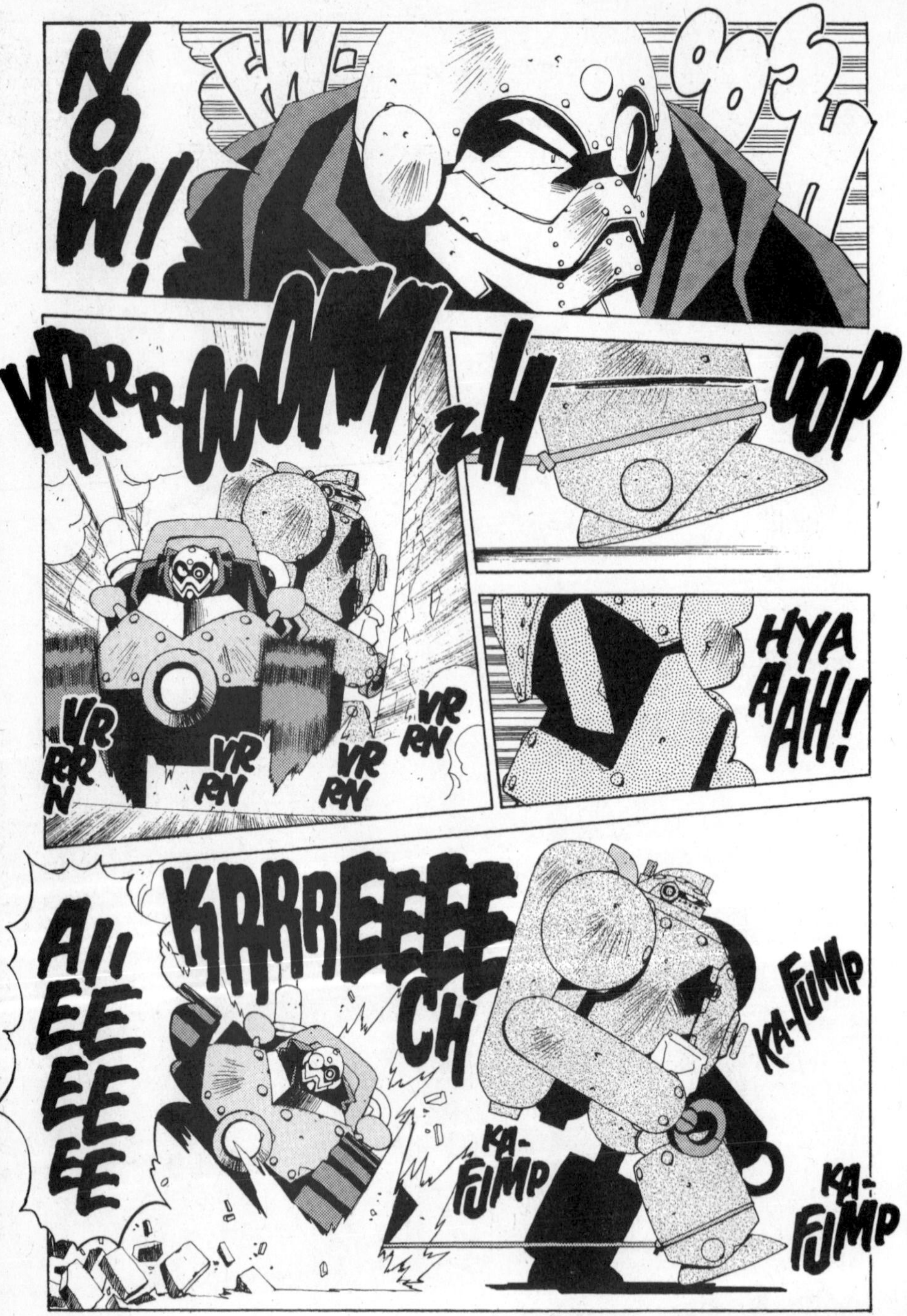
NOW!
FWOOOSH
VRRR-ROOOM
ZH
OOP
VRRRN
VRRN
VRRN
VRRN
HYAAAH!
AIIEEEEEEE
KRRREEEECH
KA-FUMP
KA-FUMP
KA-FUMP

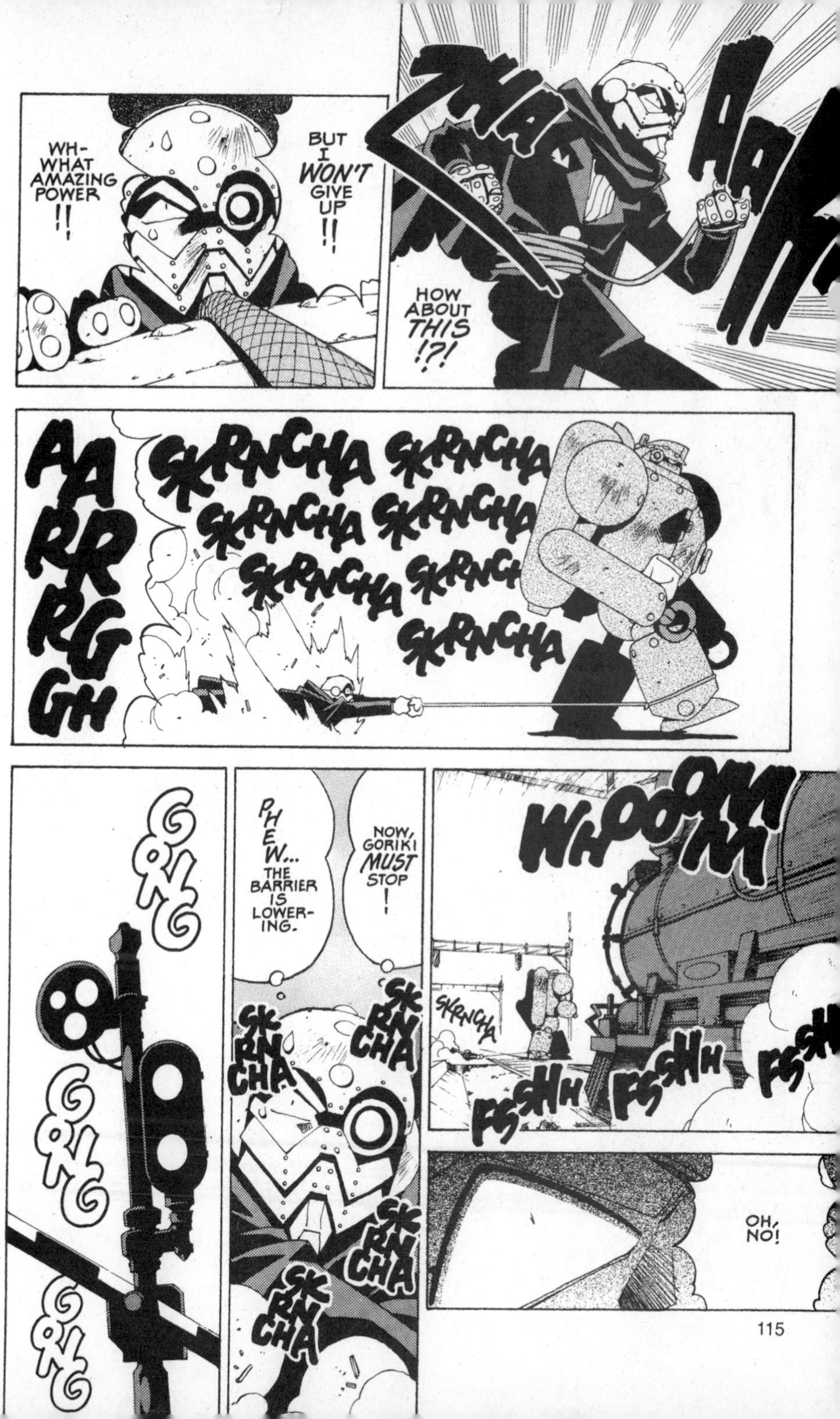
WH- WHAT AMAZING POWER !!
BUT I WON'T GIVE UP !!
ZHAAA
HOW ABOUT THIS !?!
AARRRGGH
SKRNCHA SKRNCHA SKRNCHA SKRNCHA SKRNCHA SKRNCH SKRNCHA
GONG GONG GONG
PHEW... THE BARRIER IS LOWERING.
NOW, GORIKI MUST STOP !
SKRNCHA SKRNCHA SKRNCHA SKRNCHA
WHOOOM
SKRNCHA
FSSHH FSSHH FSSH
OH, NO!

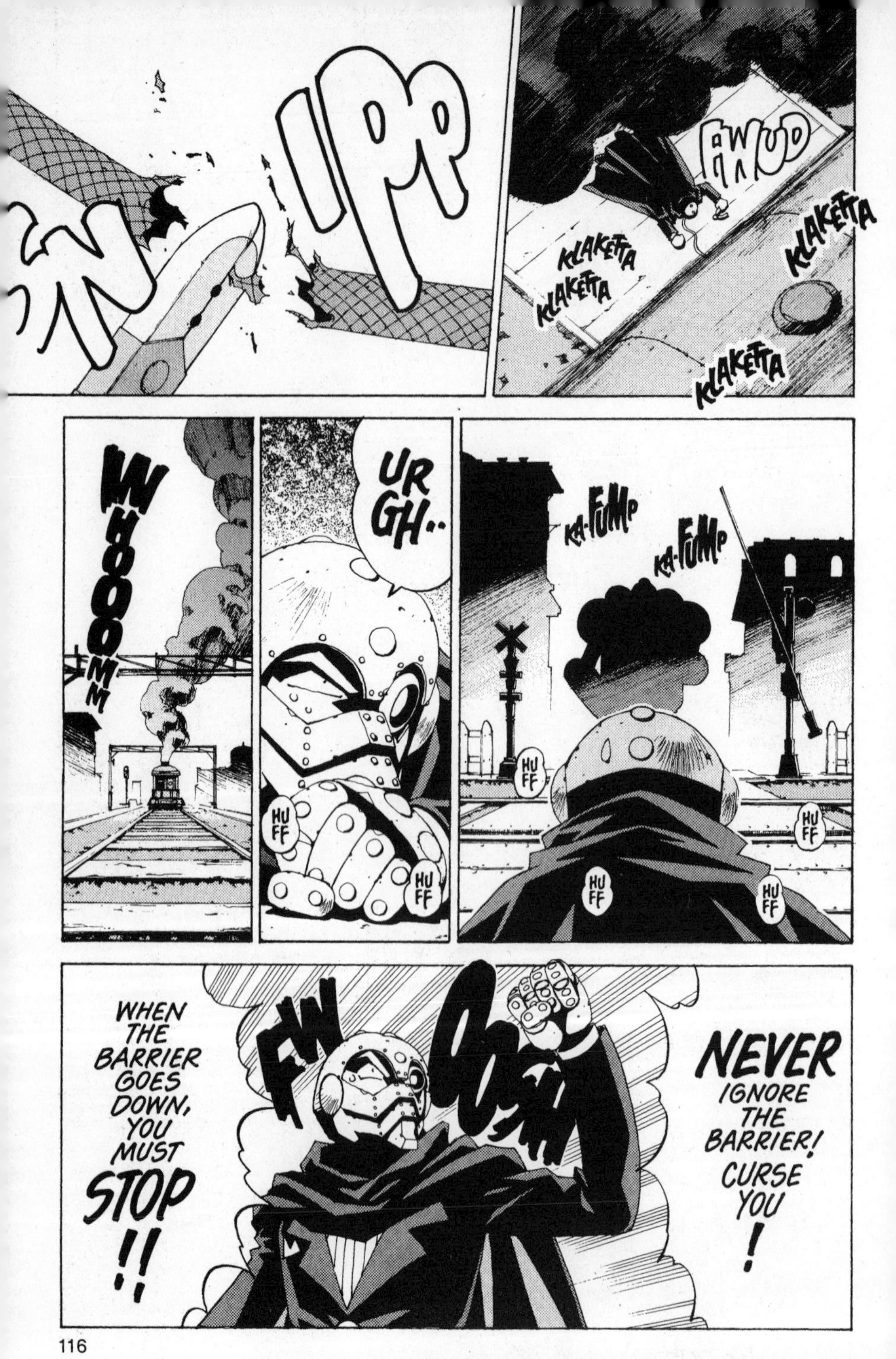
WIPP
FWUD
KLAKETTA
KLAKETTA
KLAKETTA
KLAKETTA
WHOOOOMM
URGH..
HUFF
HUFF
KA-FUMP
KA-FUMP
HUFF
HUFF
HUFF
HUFF
WHEN THE BARRIER GOES DOWN, YOU MUST STOP!!
FWOOSH
NEVER IGNORE THE BARRIER! CURSE YOU!

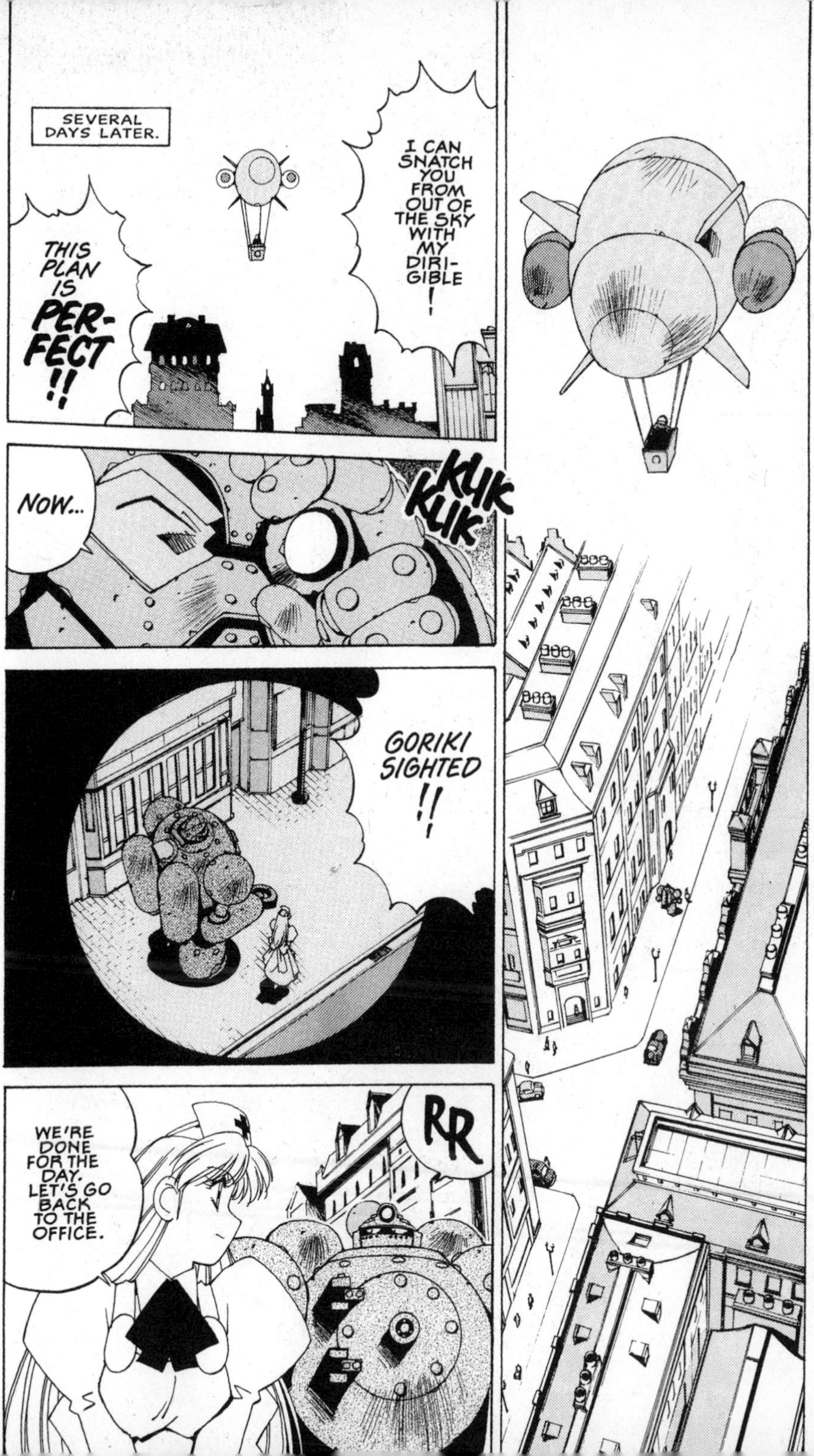
SEVERAL DAYS LATER.
THIS PLAN IS PER-FECT!!
I CAN SNATCH YOU FROM OUT OF THE SKY WITH MY DIRI-GIBLE!
NOW...
KUK KUK
GORIKI SIGHTED!!
WE'RE DONE FOR THE DAY. LET'S GO BACK TO THE OFFICE.
RR

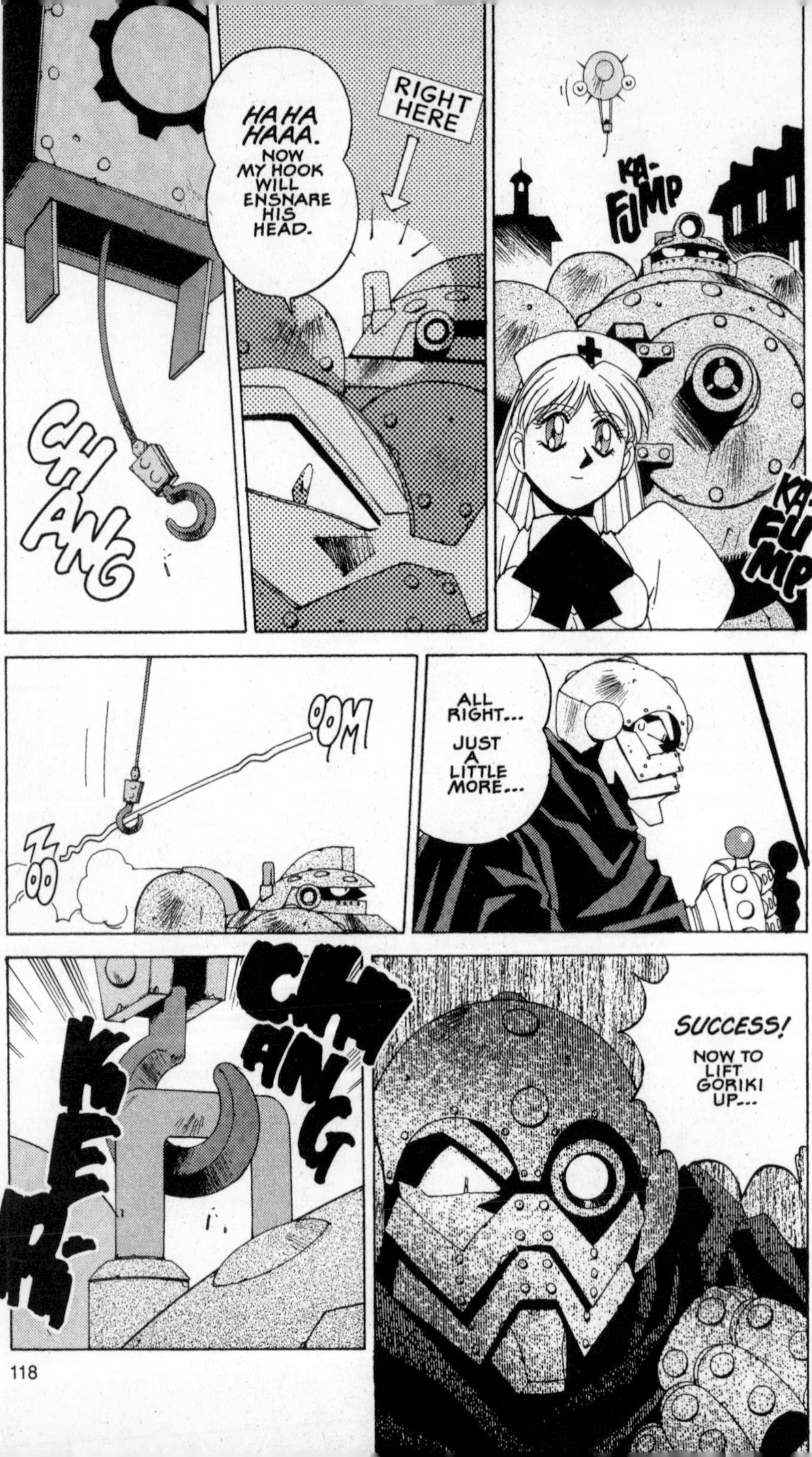
HA HA HAAA. NOW MY HOOK WILL ENSNARE HIS HEAD.
RIGHT HERE
KA-FUMP
KA-FUMP
OOM
ALL RIGHT... JUST A LITTLE MORE...
SUCCESS!
NOW TO LIFT GORIKI UP...

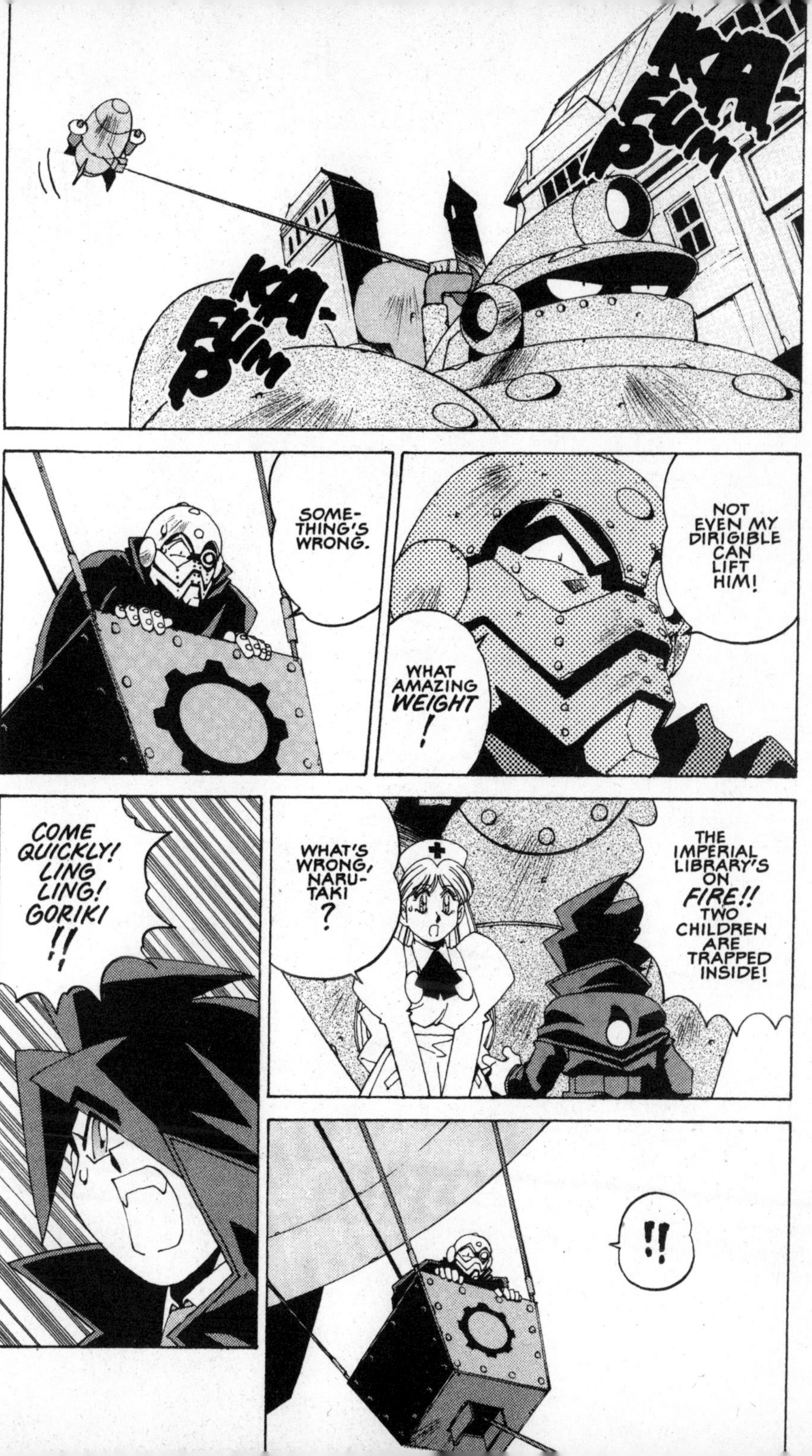
KA-FUMP
KA-FUMP
SOME-THING'S WRONG.
NOT EVEN MY DIRIGIBLE CAN LIFT HIM!
WHAT AMAZING WEIGHT!
COME QUICKLY! LING LING! GORIKI!!
WHAT'S WRONG, NARU-TAKI?
THE IMPERIAL LIBRARY'S ON FIRE!! TWO CHILDREN ARE TRAPPED INSIDE!
!!

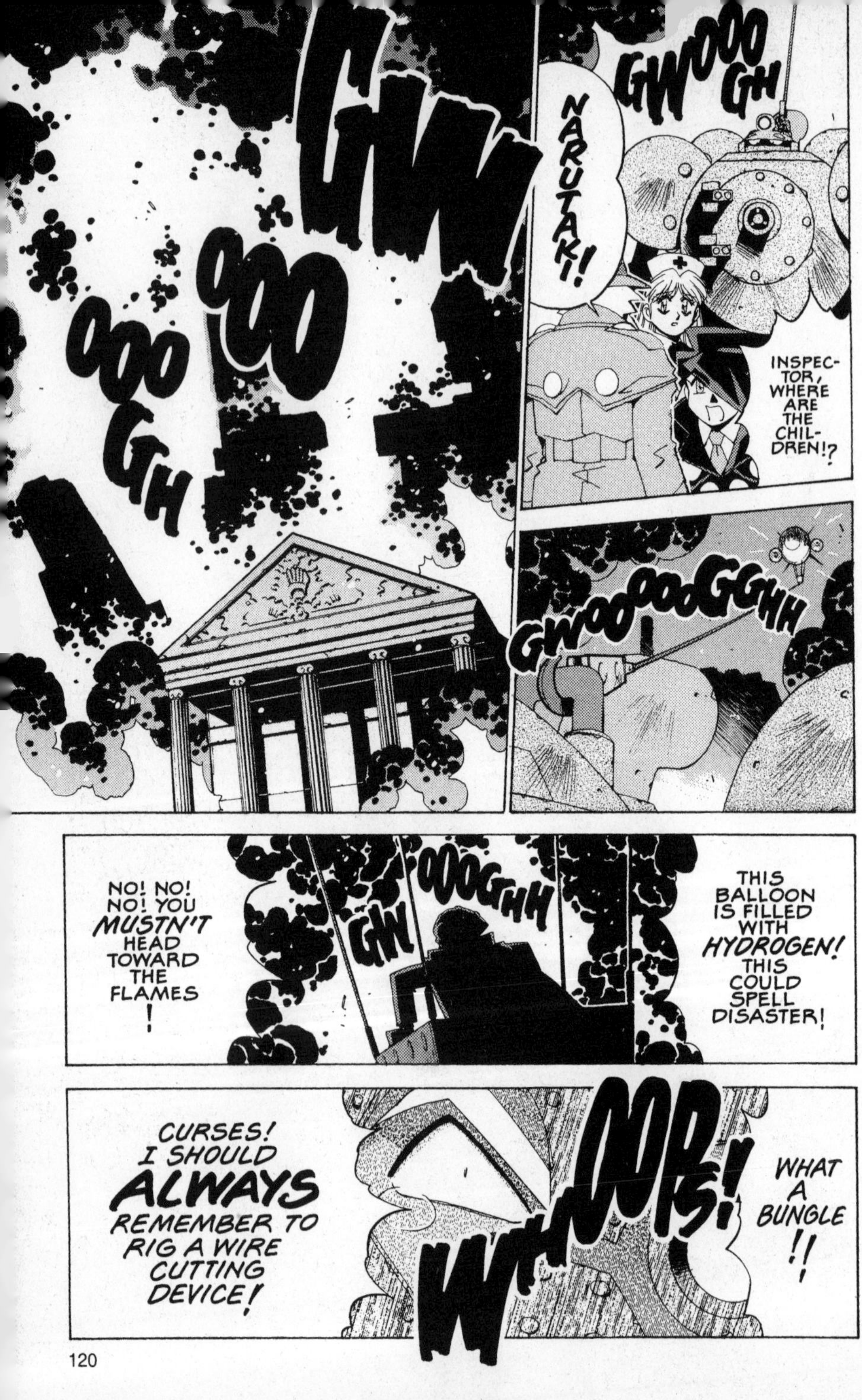
GWOOOOOOGH
GWOOOGH
NARUTAKI!
INSPECTOR, WHERE ARE THE CHILDREN!?
GWOOOOOGGHH
NO! NO! NO! YOU *MUSTN'T* HEAD TOWARD THE FLAMES!
GWOOOGHH
THIS BALLOON IS FILLED WITH *HYDROGEN!* THIS COULD SPELL DISASTER!
CURSES! I SHOULD **ALWAYS** REMEMBER TO RIG A WIRE CUTTING DEVICE!
WHOOPS!
WHAT A BUNGLE!!

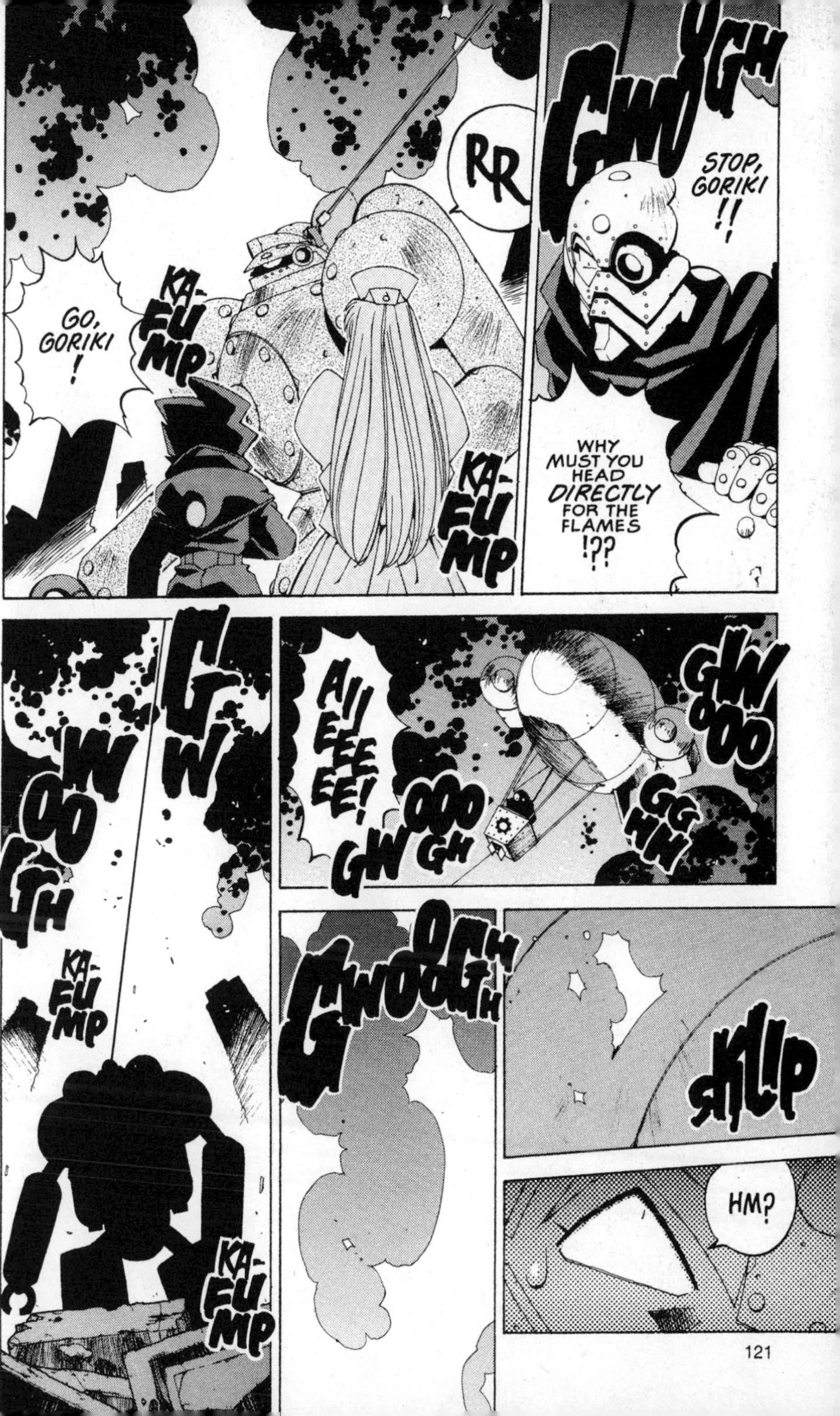
GO, GORIKI!
KA-FUMP
RR
KA-FUMP
GWOGH
STOP, GORIKI!!
WHY MUST YOU HEAD DIRECTLY FOR THE FLAMES!??
GWOOGH
GW
KA-FUMP
KA-FUMP
AIIEEEEE!
GWOOOGH
GWOOO
GGHN
GWOOOGHHH
SKLIP
HM?

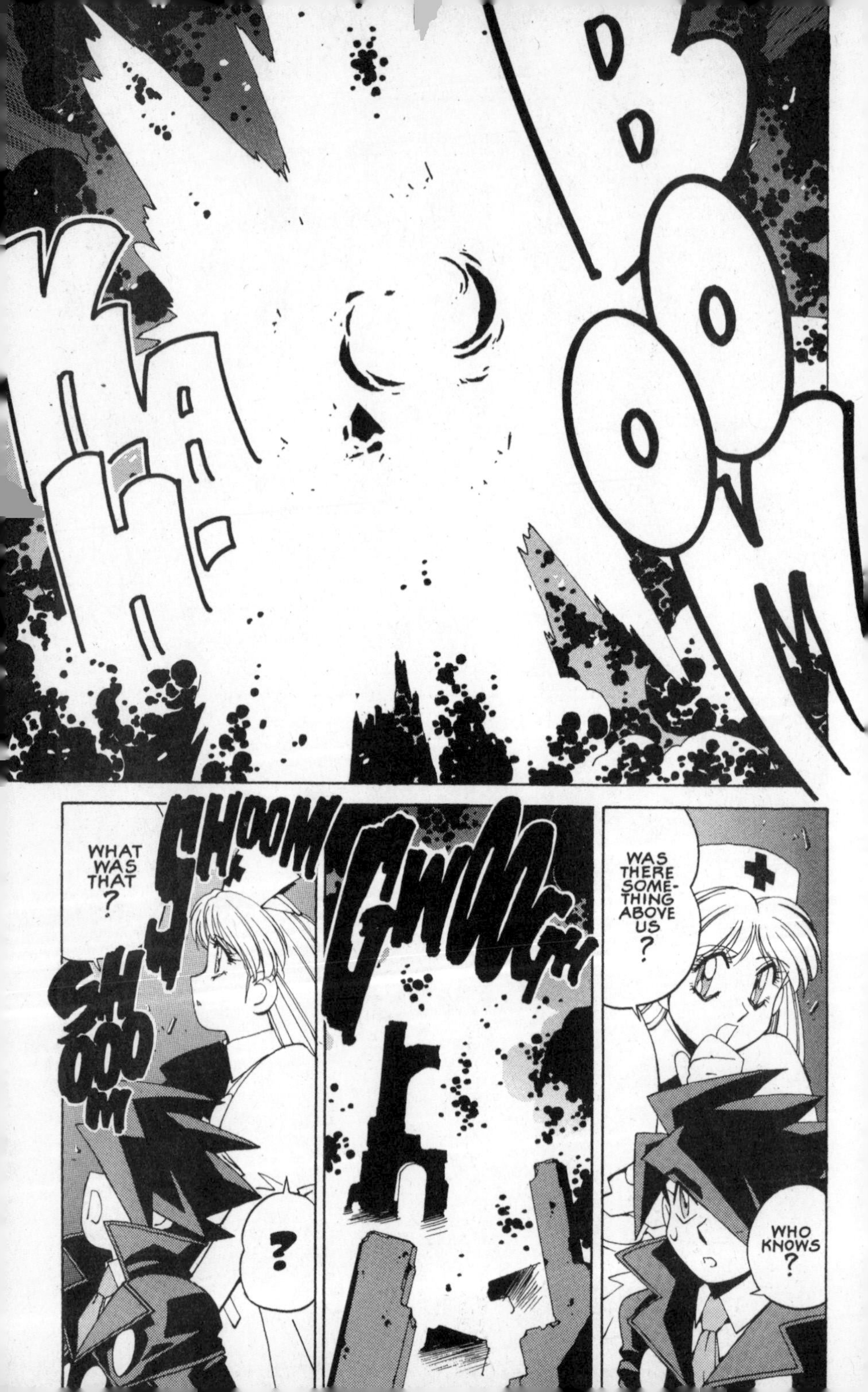
DDOOOM
SHOOM
WHAT WAS THAT?
SHOOOM
?
GWOOGH
WAS THERE SOMETHING ABOVE US?
WHO KNOWS?

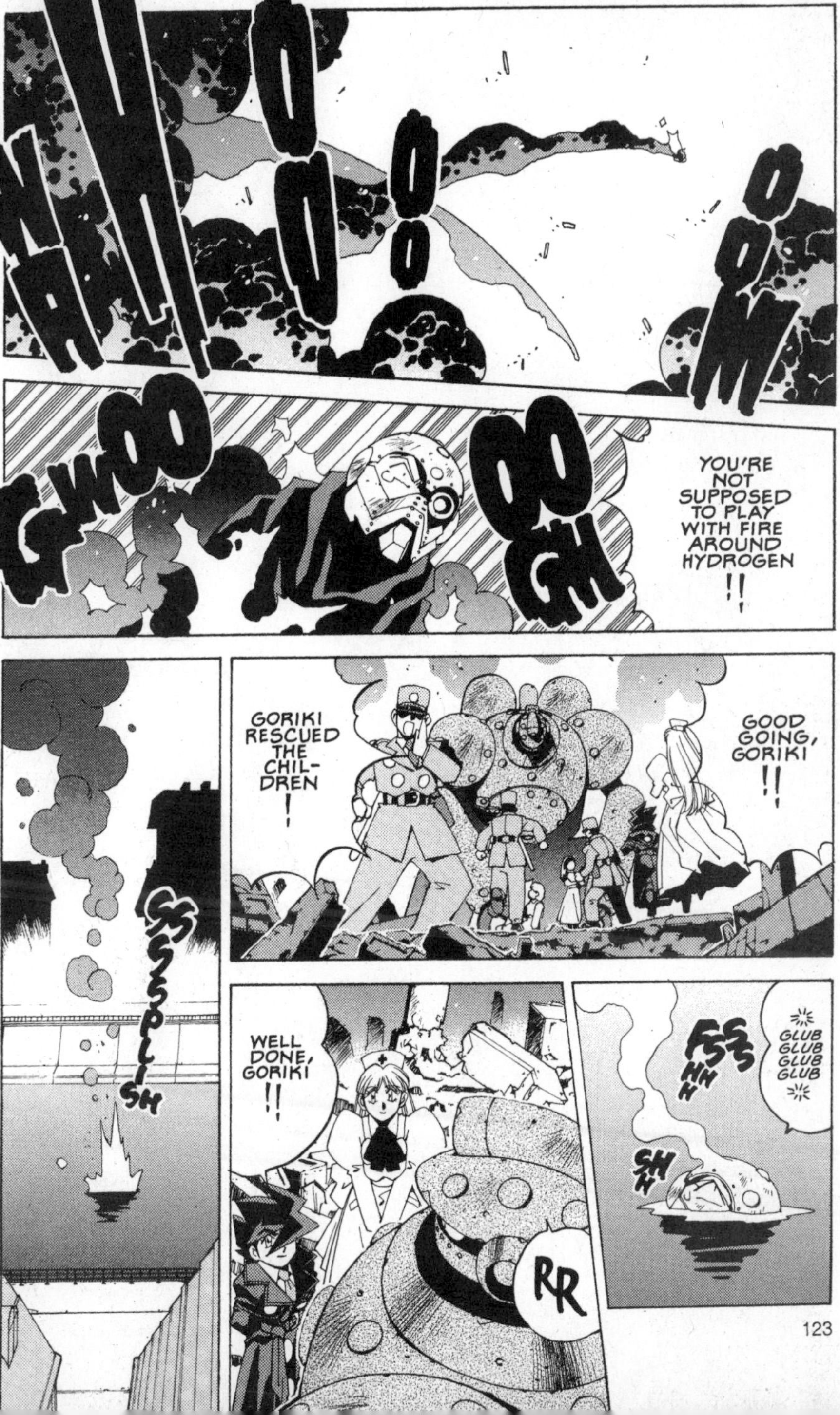
WHAHH
OOOO-OOOO
OOOM
GWOO
OOGH
YOU'RE NOT SUPPOSED TO PLAY WITH FIRE AROUND HYDROGEN !!
SSSSSPLISH
GORIKI RESCUED THE CHIL-DREN !
GOOD GOING, GORIKI !!
WELL DONE, GORIKI !!
RR
FSSS HHH
GLUB GLUB GLUB GLUB
SHH

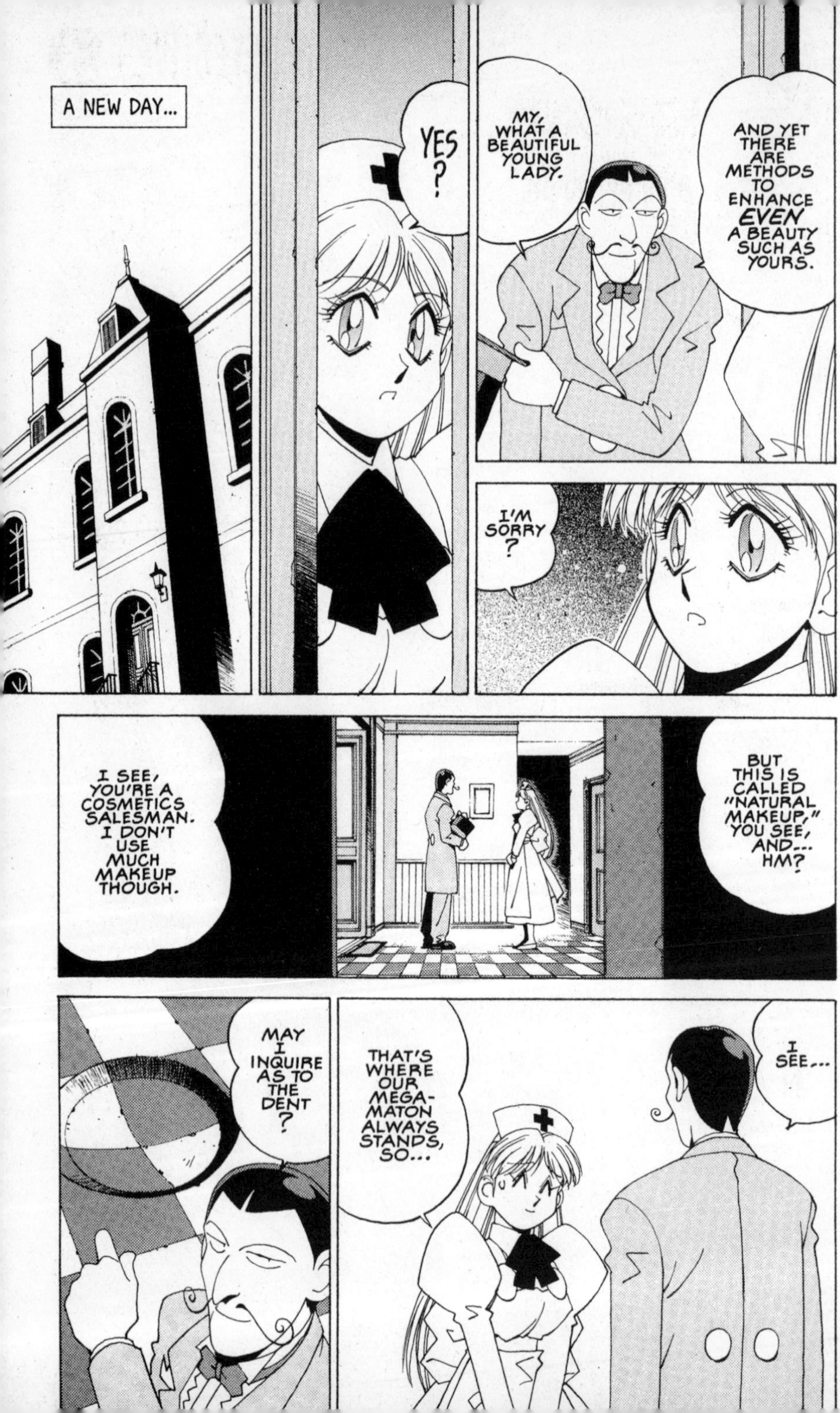
A NEW DAY...
YES?
MY, WHAT A BEAUTIFUL YOUNG LADY.
AND YET THERE ARE METHODS TO ENHANCE EVEN A BEAUTY SUCH AS YOURS.
I'M SORRY?
I SEE, YOU'RE A COSMETICS SALESMAN. I DON'T USE MUCH MAKEUP THOUGH.
BUT THIS IS CALLED "NATURAL MAKEUP," YOU SEE, AND... HM?
MAY I INQUIRE AS TO THE DENT?
THAT'S WHERE OUR MEGA-MATON ALWAYS STANDS, SO...
I SEE...

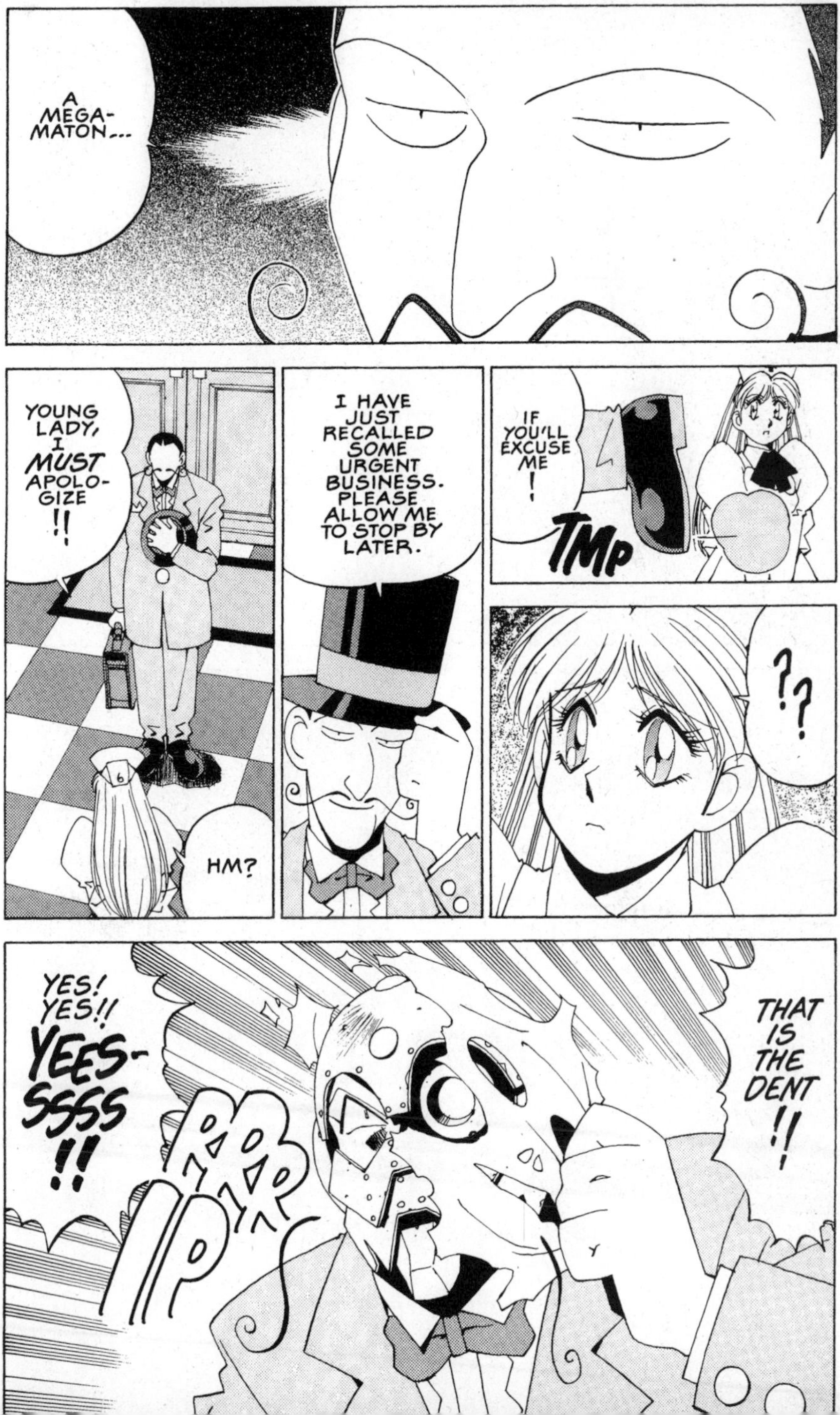
A MEGA-MATON...
YOUNG LADY, I MUST APOLOGIZE!!
HM?
I HAVE JUST RECALLED SOME URGENT BUSINESS. PLEASE ALLOW ME TO STOP BY LATER.
IF YOU'LL EXCUSE ME!
TMP
??
YES! YES!! YEES-SSSSS!!
RRRIP
THAT IS THE DENT!!

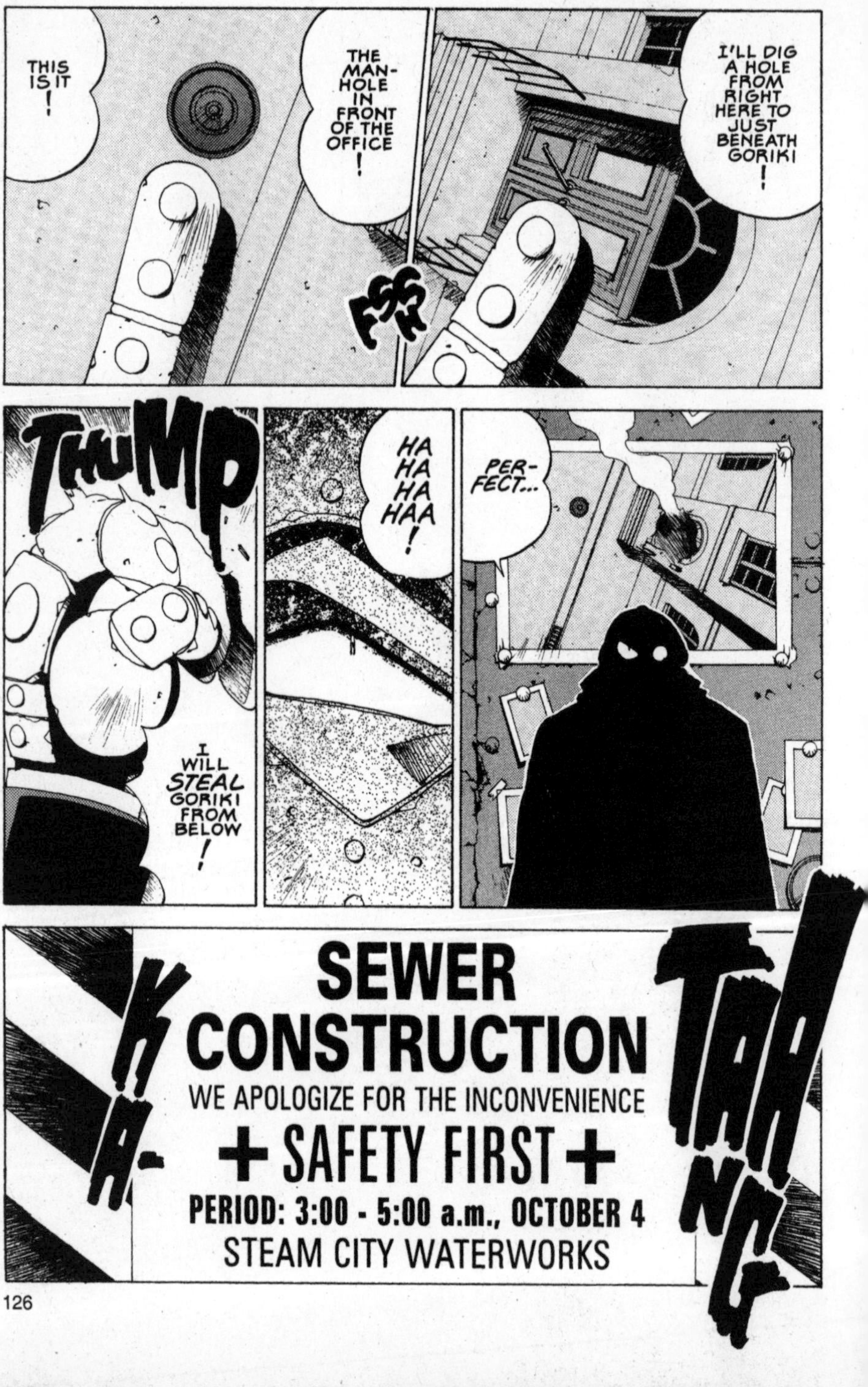

THIS IS IT!
THE MAN-HOLE IN FRONT OF THE OFFICE!
FSSH
I'LL DIG A HOLE FROM RIGHT HERE TO JUST BENEATH GORIKI!
THUMP
I WILL STEAL GORIKI FROM BELOW!
HA HA HA HAA!
PER-FECT...
SEWER CONSTRUCTION
WE APOLOGIZE FOR THE INCONVENIENCE
+ SAFETY FIRST +
PERIOD: 3:00 - 5:00 a.m., OCTOBER 4
STEAM CITY WATERWORKS
TAHNG

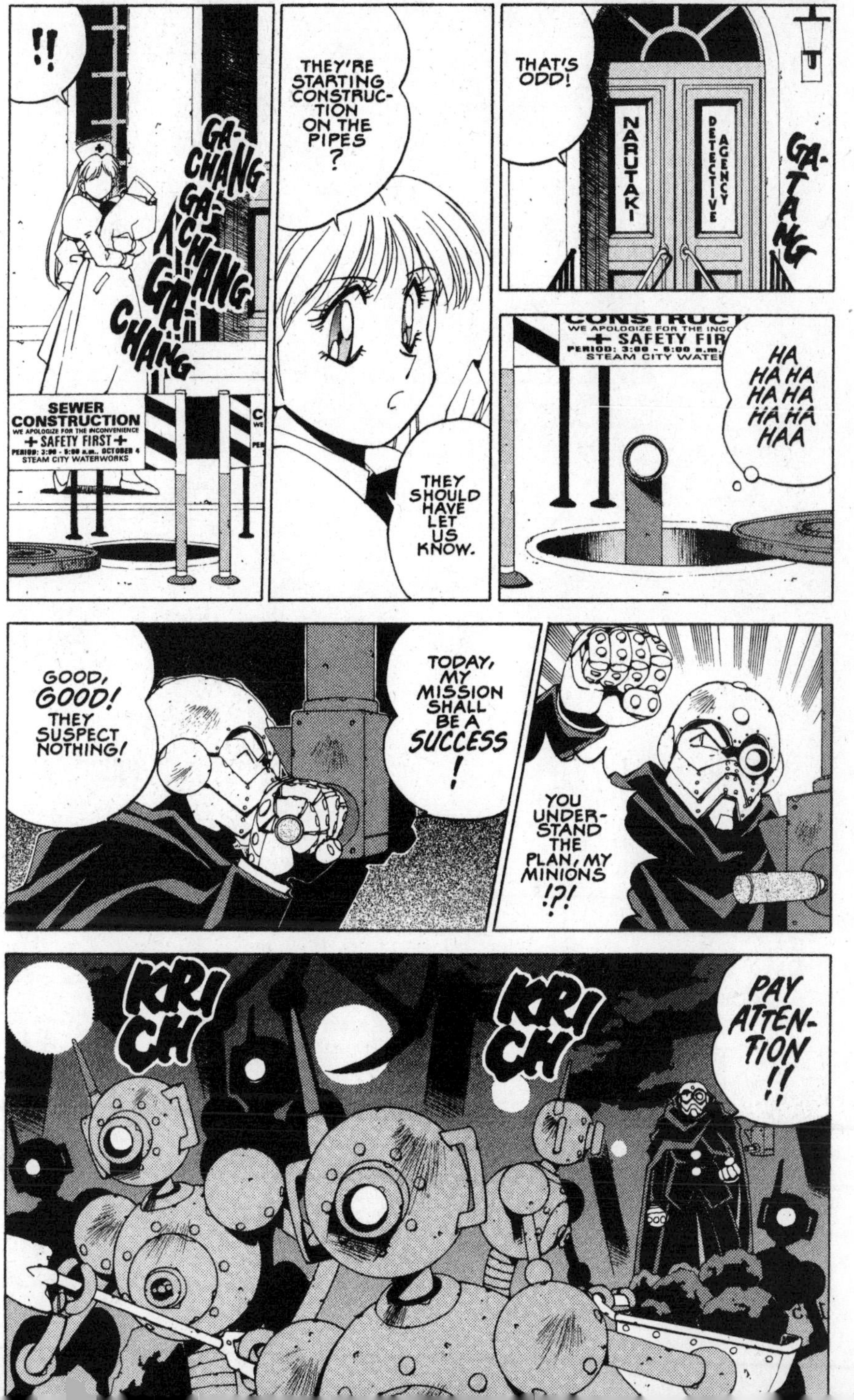
!!
GA-CHANG GA-CHANG GA-CHANG
SEWER CONSTRUCTION
WE APOLOGIZE FOR THE INCONVENIENCE
+ SAFETY FIRST +
PERIOD: 3:00 - 5:00 a.m. OCTOBER 4
STEAM CITY WATERWORKS
THEY'RE STARTING CONSTRUCTION ON THE PIPES?
THEY SHOULD HAVE LET US KNOW.
THAT'S ODD!
NARUTAKI DETECTIVE AGENCY
GA-TANG
HA HA HA HA HA HA HA HA HAA
GOOD, GOOD! THEY SUSPECT NOTHING!
TODAY, MY MISSION SHALL BE A SUCCESS!
YOU UNDERSTAND THE PLAN, MY MINIONS!?!
KRICH
KRICH
PAY ATTENTION!!

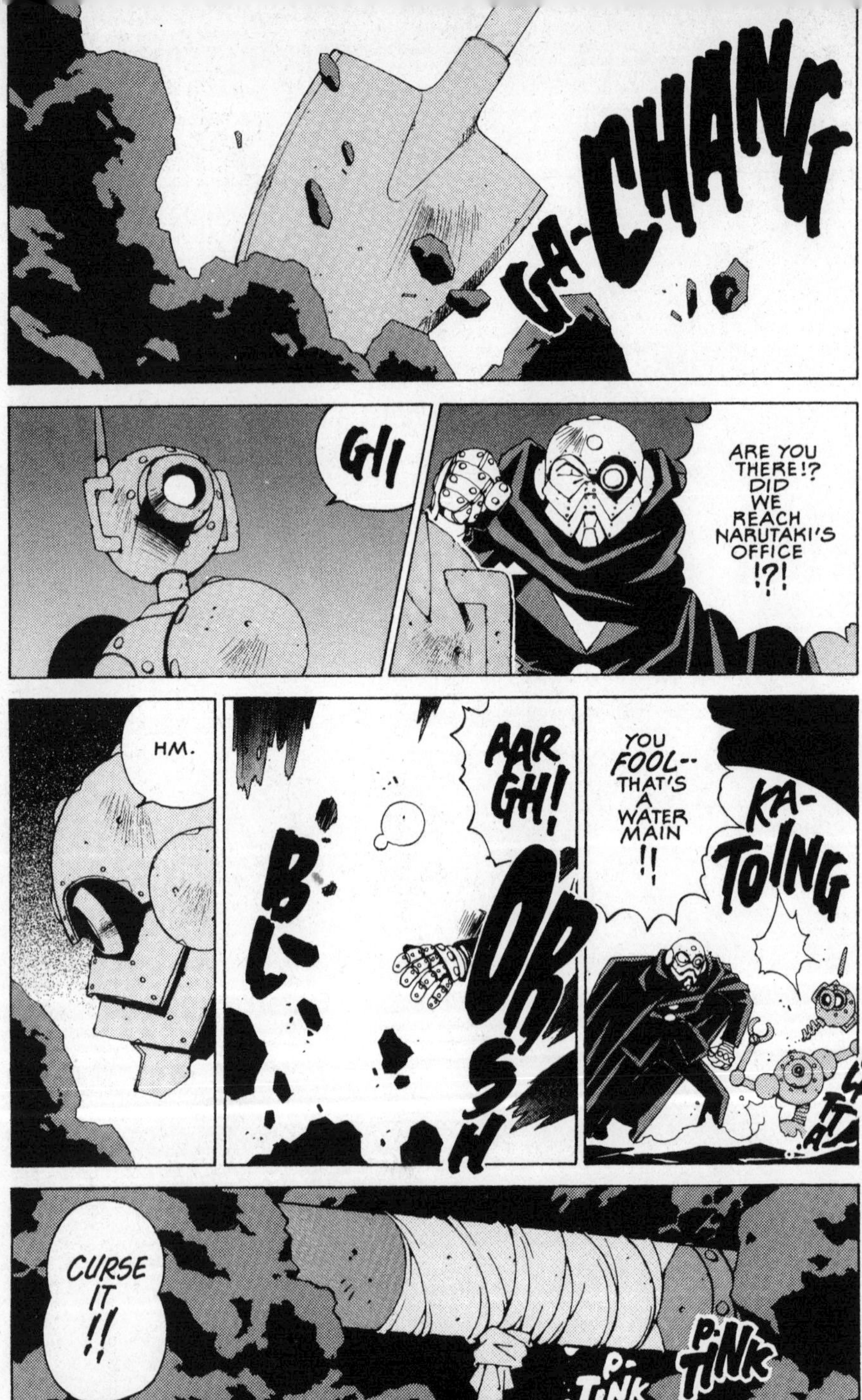
GA-CHANG
GH
ARE YOU THERE!? DID WE REACH NARUTAKI'S OFFICE !?!
HM.
AARGH!
BLORSH
YOU FOOL-- THAT'S A WATER MAIN !!
KA-TOING
KLATTA
CURSE IT !!
P-TINK
P-TINK

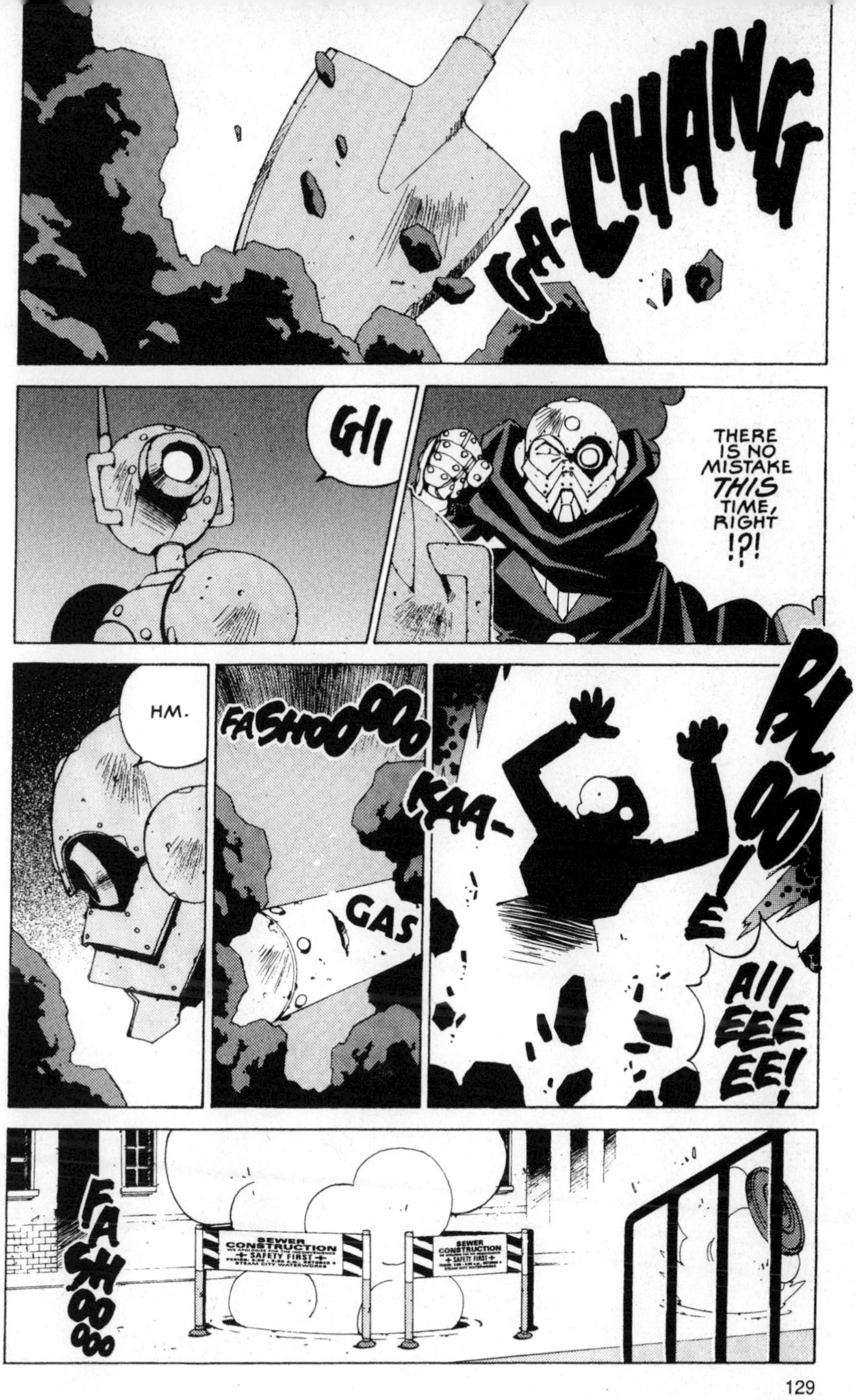
GA-CHANG
GI!
THERE IS NO MISTAKE THIS TIME, RIGHT !?!
HM.
FASHOOOOOO
GAS
KAA-
BLOOIE
AIIEEEEEE!
FASHOOOOO
SEWER CONSTRUCTION
WE APOLOGIZE FOR THE INCONVENIENCE
SAFETY FIRST
STEAM CITY WATERWORKS
SEWER CONSTRUCTION
SAFETY FIRST

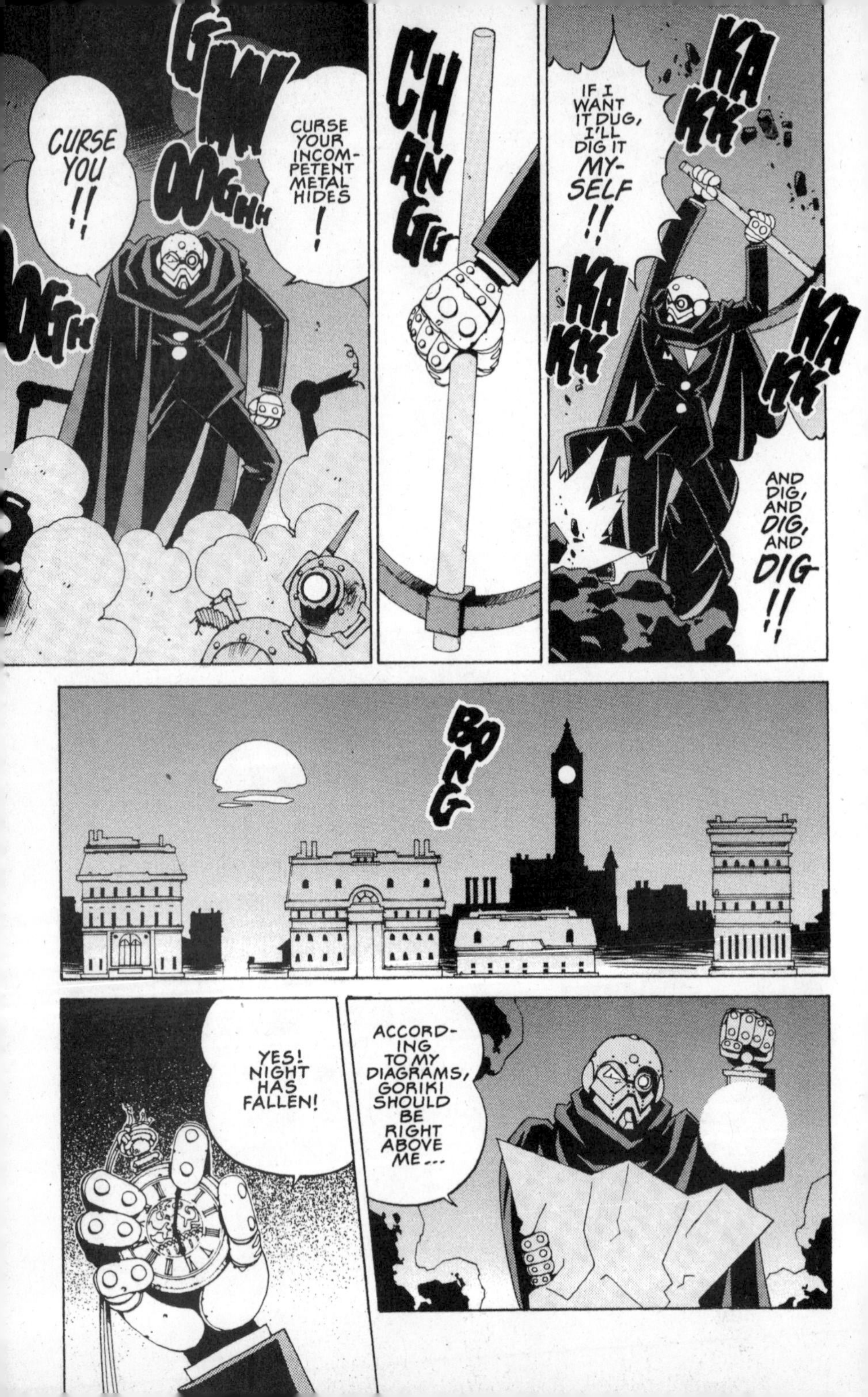
GWWOOGHH
CURSE YOU !!
CURSE YOUR INCOMPETENT METAL HIDES !
CHANGG
IF I WANT IT DUG, I'LL DIG IT MYSELF !!
KAKK
KAKK
KAKK
AND DIG, AND DIG, AND DIG !!
BONG
YES! NIGHT HAS FALLEN!
ACCORDING TO MY DIAGRAMS, GORIKI SHOULD BE RIGHT ABOVE ME...

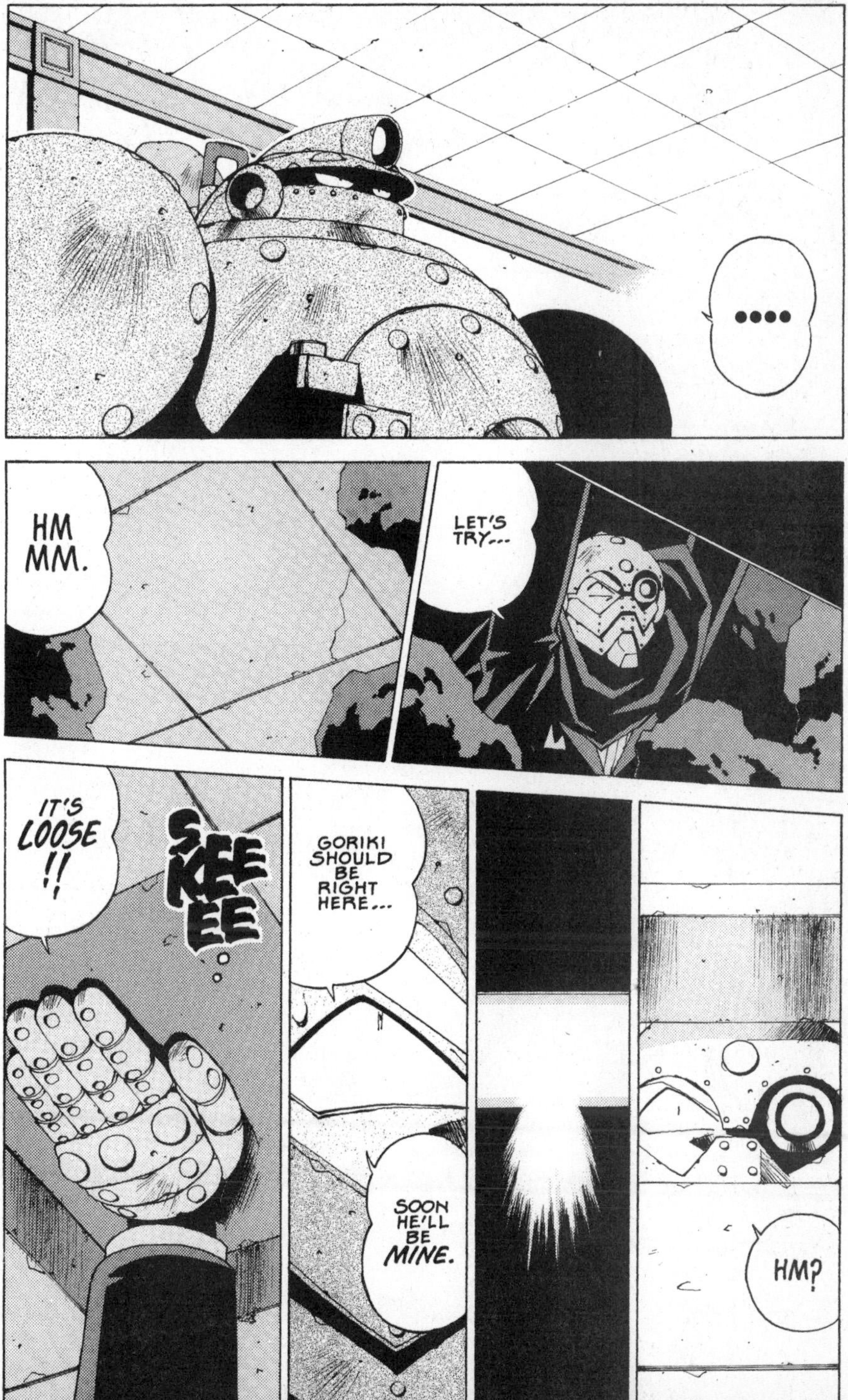

....
HM MM.
LET'S TRY...
IT'S LOOSE !!
SKEE KEE EE
GORIKI SHOULD BE RIGHT HERE...
SOON HE'LL BE MINE.
HM?

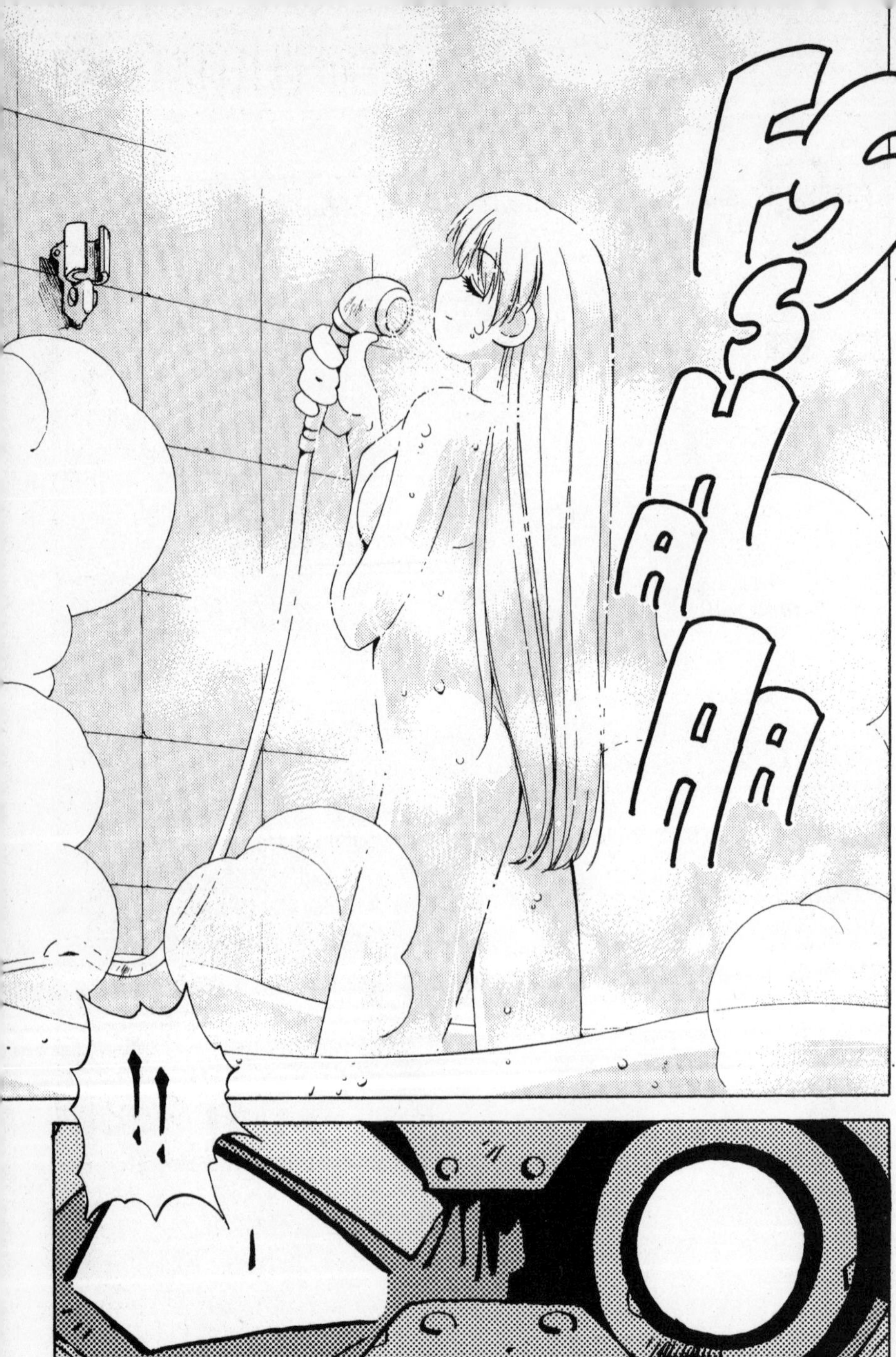
FSSHAAA
!!

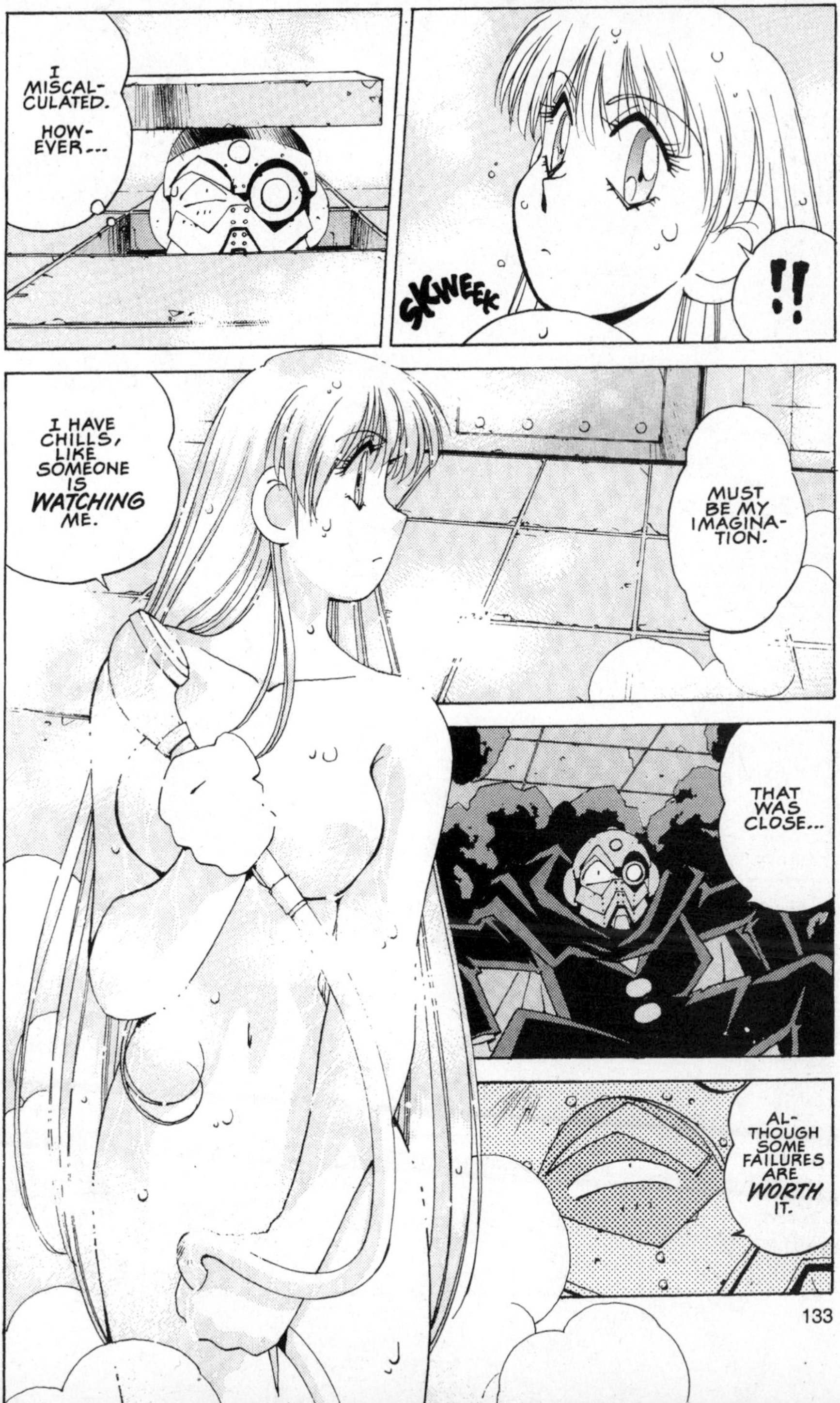
I MISCALCULATED.
HOWEVER...
SKWEEK
!!
I HAVE CHILLS, LIKE SOMEONE IS *WATCHING* ME.
MUST BE MY IMAGINATION.
THAT WAS CLOSE...
ALTHOUGH SOME FAILURES ARE *WORTH* IT.

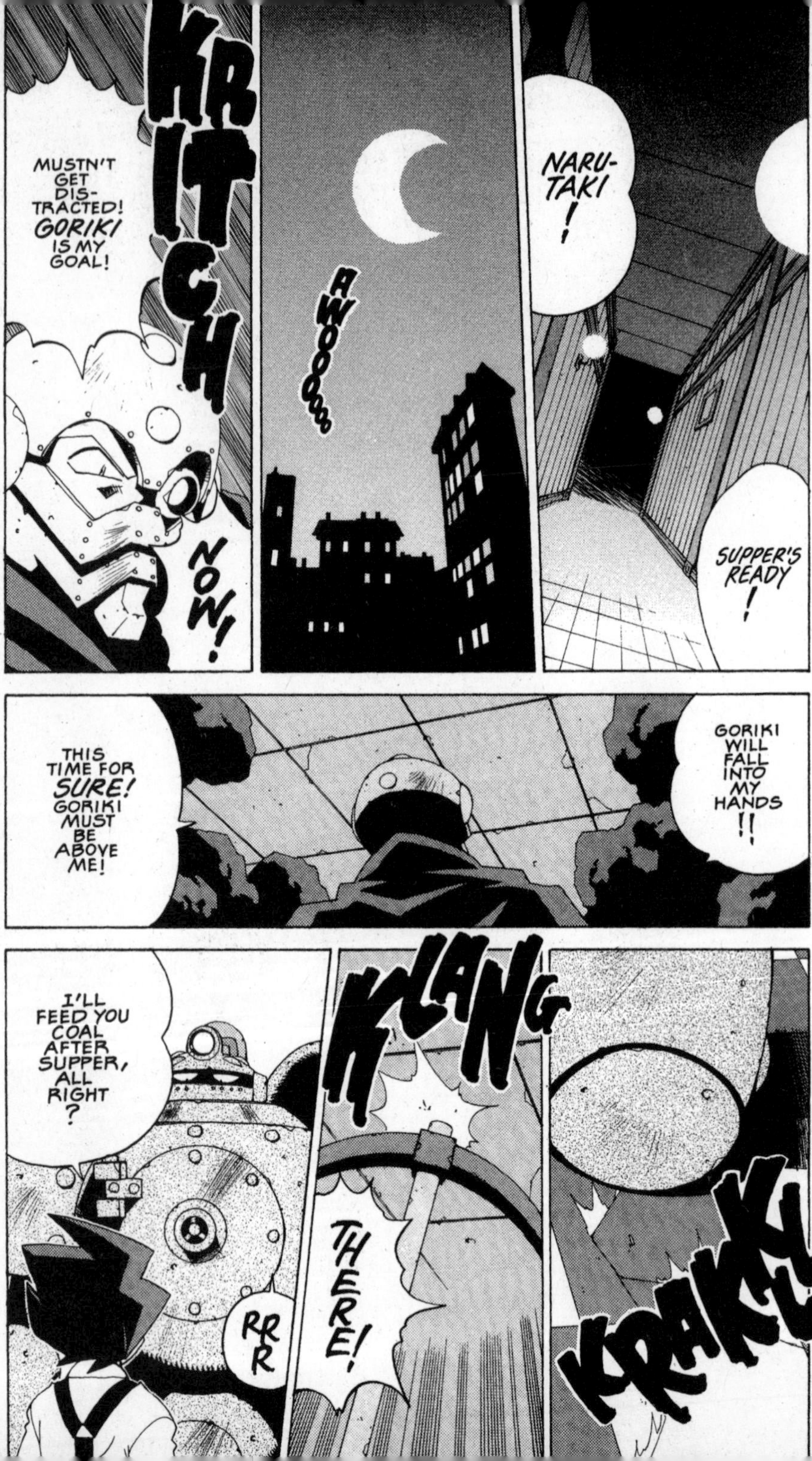
MUSTN'T GET DIS-TRACTED! GORIKI IS MY GOAL!
KRITCH
NOW!
AWOOOOooo
NARU-TAKI!
SUPPER'S READY!
THIS TIME FOR SURE! GORIKI MUST BE ABOVE ME!
GORIKI WILL FALL INTO MY HANDS!!
I'LL FEED YOU COAL AFTER SUPPER, ALL RIGHT?
RRR
KLANG
THERE!
KRAKK

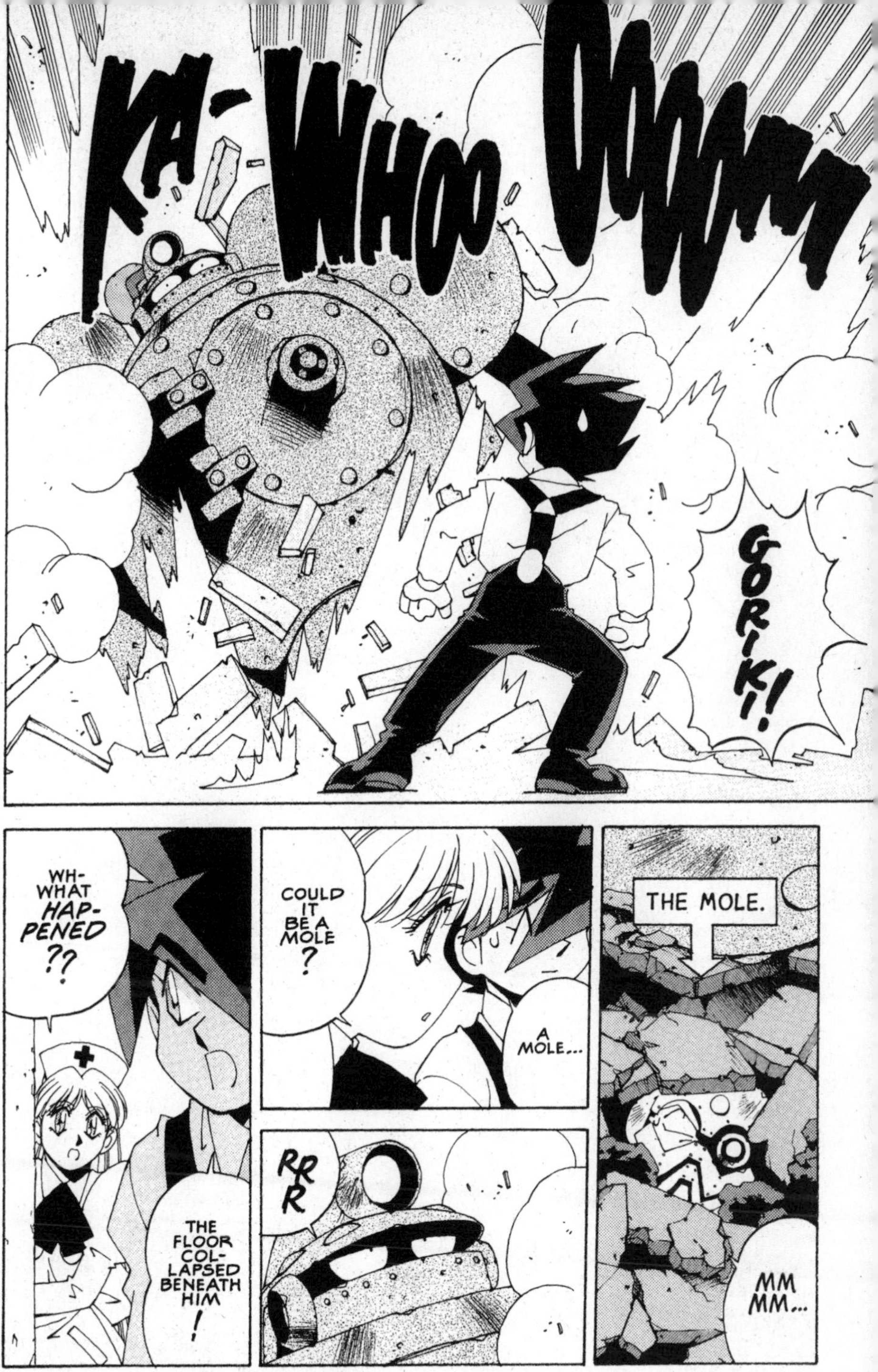
KA-WHOO OOOOOM
GORIKI!
WH-WHAT HAPPENED??
THE FLOOR COLLAPSED BENEATH HIM!
COULD IT BE A MOLE?
A MOLE...
RRR
THE MOLE.
MMMM...

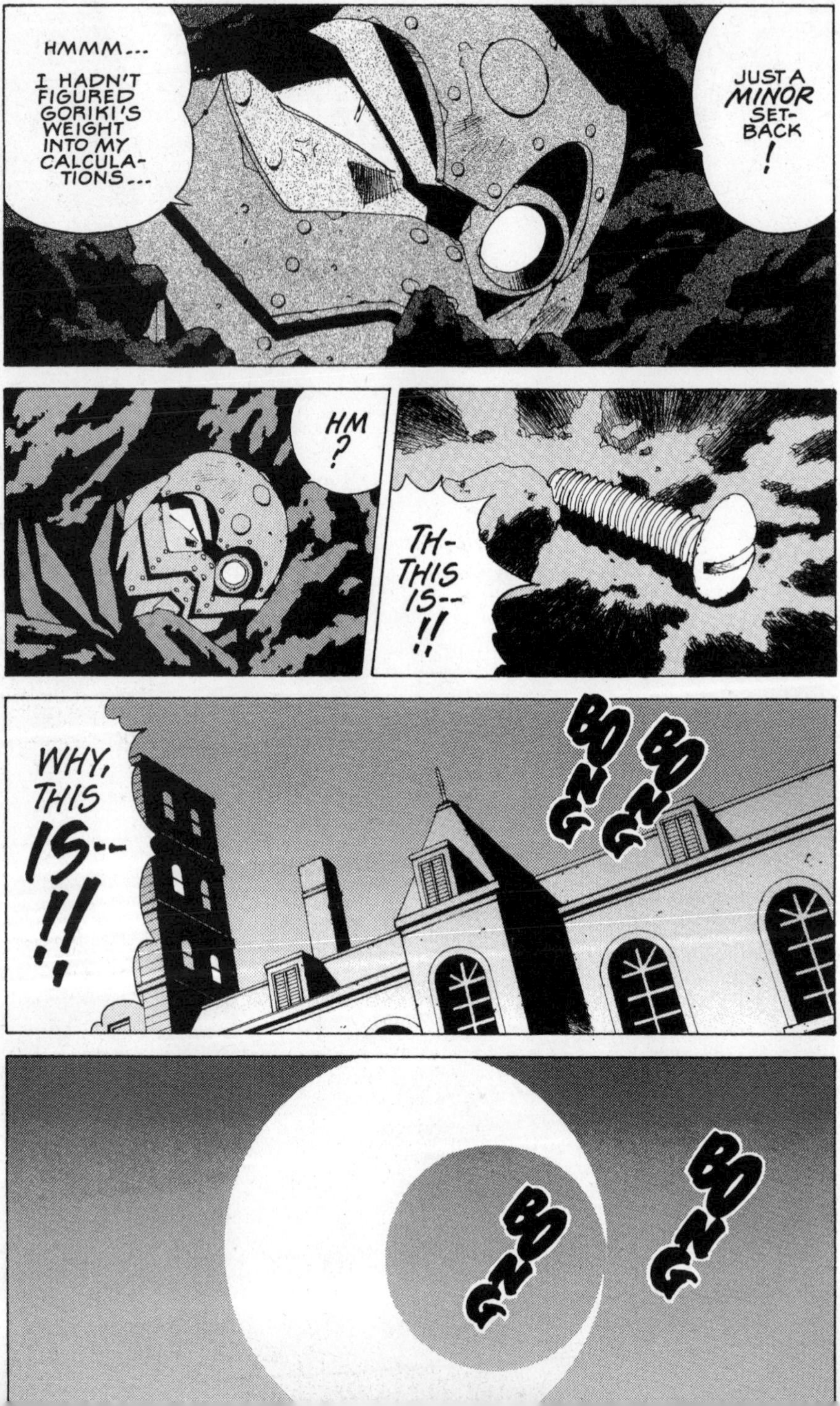
HMMM...
I HADN'T FIGURED GORIKI'S WEIGHT INTO MY CALCULATIONS...
JUST A MINOR SET-BACK!
HM?
TH-THIS IS--!!
WHY, THIS IS--!!
BONG BONG
BONG BONG

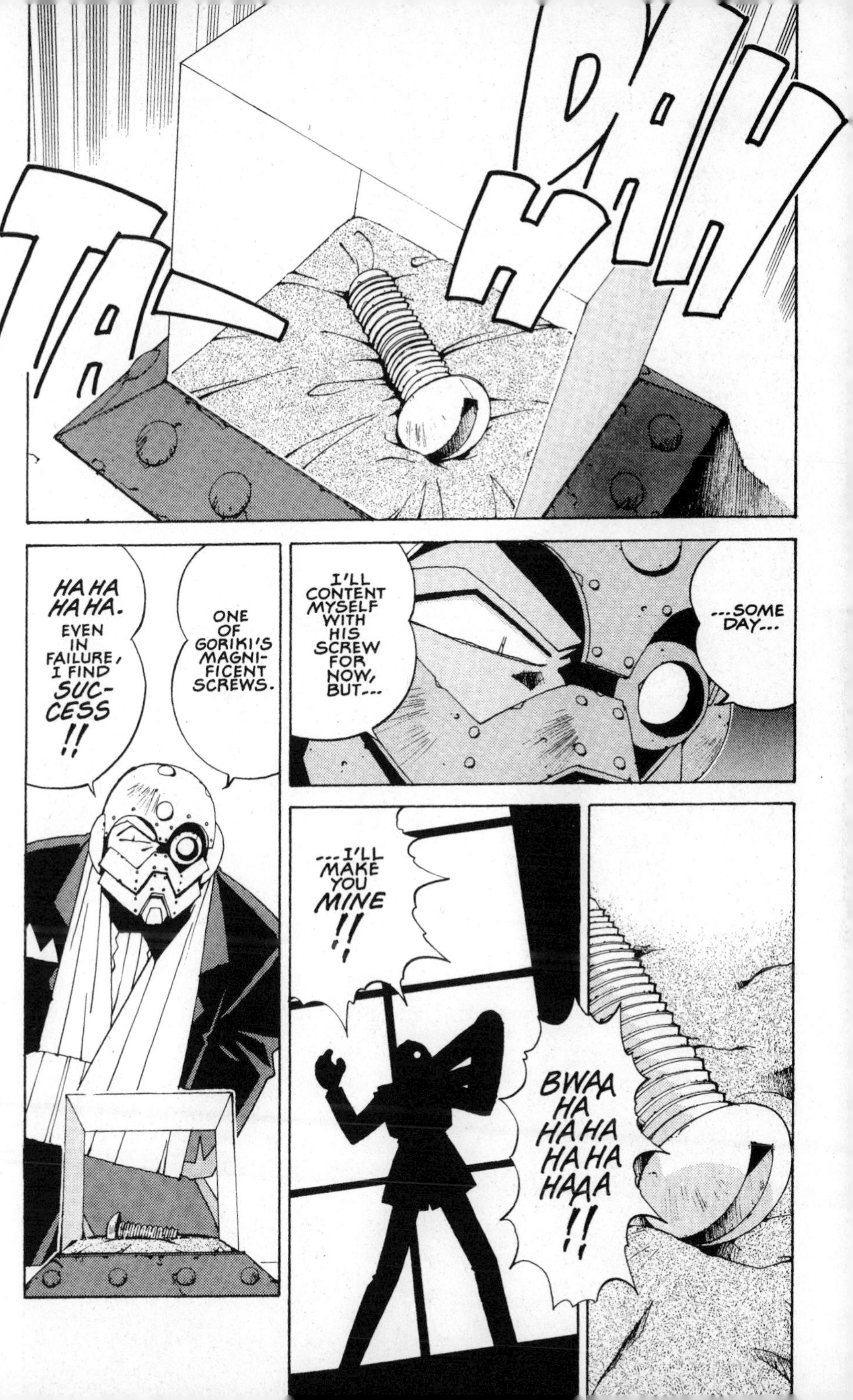
TA-
DAHHH
HA HA HA HA. EVEN IN FAILURE, I FIND SUCCESS!!
ONE OF GORIKI'S MAGNIFICENT SCREWS.
I'LL CONTENT MYSELF WITH HIS SCREW FOR NOW, BUT...
...SOME DAY...
...I'LL MAKE YOU MINE!!
BWAA HA HAHA HAHA HAAA!!

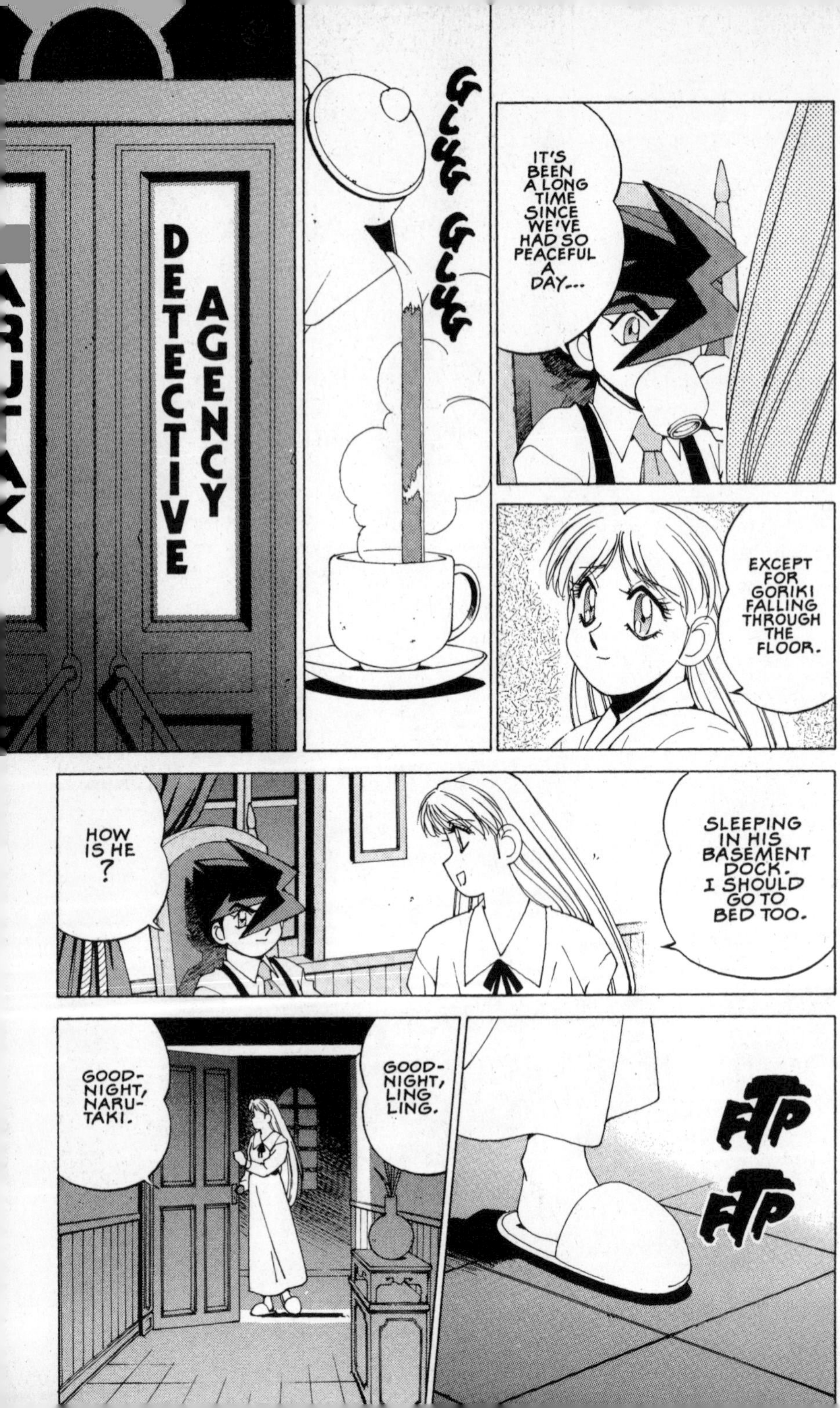
DETECTIVE AGENCY
GLUG GLUG
IT'S BEEN A LONG TIME SINCE WE'VE HAD SO PEACEFUL A DAY...
EXCEPT FOR GORIKI FALLING THROUGH THE FLOOR.
HOW IS HE?
SLEEPING IN HIS BASEMENT DOCK. I SHOULD GO TO BED TOO.
GOOD-NIGHT, NARUTAKI.
GOOD-NIGHT, LING LING.
FTP FTP

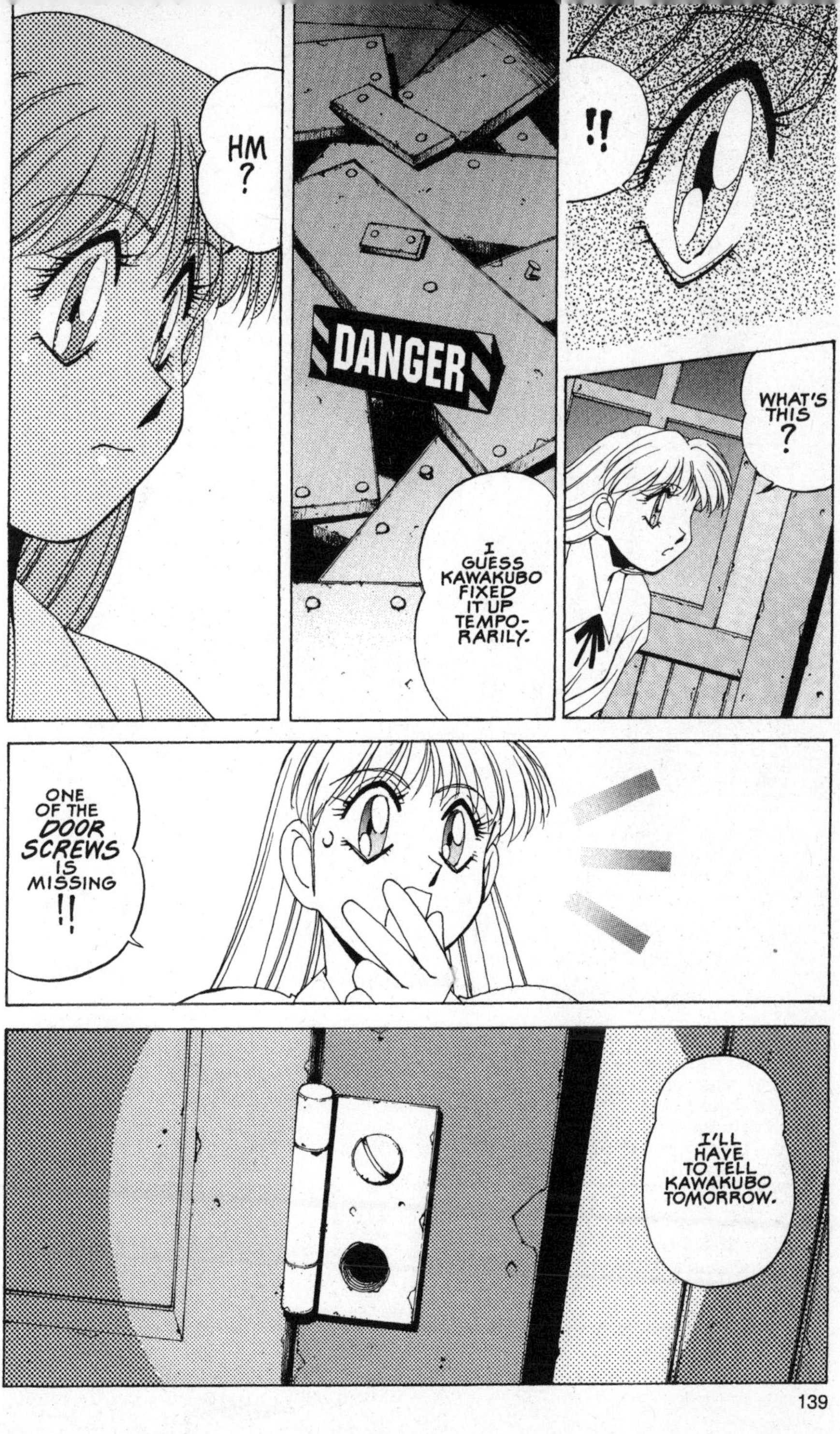
HM?
DANGER
I GUESS KAWAKUBO FIXED IT UP TEMPO-RARILY.
!!
WHAT'S THIS?
ONE OF THE DOOR SCREWS IS MISSING!!
I'LL HAVE TO TELL KAWAKUBO TOMORROW.

STEAM DETECTIVES PRESS

STEAM CITY'S LIFELINE

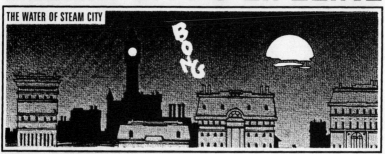

THE WATER OF STEAM CITY

BONG

Steam City is a city of water. The canal running vertically is absolutely essential for transporting goods, and the entire population depends on the underground waterworks for its water supply.
The underground water system has expanded with the increase in water usage (supplying coolant for every household's steam system is nothing to sneeze at). And gradually, the underground water system has become a giant labyrinth.
Recently, there has been a decrease in rainfall due to shifting climatic conditions, and that has given rise to a political movement advocating recycled water. The government's department of science has been researching a recycling system over the past five years, but has met little concrete success. Some are calling this project a waste of taxpayers' money. Unless there are breakthroughs and quick implementation this year there will be mounting opposition against the project. We are entering an era where we must call into question our use of water as a natural resource.
Lately, there has been a lot of excitement building about the use of natural gases based on fossil fuels as an alternative to steam power. However, this system is still being tested, and it will be quite a while before the entirety of Steam City can depend on gas.

!!
GA-CHANG
GA-CHANG
GA-CHANG
SEWER CONSTRUCTION
SAFETY FIRST
STEAM CITY WATERWORKS

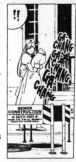

THESE SIGNS CAN BE FOUND ALL OVER STEAM CITY

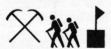

— INFORMATION —

SEWER CONSTRUCTION

3:00 a.m. - 5:00 p.m. October 4 (FRI)
LAYER DISTRICTS B6 - B8
Steam City Waterworks

Volume 013 • Issued by Steam Press Co.,Ltd.

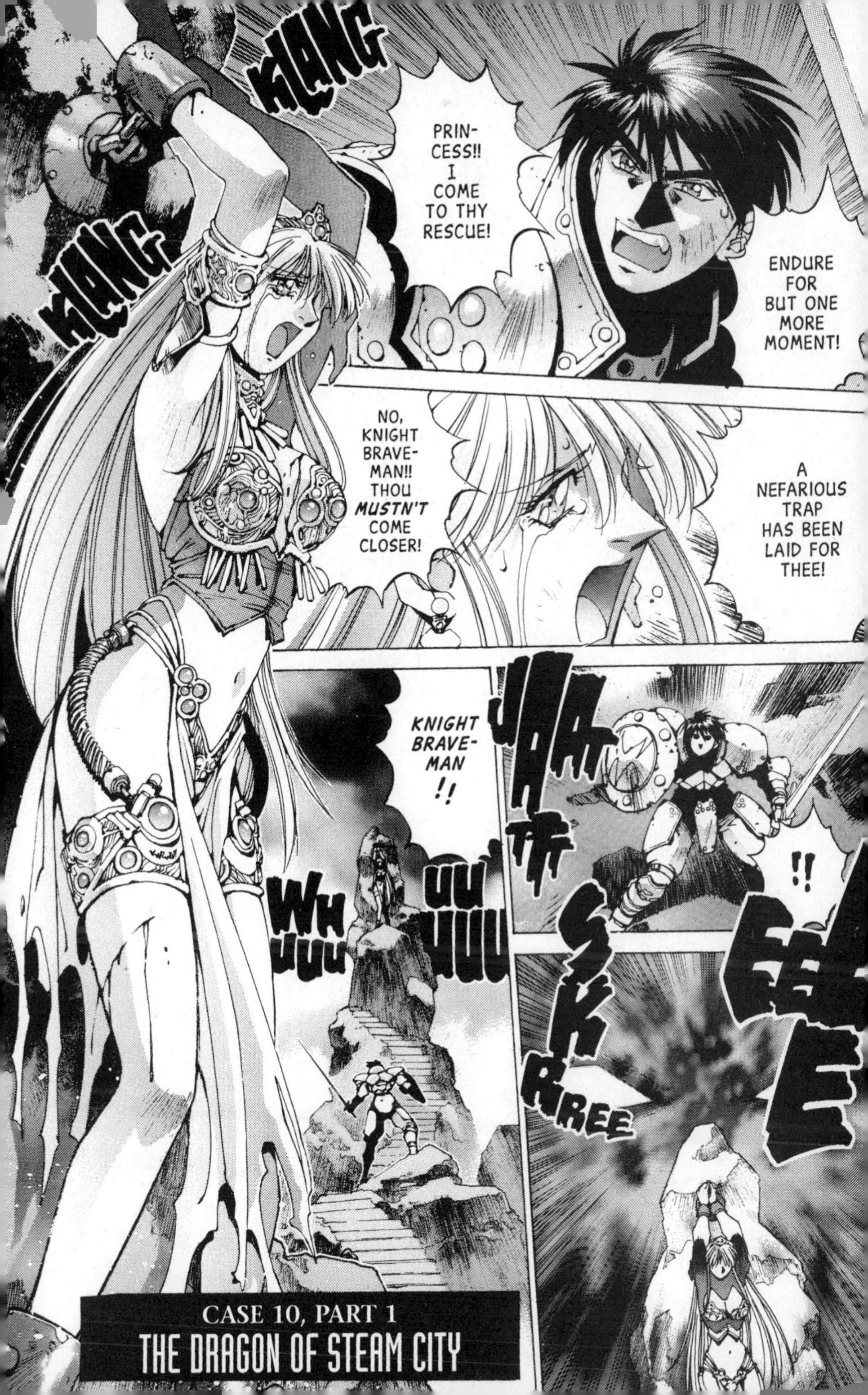
KLANG
KLANG
PRINCESS!! I COME TO THY RESCUE!
ENDURE FOR BUT ONE MORE MOMENT!
NO, KNIGHT BRAVEMAN!! THOU *MUSTN'T* COME CLOSER!
A NEFARIOUS TRAP HAS BEEN LAID FOR THEE!
KNIGHT BRAVEMAN !!
WHUUU
UUUUUU
!!
SKRREE
CASE 10, PART 1
THE DRAGON OF STEAM CITY

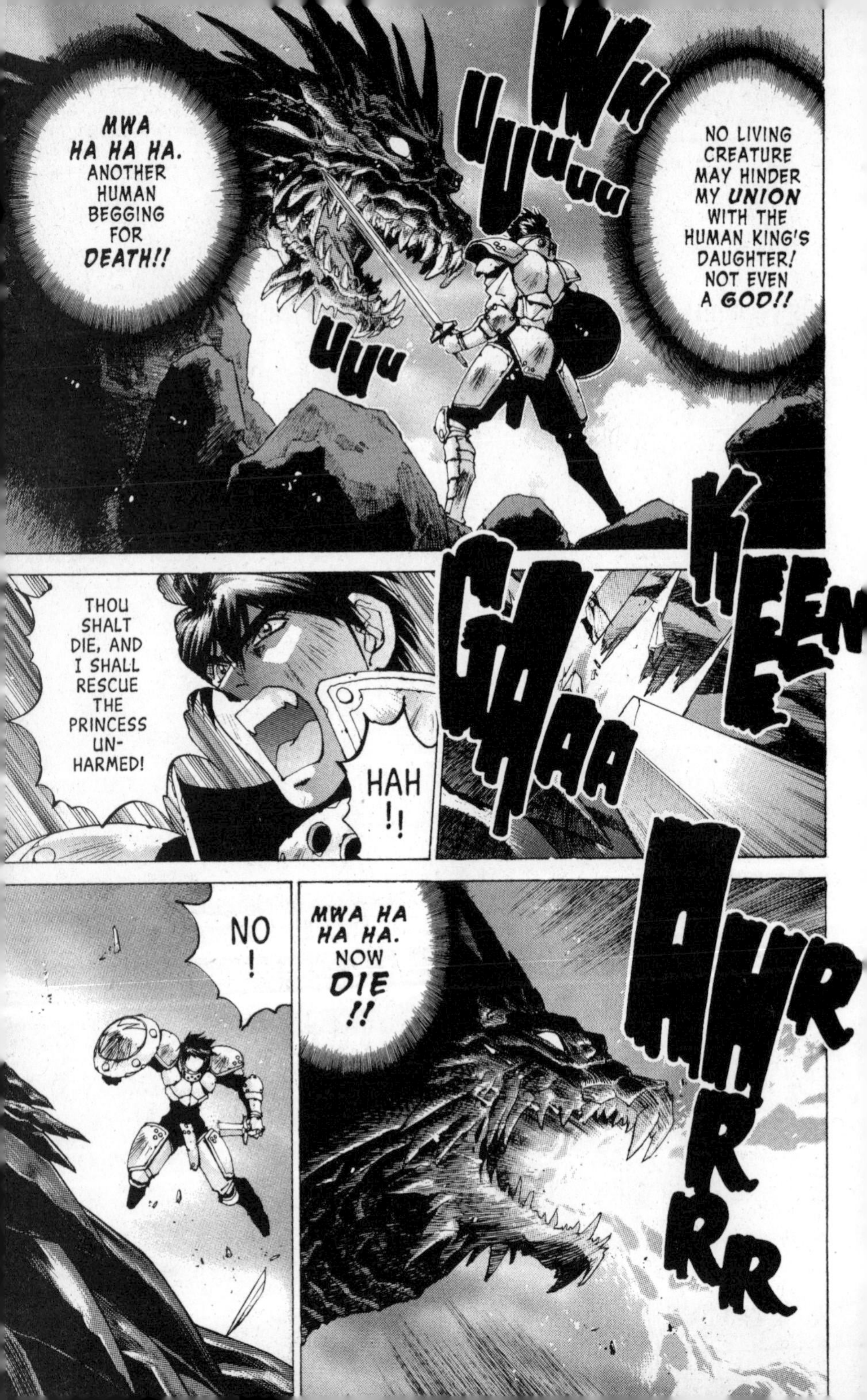
MWA HA HA HA. ANOTHER HUMAN BEGGING FOR DEATH!!
WHUUUUU
NO LIVING CREATURE MAY HINDER MY UNION WITH THE HUMAN KING'S DAUGHTER! NOT EVEN A GOD!!
UUU
THOU SHALT DIE, AND I SHALL RESCUE THE PRINCESS UN-HARMED!
HAH!!
GHAAA
KEEEN
NO!
MWA HA HA HA. NOW DIE!!
AHHRRRR

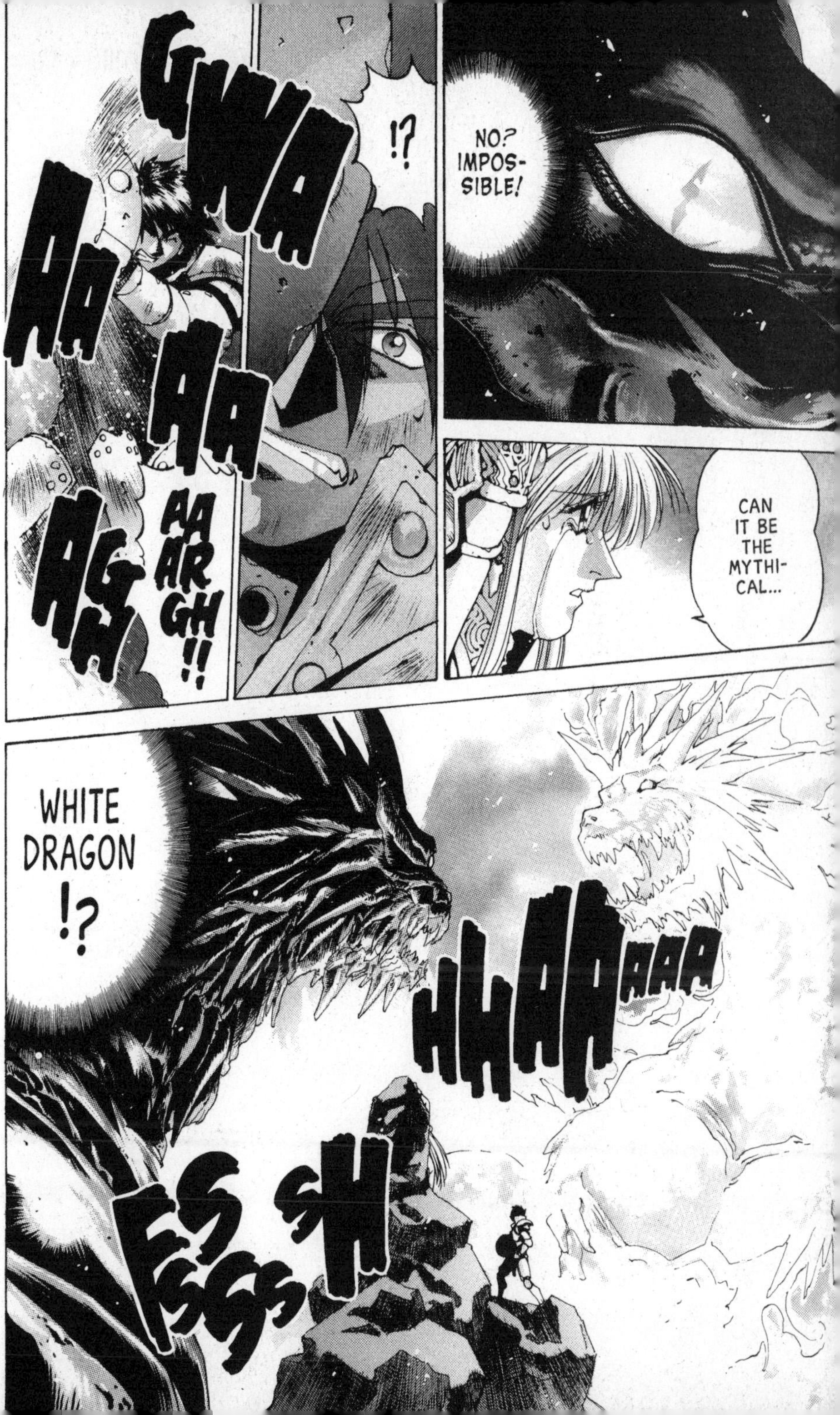
GWAAAAAAAGH
AAARGH!!
!?
NO? IMPOS-SIBLE!
CAN IT BE THE MYTHI-CAL...
WHITE DRAGON !?
HHHAAAaaa
FESSSSSH

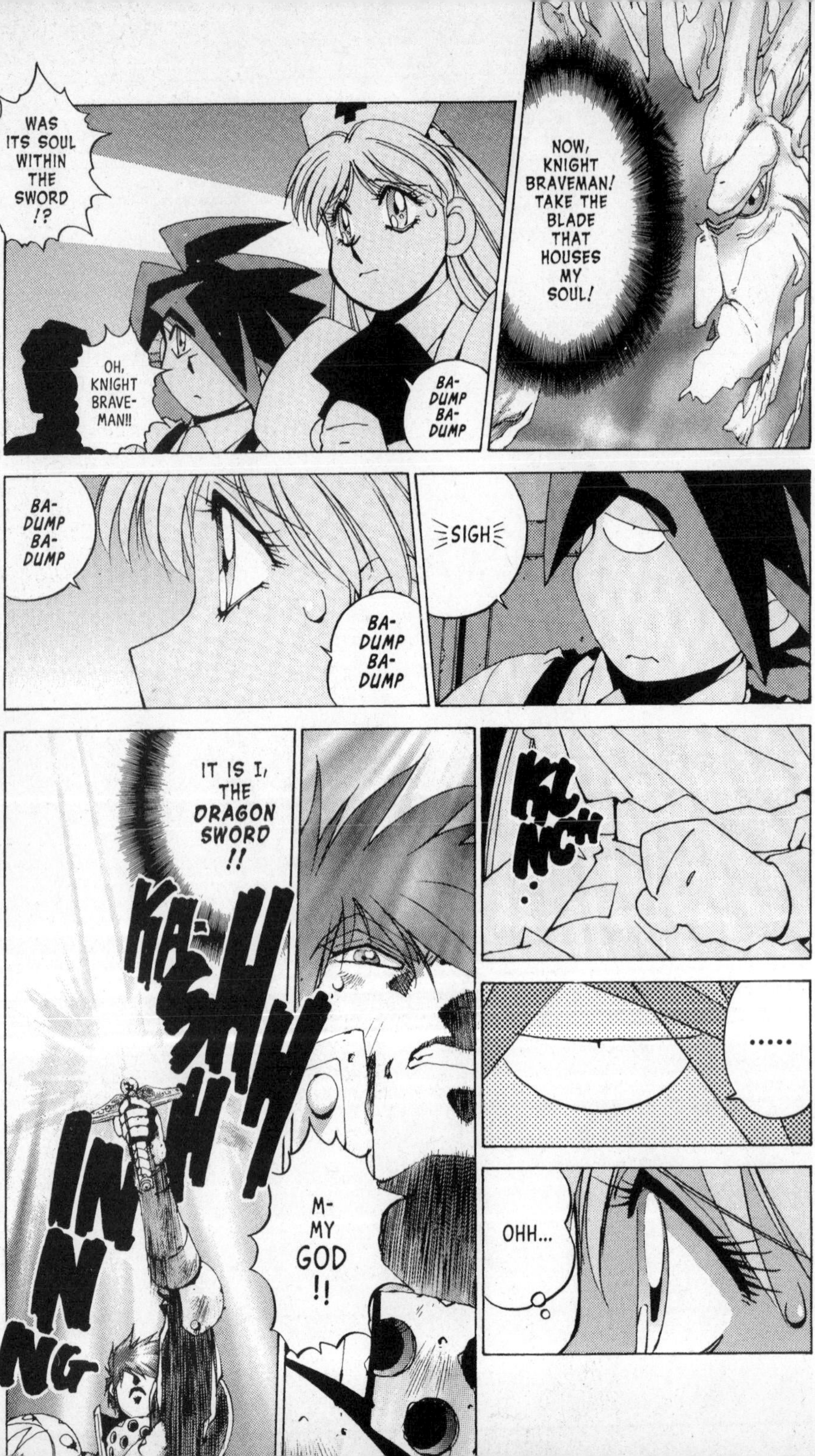
WAS ITS SOUL WITHIN THE SWORD !?
OH, KNIGHT BRAVE-MAN!!
BA-DUMP BA-DUMP
NOW, KNIGHT BRAVEMAN! TAKE THE BLADE THAT HOUSES MY SOUL!
BA-DUMP BA-DUMP
BA-DUMP BA-DUMP
SIGH
IT IS I, THE DRAGON SWORD !!
M-MY GOD !!
.....
OHH...

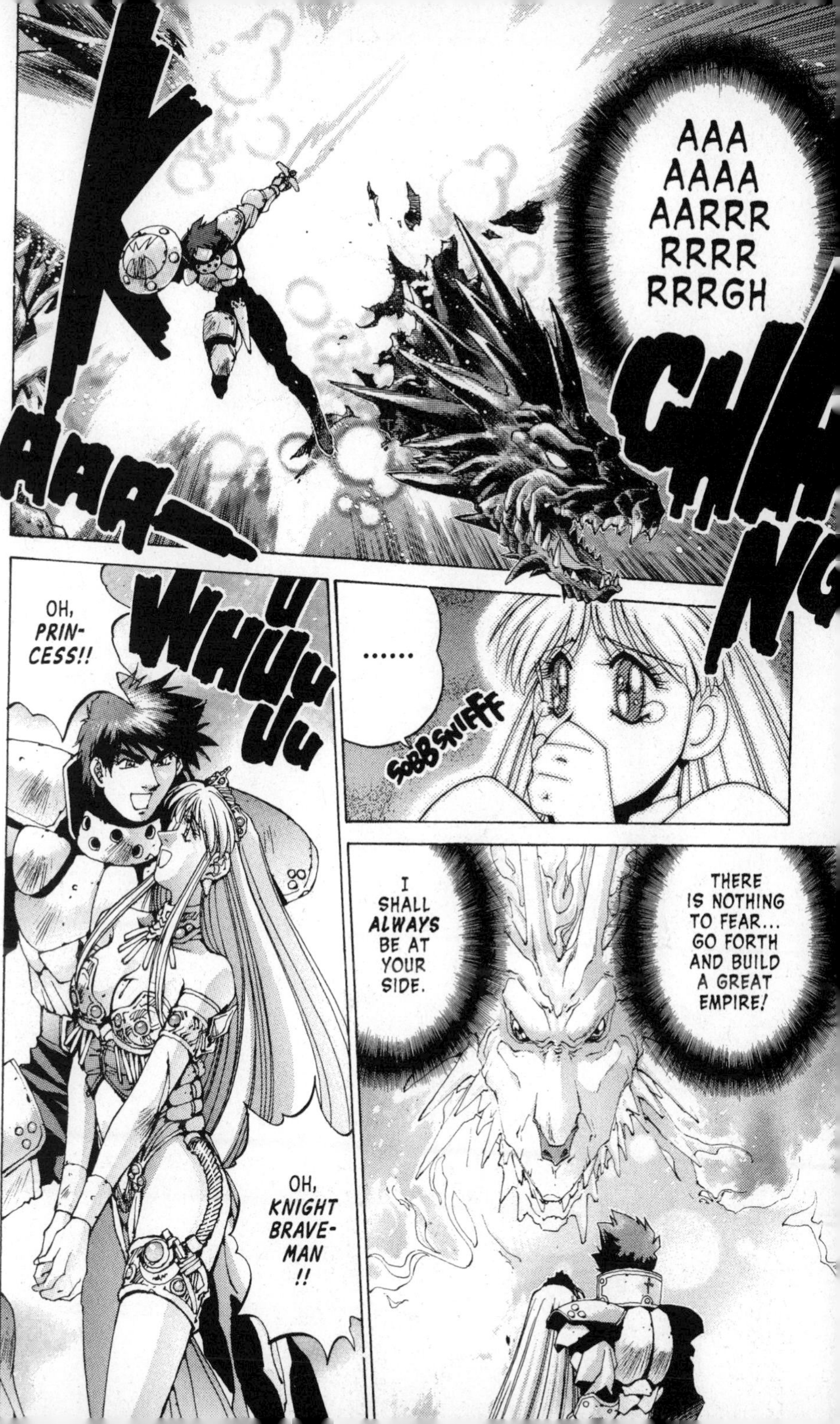

KK
AAA
AAA
AAAA
AARRR
RRRR
RRRGH
CHIING
OH, PRIN-CESS!!
WHUUU UU
......
SOBB SNIFFF
OH, KNIGHT BRAVE-MAN !!
I SHALL ALWAYS BE AT YOUR SIDE.
THERE IS NOTHING TO FEAR... GO FORTH AND BUILD A GREAT EMPIRE!

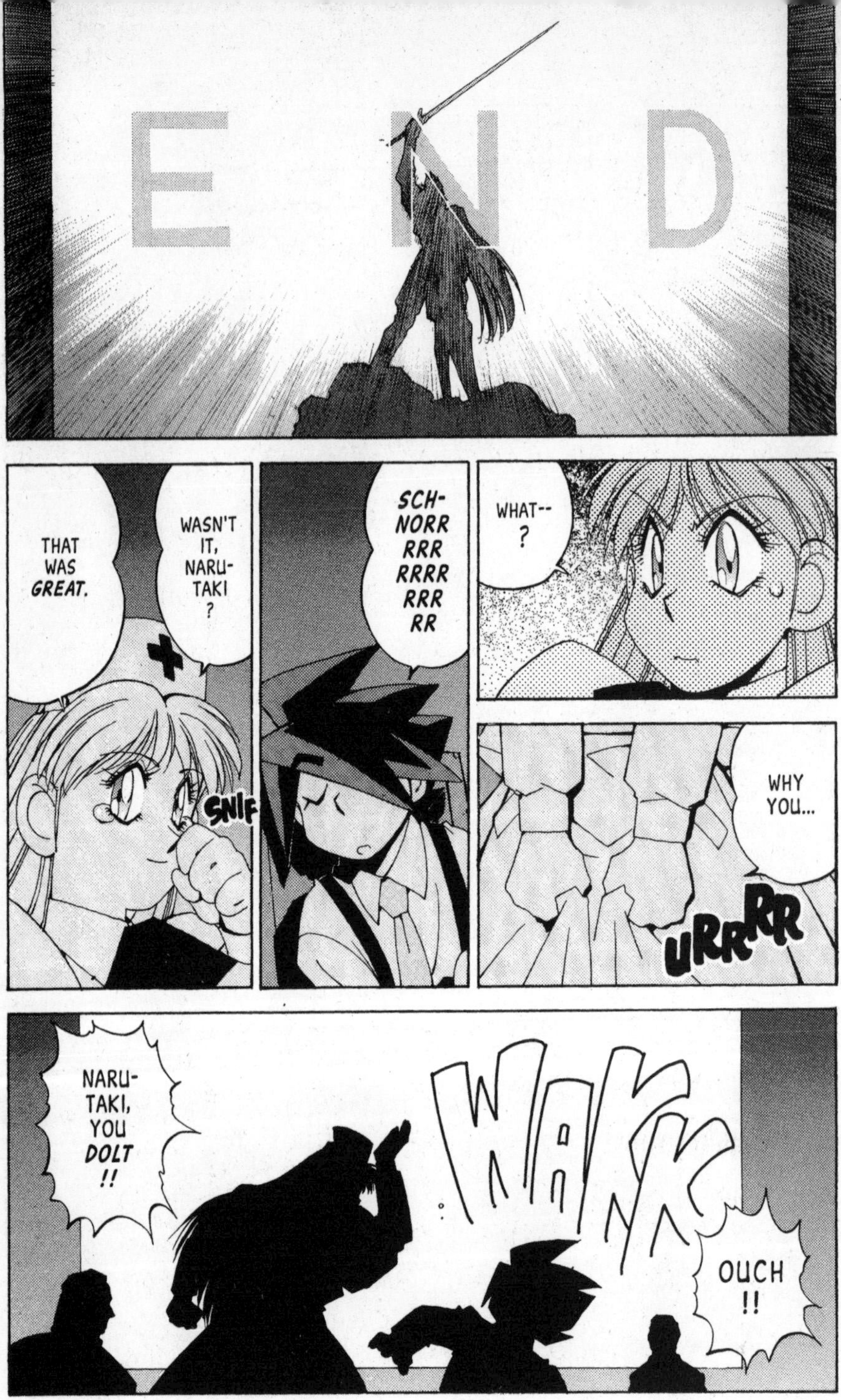
END
THAT WAS GREAT.
WASN'T IT, NARUTAKI?
SNIF
SCH-NORRRRRRRRRRRRRR
WHAT--?
WHY YOU...
URRRRR
NARUTAKI, YOU DOLT!!
WHAKK
OUCH!!

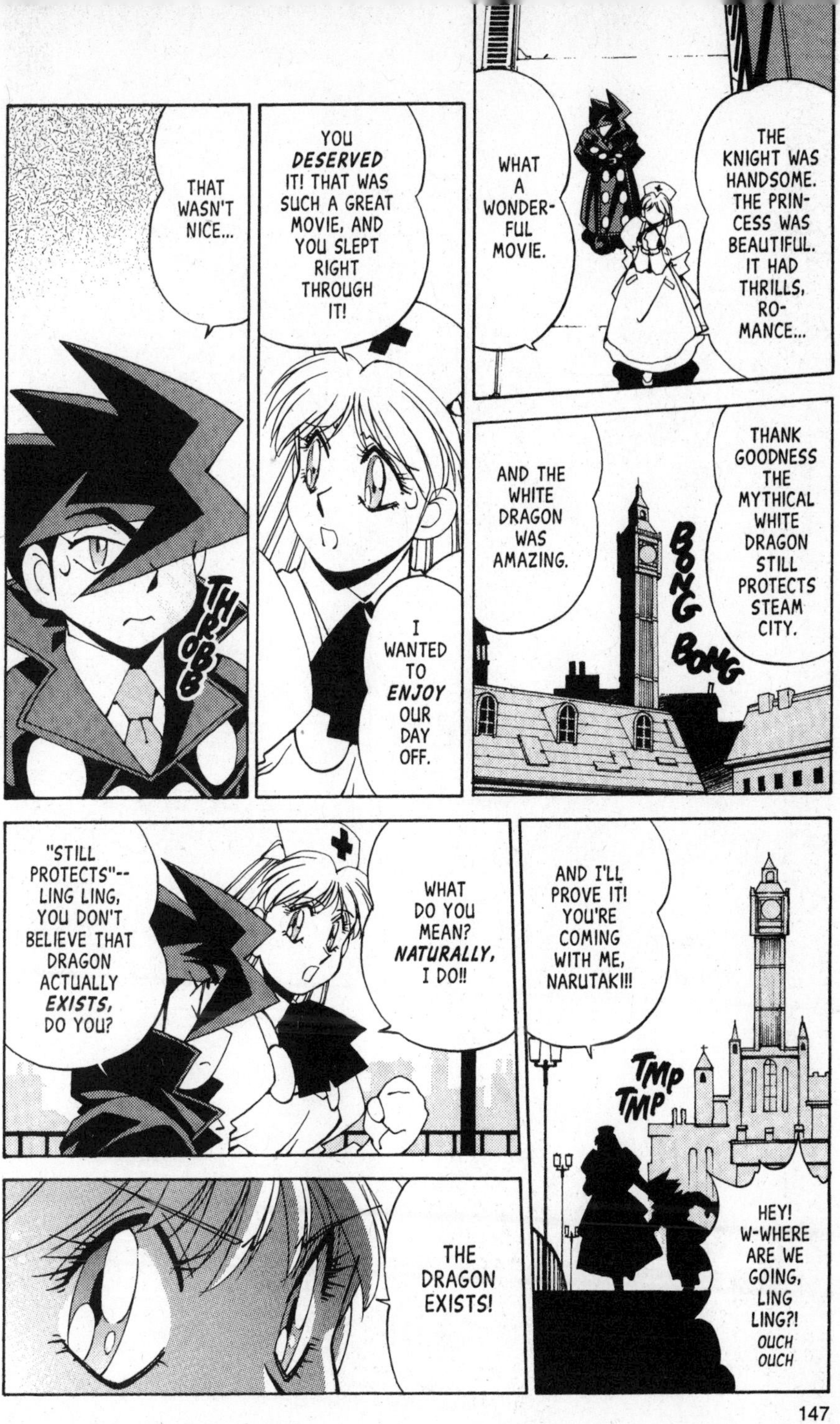
THAT WASN'T NICE...
THROBB
YOU *DESERVED* IT! THAT WAS SUCH A GREAT MOVIE, AND YOU SLEPT RIGHT THROUGH IT!
I WANTED TO *ENJOY* OUR DAY OFF.
WHAT A WONDERFUL MOVIE.
THE KNIGHT WAS HANDSOME. THE PRINCESS WAS BEAUTIFUL. IT HAD THRILLS, ROMANCE...
AND THE WHITE DRAGON WAS AMAZING.
BONG
BONG
THANK GOODNESS THE MYTHICAL WHITE DRAGON STILL PROTECTS STEAM CITY.
"STILL PROTECTS"--LING LING, YOU DON'T BELIEVE THAT DRAGON ACTUALLY *EXISTS,* DO YOU?
WHAT DO YOU MEAN? *NATURALLY,* I DO!!
THE DRAGON EXISTS!
AND I'LL PROVE IT! YOU'RE COMING WITH ME, NARUTAKI!!
TMP TMP
HEY! W-WHERE ARE WE GOING, LING LING?!
OUCH OUCH

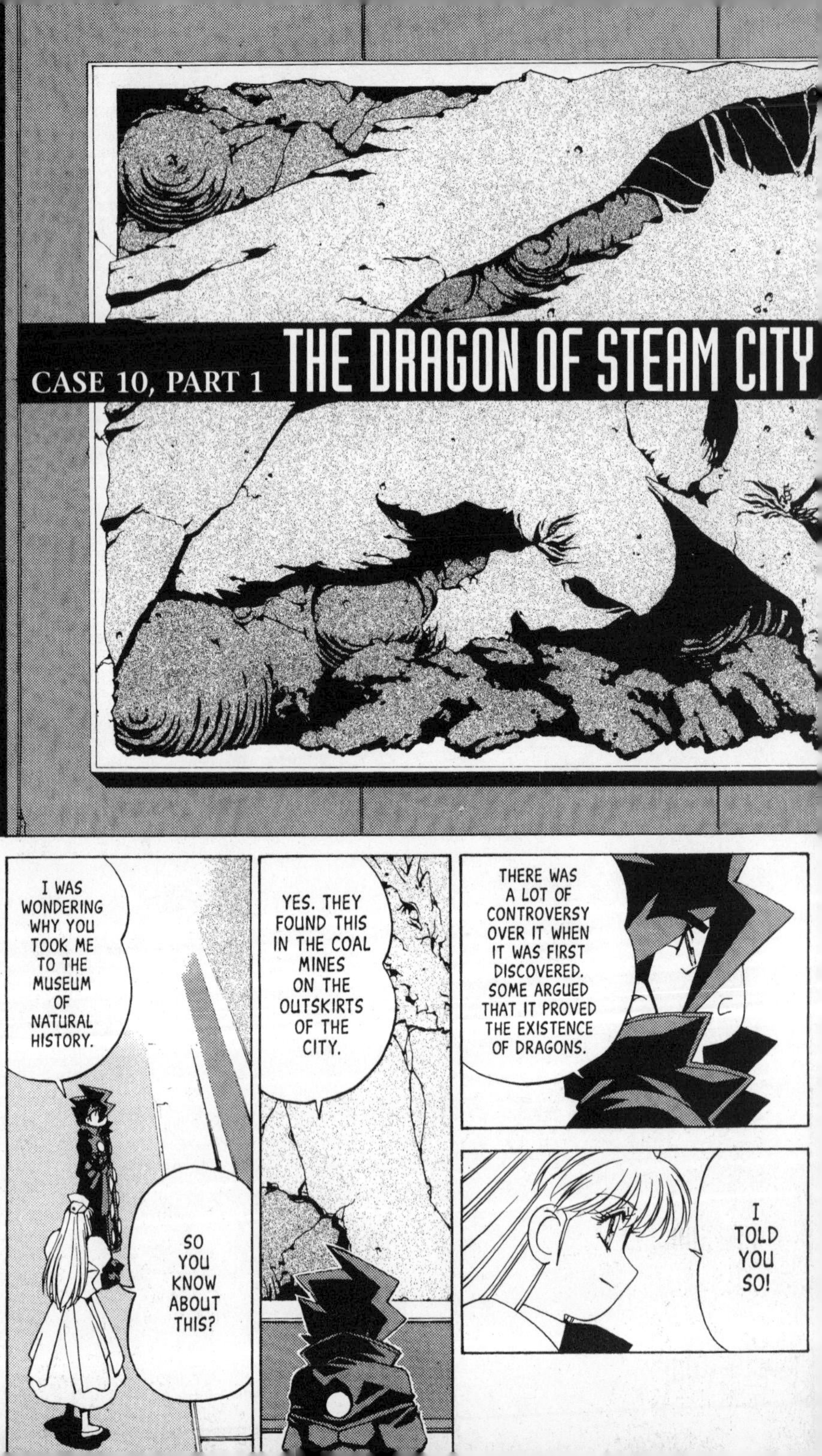
CASE 10, PART 1
THE DRAGON OF STEAM CITY
I WAS WONDERING WHY YOU TOOK ME TO THE MUSEUM OF NATURAL HISTORY.
SO YOU KNOW ABOUT THIS?
YES. THEY FOUND THIS IN THE COAL MINES ON THE OUTSKIRTS OF THE CITY.
THERE WAS A LOT OF CONTROVERSY OVER IT WHEN IT WAS FIRST DISCOVERED. SOME ARGUED THAT IT PROVED THE EXISTENCE OF DRAGONS.
I TOLD YOU SO!

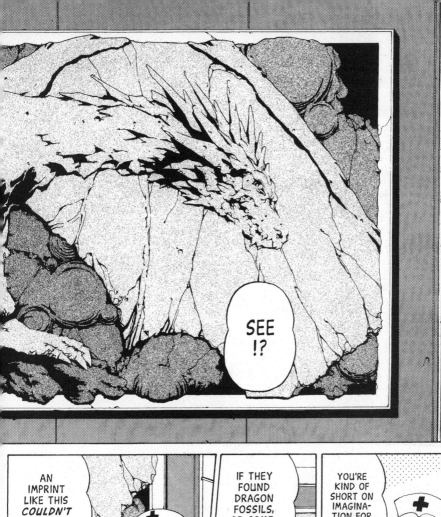

SEE !?

AN IMPRINT LIKE THIS *COULDN'T* BE FAKED.

IF THEY FOUND DRAGON FOSSILS, OR SOMETHING...

BUT A RELIEF DOESN'T PROVE ANYTHING.

YOU'RE KIND OF SHORT ON IMAGINATION FOR A KID, GEEZ.

H-H-HEY, C'MON.

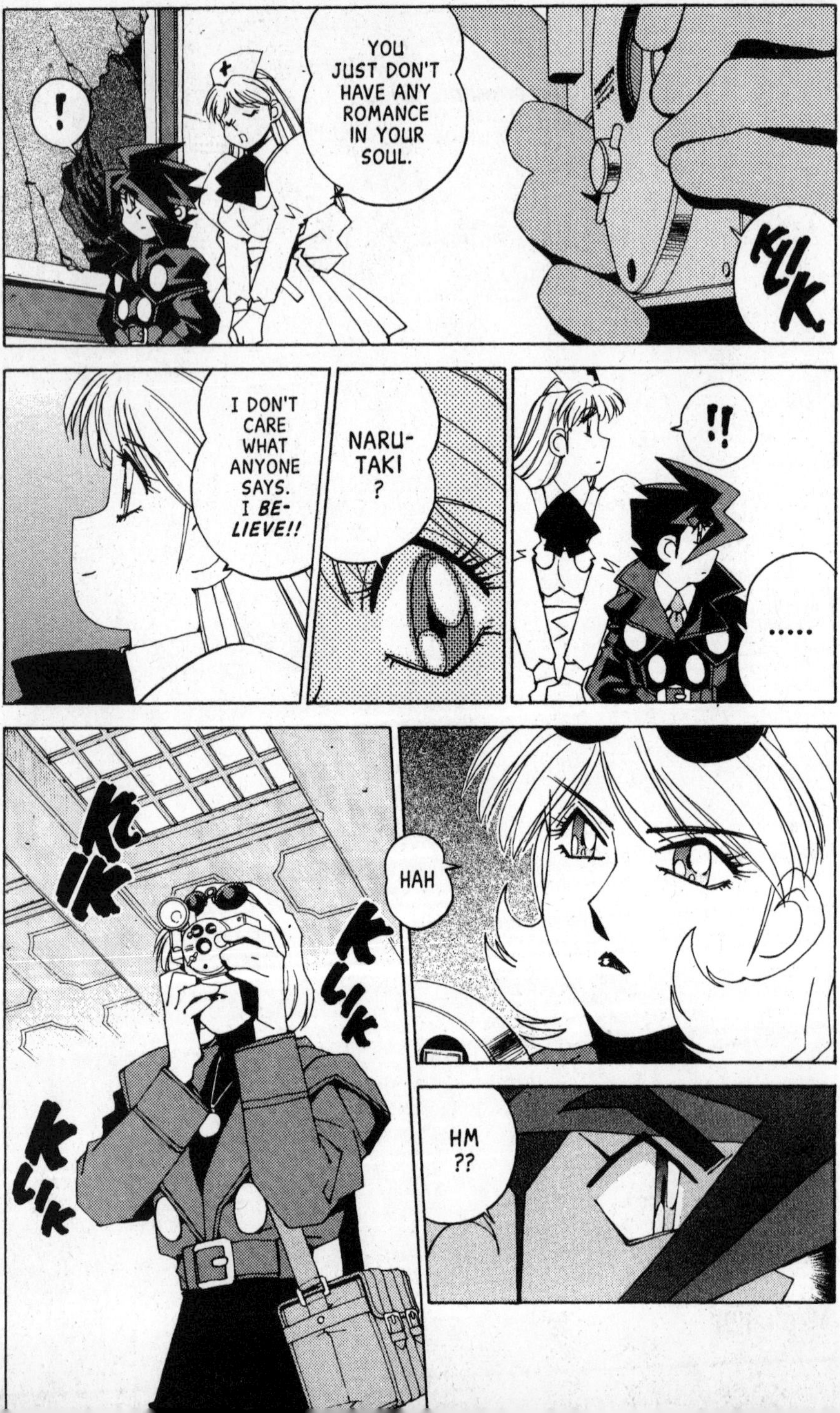
!
YOU JUST DON'T HAVE ANY ROMANCE IN YOUR SOUL.
KLIK
I DON'T CARE WHAT ANYONE SAYS. I *BE-LIEVE!!*
NARU-TAKI ?
!!
.....
KLIK
KLIK
KLIK
HAH
HM ??

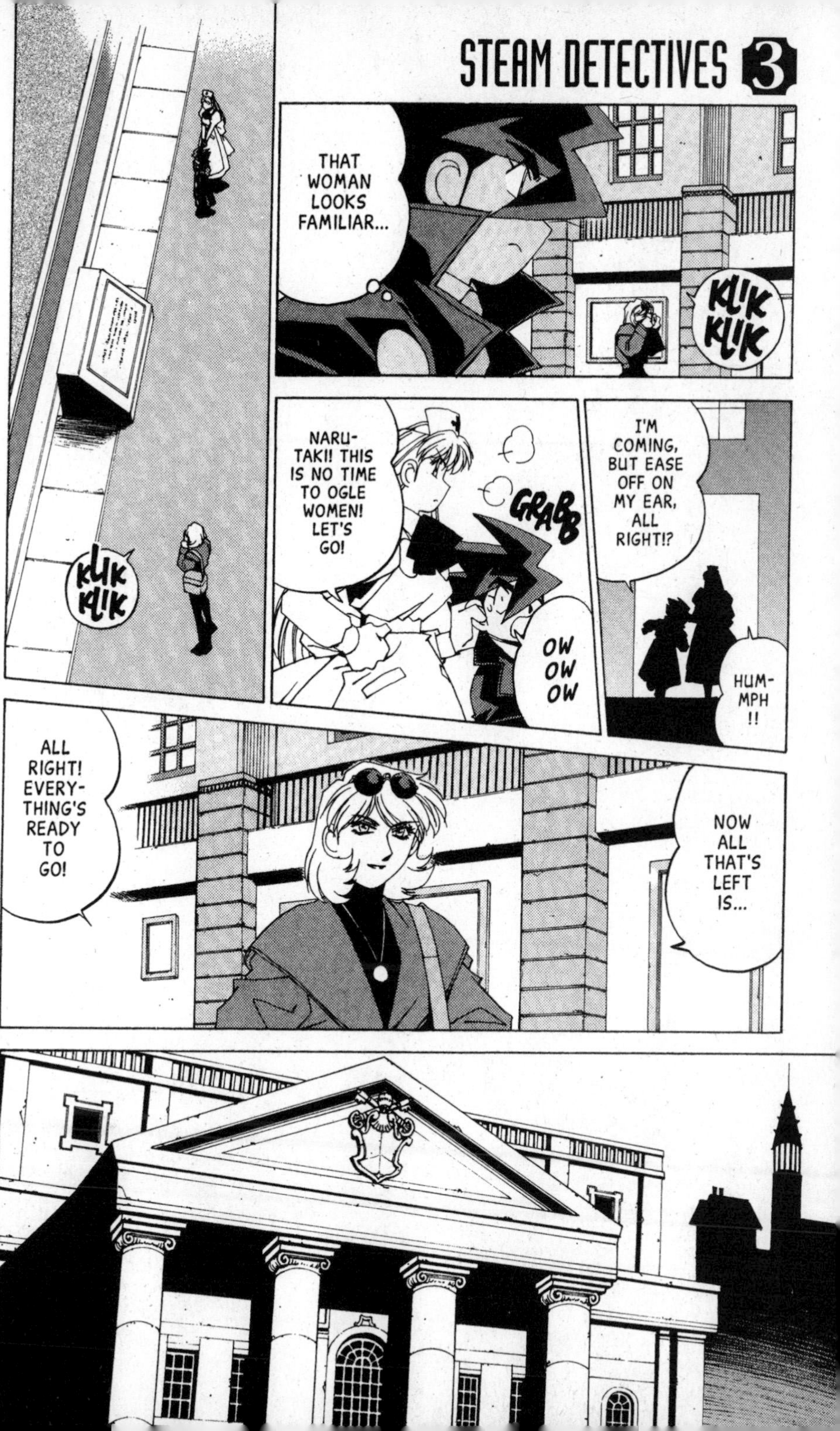
KLIK KLIK
THAT WOMAN LOOKS FAMILIAR...
KLIK KLIK
NARU-TAKI! THIS IS NO TIME TO OGLE WOMEN! LET'S GO!
GRABB
OW OW OW
I'M COMING, BUT EASE OFF ON MY EAR, ALL RIGHT!?
HUM-MPH !!
ALL RIGHT! EVERY-THING'S READY TO GO!
NOW ALL THAT'S LEFT IS...

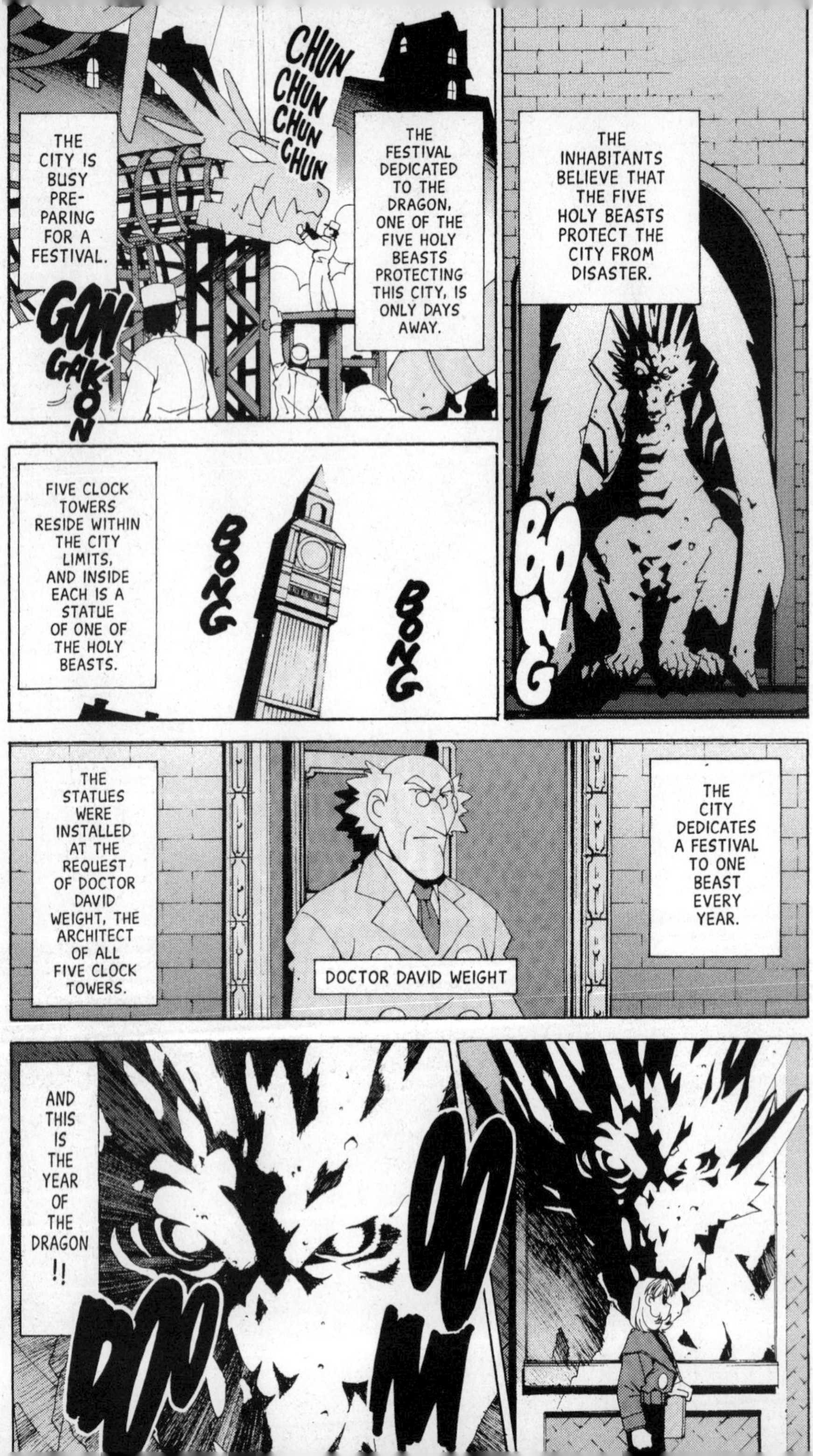
THE CITY IS BUSY PRE-PARING FOR A FESTIVAL.
CHUN CHUN CHUN CHUN
THE FESTIVAL DEDICATED TO THE DRAGON, ONE OF THE FIVE HOLY BEASTS PROTECTING THIS CITY, IS ONLY DAYS AWAY.
GON
GAKON
FIVE CLOCK TOWERS RESIDE WITHIN THE CITY LIMITS, AND INSIDE EACH IS A STATUE OF ONE OF THE HOLY BEASTS.
BONG
BONG
THE INHABITANTS BELIEVE THAT THE FIVE HOLY BEASTS PROTECT THE CITY FROM DISASTER.
BONG
THE STATUES WERE INSTALLED AT THE REQUEST OF DOCTOR DAVID WEIGHT, THE ARCHITECT OF ALL FIVE CLOCK TOWERS.
DOCTOR DAVID WEIGHT
THE CITY DEDICATES A FESTIVAL TO ONE BEAST EVERY YEAR.
AND THIS IS THE YEAR OF THE DRAGON!!
DOOOOM

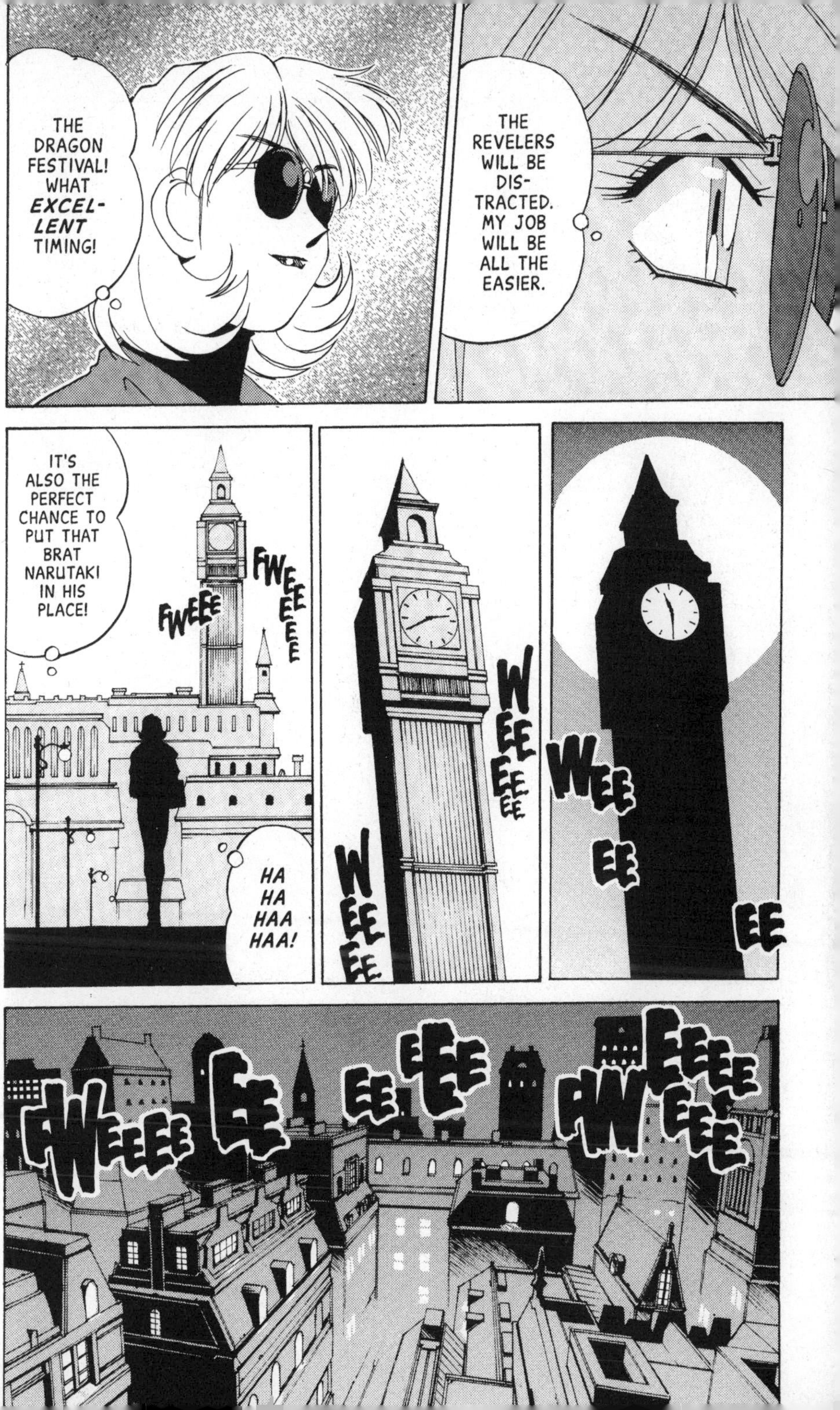
THE DRAGON FESTIVAL! WHAT *EXCEL-LENT* TIMING!
THE REVELERS WILL BE DIS-TRACTED. MY JOB WILL BE ALL THE EASIER.
IT'S ALSO THE PERFECT CHANCE TO PUT THAT BRAT NARUTAKI IN HIS PLACE!
FWEEE
FWEEEEEE
HA HA HAA HAA!
WEEEE
WEEEEEE
WEE
EE
EE
FWEEEE EE
EE EEE
FWEEEEEEEEE

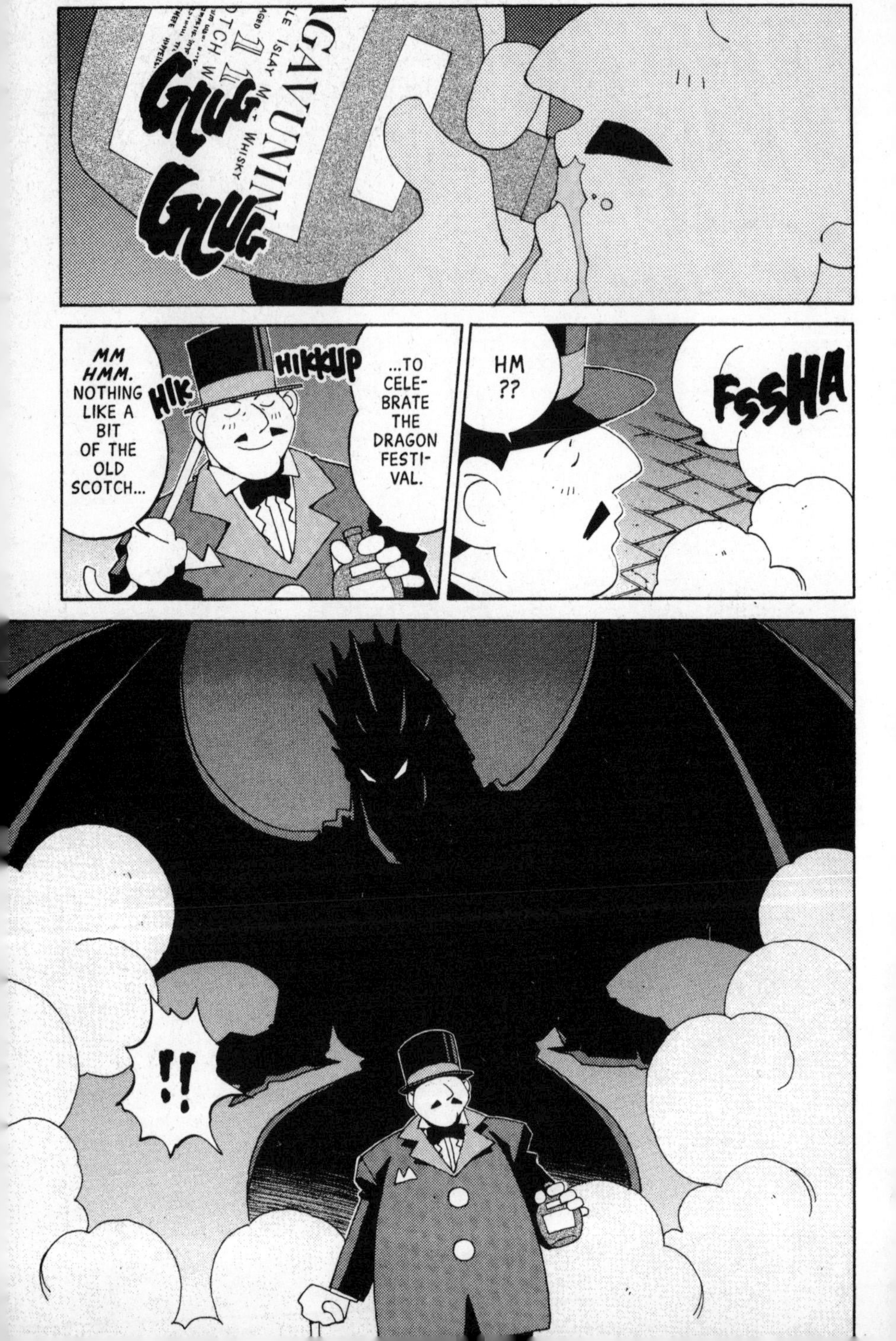
GAVUNIN
ISLAY
WHISKY
GLUG
GLUG
MM HMM. NOTHING LIKE A BIT OF THE OLD SCOTCH...
HIK
HIKKUP
...TO CELE-BRATE THE DRAGON FESTI-VAL.
HM ??
FSSHA
!!

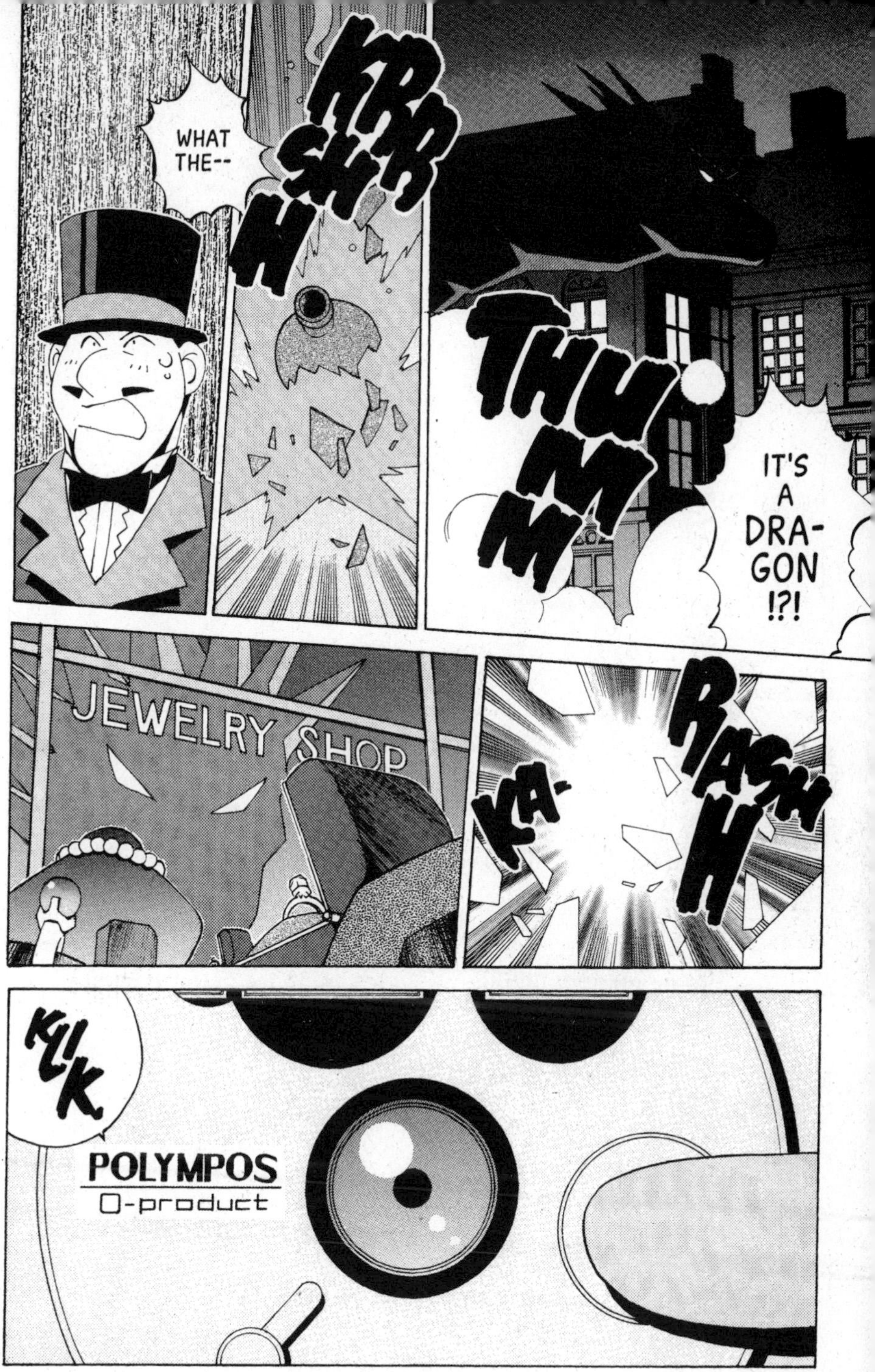
WHAT THE--
KRRSHH
THUMMM
IT'S A DRA-GON!?!
JEWELRY SHOP
KA-RASHH
KLIK
POLYMPOS
O-product

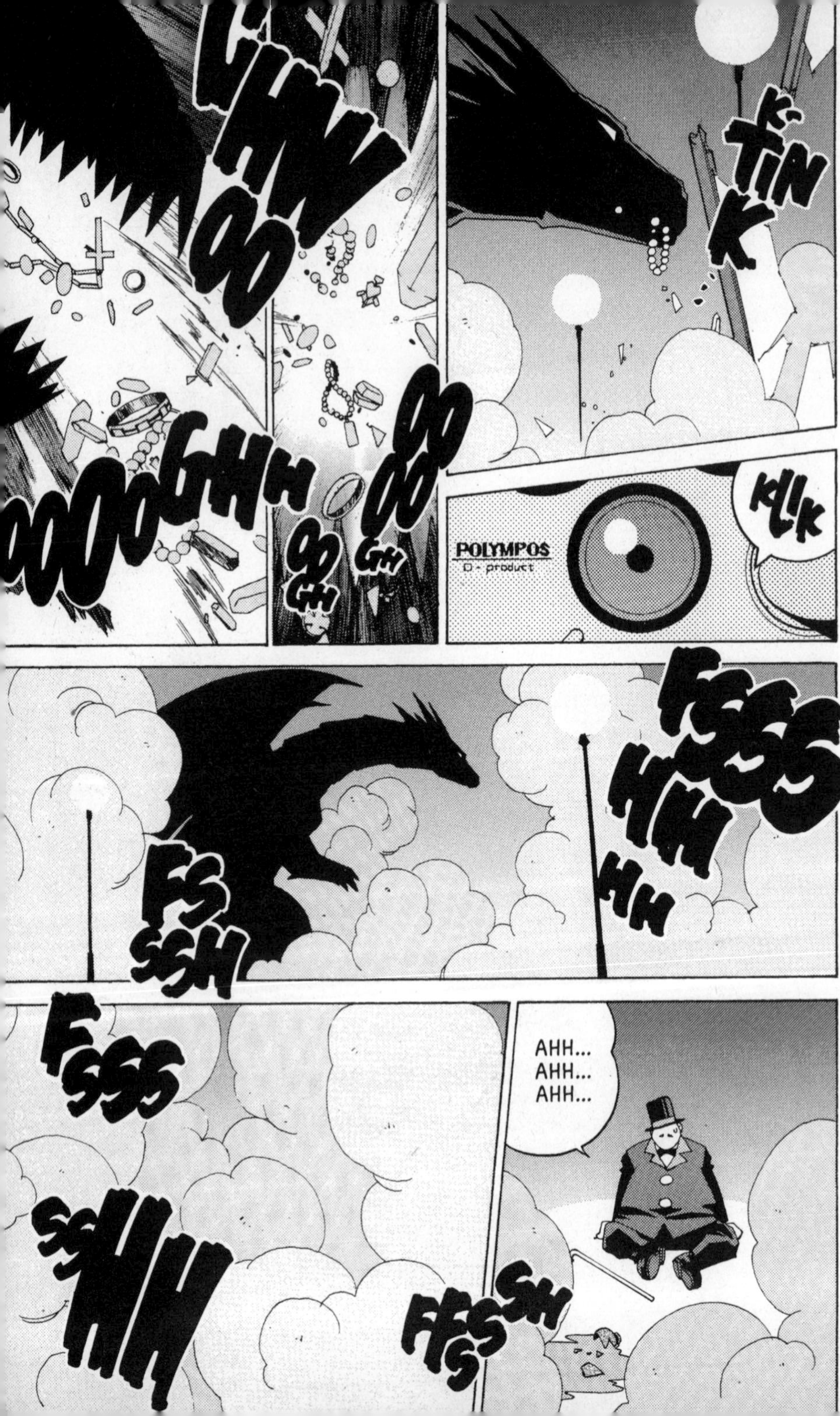
GWWOOOOOGHH
GGGGH
K-TINK
POLYMPOS
D - product
KLIK
FSSSHHH
FSSSH
FSSSS
SSHHH
FFSSSH
AHH...
AHH...
AHH...

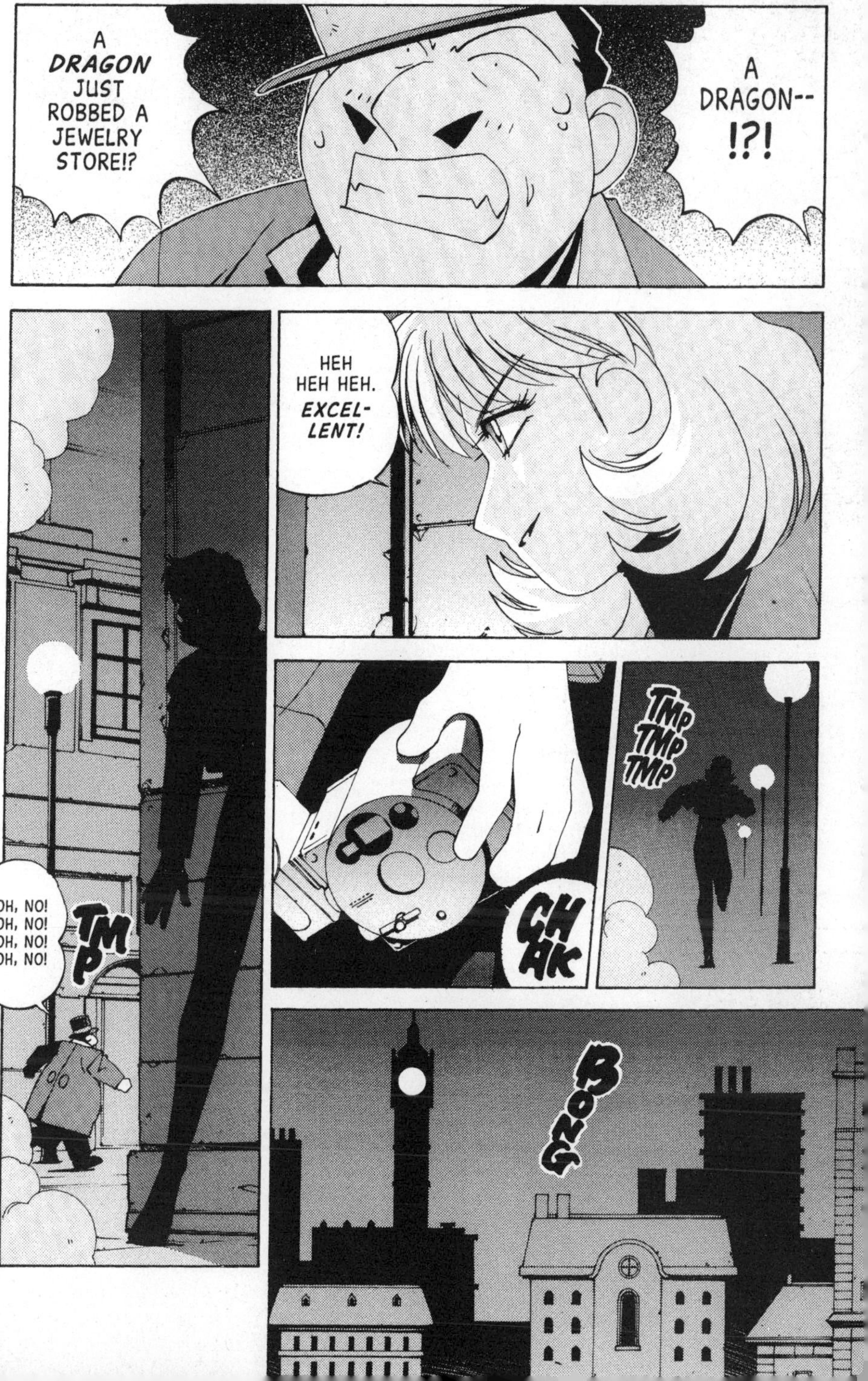
A *DRAGON* JUST ROBBED A JEWELRY STORE!?
A DRAGON-- !?!
OH, NO! OH, NO! OH, NO! OH, NO!
TMP
HEH HEH HEH. *EXCEL-LENT!*
CHAK
TMP TMP TMP
BONG

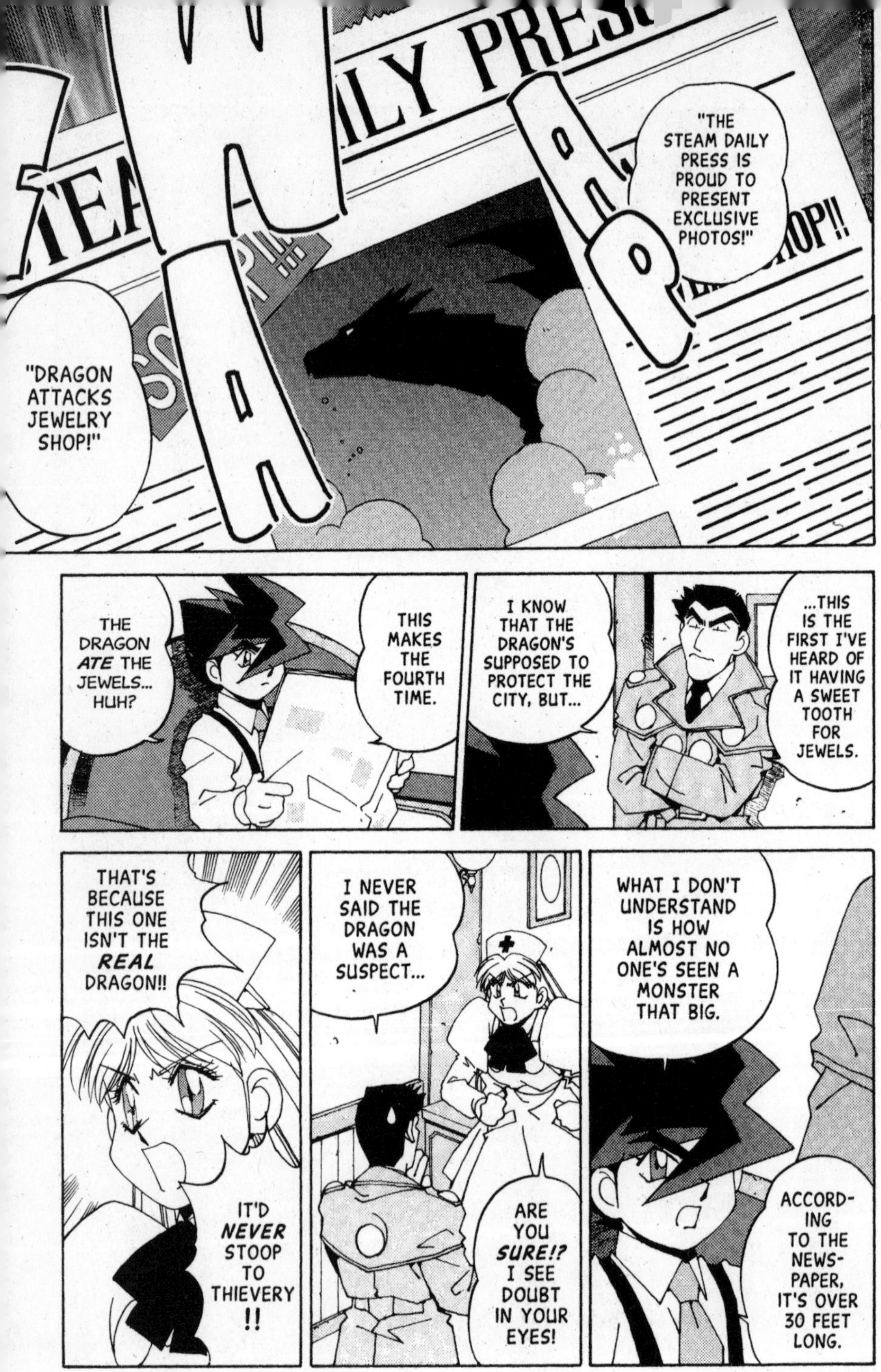
"DRAGON ATTACKS JEWELRY SHOP!"
"THE STEAM DAILY PRESS IS PROUD TO PRESENT EXCLUSIVE PHOTOS!"
THE DRAGON *ATE* THE JEWELS... HUH?
THIS MAKES THE FOURTH TIME.
I KNOW THAT THE DRAGON'S SUPPOSED TO PROTECT THE CITY, BUT...
...THIS IS THE FIRST I'VE HEARD OF IT HAVING A SWEET TOOTH FOR JEWELS.
THAT'S BECAUSE THIS ONE ISN'T THE *REAL* DRAGON!!
IT'D *NEVER* STOOP TO THIEVERY!!
I NEVER SAID THE DRAGON WAS A SUSPECT...
ARE YOU *SURE!?* I SEE DOUBT IN YOUR EYES!
WHAT I DON'T UNDERSTAND IS HOW ALMOST NO ONE'S SEEN A MONSTER THAT BIG.
ACCORDING TO THE NEWSPAPER, IT'S OVER 30 FEET LONG.

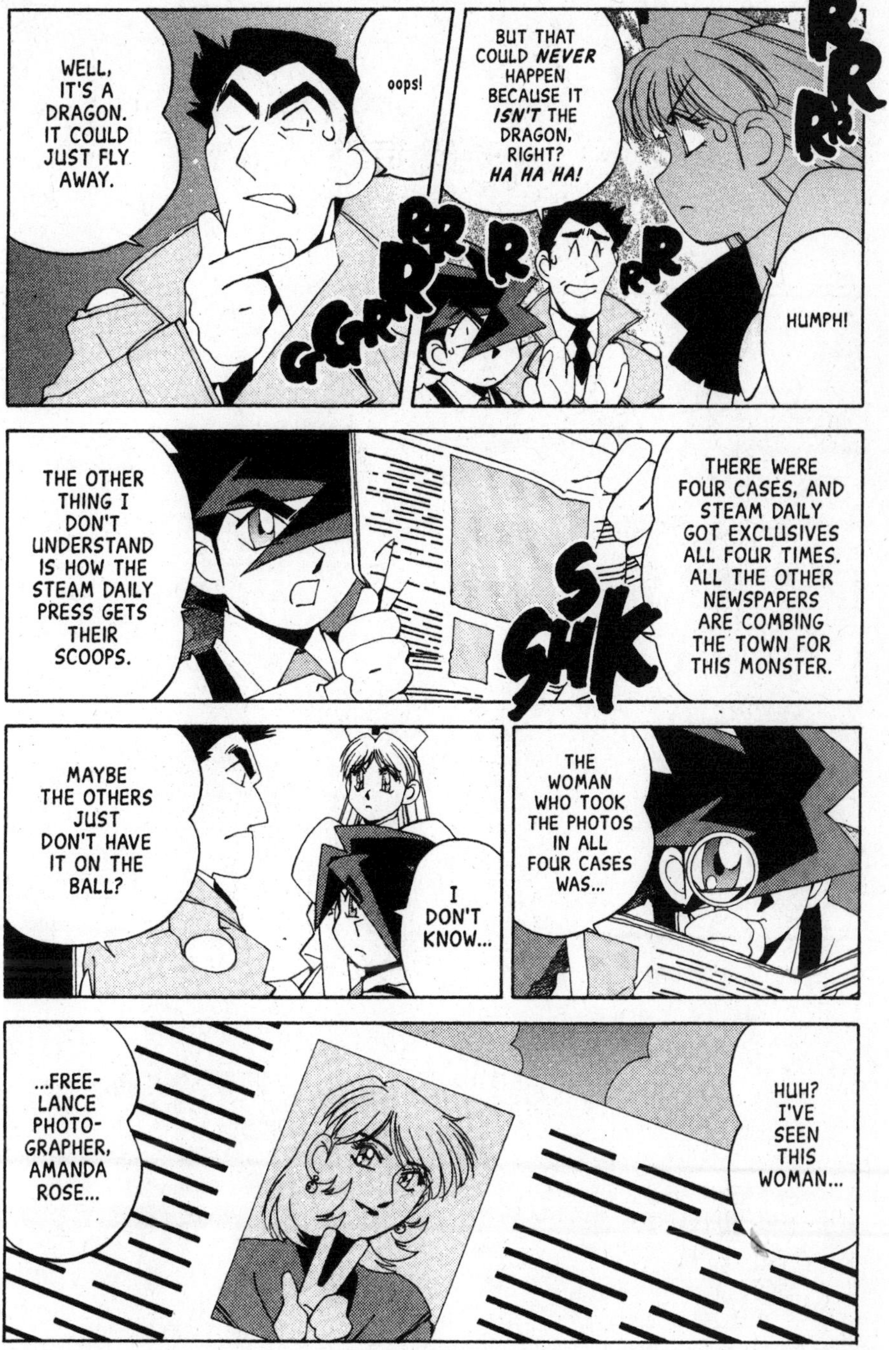
WELL, IT'S A DRAGON. IT COULD JUST FLY AWAY.
oops!
BUT THAT COULD *NEVER* HAPPEN BECAUSE IT *ISN'T* THE DRAGON, RIGHT? *HA HA HA!*
HUMPH!
THE OTHER THING I DON'T UNDERSTAND IS HOW THE STEAM DAILY PRESS GETS THEIR SCOOPS.
THERE WERE FOUR CASES, AND STEAM DAILY GOT EXCLUSIVES ALL FOUR TIMES. ALL THE OTHER NEWSPAPERS ARE COMBING THE TOWN FOR THIS MONSTER.
MAYBE THE OTHERS JUST DON'T HAVE IT ON THE BALL?
I DON'T KNOW...
THE WOMAN WHO TOOK THE PHOTOS IN ALL FOUR CASES WAS...
...FREE-LANCE PHOTO-GRAPHER, AMANDA ROSE...
HUH? I'VE SEEN THIS WOMAN...

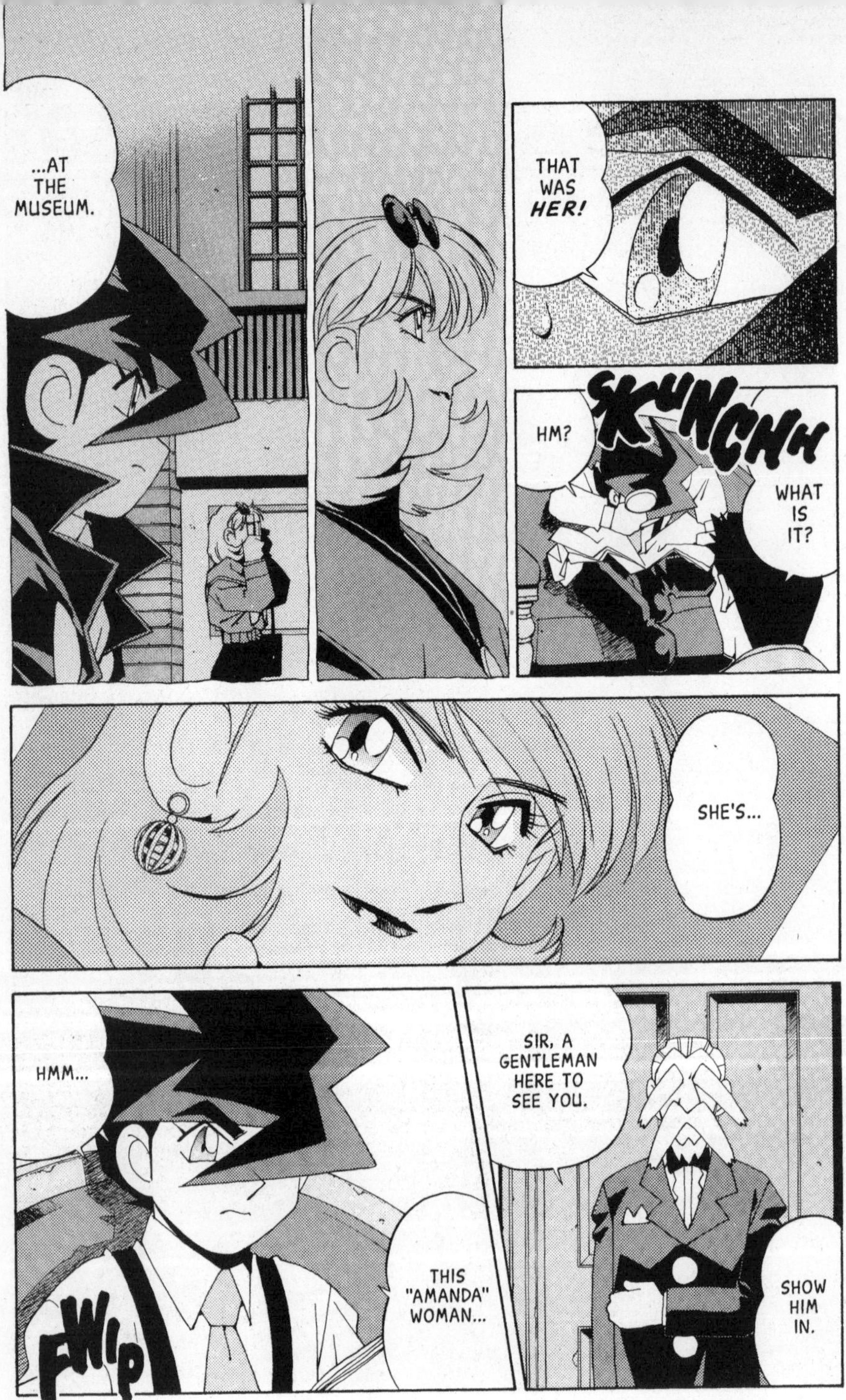
...AT THE MUSEUM.
THAT WAS *HER!*
SKUNCHH
HM?
WHAT IS IT?
SHE'S...
HMM...
FWIP
THIS "AMANDA" WOMAN...
SIR, A GENTLEMAN HERE TO SEE YOU.
SHOW HIM IN.

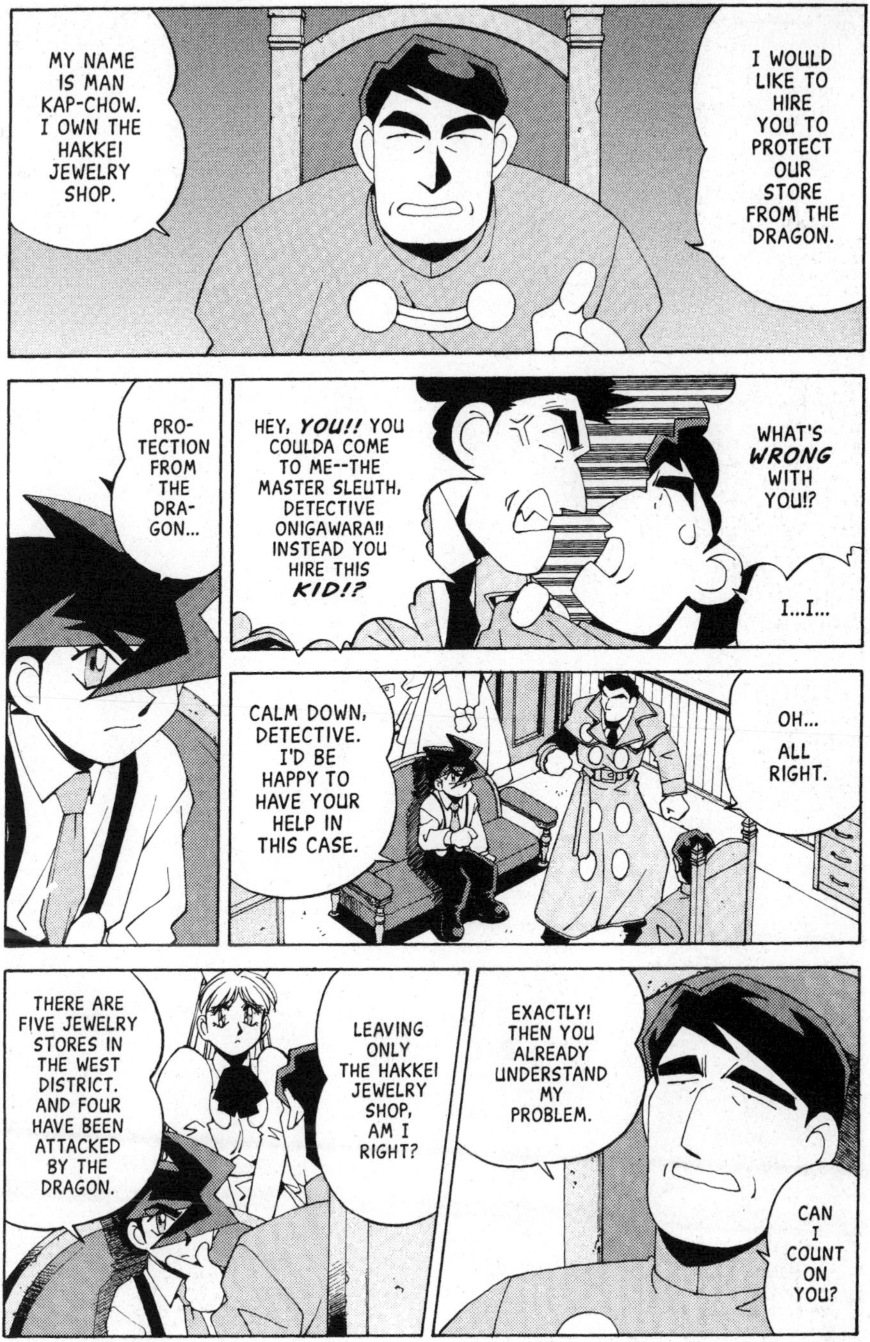
MY NAME IS MAN KAP-CHOW. I OWN THE HAKKEI JEWELRY SHOP.
I WOULD LIKE TO HIRE YOU TO PROTECT OUR STORE FROM THE DRAGON.
PRO-TECTION FROM THE DRA-GON...
HEY, *YOU!!* YOU COULDA COME TO ME--THE MASTER SLEUTH, DETECTIVE ONIGAWARA!! INSTEAD YOU HIRE THIS *KID!?*
WHAT'S *WRONG* WITH YOU!?
I...I...
CALM DOWN, DETECTIVE. I'D BE HAPPY TO HAVE YOUR HELP IN THIS CASE.
OH... ALL RIGHT.
THERE ARE FIVE JEWELRY STORES IN THE WEST DISTRICT. AND FOUR HAVE BEEN ATTACKED BY THE DRAGON.
LEAVING ONLY THE HAKKEI JEWELRY SHOP, AM I RIGHT?
EXACTLY! THEN YOU ALREADY UNDERSTAND MY PROBLEM.
CAN I COUNT ON YOU?

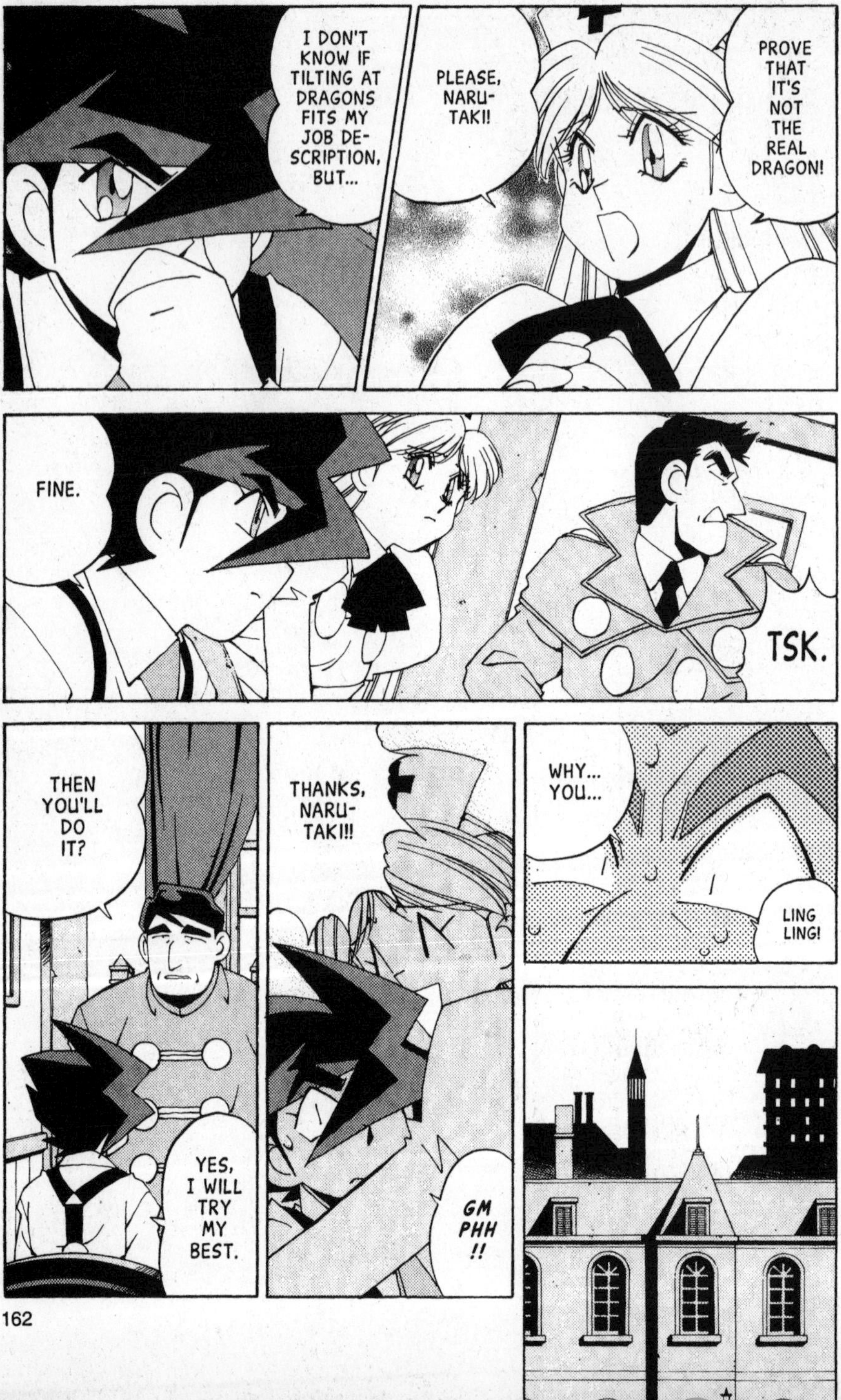
I DON'T KNOW IF TILTING AT DRAGONS FITS MY JOB DE-SCRIPTION, BUT...
PLEASE, NARU-TAKI!!
PROVE THAT IT'S NOT THE REAL DRAGON!
FINE.
TSK.
THEN YOU'LL DO IT?
YES, I WILL TRY MY BEST.
THANKS, NARU-TAKI!!
GM PHH !!
WHY... YOU...
LING LING!

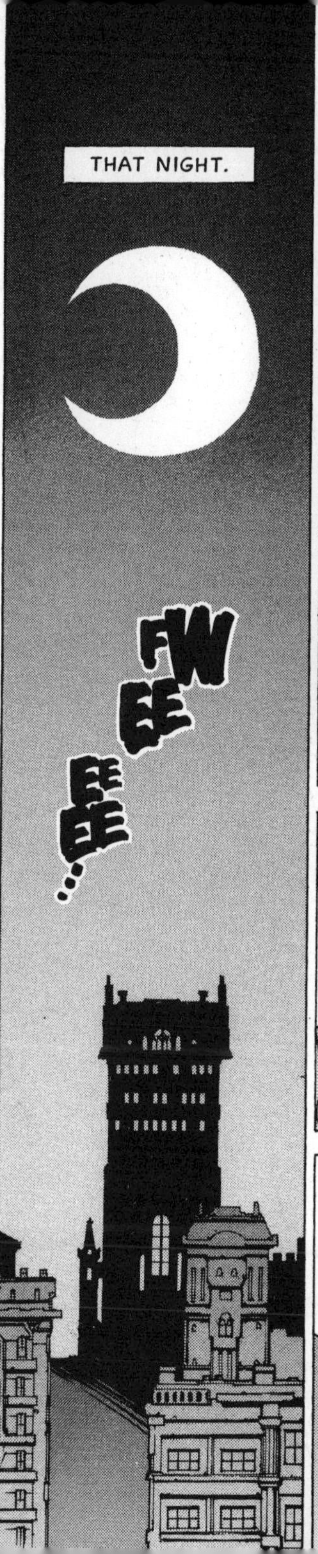
THAT NIGHT.
FWEEEEEE...

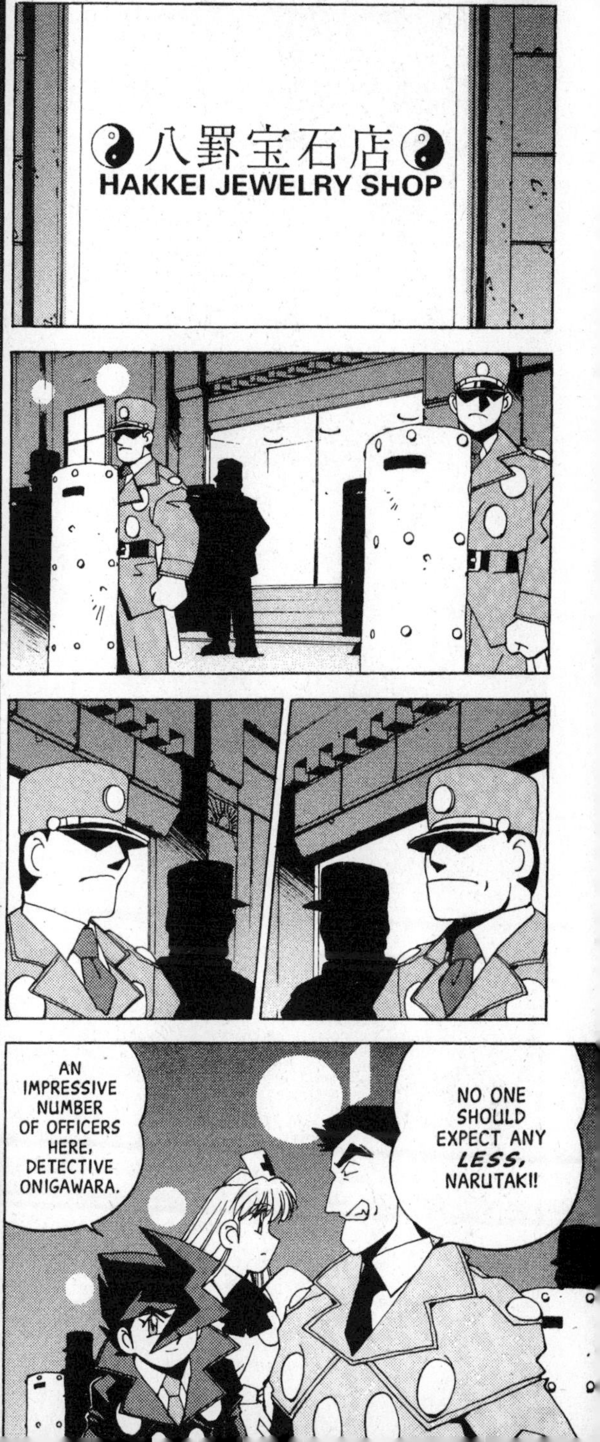
八罫宝石店
HAKKEI JEWELRY SHOP
AN IMPRESSIVE NUMBER OF OFFICERS HERE, DETECTIVE ONIGAWARA.
NO ONE SHOULD EXPECT ANY *LESS,* NARUTAKI!

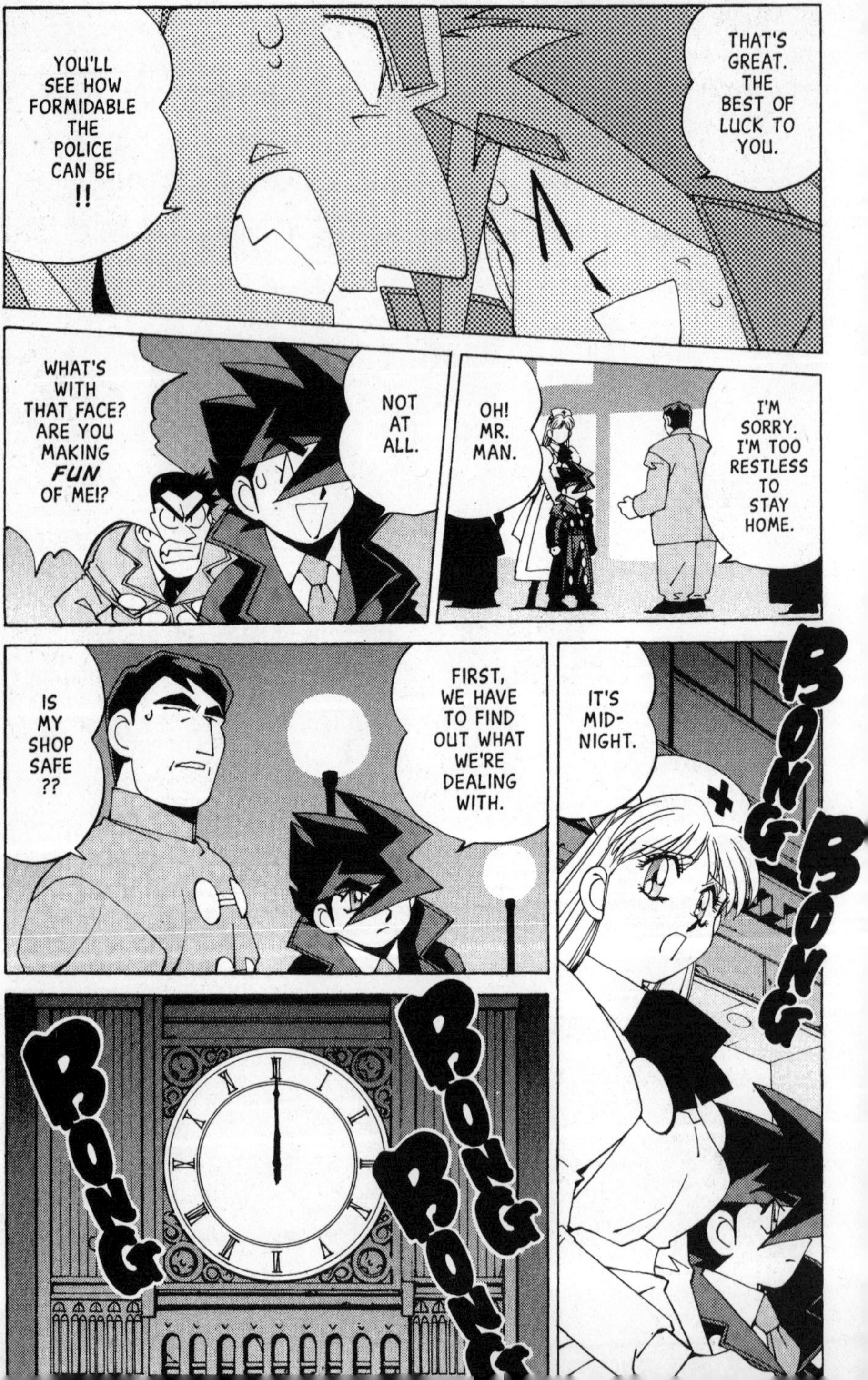
YOU'LL SEE HOW FORMIDABLE THE POLICE CAN BE !!
THAT'S GREAT. THE BEST OF LUCK TO YOU.
WHAT'S WITH THAT FACE? ARE YOU MAKING FUN OF ME!?
NOT AT ALL.
OH! MR. MAN.
I'M SORRY. I'M TOO RESTLESS TO STAY HOME.
IS MY SHOP SAFE ??
FIRST, WE HAVE TO FIND OUT WHAT WE'RE DEALING WITH.
IT'S MID-NIGHT.
BONG
BONG
BONG
BONG
BONG
BONG

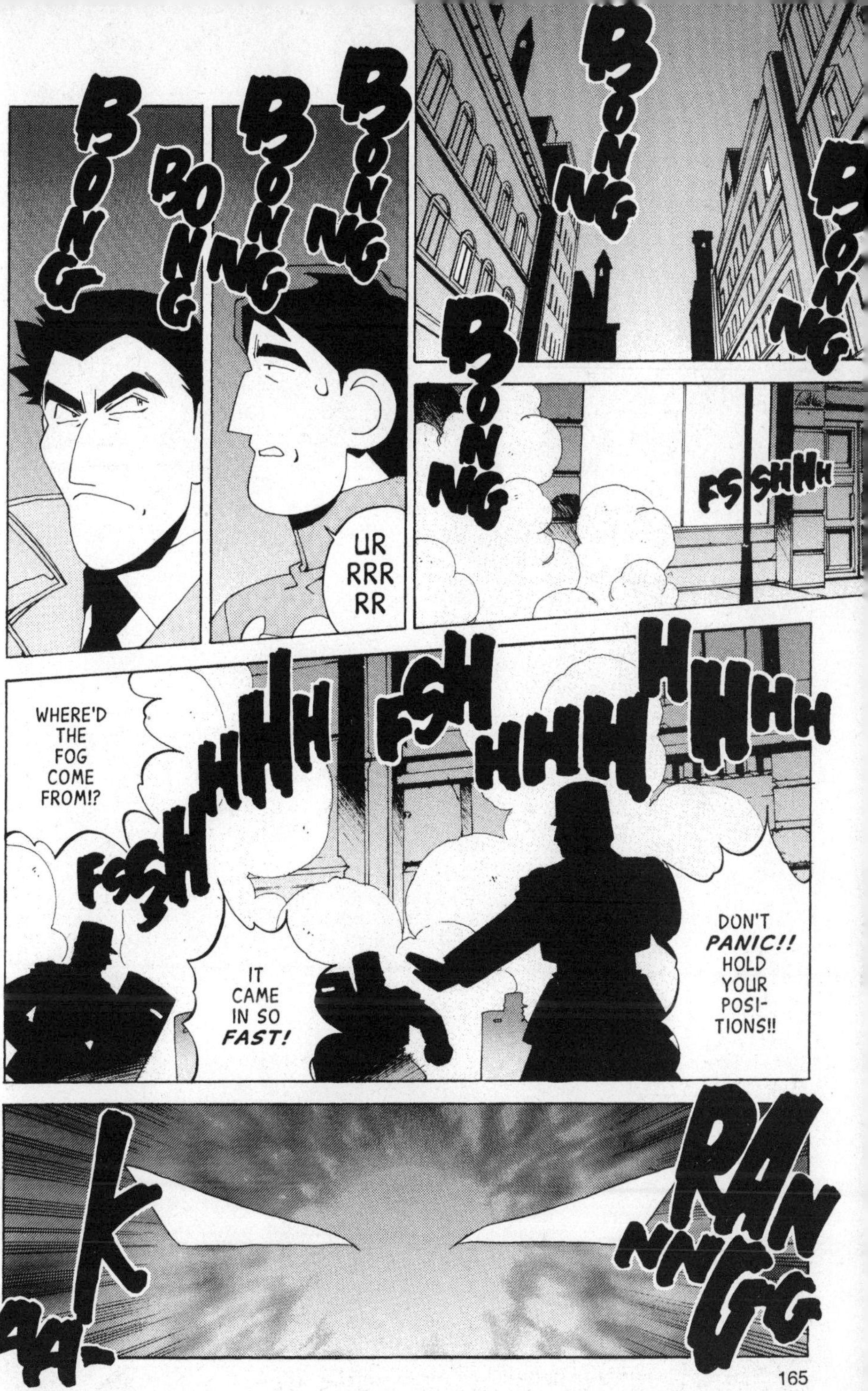
BONG
BONG
BOONG
BOONG
UR RRR RR
BOONG
BOONG
BOONG
FSSHHH
WHERE'D THE FOG COME FROM!?
FSSHHHHH
FSHHHHHHHHH
IT CAME IN SO *FAST!*
DON'T *PANIC!!* HOLD YOUR POSI-TIONS!!
KAA-
RANNNG

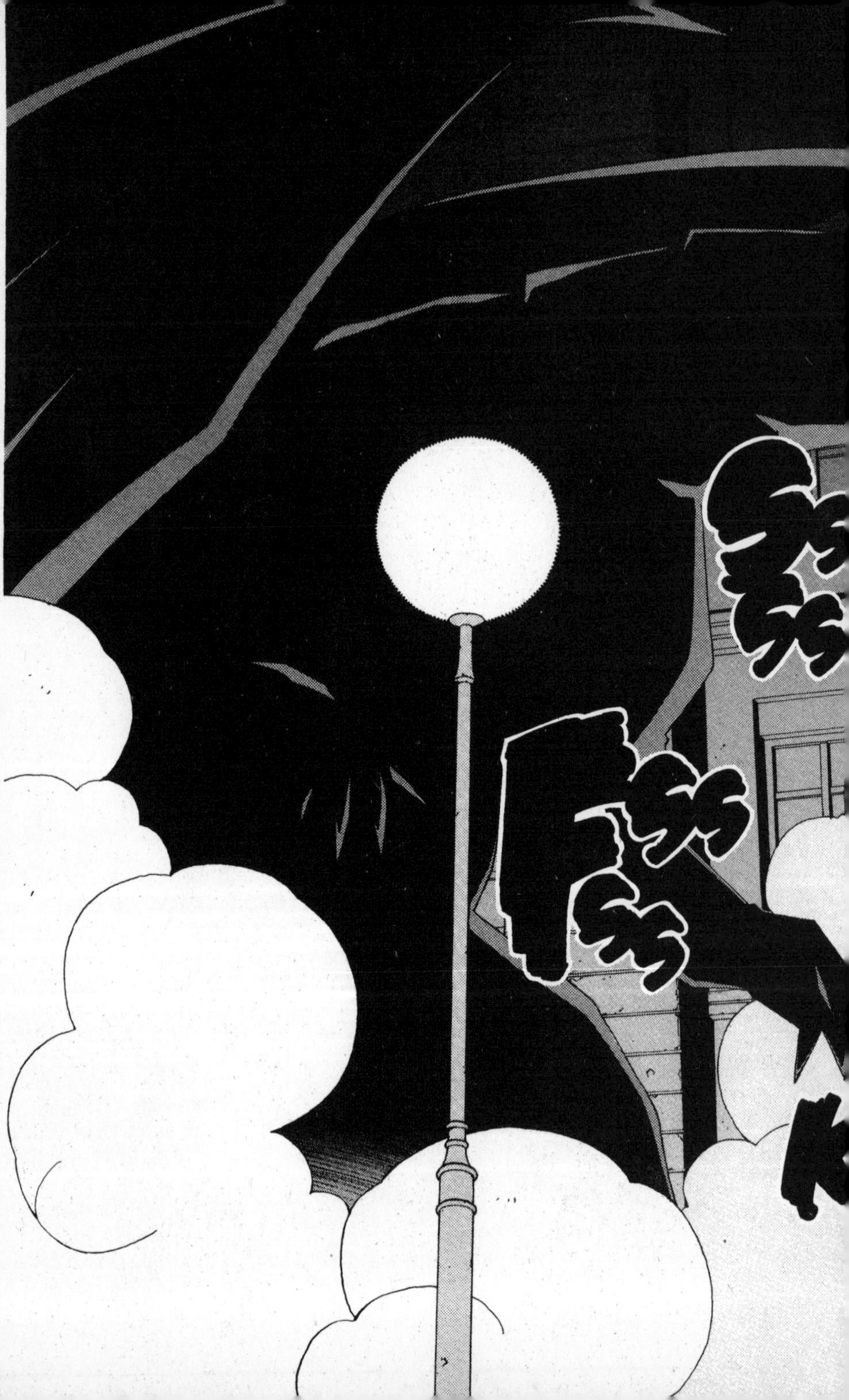

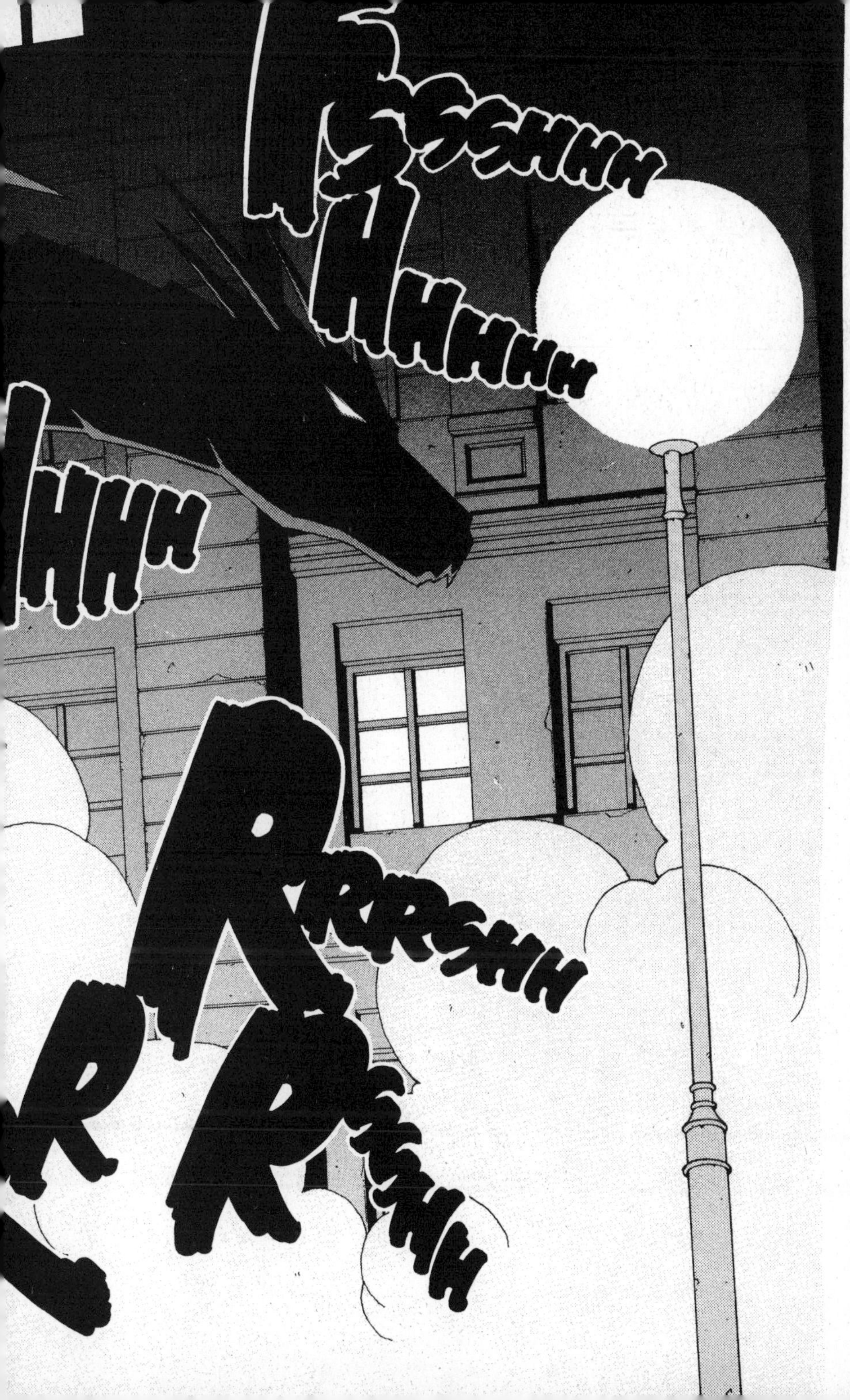
SSSHHHH
HHHHHHH
HHHH
RRRRSHHH
RRRRSHHHH

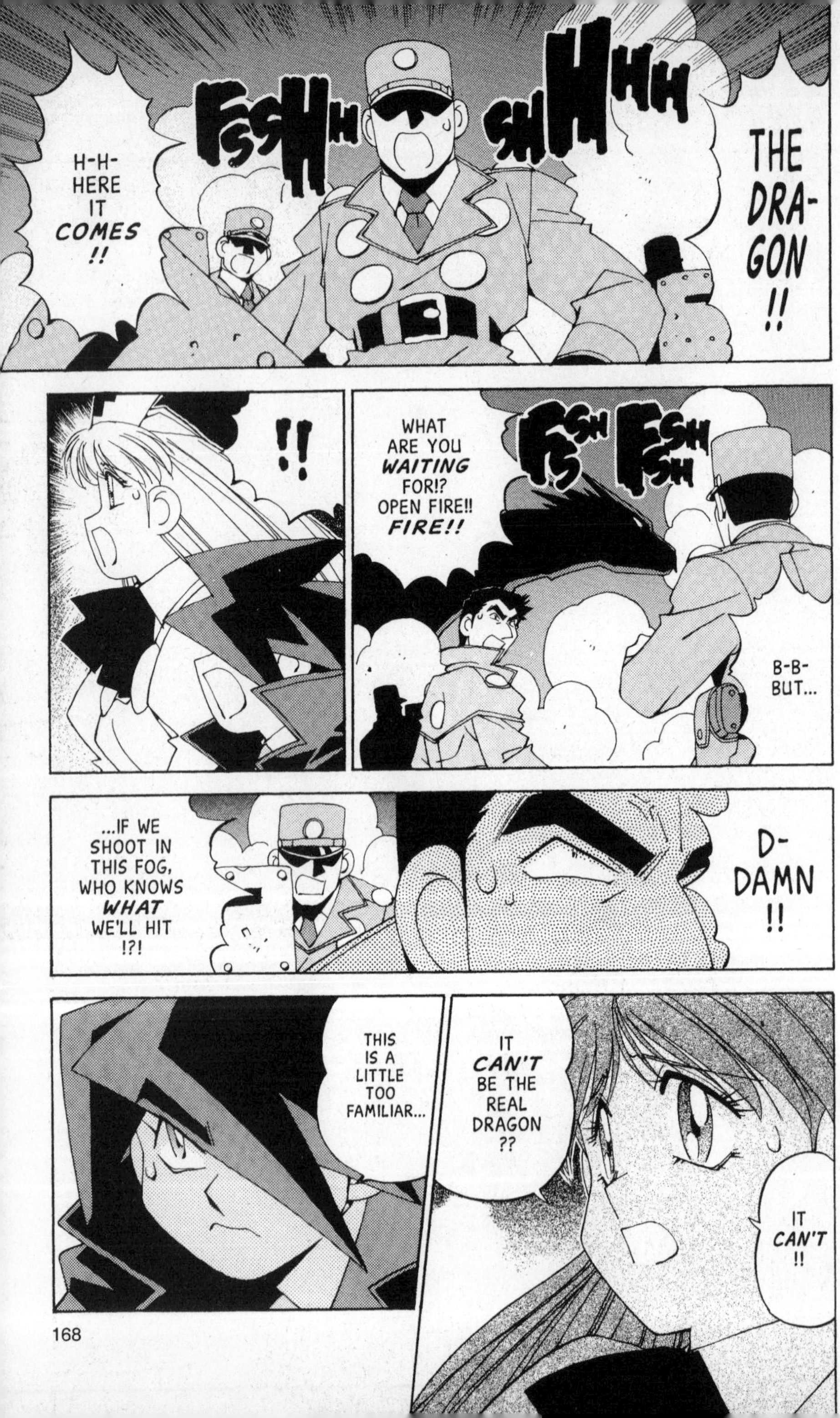
H-H-HERE IT COMES !!
FSSHH
SHHHHH
THE DRA-GON !!
!!
WHAT ARE YOU WAITING FOR!? OPEN FIRE!! FIRE!!
FSH FSH FSH FSH
B-B-BUT...
...IF WE SHOOT IN THIS FOG, WHO KNOWS WHAT WE'LL HIT !?!
D-DAMN !!
THIS IS A LITTLE TOO FAMILIAR...
IT CAN'T BE THE REAL DRAGON ??
IT CAN'T !!

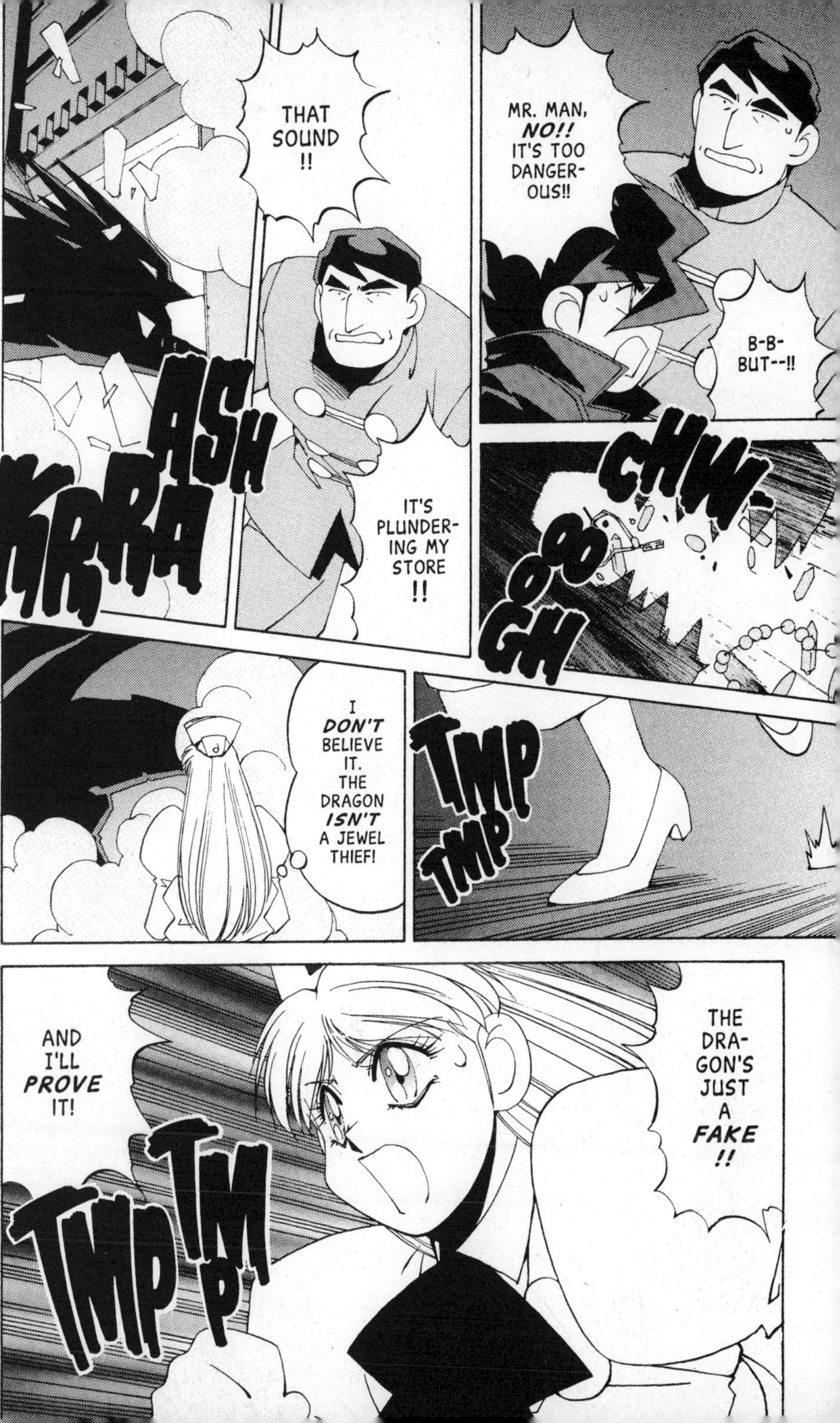
KRRAASH
THAT SOUND !!
IT'S PLUNDERING MY STORE !!
MR. MAN, *NO!!* IT'S TOO DANGEROUS!!
B-B-BUT--!!
CHW-OOOGH
I *DON'T* BELIEVE IT. THE DRAGON *ISN'T* A JEWEL THIEF!
TMP TMP
AND I'LL *PROVE* IT!
TMP TMP
THE DRAGON'S JUST A *FAKE* !!

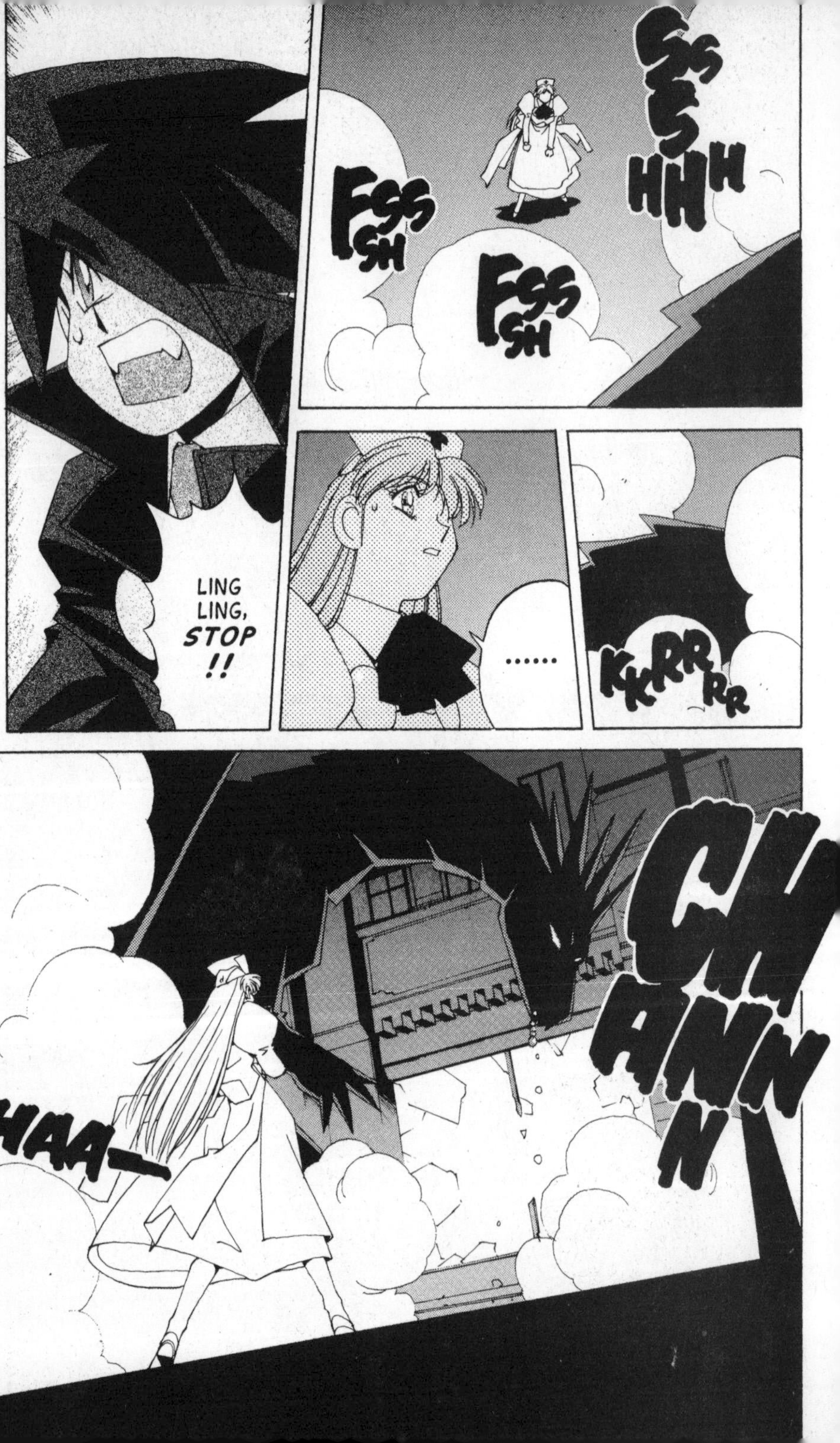
LING LING, STOP !!
FSSSH
FSSSH
SSSHHHH
......
KKRRRRR
SHAA—
CHANNNN

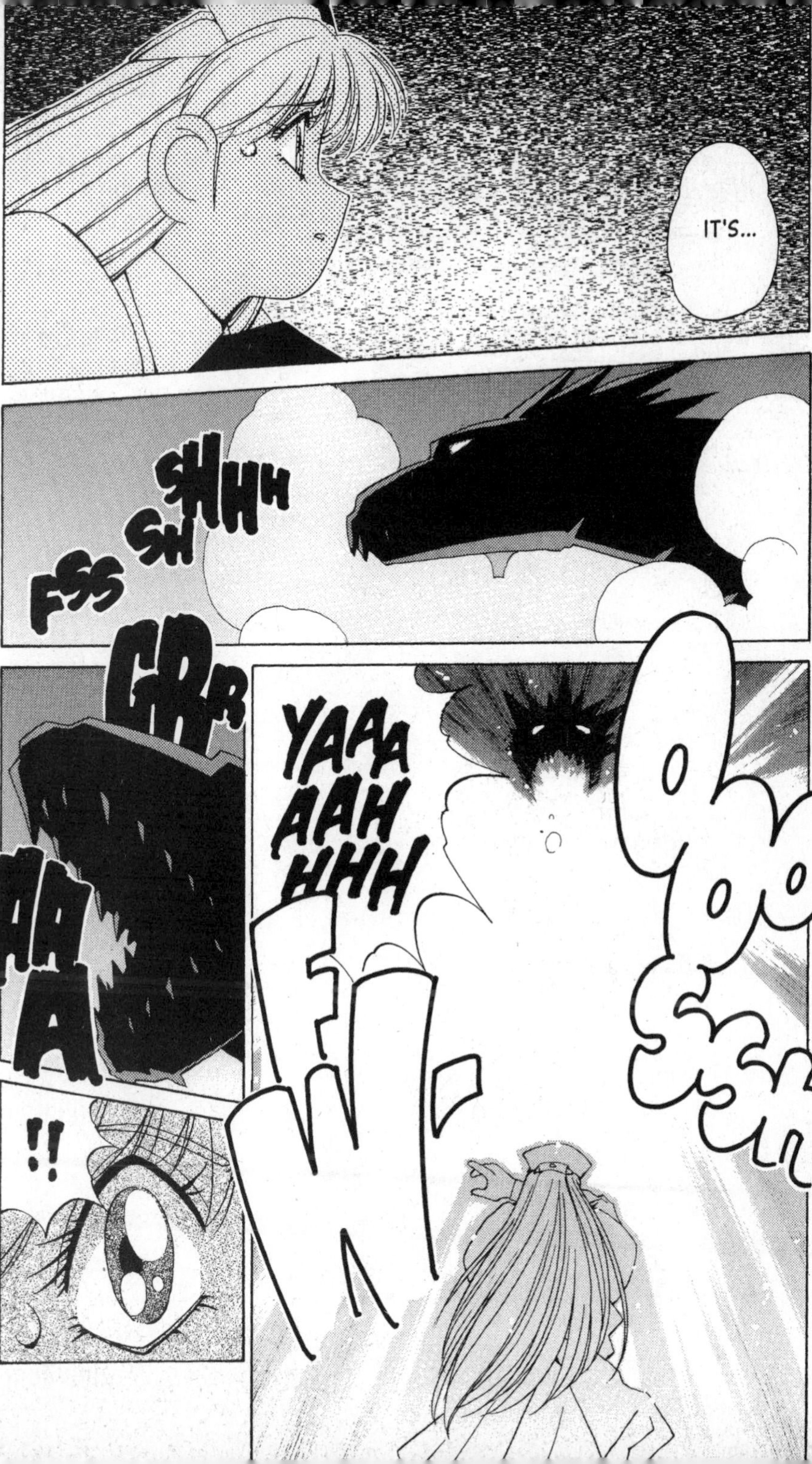
IT'S...
FSS
SH
SHHH
GRR
AAAAA
YAAAAAHHHH
!!

STEAM DETECTIVES PRESS

DRAGON SWORD, A SMASHING SUCCESS!

This year's number one movie is *Dragon Sword*!! Originally produced in honor of the Steam City Dragon Festival, the new action film ended up breaking all attendance records only three days after its opening!
Now, in its eighth week, the film is still number one, and it's breaking even more records. It's the odds-on favorite to be the top-grossing event of the year, and the notices have been unanimously favorable.

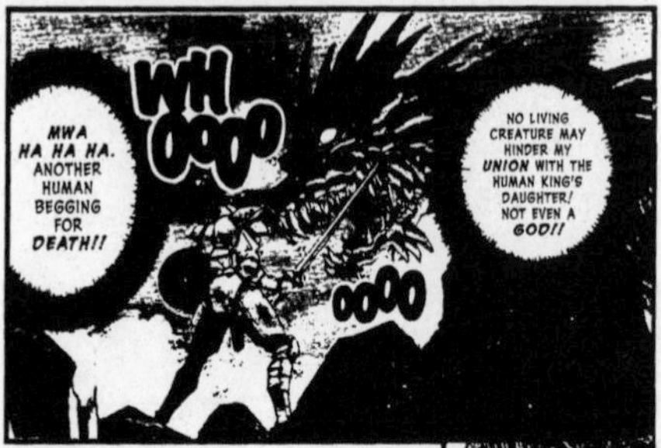
WHOOOO
MWA HA HA HA. ANOTHER HUMAN BEGGING FOR DEATH!!
NO LIVING CREATURE MAY HINDER MY UNION WITH THE HUMAN KING'S DAUGHTER! NOT EVEN A GOD!!
OOOO

From the hit film *Dragon Sword*

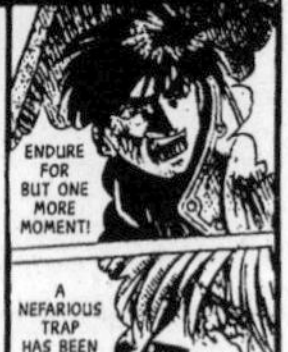
ENDURE FOR BUT ONE MORE MOMENT!
A NEFARIOUS TRAP HAS BEEN LAID FOR THEE!

WEEKLY STEAM MAGAZINE: "A miraculous 2 1/2 hours!"
PLAY STEAM BOY MAGAZINE: "A warm-hearted human drama."
STEAM TIME MAGAZINE: "I have never been so moved...never been so thrilled...never been so inspired by love!"

The film's production company, Steam Fox, recently announced that they will be releasing *Dragon Sword 2* next year. However, next year is the festival of the Simurgh, so some are criticizing the company's timing.

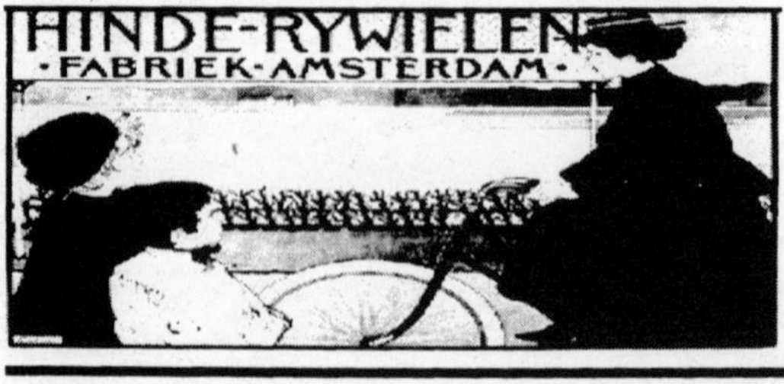
HINDE-RYWIELEN
·FABRIEK·AMSTERDAM·

PROVE YOUR LOVE WITH JEWELRY
HAKKEI JEWELRY SHOP
八卦宝石店

Volume 014 • Issued by Steam Press Co.,Ltd.

THE TRUTH BEHIND THE DRAGON

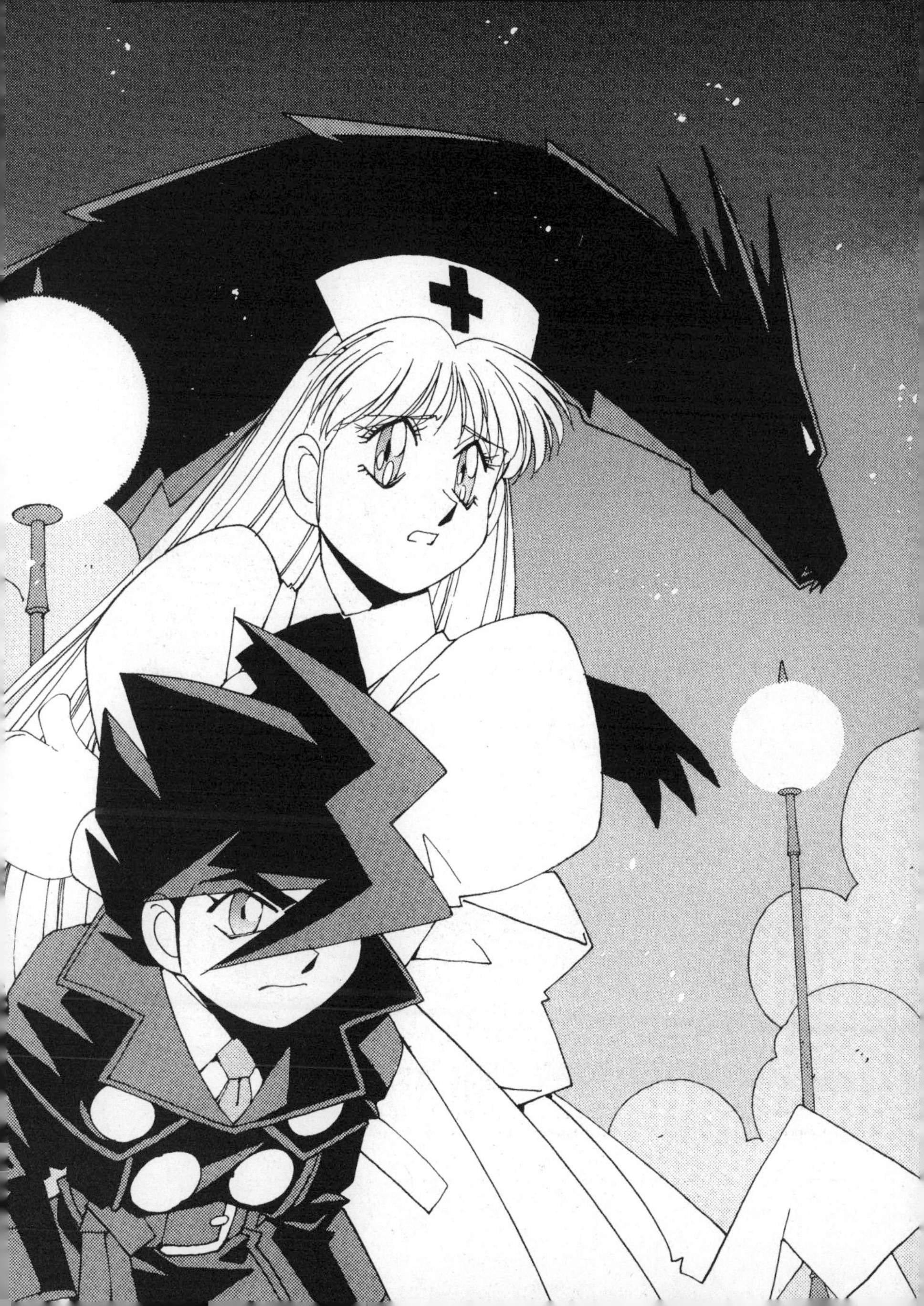

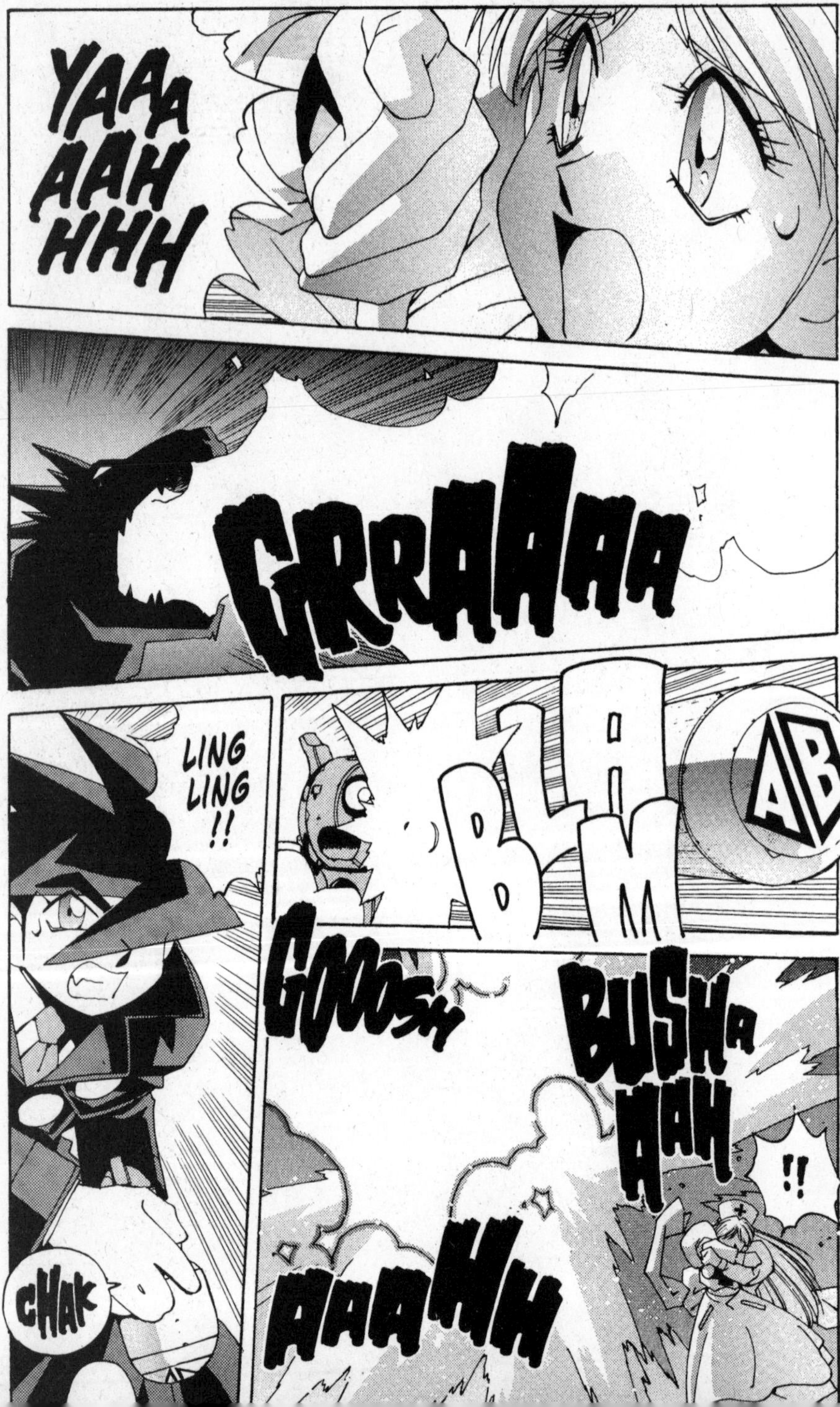
YAAAAAHHHH
GRRAAAAA
LING LING !!
BLAM
AB
CHAK
GOOOSH
BUSHAAAH
!!
AAAAHH

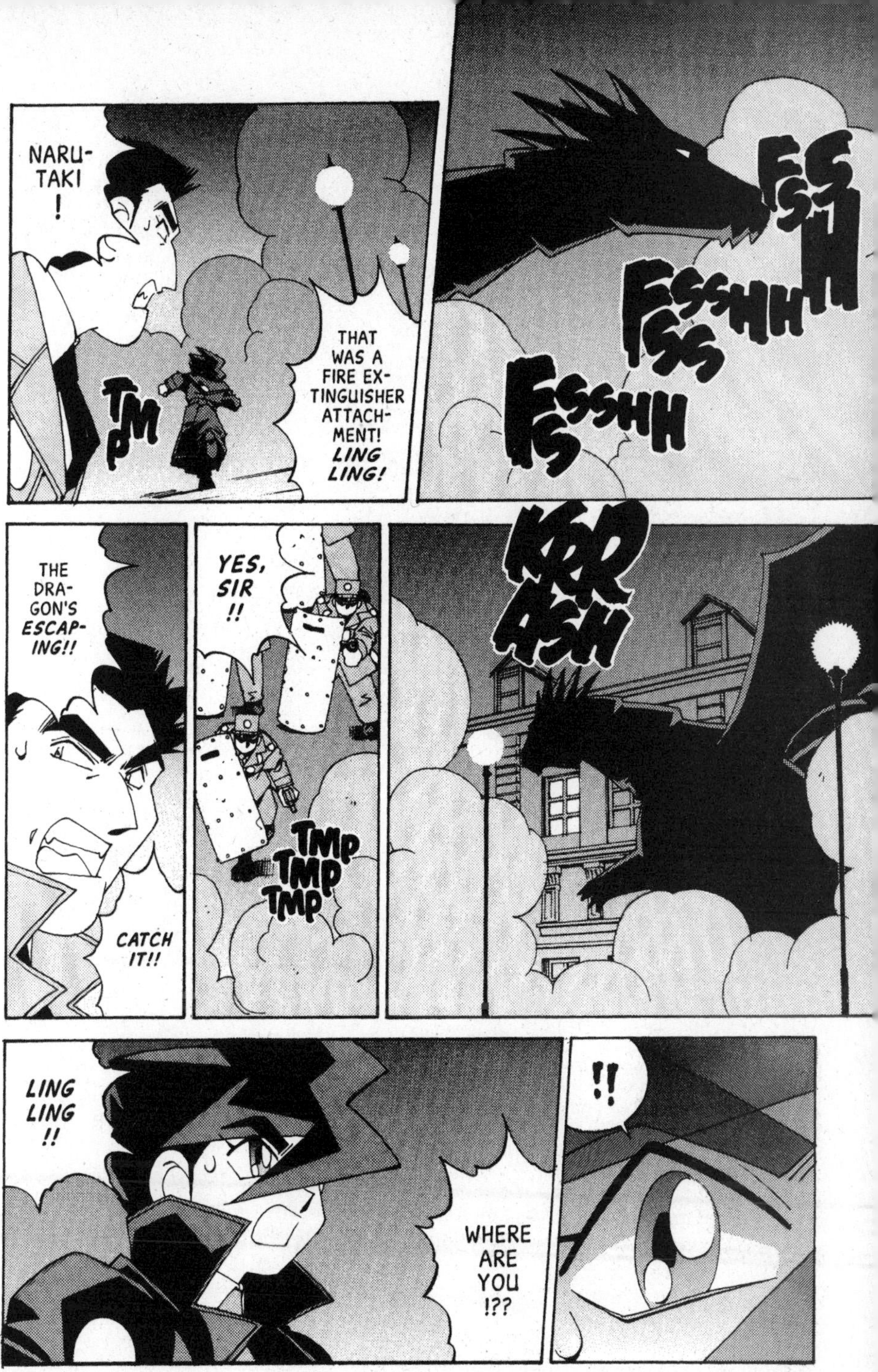
NARU-TAKI!
TMP
THAT WAS A FIRE EXTINGUISHER ATTACHMENT! *LING LING!*
FSSHH
FSSSHH
FSSSHH
THE DRAGON'S *ESCAPING!!*
CATCH IT!!
YES, SIR!!
TMP TMP TMP
KRRASH
LING LING!!
WHERE ARE YOU!??
!!

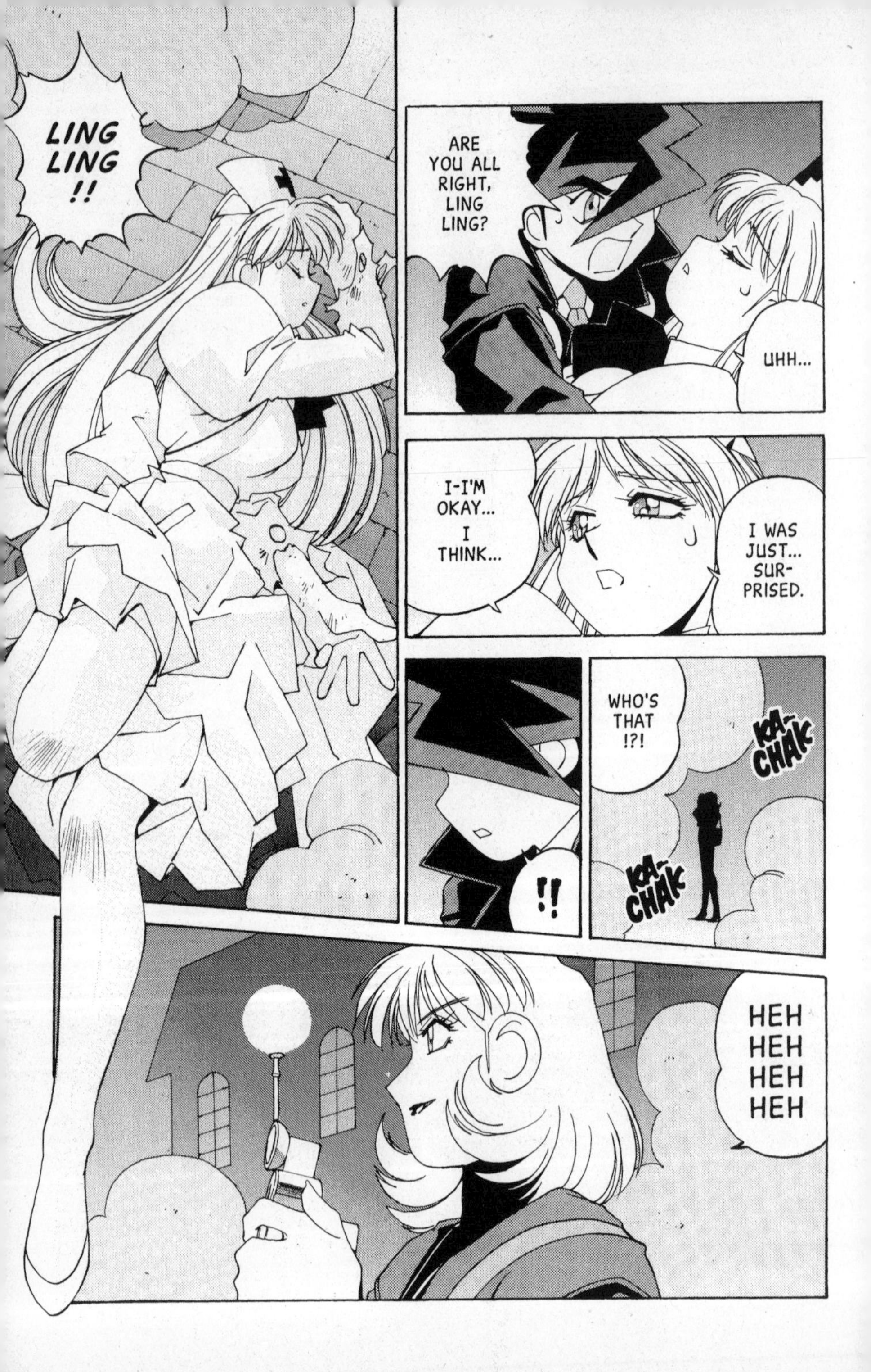
LING LING !!
ARE YOU ALL RIGHT, LING LING?
UHH...
I-I'M OKAY... I THINK...
I WAS JUST... SUR-PRISED.
!!
WHO'S THAT !?!
KA-CHAK
KA-CHAK
HEH HEH HEH HEH

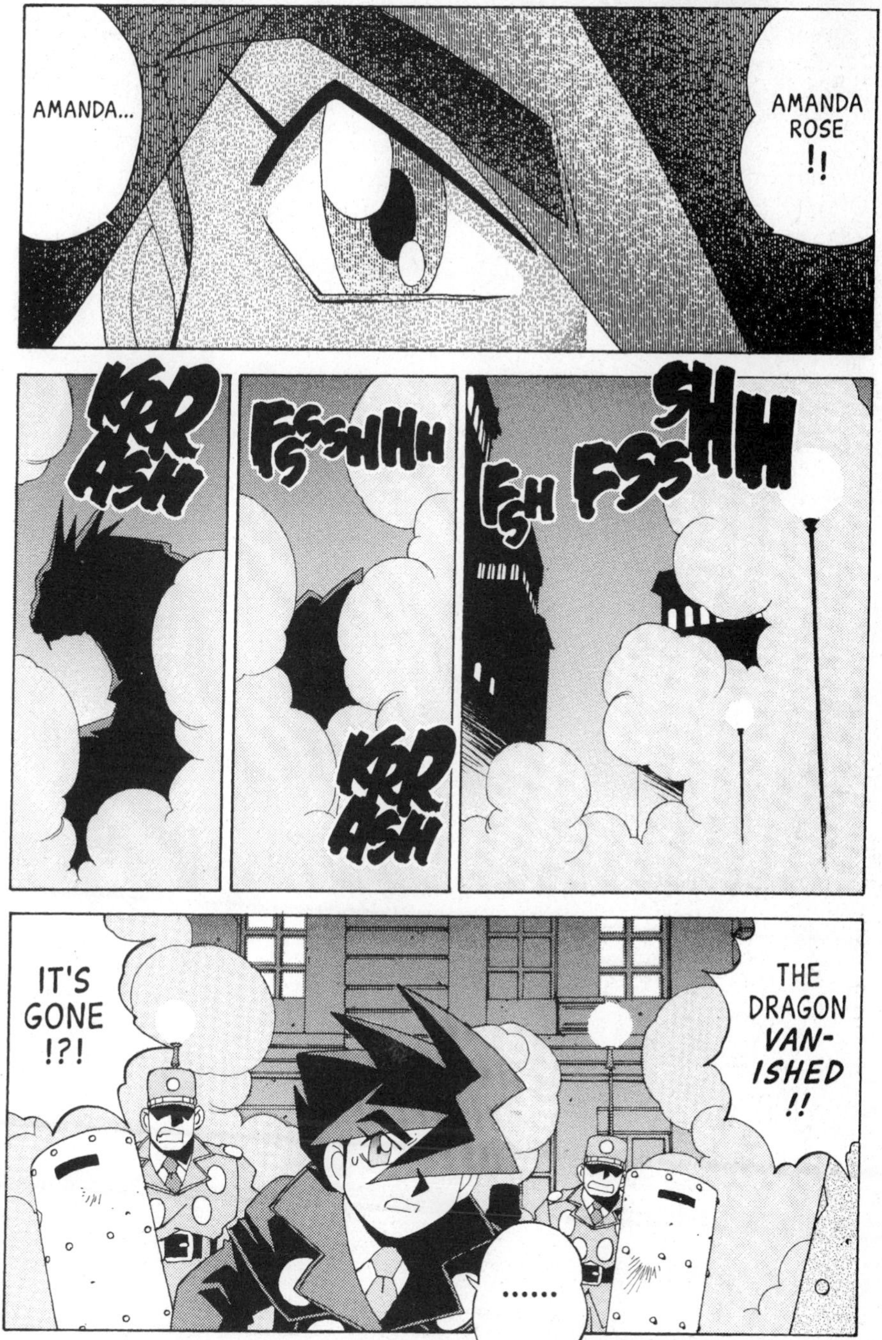
AMANDA...
AMANDA ROSE !!
KRRASH
FSSSHHH
KRRASH
FSH
FSSSHHH
IT'S GONE !?!
THE DRAGON VAN-ISHED !!
......

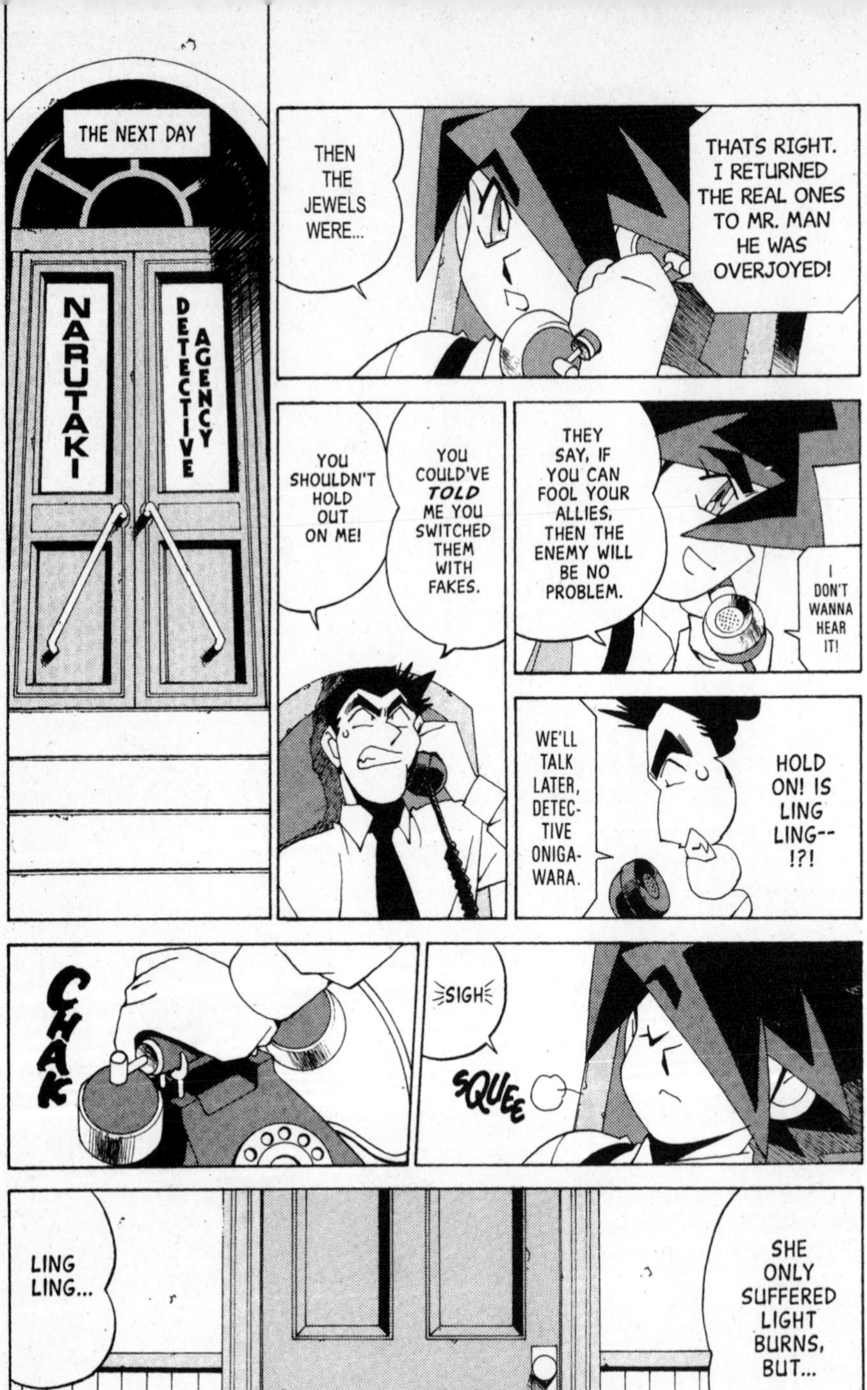
THE NEXT DAY
NARUTAKI DETECTIVE AGENCY
THEN THE JEWELS WERE...
THATS RIGHT. I RETURNED THE REAL ONES TO MR. MAN HE WAS OVERJOYED!
YOU SHOULDN'T HOLD OUT ON ME!
YOU COULD'VE *TOLD* ME YOU SWITCHED THEM WITH FAKES.
THEY SAY, IF YOU CAN FOOL YOUR ALLIES, THEN THE ENEMY WILL BE NO PROBLEM.
I DON'T WANNA HEAR IT!
WE'LL TALK LATER, DETECTIVE ONIGAWARA.
HOLD ON! IS LING LING--!?!
CHAK
SIGH
SQUEE
LING LING...
SHE ONLY SUFFERED LIGHT BURNS, BUT...

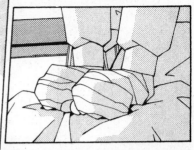

......

KAWAKUBO, I NEED TO GO OUT FOR A MOMENT. CAN YOU LOOK AFTER LING LING?

OF COURSE, SIR.

WHERE TO?

VRRR RR RMM

TO OFFICES OF THE STEAM DAILY PRESS !

VR RR MM...

179

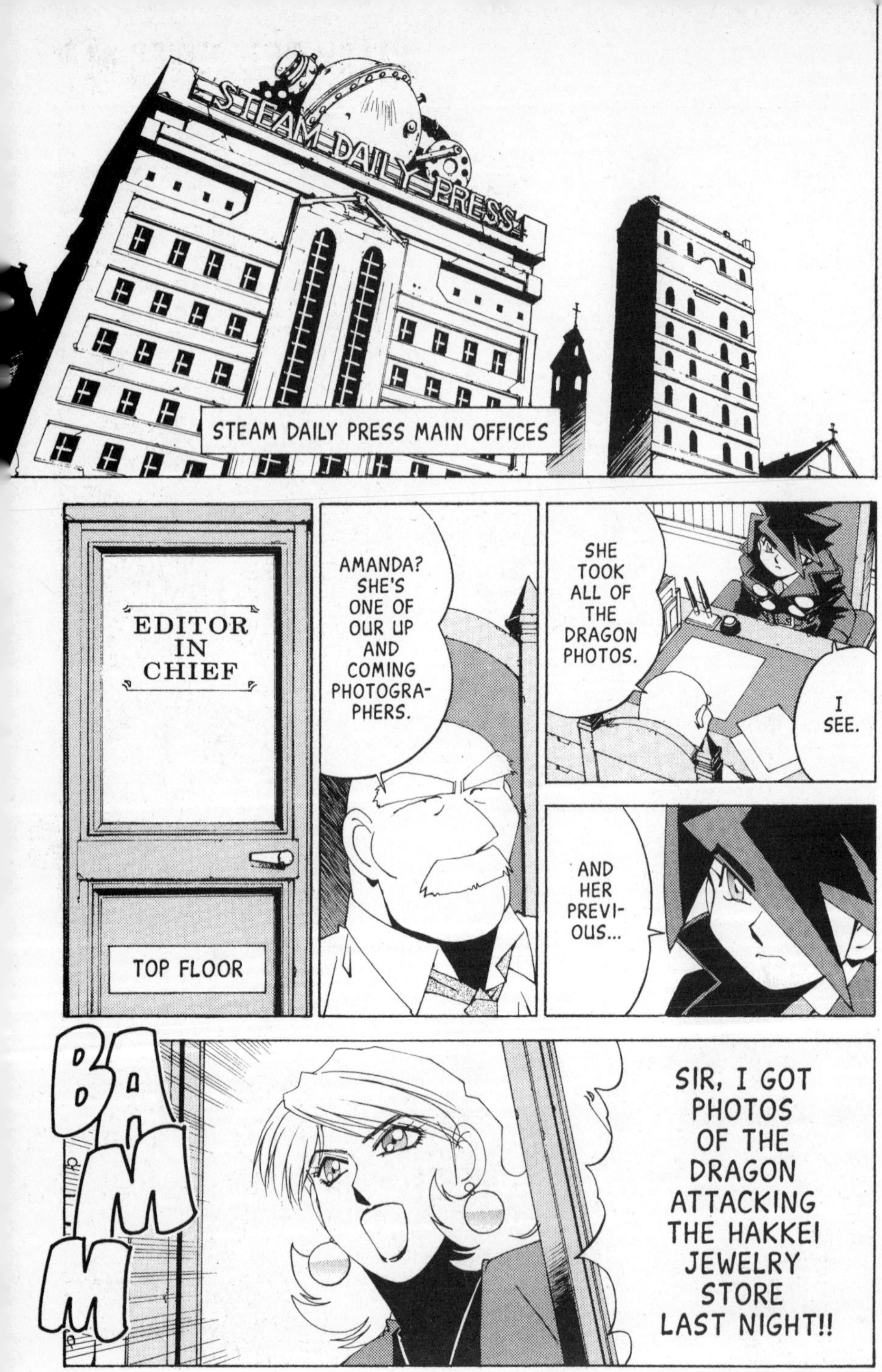
STEAM DAILY PRESS
STEAM DAILY PRESS MAIN OFFICES
EDITOR IN CHIEF
TOP FLOOR
AMANDA? SHE'S ONE OF OUR UP AND COMING PHOTOGRAPHERS.
SHE TOOK ALL OF THE DRAGON PHOTOS.
I SEE.
AND HER PREVIOUS...
BAMMM
SIR, I GOT PHOTOS OF THE DRAGON ATTACKING THE HAKKEI JEWELRY STORE LAST NIGHT!!

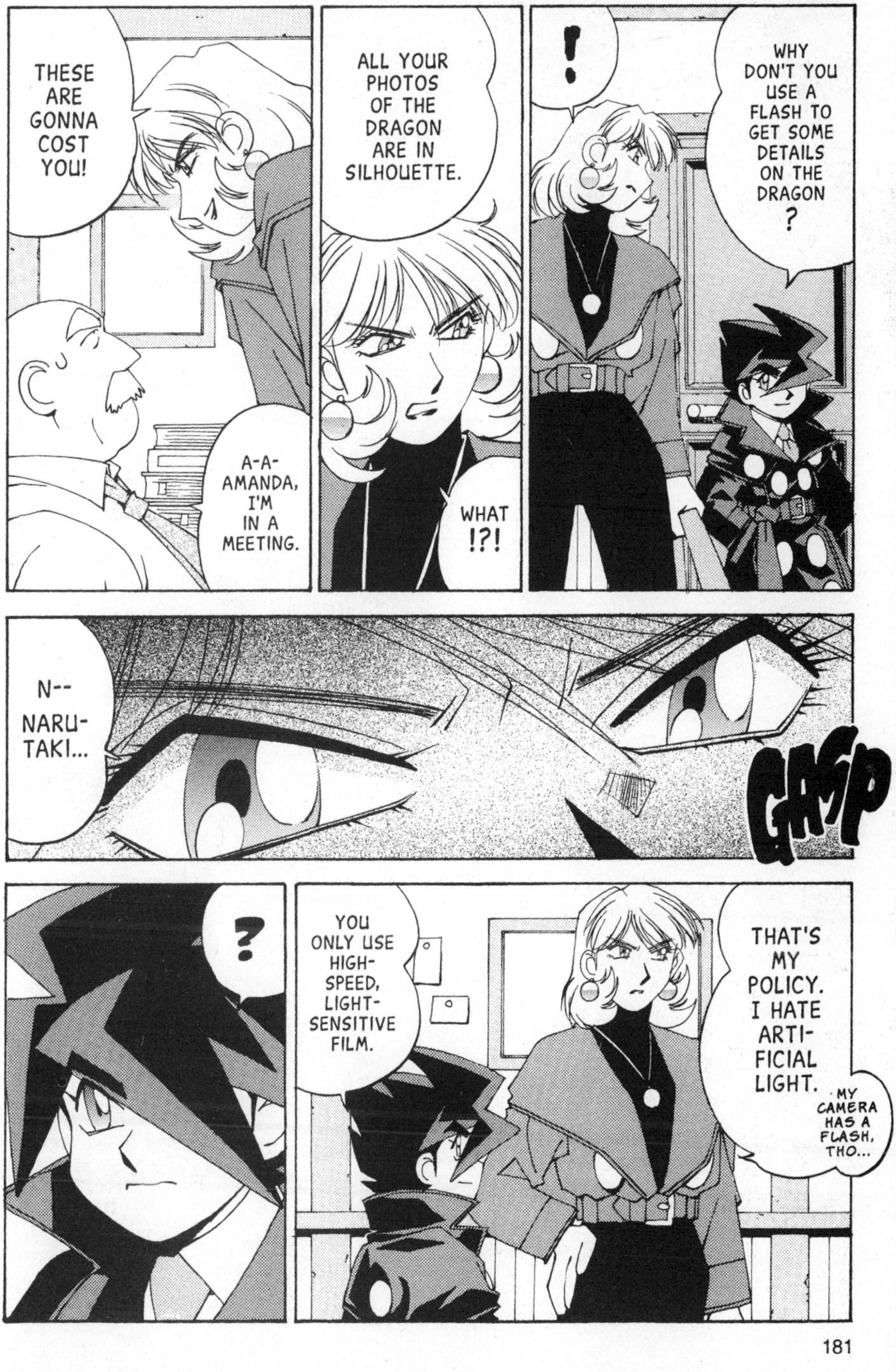
THESE ARE GONNA COST YOU!
A-A-AMANDA, I'M IN A MEETING.
ALL YOUR PHOTOS OF THE DRAGON ARE IN SILHOUETTE.
WHAT !?!
!
WHY DON'T YOU USE A FLASH TO GET SOME DETAILS ON THE DRAGON ?
N-- NARU-TAKI...
GASP
?
YOU ONLY USE HIGH-SPEED, LIGHT-SENSITIVE FILM.
THAT'S MY POLICY. I HATE ARTI-FICIAL LIGHT.
MY CAMERA HAS A FLASH, THO...

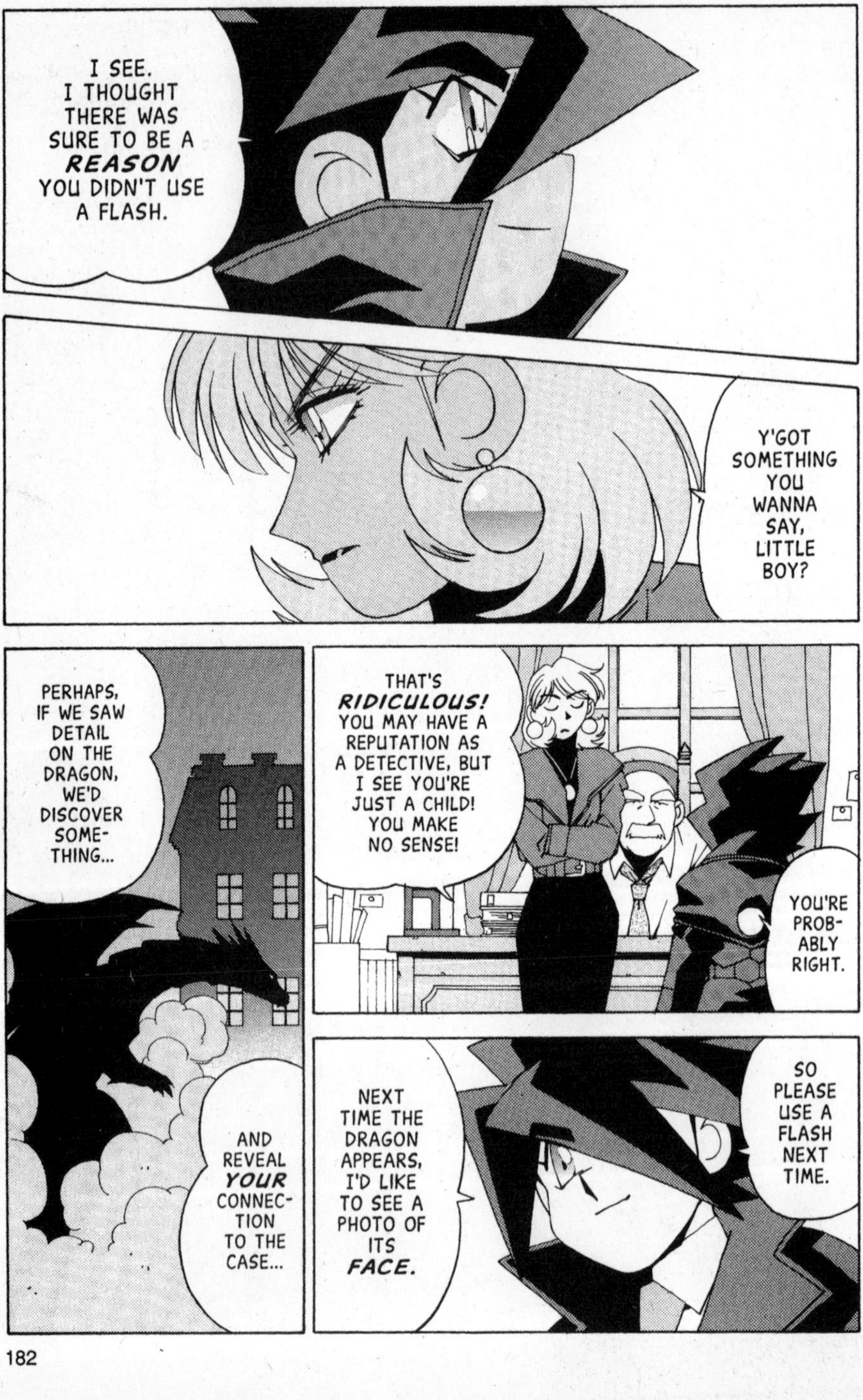
I SEE. I THOUGHT THERE WAS SURE TO BE A ***REASON*** YOU DIDN'T USE A FLASH.
Y'GOT SOMETHING YOU WANNA SAY, LITTLE BOY?
PERHAPS, IF WE SAW DETAIL ON THE DRAGON, WE'D DISCOVER SOME-THING...
AND REVEAL ***YOUR*** CONNEC-TION TO THE CASE...
THAT'S ***RIDICULOUS!*** YOU MAY HAVE A REPUTATION AS A DETECTIVE, BUT I SEE YOU'RE JUST A CHILD! YOU MAKE NO SENSE!
YOU'RE PROB-ABLY RIGHT.
NEXT TIME THE DRAGON APPEARS, I'D LIKE TO SEE A PHOTO OF ITS ***FACE.***
SO PLEASE USE A FLASH NEXT TIME.

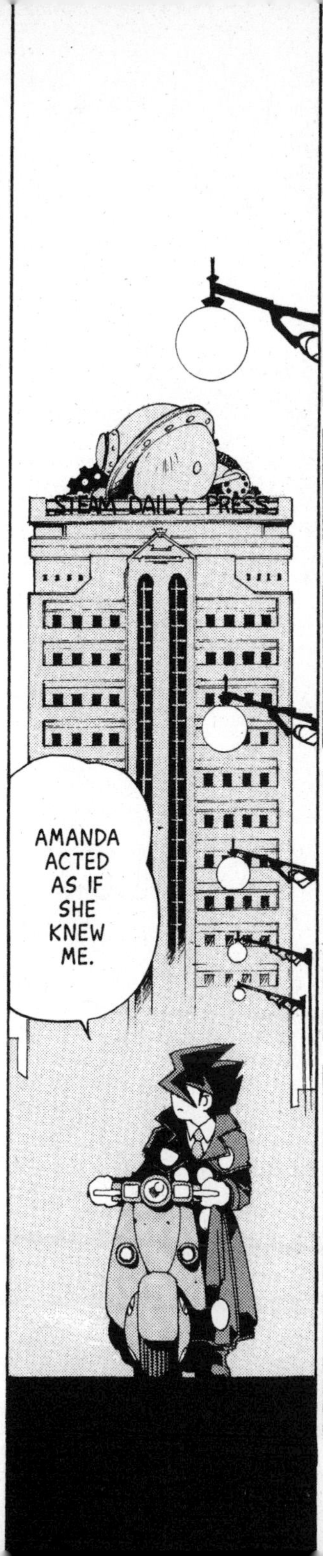
STEAM DAILY PRESS
AMANDA ACTED AS IF SHE KNEW ME.

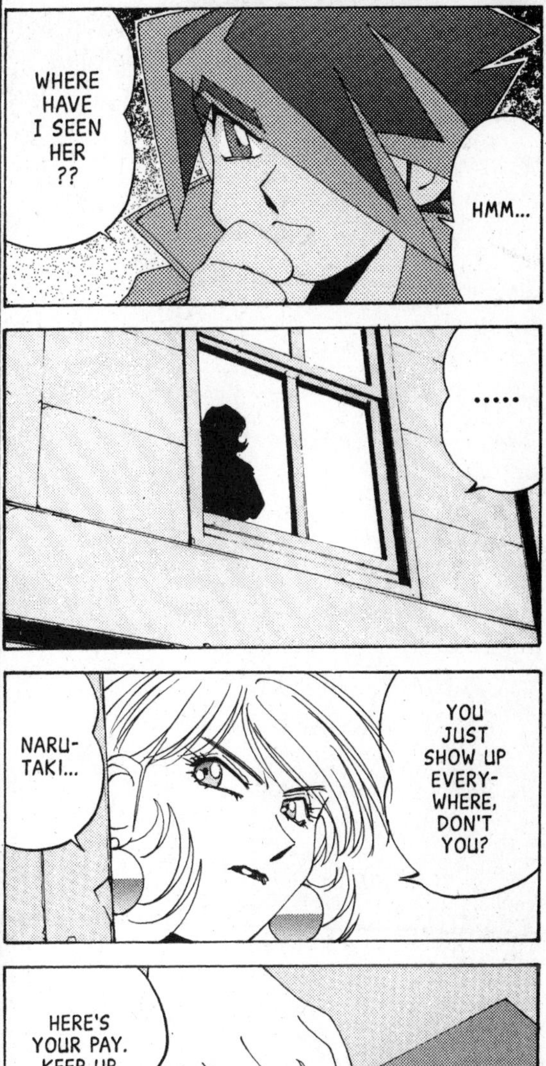
WHERE HAVE I SEEN HER ??
HMM...
.....
NARU-TAKI...
YOU JUST SHOW UP EVERY-WHERE, DON'T YOU?
HERE'S YOUR PAY. KEEP UP THE GOOD WORK.
SHHT
THANK YOU!

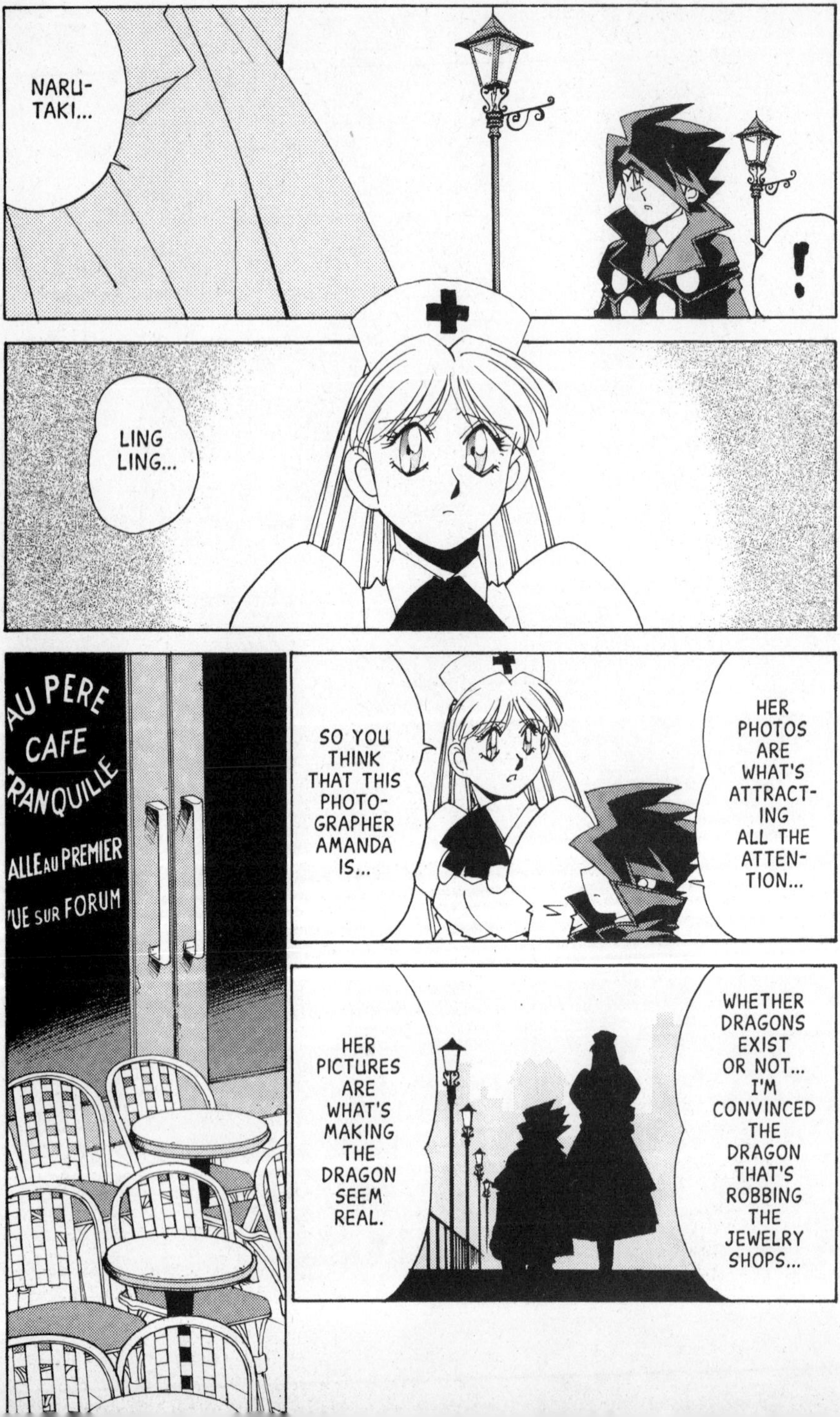
NARU-TAKI...
!
LING LING...
AU PERE CAFE TRANQUILLE
ALLE AU PREMIER
VUE SUR FORUM
SO YOU THINK THAT THIS PHOTO-GRAPHER AMANDA IS...
HER PHOTOS ARE WHAT'S ATTRACT-ING ALL THE ATTEN-TION...
HER PICTURES ARE WHAT'S MAKING THE DRAGON SEEM REAL.
WHETHER DRAGONS EXIST OR NOT... I'M CONVINCED THE DRAGON THAT'S ROBBING THE JEWELRY SHOPS...

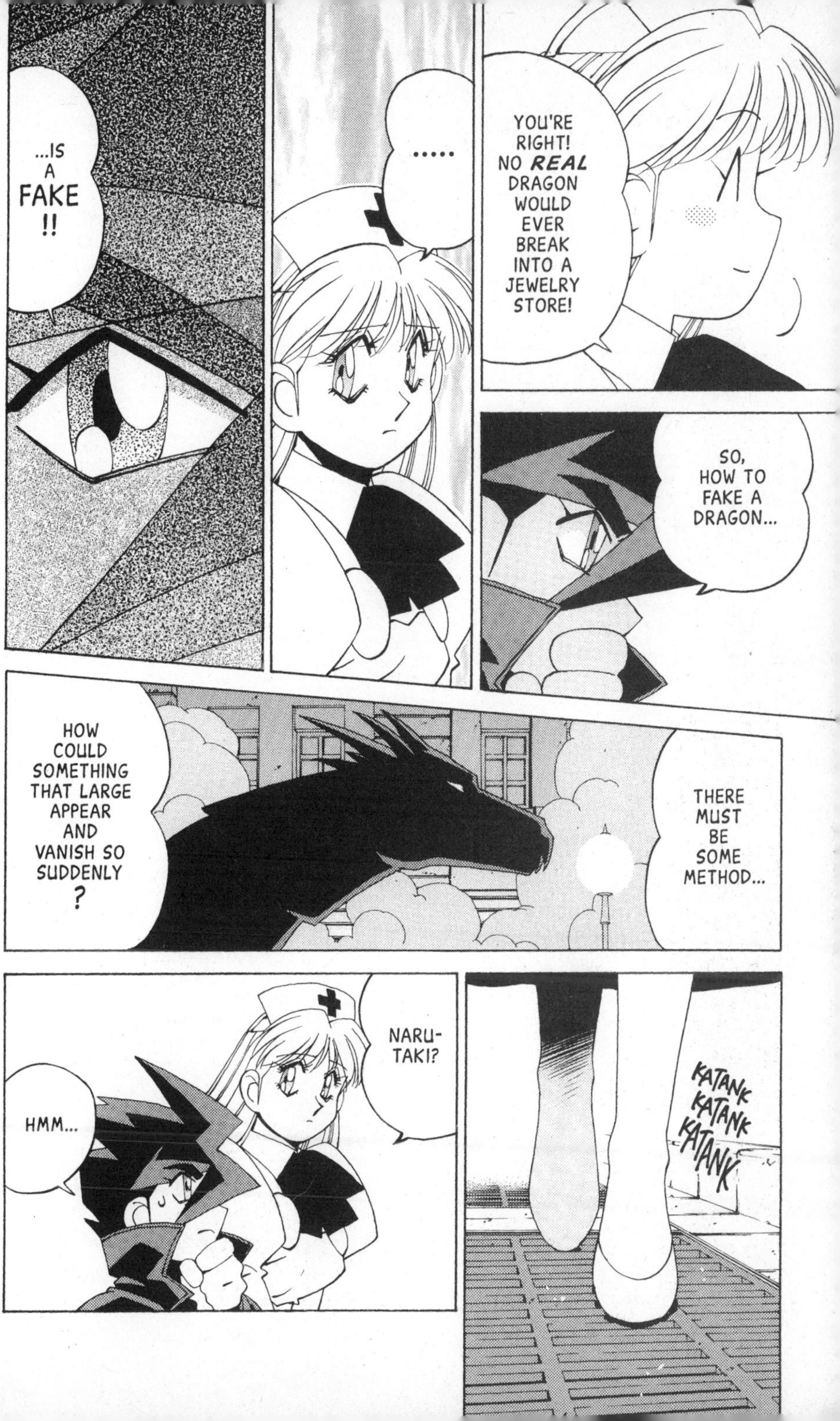
...IS A FAKE !!
.....
YOU'RE RIGHT! NO *REAL* DRAGON WOULD EVER BREAK INTO A JEWELRY STORE!
SO, HOW TO FAKE A DRAGON...
HOW COULD SOMETHING THAT LARGE APPEAR AND VANISH SO SUDDENLY ?
THERE MUST BE SOME METHOD...
HMM...
NARU-TAKI?
KATANK KATANK KATANK KATANK

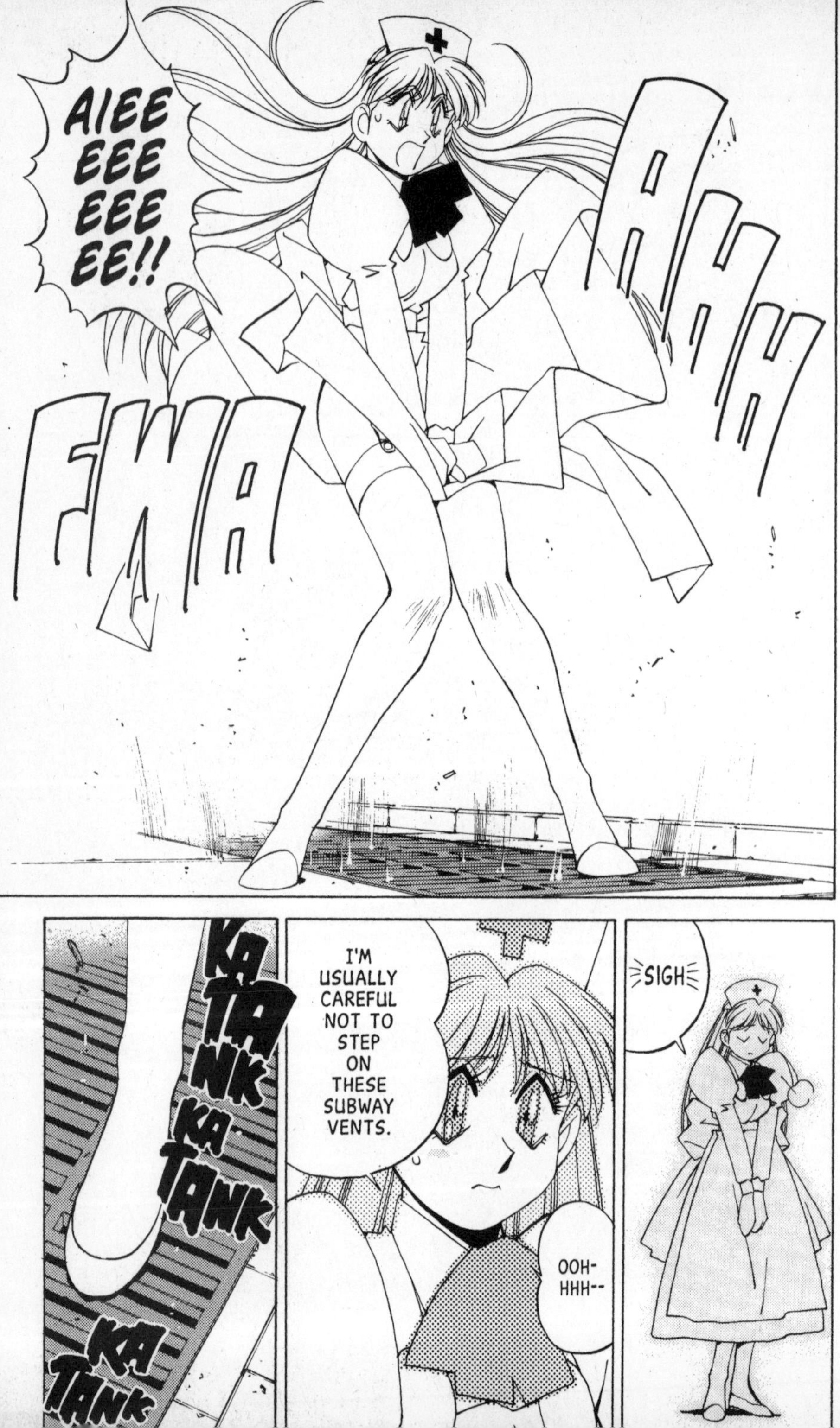
AIEE EEE EEE EE!!
FWA
AHHH
KA TANK KA TANK
KA TANK
I'M USUALLY CAREFUL NOT TO STEP ON THESE SUBWAY VENTS.
OOH-HHH--
SIGH

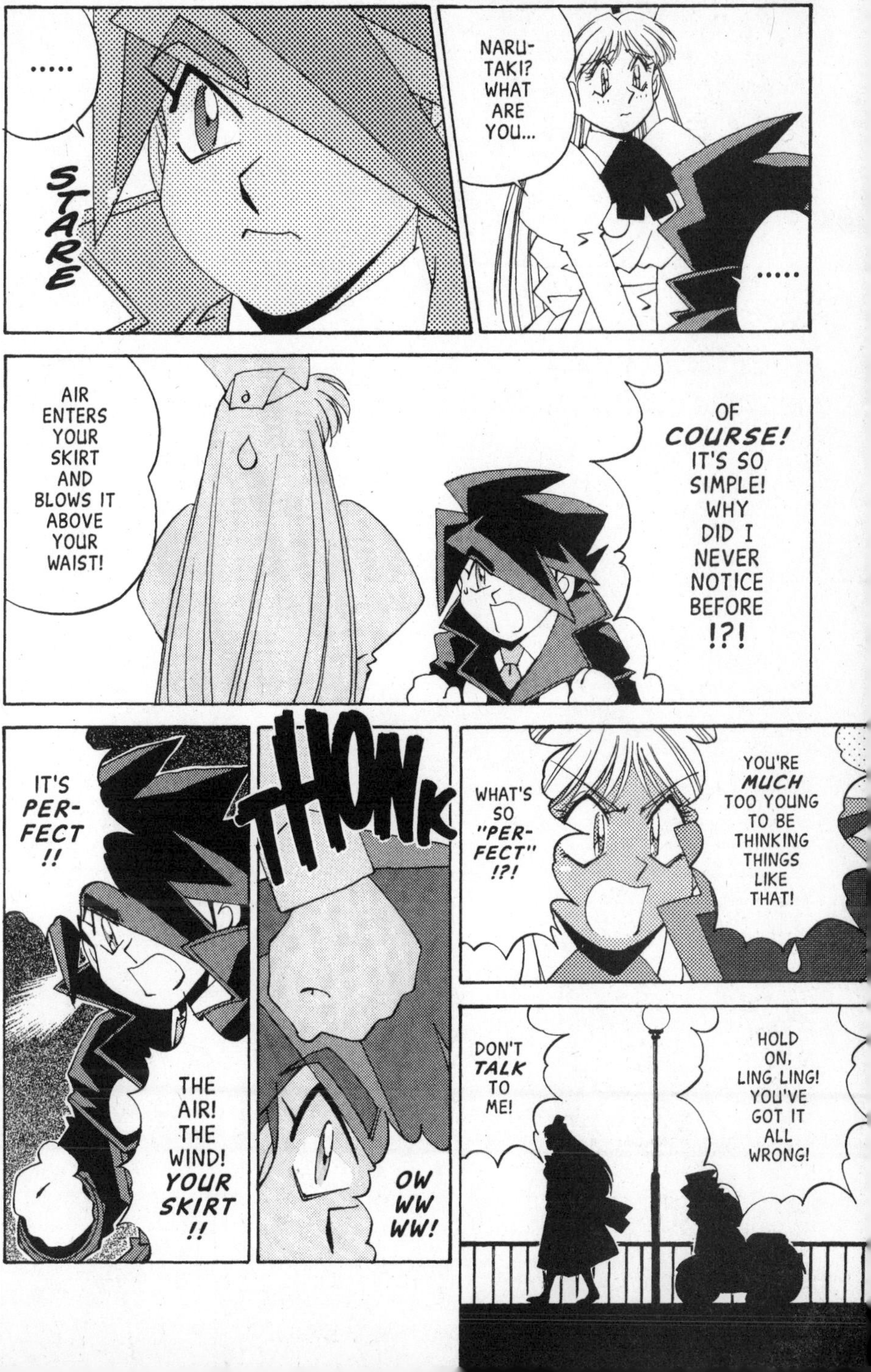
.....
STARE
NARU-TAKI? WHAT ARE YOU...
.....
AIR ENTERS YOUR SKIRT AND BLOWS IT ABOVE YOUR WAIST!
OF COURSE! IT'S SO SIMPLE! WHY DID I NEVER NOTICE BEFORE !?!
IT'S PER-FECT !!
THE AIR! THE WIND! YOUR SKIRT !!
THONK
OW WW WW!
WHAT'S SO "PER-FECT" !?!
YOU'RE MUCH TOO YOUNG TO BE THINKING THINGS LIKE THAT!
DON'T TALK TO ME!
HOLD ON, LING LING! YOU'VE GOT IT ALL WRONG!

......

BONG BONG BONG

TMP TMP

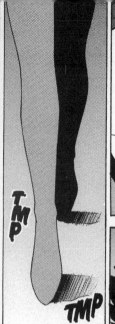

GOOD EVENING, AMANDA!

TUP

AI EEE EE!!

N-NARU-TAKI...

KRICH

WORKING LATE, I SEE. ARE YOU DRAGON HUNTING?

TH-THAT'S RIGHT! WHAT ARE YOU DOING OUT SO LATE?

ISN'T IT PAST YOUR BED-TIME?

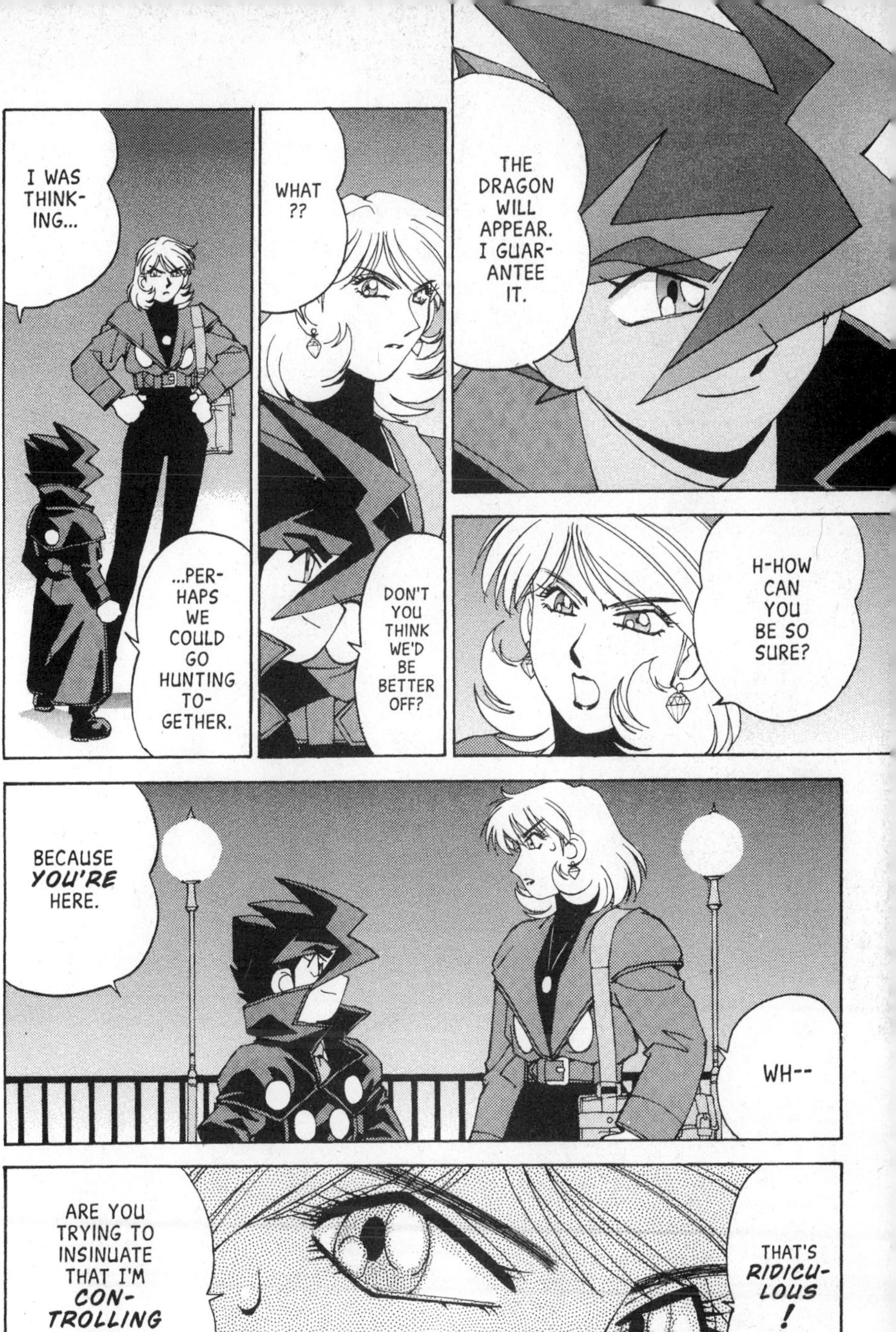
I WAS THINKING...
...PERHAPS WE COULD GO HUNTING TOGETHER.
WHAT ??
DON'T YOU THINK WE'D BE BETTER OFF?
THE DRAGON WILL APPEAR. I GUARANTEE IT.
H-HOW CAN YOU BE SO SURE?
BECAUSE *YOU'RE* HERE.
WH--
ARE YOU TRYING TO INSINUATE THAT I'M *CONTROLLING* THE DRAGON?
THAT'S *RIDICULOUS!*

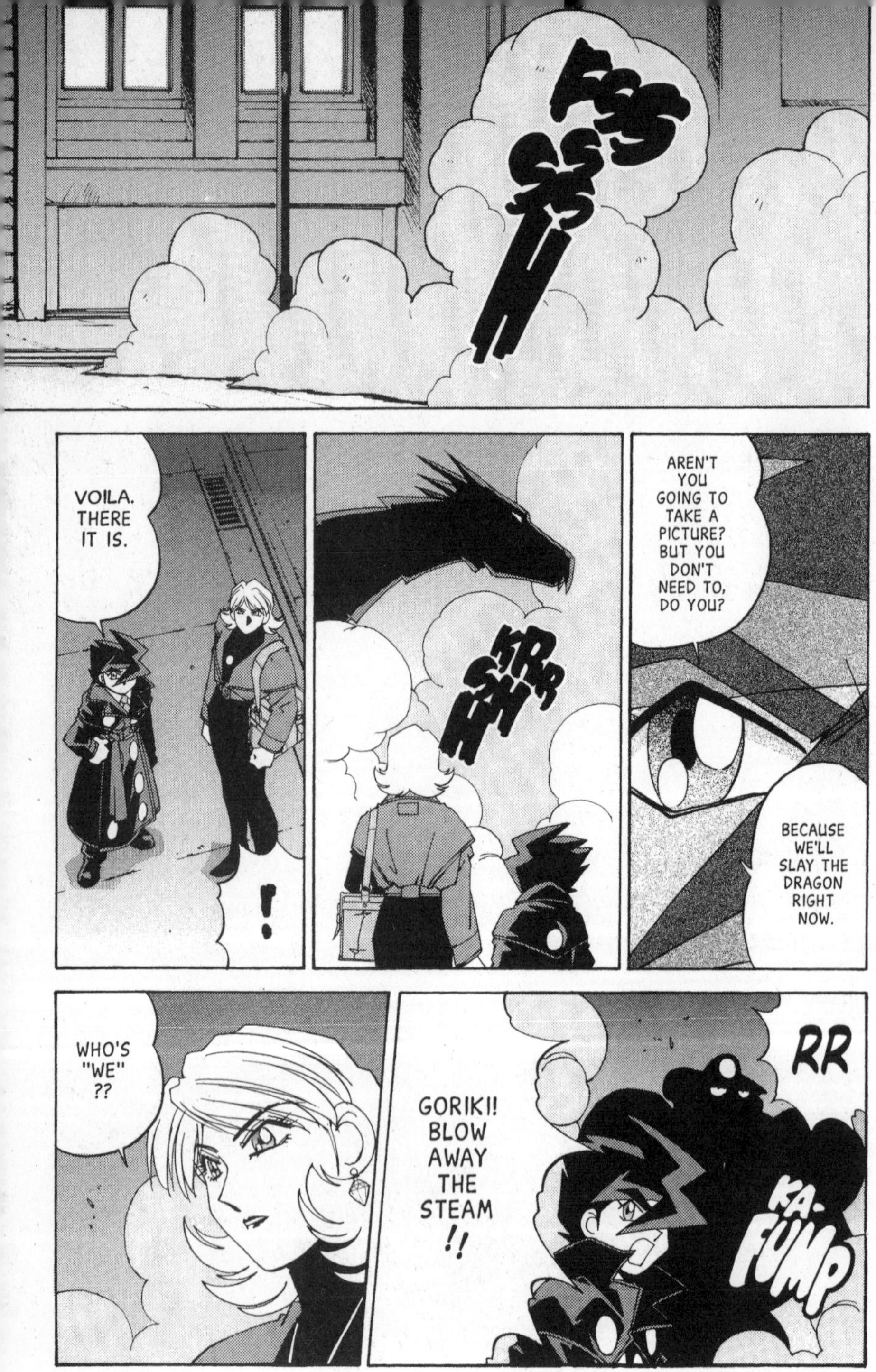
FSSSSSH
VOILA. THERE IT IS.
!
KRRR SHH
AREN'T YOU GOING TO TAKE A PICTURE? BUT YOU DON'T NEED TO, DO YOU?
BECAUSE WE'LL SLAY THE DRAGON RIGHT NOW.
WHO'S "WE" ??
GORIKI!! BLOW AWAY THE STEAM !!
RR
KA-FUMP

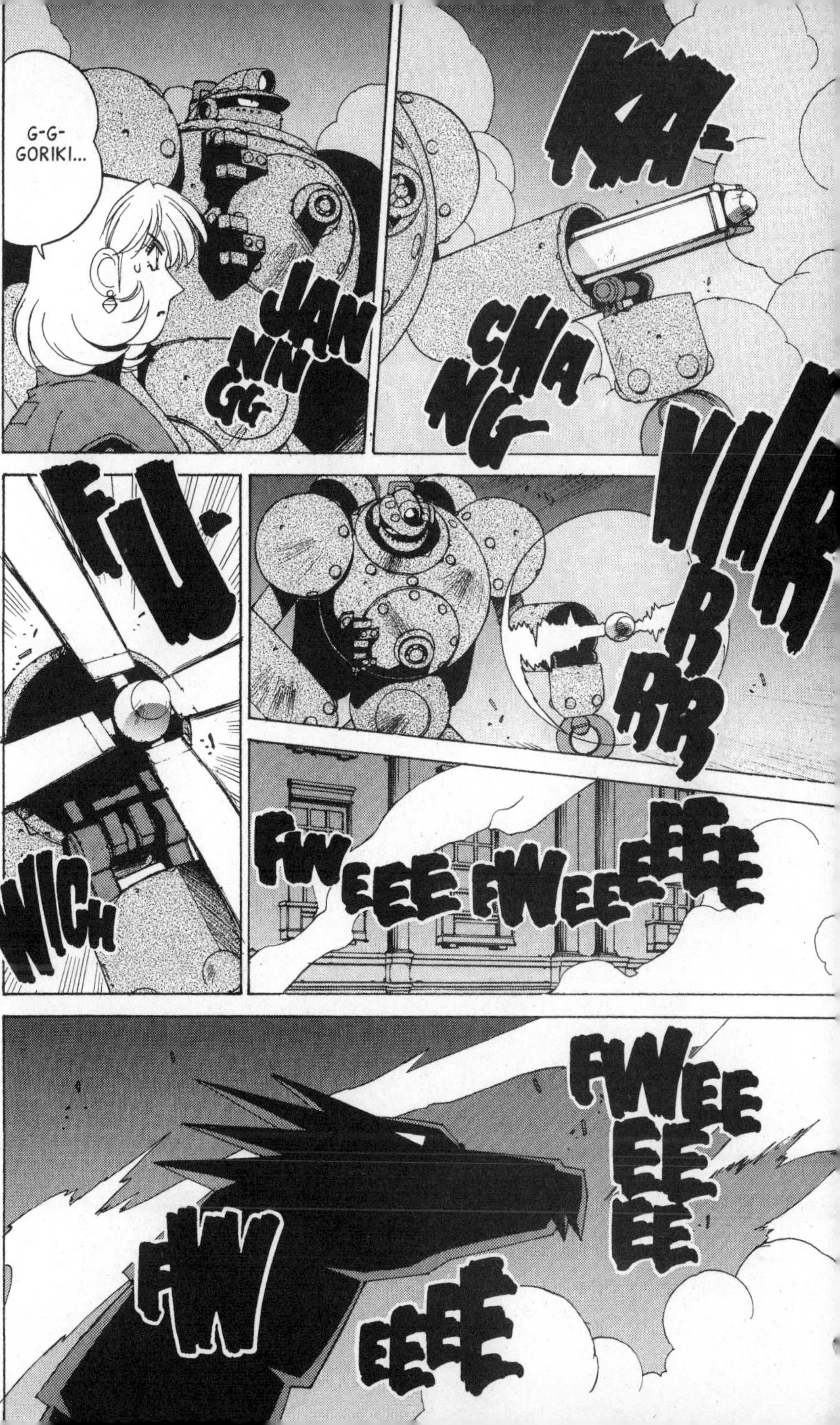
G-G-GORIKI...
JANNINGG
KA-
CHANG
FU-
WICH
VIIRRRR
FWEEE FWEEEEEEE
FWEEEEEEE
FWEEEE

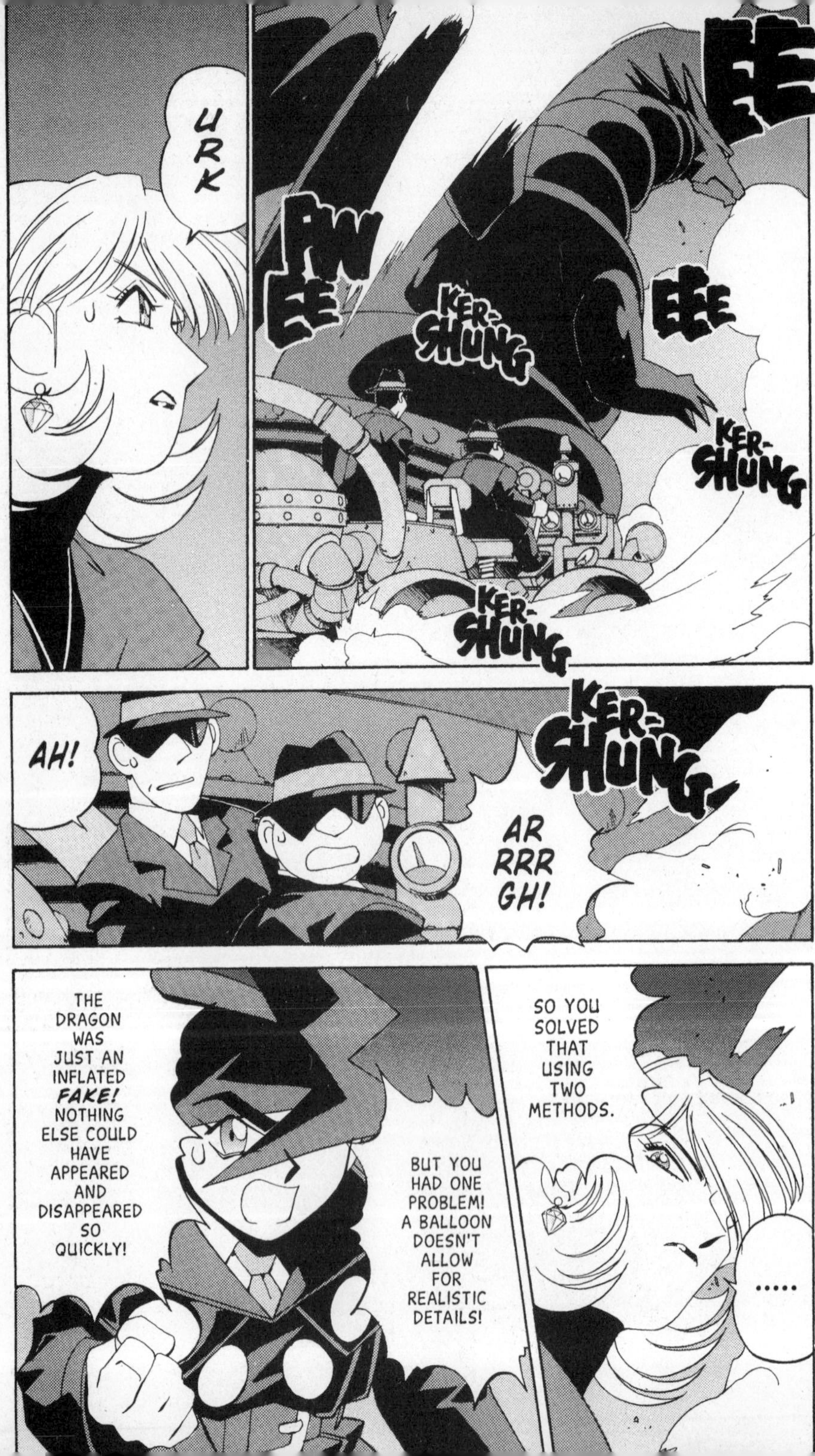
URK
PWEE
EEE
EEE
KER-SHUNG
KER-SHUNG
KER-SHUNG
AH!
KER-SHUNG-
ARRRRGH!
THE DRAGON WAS JUST AN INFLATED ***FAKE!*** NOTHING ELSE COULD HAVE APPEARED AND DISAPPEARED SO QUICKLY!
BUT YOU HAD ONE PROBLEM! A BALLOON DOESN'T ALLOW FOR REALISTIC DETAILS!
SO YOU SOLVED THAT USING TWO METHODS.
.....

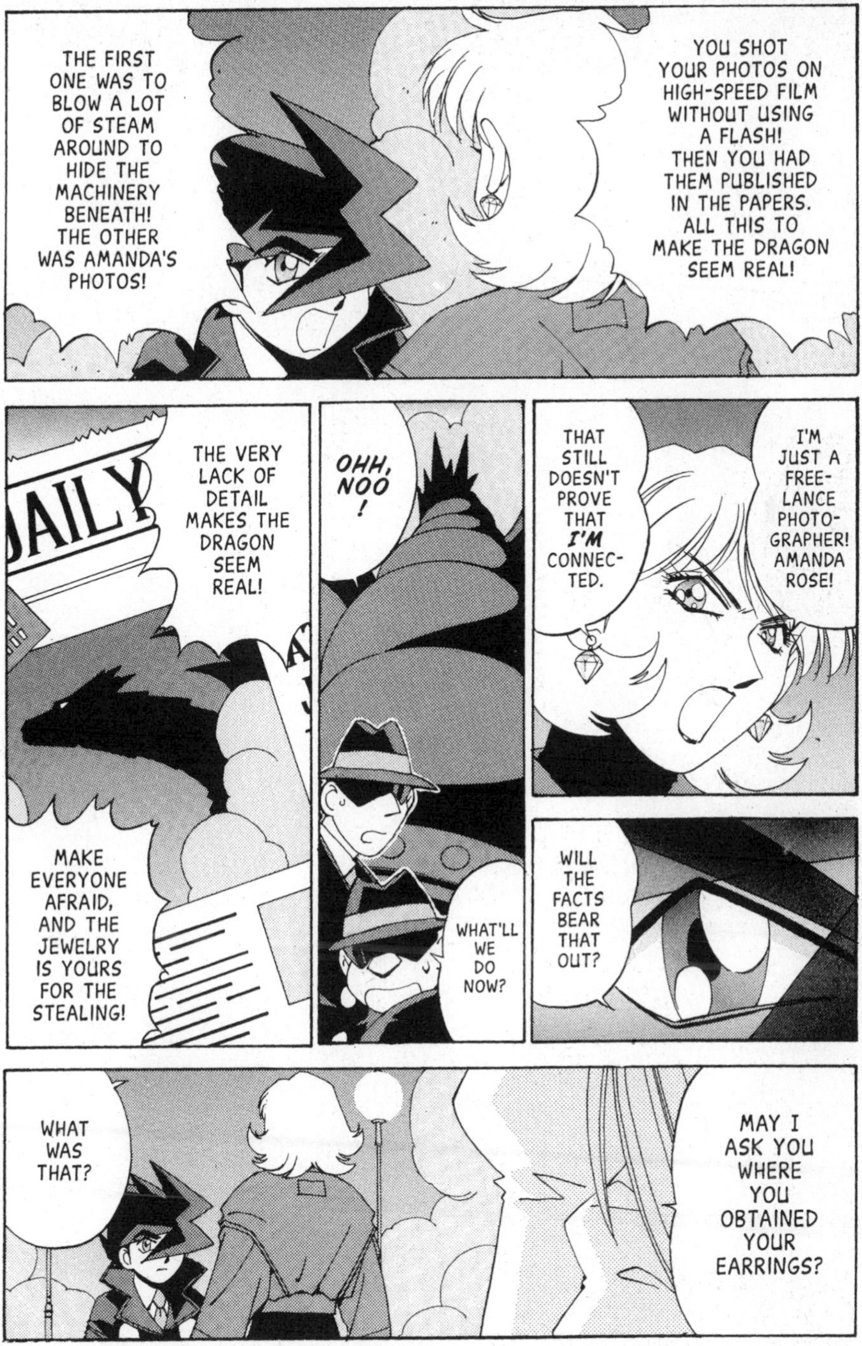
THE FIRST ONE WAS TO BLOW A LOT OF STEAM AROUND TO HIDE THE MACHINERY BENEATH! THE OTHER WAS AMANDA'S PHOTOS!
YOU SHOT YOUR PHOTOS ON HIGH-SPEED FILM WITHOUT USING A FLASH! THEN YOU HAD THEM PUBLISHED IN THE PAPERS. ALL THIS TO MAKE THE DRAGON SEEM REAL!
DAILY
THE VERY LACK OF DETAIL MAKES THE DRAGON SEEM REAL!
MAKE EVERYONE AFRAID, AND THE JEWELRY IS YOURS FOR THE STEALING!
OHH, NOO!
WHAT'LL WE DO NOW?
THAT STILL DOESN'T PROVE THAT *I'M* CONNECTED.
I'M JUST A FREE-LANCE PHOTO-GRAPHER! AMANDA ROSE!
WILL THE FACTS BEAR THAT OUT?
WHAT WAS THAT?
MAY I ASK YOU WHERE YOU OBTAINED YOUR EARRINGS?

WHAT !?!

THOSE EARRINGS ARE FROM THE HAKKEI JEWELRY STORE!

THE OWNER HAD THEM CUSTOM-MADE FOR HIS WIFE!

SNIFF

THOSE ARE THE EARRINGS! I CUT THE DIAMONDS *MYSELF!*

K-KRR

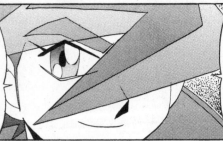

ONCE AGAIN, GEMS ARE ALL THAT ATTRACT YOU. AND YOU COULDN'T RESIST WEARING YOUR STOLEN TREASURES.

YOU EVEN WORE THEM IN THE NEWS PHOTOS. THAT'S WHEN I DEDUCED A JEWELRY HOUND LIKE YOU MIGHT BE THE CULPRIT.

IT'S TOO BAD YOUR DRAGON RESEARCH IN THE HISTORICAL MUSEUM CAME TO NOTHING.

IT'S TRUE. CRIME DOESN'T PAY.

ARE YOU LEC-TURING ME...

...LITTLE BOY?

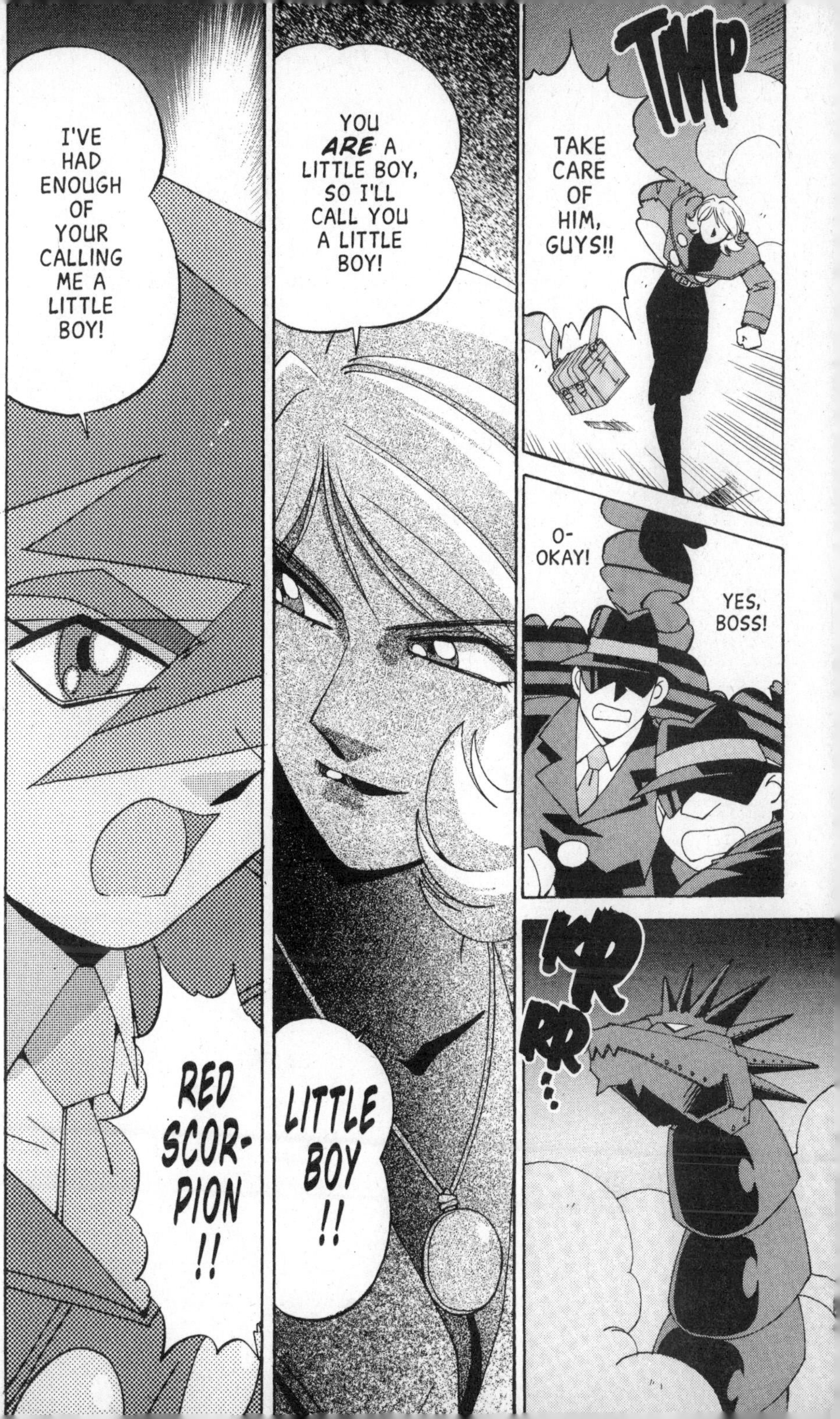
I'VE HAD ENOUGH OF YOUR CALLING ME A LITTLE BOY!
RED SCOR-PION !!
YOU ARE A LITTLE BOY, SO I'LL CALL YOU A LITTLE BOY!
LITTLE BOY !!
TMP
TAKE CARE OF HIM, GUYS!!
O-OKAY!
YES, BOSS!
KRR RR...

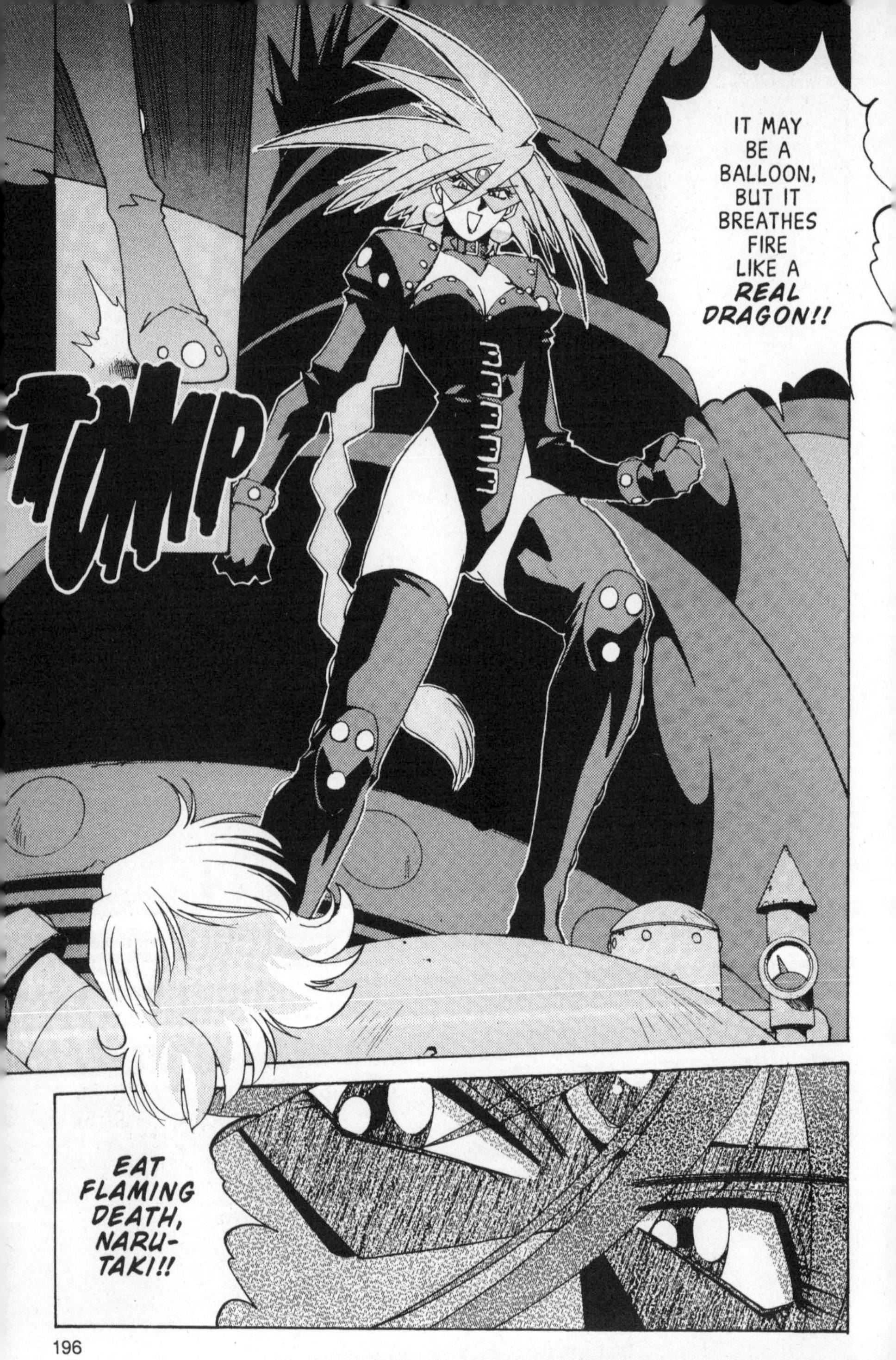
IT MAY BE A BALLOON, BUT IT BREATHES FIRE LIKE A REAL DRAGON!!
TUMP
EAT FLAMING DEATH, NARU-TAKI!!

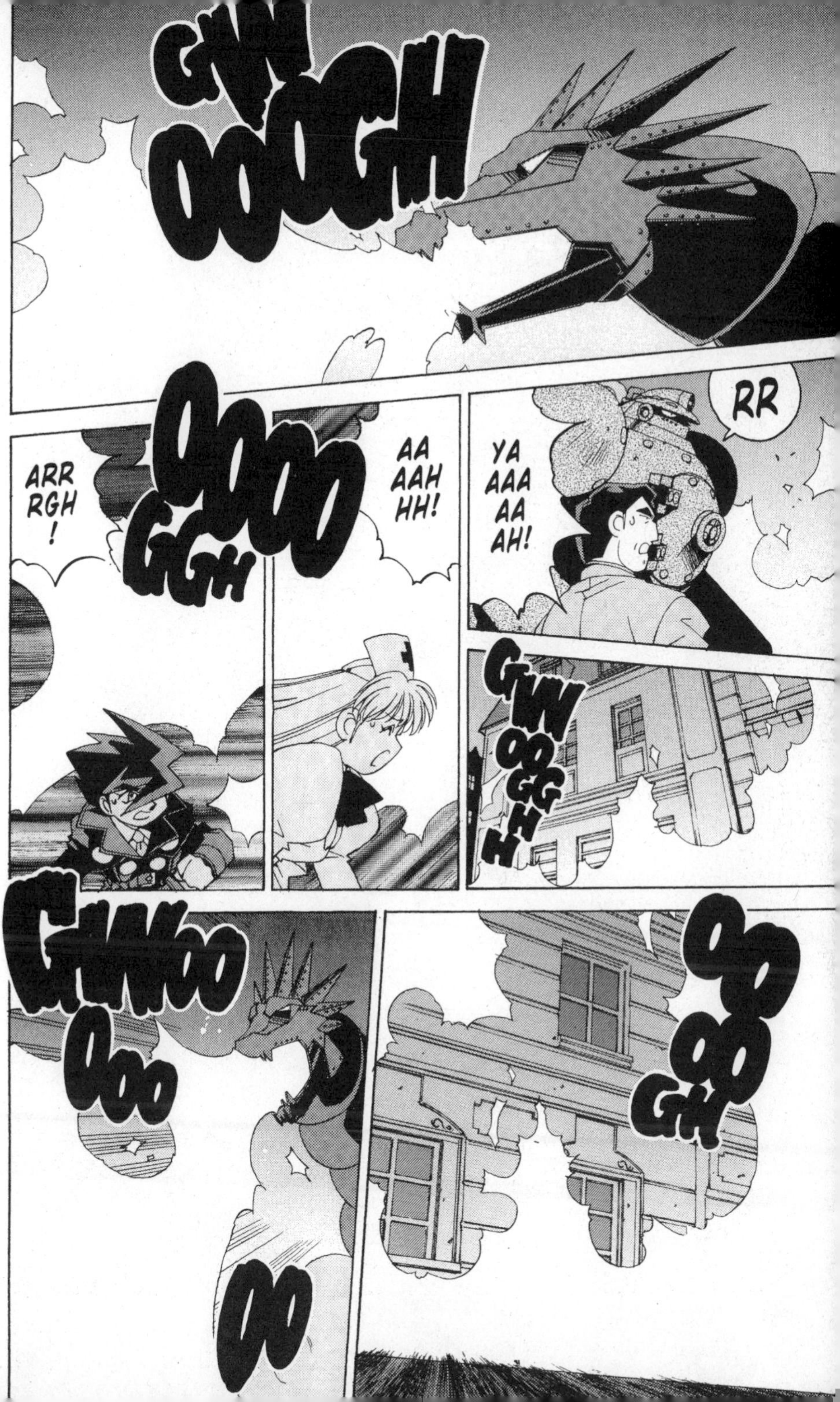
GWN
OOOGH
ARR RGH !
OOOO GGH
AA AAH HH!
YA AAA AA AH!
RR
GWW OOGGHH
GWOO OOO
OO
OO OO GH

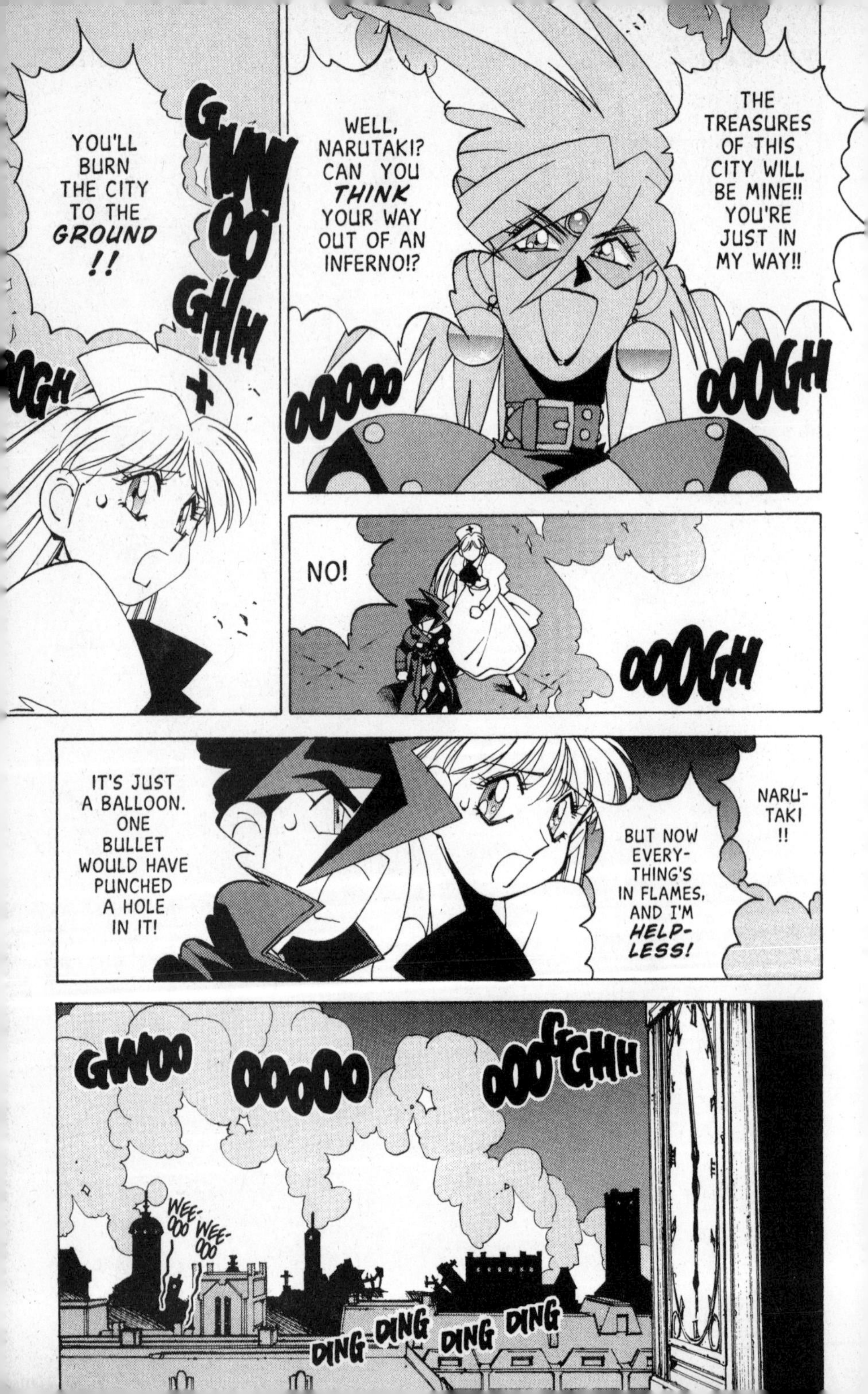
YOU'LL BURN THE CITY TO THE *GROUND* !!
GWWOOGHH
OOGH
WELL, NARUTAKI? CAN YOU *THINK* YOUR WAY OUT OF AN INFERNO!?
THE TREASURES OF THIS CITY WILL BE MINE!! YOU'RE JUST IN MY WAY!!
OOOOO
OOOGH
NO!
OOOGH
IT'S JUST A BALLOON. ONE BULLET WOULD HAVE PUNCHED A HOLE IN IT!
BUT NOW EVERY-THING'S IN FLAMES, AND I'M *HELP-LESS!*
NARU-TAKI !!
GWOO
OOOOO
OOOGGHH
WEE-OOO WEE-OOO
DING DING DING DING

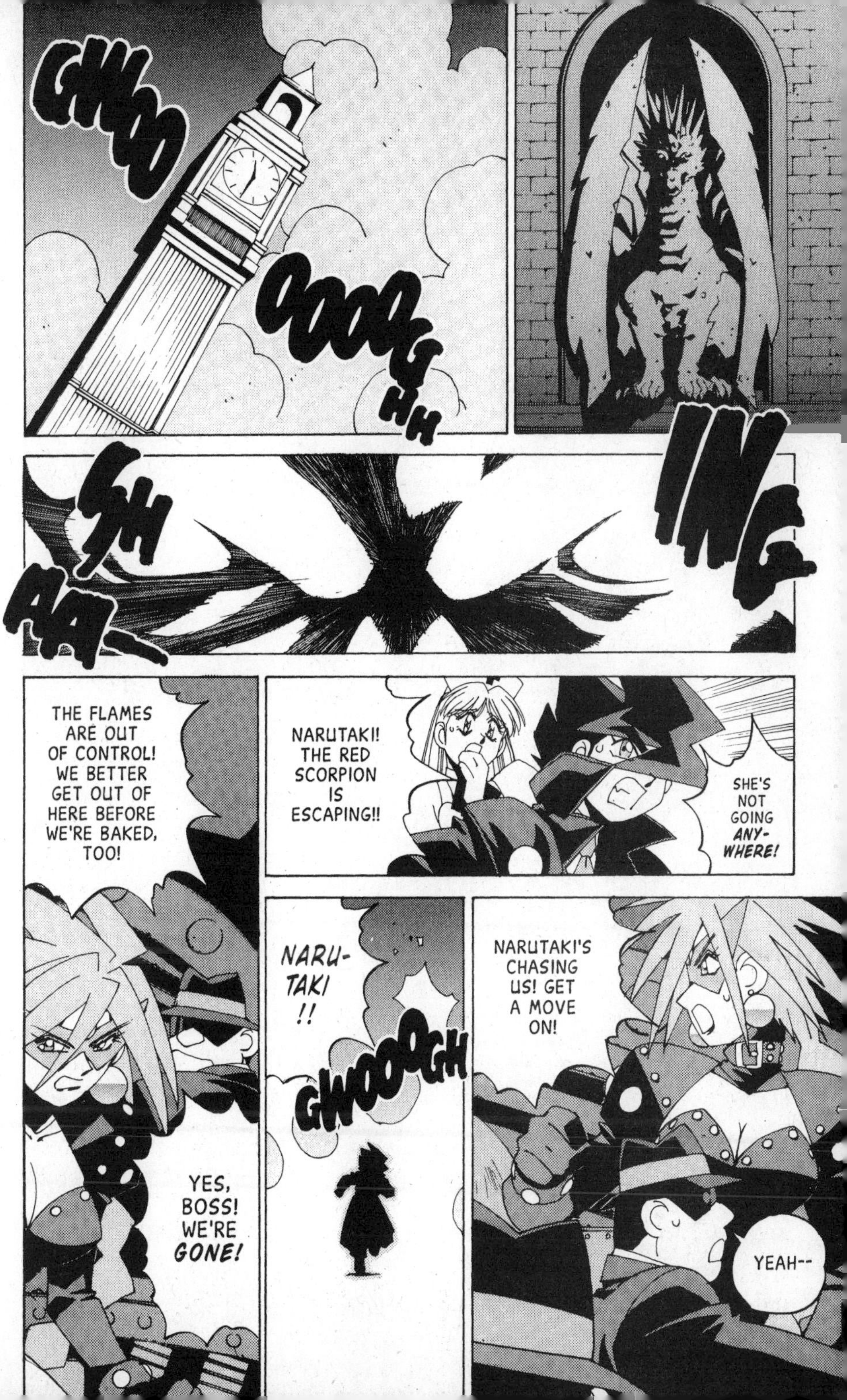
GWOO
OOOAGHH
SHAA—
ING
THE FLAMES ARE OUT OF CONTROL! WE BETTER GET OUT OF HERE BEFORE WE'RE BAKED, TOO!
NARUTAKI! THE RED SCORPION IS ESCAPING!!
SHE'S NOT GOING *ANYWHERE!*
YES, BOSS! WE'RE *GONE!*
NARUTAKI!!
GWOOOGH
NARUTAKI'S CHASING US! GET A MOVE ON!
YEAH--

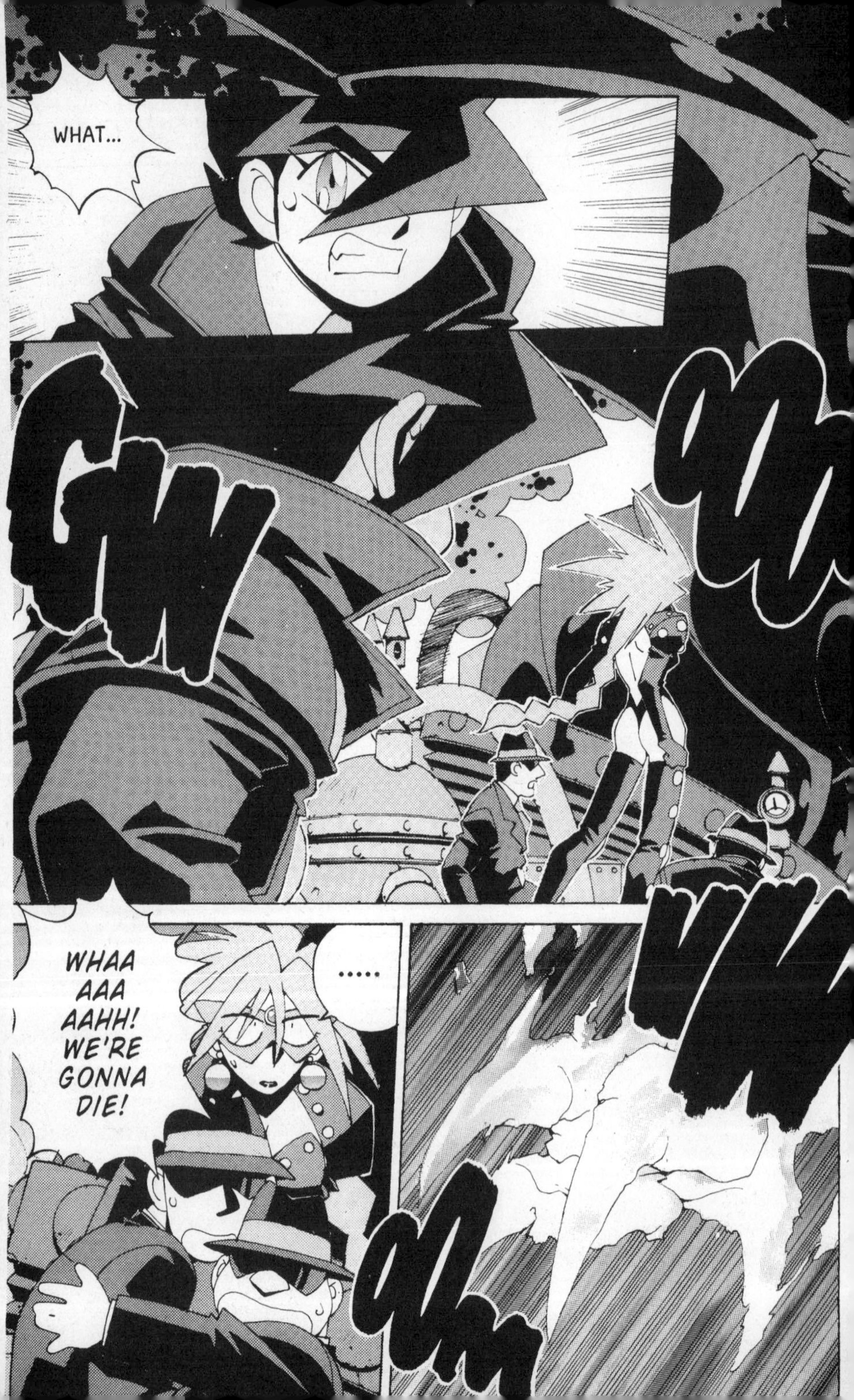
WHAT...
WHAA AAA AAHH! WE'RE GONNA DIE!
......

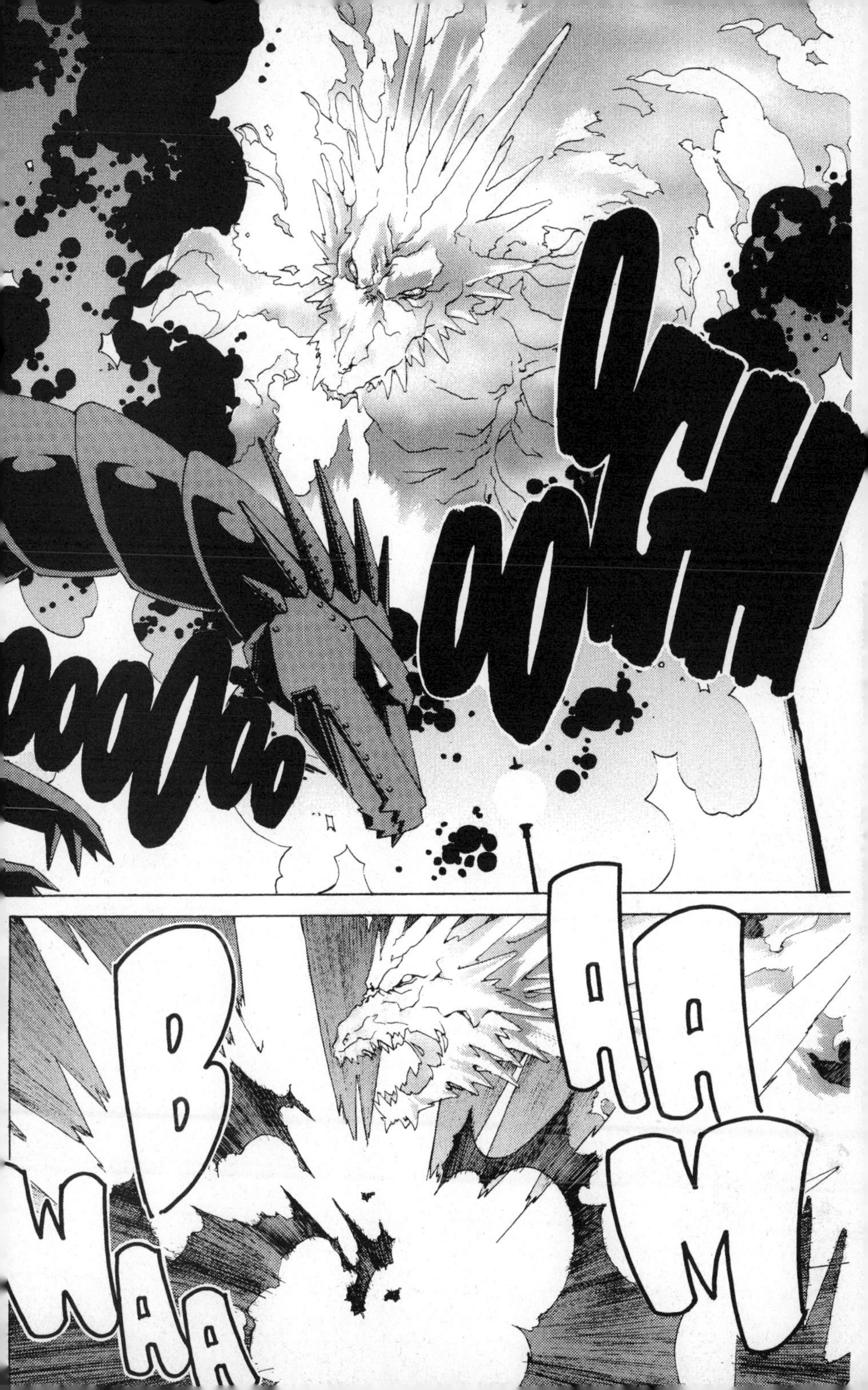
OOOOOOOOOGH
BAAAM
WAAA

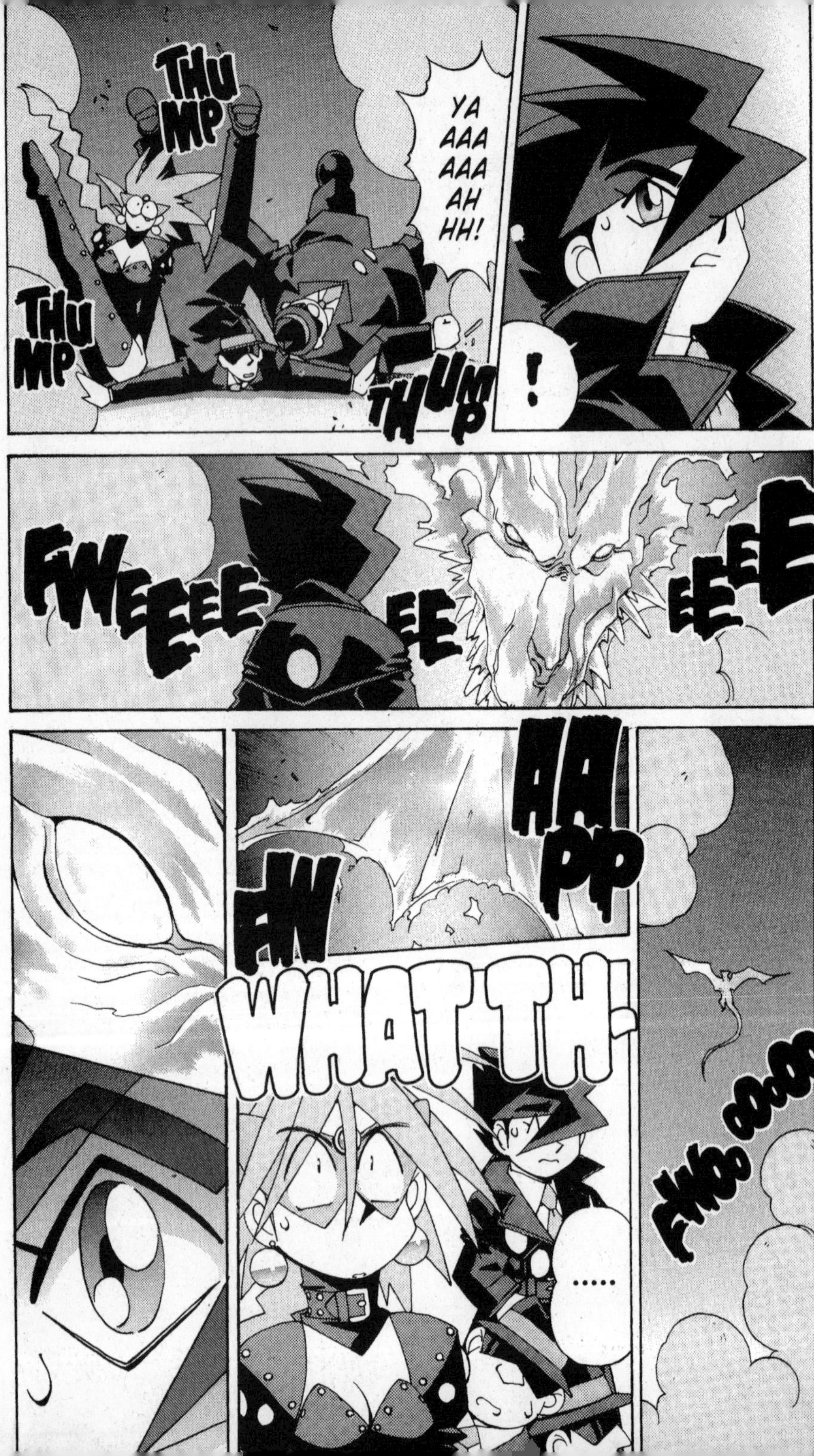
THUMP
THUMP
YAAAAAAAAHHH!
THUMP
!
FWEEEEEEEEEEEE
FWAAIPP
WHAT TH-
......
FWOOOOOOO

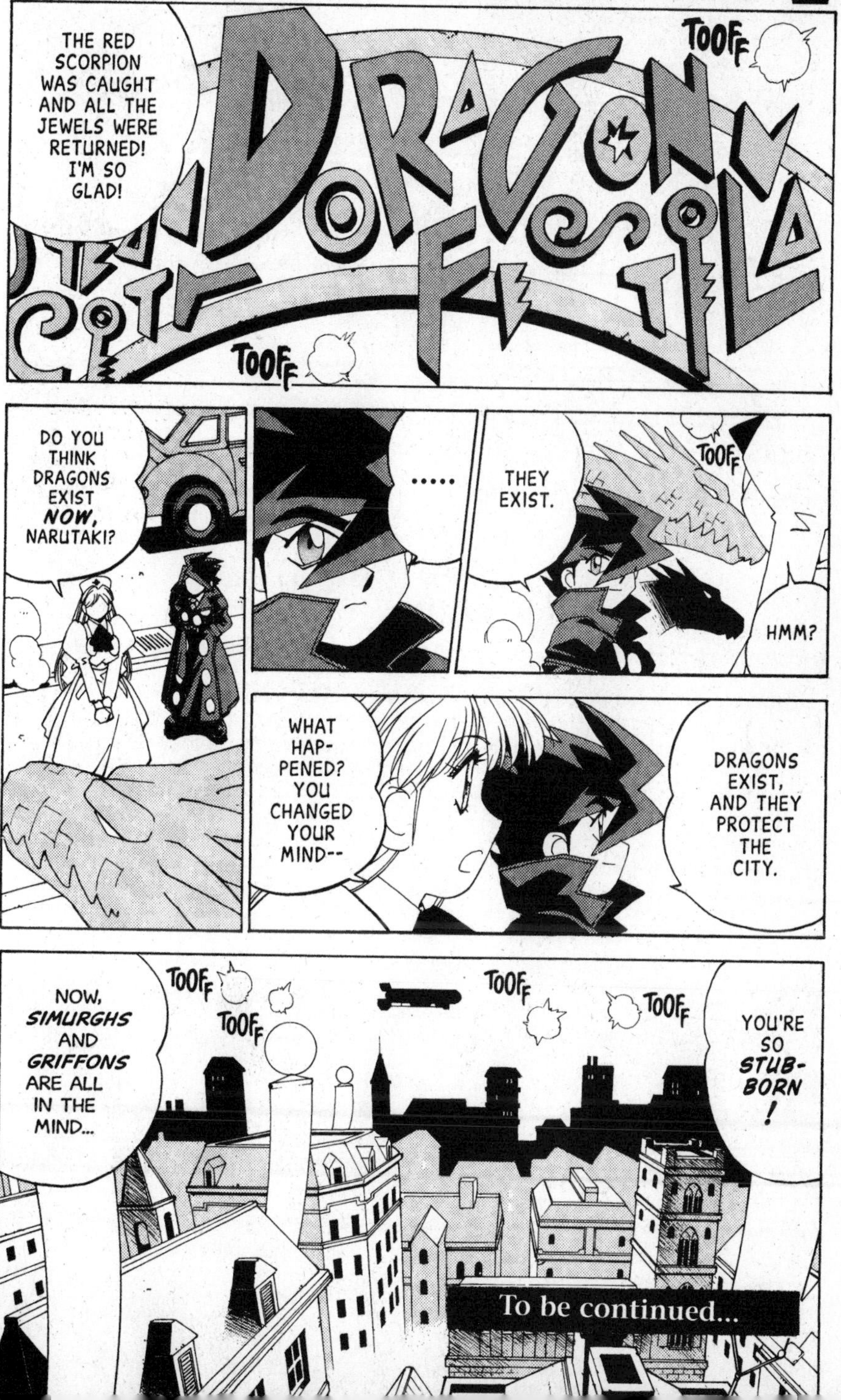
THE RED SCORPION WAS CAUGHT AND ALL THE JEWELS WERE RETURNED! I'M SO GLAD!
TOOFF
TOOFF
DO YOU THINK DRAGONS EXIST *NOW*, NARUTAKI?
.....
THEY EXIST.
TOOFF
HMM?
WHAT HAP-PENED? YOU CHANGED YOUR MIND--
DRAGONS EXIST, AND THEY PROTECT THE CITY.
NOW, *SIMURGHS* AND *GRIFFONS* ARE ALL IN THE MIND...
TOOFF
TOOFF
TOOFF
TOOFF
YOU'RE SO *STUB-BORN!*
To be continued...

STEAM DETECTIVES PRESS

**ARE DRAGONS REAL?
AN ANCIENT RELIEF OF A DRAGON!**

STEAM CITY'S HISTORICAL MUSEUM
POWERS COLLECTION EXHIBIT

Steam City's historical museum is one of the largest museums in the world, and its most treasured exhibit is the giant fossil relief of a dragon, discovered in one of the coal mines on the outskirts of the city. However, this winter, the museum will be presenting us with an even more impressive exhibit!

Over his 85-year life span, Tim Powers assembled an amazing historical collection. And because he was one of the most prominent patrons of the Steam City Historical Museum, the museum is honored to exhibit his collection for one month.

The historical museum has repeatedly requested the Powers Foundation to lend its collection for exhibit. Finally, 50 years after his death, this request has been granted.

The Powers Collection reportedly includes ancient artifacts which support theories of the existence of holy beasts, ruins from the legendary super-civilization "Japoné" which sunk beneath the waves thousands of years ago, plus many other rare items.

This collection includes extremely important archaeological artifacts. Whether you are interested in history or not, the exhibition will thrill you!! Visit the exhibition and take a journey into the past!!

EXHIBITION SCHEDULE: 13/24-1/24
INFORMATION: HISTORICAL MUSEUM/OFFICE
                 OF POWERS COLLECTION
PHONE: 4A008-094-01125B
        (CLOSED ON TUESDAYS)

HISTORICAL MUSEUM

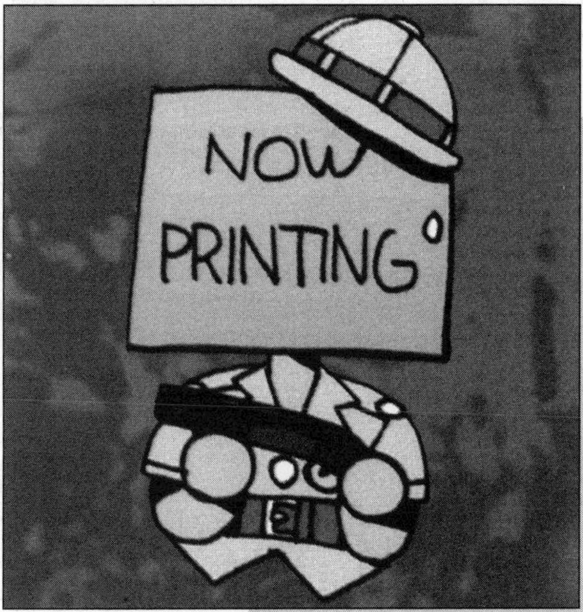
NOW PRINTING

Kia Asamiya

Details are sketchy with regard to this elusive author, but since his debut work on *Vagrants* in 1986, he has produced some very popular manga and anime including *Silent Möbius, Compiler, Assembler, Gunhed, Dark Angel, Martian Successor Nadesico, Corrector Yui*, and others. In the past several years, no less than six of his manga series have been translated into English making him one of the most widely published manga artists in America.